‘My own sort of heaven’

A LIFE OF
ROSALIE GASCOIGNE

‘My own sort of heaven’

A LIFE OF ROSALIE GASCOIGNE

Nicola Francis

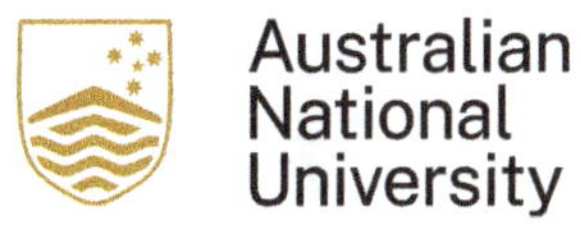

ANU PRESS

BIOGRAPHY SERIES

For my husband Allen Bryce
in Te Whanganui-a-Tara Wellington, Aotearoa New Zealand
and my sons
Ben Fawkes in Cambridge, United Kingdom
and Sacha Fawkes in Naarm Melbourne, Australia
with love and gratitude.
And in memory of my mother
Aylsa Daphne Francis, née Vahry (1914–1969),
who, like Rosalie, grew to adulthood in Tāmaki Makaurau Auckland
in the same era and left at the same time because of love and war.

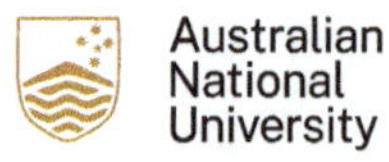

ANU PRESS

Published by ANU Press
The Australian National University
Canberra ACT 2600, Australia
Email: anupress@anu.edu.au

Available to download for free at press.anu.edu.au

ISBN (print): 9781760466558
ISBN (online): 9781760466565

WorldCat (print): 1442033175
WorldCat (online): 1442034115

DOI: 10.22459/MOSH.2024

Cover design and layout by ANU Press. Cover photograph: Rosalie Gascoigne at Toi o Tāmaki Auckland Art Gallery, July 1999.Courtesy of the Marti Friedlander Estate. Photograph: Marti Friedlander.

The Biography Series is an initiative of the National Centre of Biography at The Australian National University, ncb.anu.edu.au.

This book is published under the aegis of the Biography editorial board of ANU Press.

Contents

Foreword

Hester Gascoigne

Unlike our parents, we three children grew up without an extended family. Separated from aunts, uncles, cousins and grandparents by the Tasman Sea, there was no shared family history bouncing around our childhood. No different views on people and events, only an occasional story. So it is quite an experience to read an account of my mother's life, from her uneasy childhood to her death, as seen by someone outside the family. Some parts of Niki's book resonate strongly, some took me by surprise, of others I have different memories and interpretations.

My parents were born in New Zealand in the shadow of World War I. They scored the Great Depression and were married in Australia in the heat of World War II, the year after Darwin was bombed. When mum arrived at Mount Stromlo in 1943, the observatory had become an optical munitions factory, designing and manufacturing precision optics for sighting telescopes, artillery directors, range finders and such. Dad had relocated from Auckland to work there in 1941.

The move to Australia had a profound effect on mum. She was twenty-five, dad twenty-seven, when they married in Canberra in January 1943. Until their wedding, she had never left New Zealand. She left family, friends and the lifelong familiarity of the harbour city of Auckland, urban population c. 260,000, for Mt Stromlo, a remote hill ten kilometres west of landlocked Canberra, a country town of around 12,000 people. It was a massive culture shock.

The access road to the mountain was unsealed and graded infrequently; and, with the shortage of cars and petrol, bicycles were a popular mode of transport into 'town'. Residents relied on food deliveries from Canberra and, in those early days, shared a community fridge.

Early marriage seems to have played out in accordance with the expectations of the times. In the world of Mt Stromlo, husbands had professionally interesting lives at the observatory. Away from the observatory was a small and isolated community of very assorted women whose role was to be wives. And mothers. Astronomy came first. Some found it too hard and got out.

Mum had their first baby, Martin, in November 1943, ten months after the wedding. It was a tough introduction to motherhood, with lots of morning sickness, three days in labour and a baby who had to go immediately to Sydney for surgery. A second son, Toss (Thomas) was born eighteen months later and, after three and a half years, I was born, a much-wanted daughter. Mum recalled her visiting mother looking at her doubtfully in those early years of motherhood and saying 'you better not have any more, it takes too much out of you'.[1]

Those first years on Stromlo were consumed by the mechanics of living in a cold 'backbreaker' house with a fuel stove, a small Dux heater, an 'awful' copper for boiling clothes and three small children. She said she was not a good housekeeper.

She found connection in the landscape, seeking detail, and collecting interesting things to take home and look at. Indeed, the landscape became her firm friend and inspiration. She was a knitter, sewer and embroiderer. Probably like many women then, she was motivated by shortages of things to buy, lack of money, keeping her hands moving and providing for her family. It provided a creative outlet, of sorts.

I have a collection of her creations saved from that time: clothes, toys and knitted jumpers; embroidered serviettes on colourful check cotton with individual motifs of initials and flowers; a hand-stitched calico doll; an embroidered tea-cosy inspired by a pattern in a magazine; a cheerful sampler of stitches and colours. There's the Christmas fairy, now some seventy-five years old, made to distract two little boys in the challenging Stromlo house. 'If you're *very* good the Christmas fairy might come.' The hand-size fairy still flies at Christmas, to entertain her great-grand-twins (and me).

---

1 The quotes by my mother are from the extended interview by Robin Hughes. See Hughes et al., 'Rosalie Gascoigne Artist'.

And, of course, there is the patchwork quilt, in which she could indulge her love of flowers. She sewed it at night when the children were in bed to keep her company while dad was up at the observatory. It's a family history in fabric, spanning seventeen years, arranged and ordered in a grid of hexagons of colour and flowery prints.

There is family history, too, in her handwritten cookery book, the first of two green books she kept. The battered old recipe book covers the Stromlo era through recipes, random lists and household hints.

There are recipes from her mother, sister, sister-in-law and neighbours. She recorded the heights of the growing little boys and made notes on pocket money paid. There are names and dates of roses planted; the 1948 weekly egg count from the prolific chooks; and an itemised shopping list from J. B. Young, the pioneer department store down the hill in Canberra. She recorded the preferred shades of Holeproof stockings for her mother (Royalty) and sister (Sweet Adeline). And she collected household hints, many of which suggest the shortages of the times—how to bleach sheets, press trousers, patch lino, wash flour bags, etc.

After seventeen years on Stromlo, it was time to move. The university offered a couple of alternatives from its stock of staff housing and in 1960 she chose a newly built house in a new part of the suburb of Deakin.

The awkward Deakin house saw the end of our school days. We headed to university. Mum's interests in collecting and Ikebana were shifting rapidly to experiments with art forms. Her collections of farm iron and other materials accumulated in the garden. There was no space in the house to spread and create.

From the early 1960s until 1975, dad was a major player in the planning, construction and commissioning of the Anglo-Australian Telescope (AAT) at Siding Spring, New South Wales. He was frequently away and consumed by the project. However, they needed a solution to the manifest inadequacies of the Deakin house.

They bought a block in the new suburb of Pearce. Architect Theo Bischoff designed their house to their brief. Completed in 1969, this was the third and final house of their marriage. It had places to test finished art works and plenty of garden. It was not big (less housework) and it was post-child—

I was the only one of the three to live there and closely observed her early art making. In due course, a studio was added to accommodate mum's growing art practice and move it out of the dining room.

While dad was absorbed in the AAT, mum filled her life making art. She once said in an interview that she always wanted children but that wasn't enough. Given the opportunity, she seized on art and did it everywhere. 'I've never seen obsession like it', said dad, the obsessed scientist.

In her second green book, covered in a Marimekko fabric, mum collected quotes that struck a chord, mostly about art and the creative process. This book points to her life as an artist, just as the battered green recipe book points to her newly married life, motherhood and sustaining her family.

She recorded a quote that could apply equally to scientists. Author Murray Bail wrote:

> Writers and artists are not very good people to live with, they are preoccupied, bad tempered, superior, and conscious of preserving a clear shape of themselves. It makes them selfish and obnoxious.

She used to talk to art students in a know-thyself-and-be-true-to-thyself kind of way. Thus, the quote by Picasso, talking of young artists: 'The important thing is that they start out with what belongs to them, is in them and not with that which belongs to others or what others discovered.'

Often in the Pearce house she would roll out of bed and into the studio to surprise the piece she had been working on the day before. Sometimes it just fell off the wall (metaphorically), a proper nothing or as Rauschenberg put it, there are 'works and don't works', all part of development.

Dad retired in 1980. As art took over mum's life, his life evolved from absorption in his science to sometime studio hand, then archivist. It was a challenging transition, but when all is said and done, he was proud of her achievements and the part he played.

In her last year, 1999, I accompanied mum on a trip to Auckland, where she had been reclaimed as a New Zealand artist for two exhibitions. When I look at the photographs of her addressing a packed audience at the Auckland Art Gallery, I remember a sea of women seeking affirmation for their own art making as she talked about her evolution as an artist: 'Start out with what belongs to you.'

Mum died in 1999, yet interest in her life and work grows and prices for her work continue to rise. There has been a notable absence of easily accessible accounts of her life and art for people who would like to know more. For that reason alone it is especially pleasing to see Niki's work come to fruition. I congratulate Niki on clearing the many hurdles and seeing her thesis through to publication. My thanks goes also to ANU Press for recognising and then seizing the opportunity to produce this book. May there be many more!

Hester Gascoigne
Canberra
October 2023

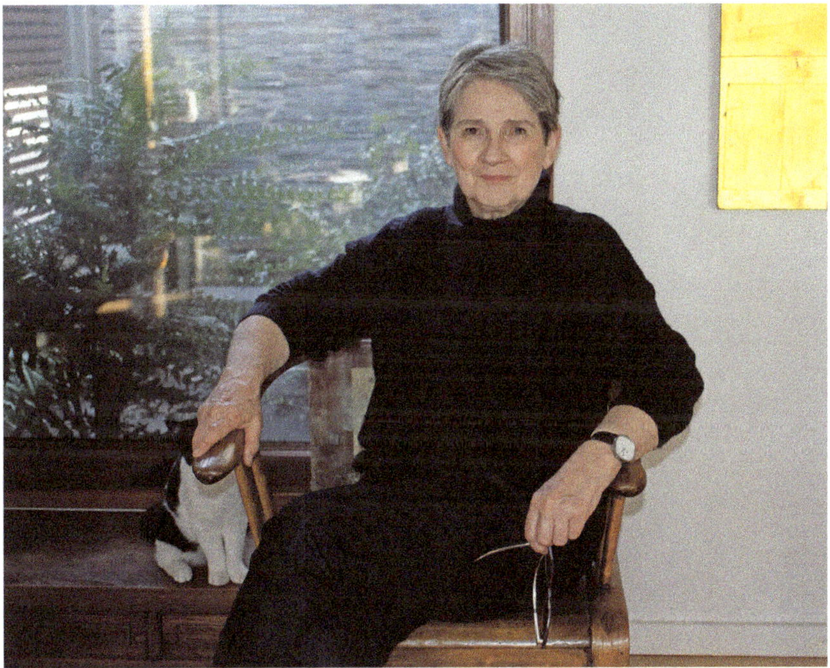

Figure 0.0: Hester Gascoigne at home in Canberra, 2023.
Photograph: Sally Colahan Griffin. Source: Courtesy of Sally Colahan Griffin and Hester Gascoigne.

Acknowledgement of Country and recognition of mana whenua

I acknowledge the Ngunnawal and Ngambri people who are the Traditional Owners of the lands of the Canberra region on which I prepared the thesis on which this book is based, and Te Ātiawa, the iwi (tribe) with mana whenua (authority over the land) of the lands on which I have prepared this book, Te Whanganui-ā-Tara Wellington and Te Awa Kairangi Lower Hutt.

I extend this respect to all Indigenous peoples of Australia and the Torres Strait Islands, and to all iwi in Aotearoa New Zealand.

I recognise that the Ngunnawal and Ngambri people, the Traditional Owners of the land and waterways on which Rosalie Gascoigne made her art, are part of the oldest continuous living culture in human history, and that their deep and enduring spiritual connections and relationship with the land, waterways, air and sky inspired her in her art making.

I recognise, too, the special relationship that Ngāti Whātua, iwi of the parts of Tāmaki Makaurau Auckland where both Rosalie and I grew up, have with the land, waterways, harbours, skies and air, which nurtured Rosalie's love of nature and developing visual acuity.

Notes about naming, copyright and placenames

Rather than switch between her birth name and the one she took on marriage, I have chosen to refer to Rosalie Gascoigne as 'Rosalie' throughout the book, as it is the one name she used throughout her life, despite the fact that it implies an intimacy that does not exist. This practice also avoids confusion with other members of the Gascoigne family who feature in the book.

Copyright complexities have meant I have been unable to include images of Rosalie's work in this biography; however, all her work can be seen in *Rosalie Gascoigne: A Catalogue* by her son Martin Gascoigne (1943–2024), downloadable at no cost from ANU Press.

In Aotearoa New Zealand, where I am writing, in 2024 it is respectful to tangata whenua (the people of the land)—Māori—to include te reo Māori (Māori language) placenames alongside settler colonial names. I consider this best practice and it is my preferred practice. However, it seems anachronistic to do so when writing about times when such practice was far in the future, so I have used te reo placenames alongside settler colonial names in my own reflections and when appropriate.

Words of gratitude

Just as Rosalie said 'art isn't for sissies', writing a biography is not for the faint-hearted.[1] I cannot imagine having completed this book without the help of the many people who have contributed and supported me along the way.

This book has had two distinct lives: it is based on the thesis I wrote for my doctor of philosophy at the National Centre of Biography, School of History, The Australian National University. Now, seven years after graduation, I have adapted the thesis into a book for publication. I thank my friend and former fellow PhD candidate Dr Sophie Scott-Brown for nudging me into action. Thanks also to Professor Melanie Nolan, my initial PhD supervisor and chair of the Biography editorial board at ANU Press for being open to the idea.

I am deeply indebted to Rosalie's daughter Hester Gascoigne for her warmth and assistance throughout the years of research, writing and manuscript preparation. I can only begin to imagine the inherent challenges in having a total stranger turn up wanting to write your mother's life, yet Hester has been helpful, supportive and encouraging. Ben Gascoigne gave me precious time shortly before his death in March 2010, and both Toss Gascoigne and Martin Gascoigne made time to talk with me. The Gascoigne family kindly provided me with family photographs.

For the doctoral thesis, Professor Melanie Nolan midwifed my application, set me on track with my research and gave me a job I loved at the *Australian Dictionary of Biography* for the first four years of my candidature. Professor Nicholas Brown provided valuable insights into Canberra's history, an

1 In 1998, Rosalie Gascoigne told Robin Hughes: 'Bette Davis once said—the actress—"Old age isn't for sissies". Well, I'll tell you, I'm here to tell you that art isn't for sissies, either. It's hard yakka. It's hard grind. And it's a very isolated, isolating sort of way to live. You know, you give up a lot for art.' See Hughes et al., 'Rosalie Gascoigne Artist', tape 7.

important component of Rosalie's story. Helen Ennis, former William Dobell Professor of Art History at ANU, encouraged and enabled a visual arts perspective that was crucial to appropriately honouring Rosalie, and continued to support and encourage me in the preparation of the book manuscript: I am enormously grateful for her wisdom, warmth and professionalism. Thanks to Dr Karen Fox, Dr Rani Kerin and Dr Christine Winter for their ready willingness, during the thesis process, to read my work and provide me with timely feedback.

Other academics at the School of History, ANU, talked through specific angles, provided guidance at particular points or just had friendly, encouraging chats, which meant a lot to me, including Pat Jalland, Tom Griffiths, Peter Read, Angela Woollacott, Frank Bongiorno, Karen Downing, Tim Rowse, Malcolm Allbrook, Mary Anne Jebb, Allison Cadzow, Ann McGrath, Jeanine Leane, Carolyn Strange and Kynan Gentry. Professor Ann Evans, dean of Higher Degree Research at ANU, deserves a special mention for the support she provided.

I am also grateful to academics from other universities: in particular, Professor Leonard Bell, art historian at the University of Auckland, who shared his thoughts on writing about expatriate artists and introduced me to the work of Czech-born philosopher Vilèm Flusser on migration, displacement and creativity, which has been central to this work. Len continued to support and encourage me in the publication of this manuscript and, as artistic/literary executor of Aotearoa New Zealand photographer the late Marti Friedlander, generously gave me permission to use Marti's photos of Rosalie in the book, including the cover photo.

Professor Jen Webb at the University of Canberra enlightened me about subjectivity in plain English when I struggled with it after years out of academia; Emeritus Professor Carolyn Steedman FBA, from Warwick University, talked with me about writing women's lives; Humphrey McQueen gave me sterling advice about writing and talked with me about the history of Australian art taste and structures; and Dr Denise Ferris, ANU School of Art, encouraged me with her interest in this project.

Dr Milton Cameron, having written about the Gascoigne's house in his own doctoral thesis and subsequent book, was immensely helpful during the thesis process and later willingly assisted with research in Canberra for the book manuscript preparation, as I no longer live in Australia.[2] British writer Vici MacDonald, author of the first published biographical book about Rosalie, kindly shared her experience of researching and writing about Rosalie back in 1997, and warmly encouraged my venture.

People on both sides of the Tasman Sea made time to talk with me about Rosalie during my thesis research: the late Jan Brown, Harriet Barry, the late Rosemary Dobson, Hester Gascoigne, Toss Gascoigne, Martin Gascoigne, Mary Eagle, Marie Hagerty, Peter Vandermark, Mary Riek, Leeanne Crisp and Dawn Waterhouse in Canberra; Kelly Gellatly and the late James Mollison in Melbourne; Ian North and Paul Greenaway in Adelaide; Katrina Rumley from Moree; the late Marti Friedlander, Louise Pether, the late Ron Brownson and Rob Gardiner in Auckland; and Gregory O'Brien and the late Peter McLeavey in Wellington. The novelist Josephine Humphreys from Charleston, South Carolina, kindly shared her time, memories of Rosalie and encouragement.

I am extremely grateful to the ANU Press Publication Subsidy Committee, chaired by ANU Librarian Roxanne Missingham, for their generous grant towards editing costs.

ANU provides first-rate support services to its students; Hans-Jörg Kraus and Emily Rutherford of the Information Literacy Program at ANU were especially helpful.

Libraries and librarians deserve much gratitude. The librarians at ANU—at Chifley, Menzies, Art and Music, and Hancock—were helpful to the nth degree, as were librarians at the National Library of Australia, the National Library of New Zealand in Te Whanganui-a-Tara Wellington, the Australian Capital Territory Heritage Library and the National Gallery of Australia Research Library. Thanks also to Caroline McBride at the Auckland Art Gallery Toi o Tāmaki Library and Archive, and to Lisa Zito at the National Gallery of Victoria Library and Archive.

Visits to archives provided endless hours of interesting research and engagement with archivists passionate about their work and keen to help. At the Epsom Girls' Grammar School archive, Christine Black and her committed team of volunteers provided superb professional assistance mixed with good dollops of reminiscence and laughter. Stephen Innes,

2 Cameron, 'Experiments in Modern Living'; Cameron, 'Where Science Meets Art'.

friend and then special collections manager at the University of Auckland library, assisted with details of Rosalie's time at university. Other archivists who unstintingly contributed to my research for the thesis include Kathryn McLeod at the National Film and Sound Archive, Canberra; Isobel Laing, Cheltenham Ladies College, UK; Natalie Clay and Jonathon Newport of Archives New Zealand Te Rua Mahara o te Kāwanatanga, Wellington; Isobel Gillon, Auckland Girls' Grammar School Archives; Auckland Council Archives staff; ANU Archives; and Isabel Sutherland, Auckland Anglican Diocesan Archives.

More recently, in the absence of a current archivist at Epsom Girls' Grammar School, Deputy Principal Patricia Milner, OGA Treasurer Julie Goodyear and Sue Morse of the EGGS Foundation enabled access to archival information and images for my cousin Peter Vahry on my behalf.

Images are important when telling the story of an artist's life. The lack of images of Rosalie's art available for use in the book meant other images related to her life and the places she lived were more important. I am enormously grateful to Leonard Bell, literary/artistic executor for Marti Friedlander, for permission to use Marti's photograph of Rosalie for the cover image, and to Auckland University Press for providing me with the image. Also in Auckland, Keith Giles of Auckland Heritage Libraries gave permission and provided me with high resolution images of Auckland during Rosalie's years there to illustrate the first few chapters. My thanks to Jude Tewnion of *Stuff* and Janette Dalley of New Zealand Media and Entertainment for permission to use newspaper images from their archives; the *Truth* Archive at Auckland War Memorial Museum Tāmaki Paenga Hira for permission to use *Truth* article images and for the images themselves; and Dennis Kerins, researcher and trustee, New Zealand War Graves Trust, for the image of Rosalie's uncle Harry Metcalfe's war grave in France.

Matt Kelso was a delight to communicate with about Rosalie and generously provided the images of Rosalie talking with Michael Taylor and of James Mollison.

Ngā mihi nui (many thanks) to Wellington Te Whanganui-a-Tara photographer Shaun Waugh for the image, and permission to use it, of the green velvet chaise longue on which Rosalie and Peter McLeavey sat in 1983 when she visited Te Whanganui-a-Tara Wellington for her exhibition at the then National Gallery and purchased a Colin McCahon painting from the McLeavey Gallery.

Happily, my friend Sally Colahan Griffin, who visited family in Canberra in 2023, was able to call on Hester Gascoigne, who kindly welcomed her and allowed photographs of some of her mother's treasures.

Catherine Ziegler and Sarah Lethbridge at ANU Archives were both very helpful in identifying and supplying me with photographs. Katrina Hatherley from Wellington's Alexander Turnbull Library organised photos for me and reminisced about meeting Rosalie in Canberra.

I am indebted to Kelly Gellatly and the National Gallery of Victoria for permission to include quotes from Kelly's book *Rosalie Gascoigne* (2008) and to the National Film and Sound Archive of Australia for permission to include quotes from *Australian Biography: Rosalie Gascoigne* (1998), Film Australia Collection, National Film and Sound Archive of Australia.

Rosalie said that art is 'hard yakka ... hard grind ... isolated, isolating'. So too, at times, was my experience of writing the original thesis. My thanks, love and gratitude to my fellow higher degree research candidates in the School of History and elsewhere on campus for their staunch friendship, intellectual support and for the fun times we shared: Kimberley Doyle, Maria Haenga-Collins, Jacqui Donegan, Alessandro Antonello, Meggie Hutchison, Alexis Bergantz, Arnold Ellem, Robyn Curtis, Murray Chisholm, Shannyn Palmer, Julia Torpey, Brett Goodin, Shelley Richardson, Yves Rees, Sophie Scott-Brown, Alexandra Roginski and Fiona Fraser; Stephanie Kizimchuk at the School of Literature, Languages and Linguistics; and Anne Masters, Matt Higgins and Lisa Clunie at the School of Art.

Other friends on both sides of the Tasman Sea provided me with accommodation on research trips, friendship and support, in particular Catriona Cairns, Sandra Fuller, Elizabeth McKenzie, Margaret Bearsley, Liz Geering and my cousin Liz Sinclair. I love you all—and anyone I have forgotten to name!

My sister Canberra members of the Australian Women's Archive Project Committee supported, inspired and encouraged me by providing me the opportunity to write more history for the Australian Women's Register. I particularly thank Anne Buttsworth for her support.

I remember and honour my mother-in-law, Nancy Bryce (19 March 1914 – 25 February 2015), who encouraged me in my endeavours and longed to see me complete the thesis, but died just before I managed it. I remember, too, my dear friend Mae Cairns who was almost as excited by my topic as I was but who died at Wellington Harbour in February 2012.

I am beholden to my brother Kerry Francis for the beautiful maps of Rosalie's Auckland and Canberra, which he made for me in the midst of his own busy academic year.

Huge gratitude to my editor Dr Rani Kerin, the best editor a historian and writer could hope for. During the final stages of manuscript preparation, after an accident that left me with a brain injury and concussion, Rani's compassion, understanding and patience sustained me and enabled the manuscript to be completed.

Thanks to the staff at ANU Press for guiding me through the process of preparing the book for publication—special thanks to Dr Nathan Hollier and Elouise Ball for coordinating and managing the process; and to Teresa Prowse for her beautiful cover design and the wonderful job she did designing the pages of the book, made complex by the many images.

I remember with loads of love the people who nurtured the historian in me from a young age and gave me a taste for women's stories: my maternal grandmother Mary Christina 'Daisy' Vahry, née Haswell (1883–1974), and her cousins Myra, Annie, Elsie and Hilda Lang, who entranced me with stories of our family's journey from the Highlands of Scotland after the land clearances, to Nova Scotia and then on to Waipū in Northland, Aotearoa New Zealand. My parents, Basil Stuart Francis (1913–1997) and Aylsa Daphne Francis, née Vahry (1914–1969), enriched my life with a love of books, reading, libraries and people's life stories.

I thank my wonderful sons who always inspire me: Ben Fawkes in Cambridge, United Kingdom, who led me to my topic; and Sacha Fawkes in Naarm Melbourne.

The last bouquet of gratitude goes to my beloved, Allen Bryce, who is ever constant in his belief in me, ever loving, ever supportive and always good-humoured. Without him, this could never have been.

Abbreviations

AAT	Anglo-Australian Telescope
ABC	Australian Broadcasting Corporation
ACT	Australian Capital Territory
AGNSW	Art Gallery of New South Wales
AM	Member of the Order of Australia
ANG	Australian National Gallery
ANU	The Australian National University
AO	Officer of the Order of Australia
AUC	Auckland University College
CAAB	Commonwealth Arts Advisory Board
CSIRO	Commonwealth Scientific and Industrial Research Organisation
EGGS	Epsom Girls' Grammar School
HSC	Horticultural Society of Canberra
ICMMA	International Council of the Museum of Modern Art
MOMA	Museum of Modern Art (New York)
NCDC	National Capital Development Commission
NGA	National Gallery of Australia
NGV	National Gallery of Victoria (Melbourne)
SPHWC	Society for the Protection of the Health of Women and Children (Aotearoa New Zealand)
VAB	Visual Arts Board (of the Australia Council)
VAD	Voluntary Aid Detachment
WGHS	Whangārei Girls' High School (Aotearoa New Zealand)
YWCA	Young Women's Christian Association

List of figures

Prologue

Rosalie Gascoigne first exhibited her art in 1974 at the age of fifty-seven. Within four years the National Gallery of Victoria had mounted a survey of her work. Just four years later, in 1982, she became the first Australian woman selected to represent Australia at the prestigious Venice Biennale. By the time of her death in 1999, her work had been exhibited in all the major art museums in Australia and Aotearoa New Zealand, as well as in New York's Metropolitan Museum of Art, and in Germany, Scandinavia and parts of Asia. In 2013, her work *Monaro* was shown in London's Royal Academy of Arts as part of the *Australia* exhibition, a survey of Australian art from 1800 to the present day. In 2021, she was part of the National Gallery of Australia's *Know My Name* exhibition that celebrated the work of women artists and aimed to enhance understanding of their contribution to Australia's cultural life. In 1998 Rosalie told Robin Hughes: 'I never considered myself an artist. I did what I did because I had to do it. Because I wanted to do it, because I wanted something to look at.'[1] Her need for 'something to look at' saw Rosalie become one of Australia's most celebrated contemporary artists.

Her story is inspiring, especially I think for women. At an age when women often begin to be overlooked, certainly in the 1970s but still now fifty years later, Rosalie stared down that likelihood and beat the odds. She became more visible. Despite having no formal art training in the academy, she achieved an international reputation. Public galleries as well as private collectors in Australia and Aotearoa New Zealand collected her work from the time of her first solo exhibition in 1974.

1 Hughes et al., 'Rosalie Gascoigne Artist', tape 4.

At the time of writing, the record of Rosalie Gascoigne's life has been primarily written by art historians or curators for catalogues accompanying exhibitions of her work who, of course, are focused on her work. They tend to cast only brief glances at the wider aspects of her life. In addition, her son Martin has written and published privately two family histories—a history of both his parents' Aotearoa New Zealand families, and another specifically about his mother's Aotearoa New Zealand origins.[2] In 2019, Martin published *Rosalie Gascoigne: A Catalogue Raisonné.*[3] British writer Vici MacDonald published a monograph rich in Rosalie's words and images.[4] I understand that Hannah Fink, a close Gascoigne family friend and art writer, is about to publish a biography that she commenced in 1997 while Rosalie still lived. Nothing substantial has been written by people who offer a perspective on her life from outside the family. Several interviews with Rosalie about her life exist in written and audiovisual forms, including the *Australian Biography* series created by Film Australia and the National Film and Sound Archive, with Robin Hughes as interviewer.[5] Through these we hear Rosalie's own voice reflecting on her past, making sense of the present, albeit mediated through interviewers and editors.

In many of the interviews conducted from 1978 onwards when she was beginning to achieve recognition, Rosalie recounts her life using recurrent themes of misfit, outsider and affinity with nature. Caroline Daley, in her study of gender and oral history, highlights the importance of analysing recurrent themes because 'what women remember and retell, and how they tell it, tells us much about their individual experiences and their understanding of their cultural place within their community'.[6] The emphases in Rosalie's story changed slightly as she achieved more and more recognition in the art world. Everyone does this: to make sense of our past in light of the changing present, and in consideration of our audience, we vary our narratives.

---

2 Gascoigne, *New Zealand Lives*; Gascoigne, *Rosalie Gascoigne: Her New Zealand Origins.*

3 Gascoigne, *Rosalie Gascoigne: A Catalogue Raisonné.*

4 MacDonald and Gascoigne, *Rosalie Gascoigne.*

5 Feneley and Gascoigne, 'Express Highlights'; Rosalie Gascoigne, interview by Stephen Feneley, 4 December 1997; Frost, 'Rosalie Gascoigne', 19–21; Gascoigne, interview by Topliss; Gascoigne, interview by North; Gascoigne, interview by Gleeson; Hughes et al., 'Rosalie Gascoigne Artist'; 'Know My Name Episode 6: Rosalie Gascoigne'; *Survey 2: Rosalie Gascoigne*; McDonald, 'There Are Only Lovers', 10–13; Mollison and Heath, 'Rosalie Gascoigne'.

6 Daley, 'He Would Know'.

Luisa Passerini wrote that 'all autobiographical memory is true: it is up to the interpreter to discover in which sense, where and for purpose'.[7] My approach does not deny the truth of Rosalie's self-narrative, despite its variance from some contemporary sources. I explore the stories she told and assess in what senses they were 'true'.

My research shaped the questions I asked of Rosalie's self-narrative. But what prompted me to undertake this study in the first place? My mother grew up in Tāmaki Makaurau Auckland during the same era as Rosalie; however, as the daughter of an enemy alien, she had a very different life. Rosalie and I grew up in adjacent Tāmaki Makaurau Auckland suburbs, attended the same high school, although decades apart. All my life I have collected shells, beachcombed and made installation art from found objects. As a woman in the latter half of my life, just as Rosalie was at the time of her first solo exhibition, her story inspired me when I saw first her art—at City Gallery Wellington in 2004, a few months before I moved to Canberra for my partner's work. Her art hit me in the solar plexus, just as Fred Williams's paintings of hillsides and trees did to Rosalie when she first saw them.[8] Her descriptions of the Canberra hinterland, its light and colour, its great blonde paddocks and raucous birds, eased some of my misgivings about moving across the Tasman.

Rosalie's story is admired by many people I met during the years of my doctoral research. As my research progressed, I became aware that there was more to her story than she revealed. Her life was complex, but her telling of it was simple, straightforward and thematically consistent.

More recently, as I prepared this book for publication, several people commented how much they enjoyed talking about Rosalie again and having her re-enter their lives through my contact over sources, photographs or archives. As a result, most people I contacted were generous with the offer of photographs and with permission to use their images, words and thoughts. I view such generosity as responses to Rosalie, to her art and her life—as tributes to a remarkable woman who had difficult times in her early life, but who found her own 'sort of heaven'; and to an artist whose work achieved international recognition, but who remained humble and unpretentious.

7 Passerini, 'Women's Personal Narratives', 189–97.

8 Hughes et al., 'Rosalie Gascoigne Artist', tape 3.

In the narratives Rosalie told about her life, she consistently presented herself as a misfit and outsider. Yet, some of the detail of her life suggests she was a social insider: a child who, although her family of origin was riven with complex difficulties, enjoyed financial stability, attended good schools, achieved well academically, and was outgoing and popular with adults and children. In many respects she enjoyed a privileged background, which made a university education and teacher training possible. Likewise, a stable marriage with a degree of affluence permitted her the time and space to explore her artistic sensibility; and she was able to access circles in which recognition came quickly and fully. A dearth of sources about her inner life inhibits understanding of whether she felt like an outsider at the time, or whether such feelings were the result of later reflection. Historian Barbara Caine describes a new literary approach to sources such as letters and diaries that recognises that authors are 'engaged in a literary exercise, constructing and representing themselves' in various ways.[9]

Using her memories, Rosalie reinterpreted her life in light of her artistic success. Historians and other academics have extensively engaged with matters of memory and its reinterpretation. Diverse experts in the field of biography such as Carolyn Steedman, Nicola King, James Olney, Jonathon Boyarin and Charles Fernyhough agree that people constantly reinterpret their lives.[10] King, an English academic who specialises in autobiography and memory, emphasises the importance of hindsight in creating significance.[11] Fernyhough, a psychologist, suggests that early memories often function as creation myths.[12] Rosalie's early memories of not fitting in, reinterpreted through the course of her life, could be viewed as 'myths of creation'—memories reinterpreted to fit her later narrative of the outsider artist. She often quoted Picasso as saying artists are born not made.[13] She told Vici MacDonald: 'As Picasso said, you don't become an artist, you're born one.'[14] Just as early in her career she made frames from discards for postcards of favourite artworks, Rosalie created a frame for her lived life from reinterpreted memories that fitted with her understanding of herself as an artist.

9 Caine, *Biography and History*, 98.

10 Steedman, *Past Tenses*; King, *Memory, Narrative, Identity*; Olney, *Memory & Narrative*; Boyarin, ed., *Remapping Memory*; Fernyhough, *Pieces of Light*.

11 Egan, 'Review of Nicola King', 922.

12 Fernyhough, *Pieces of Light*.

13 Hughes et al., 'Rosalie Gascoigne Artist', tape 8.

14 MacDonald and Gascoigne, *Rosalie Gascoigne*, 38.

This biography is not a work of art history.[15] It is an historical approach to Rosalie's life that presents a contextualised, contingent and critical account of what led her to create her art. It is contextualised within limits. In the epilogue, I place Rosalie in the wider context of challenges facing creative women. This biography is an attempt to assemble a more comprehensive picture of who she was and how she came to be an acclaimed artist making work 'about the pleasures of the eye' that was born of her adjustment to a new country, her feeling of being a misfit and outsider for much of her life and her affinity with nature.[16] I use the frame of her life that she created in interviews once she achieved fame as an artist, and her own words, as much as possible. That is, I have written the biography on her terms, not mine, not ours.

'I'd never been out of New Zealand before'[17]

It is January 1943. Newly married Rosalie Gascoigne stands on the crumbly, reddish-brown earth of Mt Stromlo, just outside Canberra, the national capital of Australia. Under the 'huge sky and lots of air' she is looking at the unfamiliar land of the ancient limestone of the Monaro Plain spread out before her. It seems endless with its high horizons, undulating plains and swaying golden grasslands.

She has been here only a few weeks, having left her home in the harbour city of Auckland on Aotearoa New Zealand's North Island. Here, there is no harbour, no Rangitoto, the iconic island in Auckland's Waitematā Harbour. 'Everything [is] different from New Zealand … the big birds like the currawongs and magpies squashed and toppled the bushes', while brightly coloured parrots scream raucously against bright blue skies. And it is hot, unlike anything she has known in Auckland: 'the sun [hits] you like a hammer'.[18]

The previous weeks have been a whirlwind. Rosalie has left behind her family, good friends and Auckland's familiarity. In a matter of a few days, she has journeyed by flying boat from Auckland to Sydney, then by train to Canberra; married; taken her husband Ben Gascoigne's name; honeymooned

15 For art history, see Gascoigne, *Rosalie Gascoigne: A Catalogue Raisonné*.
16 'Know My Name Episode 6: Rosalie Gascoigne'.
17 Hughes et al., 'Rosalie Gascoigne Artist', tape 6.
18 Ibid., tape 2.

in Sydney; and returned to Mt Stromlo, the scientific community where Ben works. The land she casts her eyes over is as unfamiliar as the life in which she finds herself. It is her first time outside of Aotearoa New Zealand. Like D. H. Lawrence's 'bird blown out of its own latitude', Rosalie is unsettled by the strange landscape.[19]

'Everything was different from New Zealand'[20]

> I had to make a friend in a strange country … I had to discard the New Zealand landscape, which I was passionately fond of. And make friends with this one. Which takes some years if you're not a tree, not a something, no harbour, no Rangitoto, no nothing. All the things that were built into you had disappeared … I was fairly desperate for something that I could associate with. And well, nature was my friend.[21]

Czech-born philosopher and exile (to Brazil) from Nazi tyranny in Europe, Vilém Flusser contended that all migration is exile and that exile is the incubator of creativity because the shock of difference enables exiles and migrants to see their new country with fresh eyes.[22] Flusser wrote that in our familiar surroundings we notice only change, whereas in a new place we see things with a fresh focus that can stimulate creativity.[23] He claimed that familiarity anaesthetises: 'it smooths the sharp edges of all phenomena … so that I can no longer bump against them'.[24]

During her childhood in Aotearoa New Zealand, Rosalie had developed an affinity with nature and a heightened visual awareness. Both stood her in good stead in the new environment, ameliorating her feelings of dislocation and isolation during the first years on Stromlo. In Flusser's terms, she transformed the data about the new landscape into 'meaningful messages'

19 Lawrence, *The Rainbow*, 296.
20 Hughes et al., 'Rosalie Gascoigne Artist', tape 2.
21 Hughes et al., 'Rosalie Gascoigne Artist', tape 8.
22 Flusser, 'Exile and Creativity', 81–7.
23 Ibid., 86.
24 Flusser, 'The Challenge of the Migrant', 13.

in a creative process.[25] Rosalie sought solace in nature. She called nature her friend.[26] Her acute visual awareness became crucial to her survival. Flusser considered this 'data processing' to be urgent:

> A matter of life and death. If [she] is not able to process the data, [she] will be swamped and consumed by the waves of exile breaking over [her]. Data processing is synonymous with creation.[27]

While Rosalie's absorption of the different landscape may not have been a matter of literal life and death, it animated her creative impulses and formed a basis for her artistic practice.

During her first ten years in Australia, Rosalie's success at gardening and flower arranging led her to ikebana and then, seeking more permanence for her creations, she began to make compositions with weathered objects she found in the Canberra hinterland, 'the readily available thing … readily available because people have been using it … the stuff of our life'.[28]

Rosalie's affinity with nature led her into making art with plant material she found in the terrain around Canberra—large bushes, stalks, grasses, dried flowers. She branched out into collecting discarded, weathered, used things, worn by nature or human use. These she would assemble, finding shape and form within the material itself as learned in ikebana. Rosalie was not interested in the materials' history. She shunned nostalgia. Her art was a felt response to the materials and sometimes the environment in which she found them:

> at the beginning you like the material, it works a bit visually for you, and putting it with something else gets a little bit exciting. But that is not enough—you have to work into it something you genuinely felt. It is not a question of just making pictures … It is expressing something in the end. But at first you are seduced by the visual thing of it.[29]

25 Flusser, 'Exile and Creativity', 81–3.

26 Hughes et al., 'Rosalie Gascoigne Artist', tape 1: 'Nature Was My Friend'; Feneley and Gascoigne, 'Express Highlights': 'And well, nature was a friend.'

27 Flusser, 'Exile and Creativity', 83.

28 Gascoigne, interview by Gleeson. Note, when Gleeson asked Rosalie: 'And the material that you work with is material that you have searched for and found almost anywhere?' Rosalie responded: 'I have not searched for it—I have found it. I just look at what's about.'

29 Gascoigne, interview by Gleeson.

Context and contingency

> Biography can be seen as the archetypal 'contingent narrative' and the one best able to show the great importance of particular locations and circumstances and the multiple layers of historical change and experience.[30]

Contingency is a feature of all lives, as is context. The time and place in which Rosalie achieved recognition and acclaim as an artist are crucial parts of her story. Canberra's exponential growth from the 1950s, as a result of Prime Minister Robert Menzies's commitment to build a national capital befitting Australia, saw it develop from a small country town to a city with major national cultural and heritage institutions. After its foundation in 1913, development was hindered by world wars I and II and the 1930s Depression. With the transfer of public service offices, the expansion of The Australian National University (ANU) and the development of the Commonwealth Scientific and Industrial Research Organisation (CSIRO), the city became home to a highly educated mix of academics, scientists, writers, researchers, politicians and high-level administrators from the 1950s. Rosalie's husband's position as a scientist and then academic when ANU took over the Commonwealth Observatory based on Mt Stromlo in 1957 meant that Rosalie was part of an intellectual milieu, albeit with the status of 'wife'—against which she railed. A further influx of poets, artists, craftspeople and arts administrators arrived with the opening of national arts, heritage and cultural institutions in the early 1970s. Some of these people shared Rosalie's environmental and artistic sensibilities and became her friends.

Crucially, changes in the Australian art world became significant in Rosalie's recognition: the commercialisation of art and the rise of Canberra's dealer galleries; changing art tastes; and, in particular, the growth of art bureaucracies around the Australian National Gallery (ANG, later the National Gallery of Australia) and public state galleries. New ways of showing, selling and buying art developed with the increase in dealer galleries and move away from art society exhibitions, which is where public institutions had previously bought for their collections.[31] Rosalie held her first solo exhibition in 1974

30 Caine, *Biography and History*, 2.
31 McQueen, *Suburbs of the Sacred*, 153.

in one of these dealer galleries and was elated when James Mollison, then acting director of the yet-to-be-built ANG, purchased two works. A few months later he purchased two additional works.[32]

Bernard Smith's *Australian Painting* (1962), Humphrey McQueen's *Suburbs of the Sacred* (1988) and Andrew Sayers's *Australian Art* (2001) all attest to the power of curators, critics and dealers in Australia's growing art industry during this period.

In terms of art tastes, the primacy of painting and sculpture waned during the 1950s and 1960s, opening the way for artists to achieve recognition in other media and genres. Rosalie's assemblages of discarded objects, through which she expressed her feelings for the land, related to a long tradition of landscape art in Australia but also extended it. While she fitted into this tradition, she adapted to it in a new way. Her practice intersected with increased acceptance of other ways of making art, including installation and assemblage, that flourished in Australia in the 1960s. She brought landscape and environmental sensibility together with contemporary art approaches.

These changes, together with increased funding for public galleries and the opening of the ANG, set the scene for growing ranks of curators, each of whom needed artists and styles to promote.[33] Enter James Mollison, a young curator destined to become foundation director of the ANG, who befriended Rosalie and Ben through their elder son Martin. Mollison was to become key in Rosalie's artistic development and recognition.

Rosalie's timing was auspicious. She entered the industry at a moment when the doors had been thrown open in terms of style, when there were increased opportunities to exhibit so that her work was more visible to buyers from public institutions, and when young curators were on the hunt for talent.

***

32 The four works purchased by Mollison for the Philip Morris Collection were *Back Verandah*, 1974 (045 in Gascoigne, *Rosalie Gascoigne: A Catalogue Raisonné*, 156); *The Dredge* (065 in *Catalogue Raisonné*, 160); *Woolshed*, 1974 (071 in *Catalogue Raisonné*, 161); *Bowl of Balls*, 1974–75 (075 in *Catalogue Raisonné*, 162).

33 McQueen, *Suburbs of the Sacred*, 153.

Rosalie and Ben met over a bridge table at a mutual friend's place in Remuera, Auckland, while they were both students at Auckland University College. Ben's doctoral study in Bristol, England, led him to be recruited for wartime optics work at the observatory on Mt Stromlo, and he started work there in late 1941. The couple corresponded regularly but had not seen each other for sixteen months prior to their marriage.

On Stromlo, Rosalie struggled to fit in. A university-educated high school teacher in Auckland, living within an easy tram ride to the city with its cinemas, dances, galleries and friends, she found herself expected to keep house in a tiny scientific community with no transport apart from one bus a day to the then small town of Canberra, population eleven thousand.

Now we know her as Rosalie Gascoigne, an acclaimed artist. However, she travelled a long road to that recognition and, indeed, to her own identification as an artist. In 1998, she expressed some of her struggles to Robin Hughes for Film Australia's *Australian Biography* series: 'You peel yourself like an onion to make visible what you really are. And I didn't know what I was. I just knew I was out of step and always looking.'[34]

A lone marigold pushing its way through weeds in her Stromlo garden inspired her to take up gardening. That led to flower arranging, specifically to Sogetsu Ikebana, an art form popularised by Norman Sparnon who had learned it in Japan and founded schools throughout Australia and New Zealand in the 1960s.

Eventually tiring of ikebana, seeking more permanence but having learnt composition and form from the Japanese art, Rosalie began making art from objects she found in the countryside around Canberra, including the local rubbish tip (see Figure 0.1). From there her rise in the art world was stellar but her self-identification as an artist took decades. To Hughes she voiced her joy at the artistic success that enabled her identification and recognition as an artist: 'I got my own sort of heaven.'[35] It was, she would insist, a hard-won heaven:

> I spent a lot of time … restless and out of step with everybody … And then I came to this thing I could do and it grew. And all you had to do was, as it were, hang loose and just use your eye.[36]

34 Hughes et al., 'Rosalie Gascoigne Artist', tape 8.

35 Ibid., tape 4.

36 Ibid, tape 8.

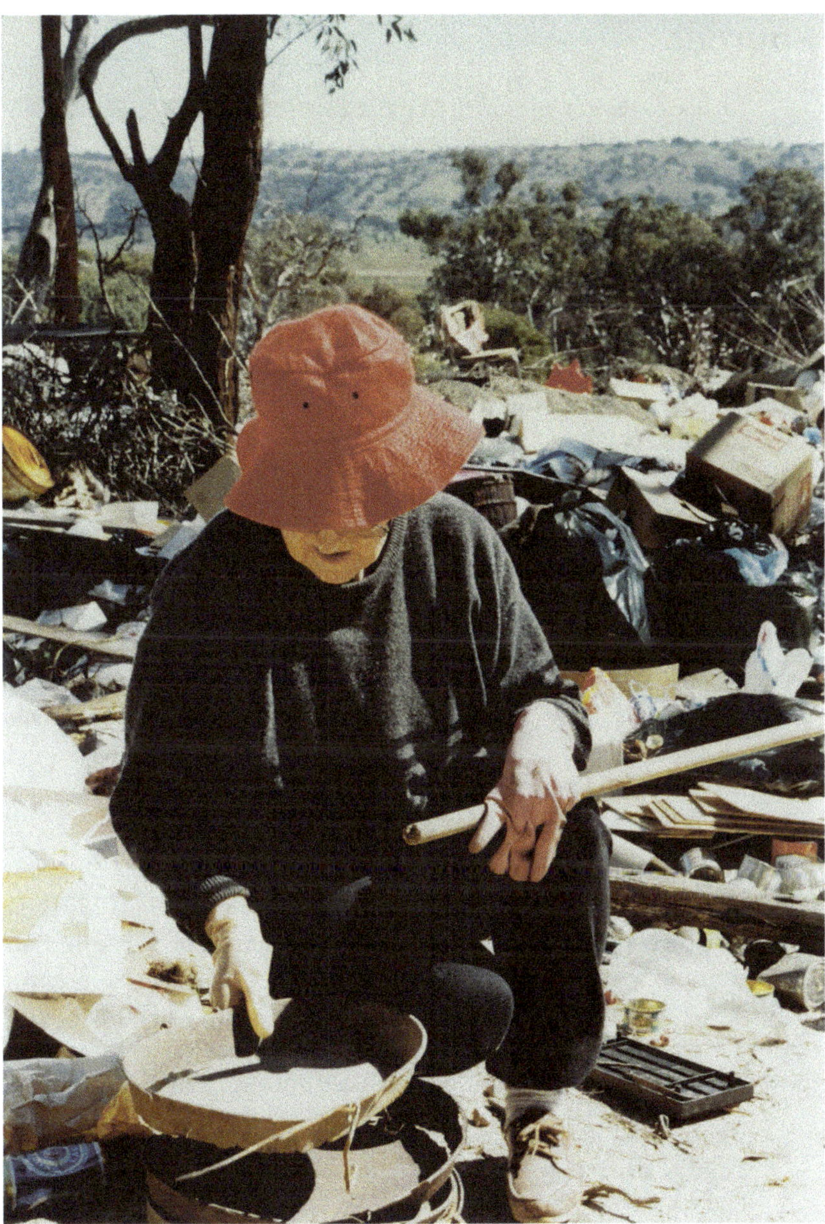

Figure 0.1: Rosalie exploring materials at a local rubbish tip, 1980s or 1990s.

Source: Courtesy of Gascoigne family.

Sources

> I like collecting. I use what I find out there, take what is available from tips and what has been dumped.[37]

A major challenge in writing this biography has been a scarcity of sources. Somebody wrestling with her role as a housewife does not usually accumulate orderly boxes of personal papers. Where there are personal papers, I did not have access to them. This is not, like Janet Malcolm's *Silent Woman*, an account of the issue of biographer's access. It is a historical biography.[38] Given this situation, I took heart from Rosalie's comment: 'there is virtue in scarcity; I don't need a lot of props. Scarcity leads to saying more with less and a higher acceptance of faults.'[39]

Rosalie collected materials for her art, and I gathered what I could for this narrative of her life. In a 1994 Australian Broadcasting Corporation (ABC) interview on the *Arts Today* program, Rosalie resorted to a womanly, domestic metaphor to describe her love of collecting materials and how she saw that as a quite distinct part of her work:

> Collecting is a separate part of my oeuvre. I enjoy going out as a woman who enjoys going out with her basket shopping. You take what you think is nice or what is interesting and you don't care about the art form. That's a separate life altogether. So you collect all this stuff and you never ever throw it away, or hardly ever, because you're not going to get it again.[40]

Interviews with Rosalie, particularly those by North, Hughes, Mollison, Topliss, Jelbart and Heath, provide a rich collection of her reflections and recounting of her life. From the beginning, I aimed to keep her at the heart of my project and to make her voice heard. While this sounds obvious for a biography, impressionist painter Edouard Manet understood the difficulties in such a venture. He has been quoted as saying:

> You would hardly believe how difficult it is to place a figure alone on a canvas, and to concentrate all the interest on this single and unique figure and still keep it living and real.[41]

---

37 Mollison and Heath, 'Rosalie Gascoigne', 7–8.

38 Malcolm, *The Silent Woman*.

39 Ibid., 8.

40 'Know My Name Episode 6: Rosalie Gascoigne'. See Figure 0.2.

41 Quotation attributed to Edouard Manet (1880) in many sources but I have been unable to locate the original source. Examples include reports of the *Manet: Portraying Life* exhibition held at the Royal Academy, London, in 2013, such as Sugar, 'Manet Portraying Life', 16–17.

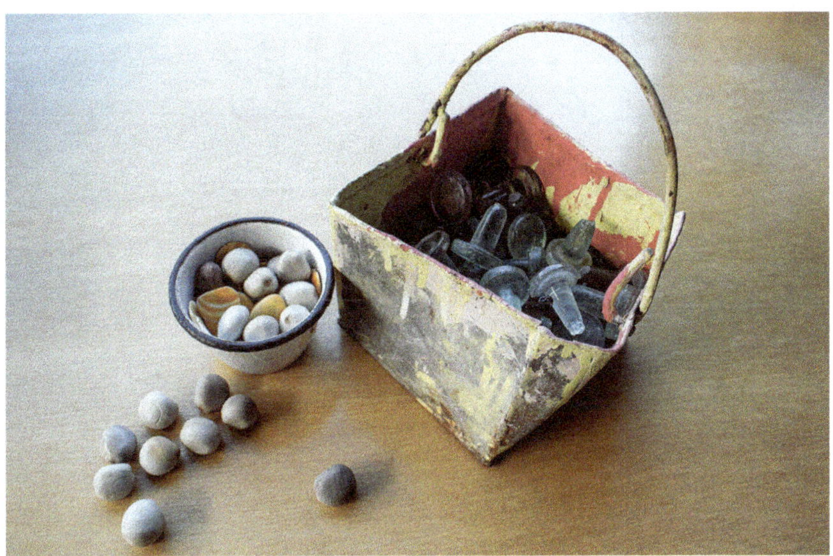

Figure 0.2: Items collected by Rosalie, at Hester Gascoigne's home, 2023.
Source: Photograph and courtesy: Sally Colahan Griffin.

I have attempted to stay in tune with Rosalie's voice and presence through listening to (and watching where possible) her interviews, and standing in the presence of her art.

I have arranged the biography in three chronological parts. Rosalie's visual awareness and love of the natural world—her friendship with nature—are threaded through the narrative, adding texture to her life and providing the foundation for her artistic practice.

A story frequently told about Rosalie is that of an older woman 'discovering herself' later in life through art: a woman with no formal art training creating art later in life and shooting to fame. Her story is more complex than that. This is the first comprehensive historical biography of Rosalie Gascoigne. In this version of Rosalie's story, I use the frames she herself created and examine the context of her stellar rise, as her life intersected with historical changes in Australia in the 1960s and 1970s.

Unfortunately, because of copyright complexities, this book contains no images of Rosalie's work, however, all her work can be seen in *Rosalie Gascoigne: A Catalogue Raisonné* by her son Martin Gascoigne, downloadable at no cost from ANU Press.[42]

42 Gascoigne, *Rosalie Gascoigne: A Catalogue Raisonné*.

PART I

1917–43

AUCKLAND

Light and shadow

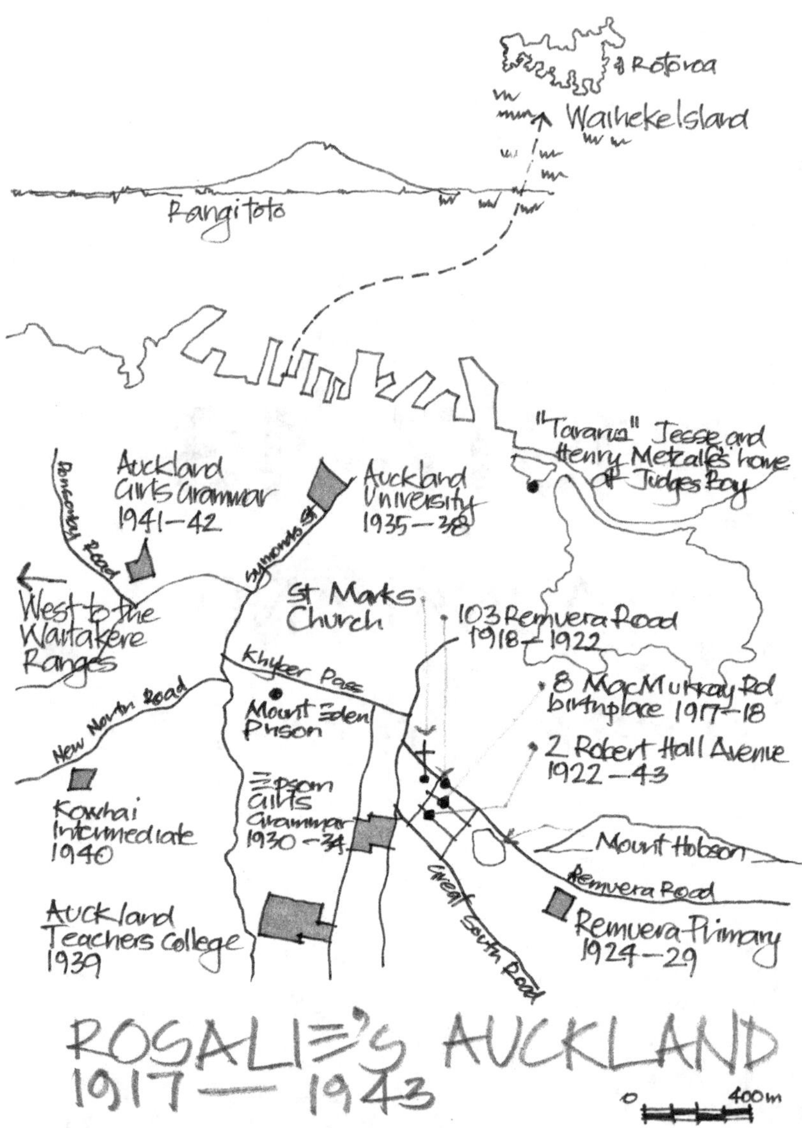

Map 1: Rosalie's Auckland, 1917–43.

Source: Map drawn by Kerry Francis, architect and academic, Tāmaki Makaurau Auckland, Aotearoa New Zealand. Courtesy of Kerry Francis.

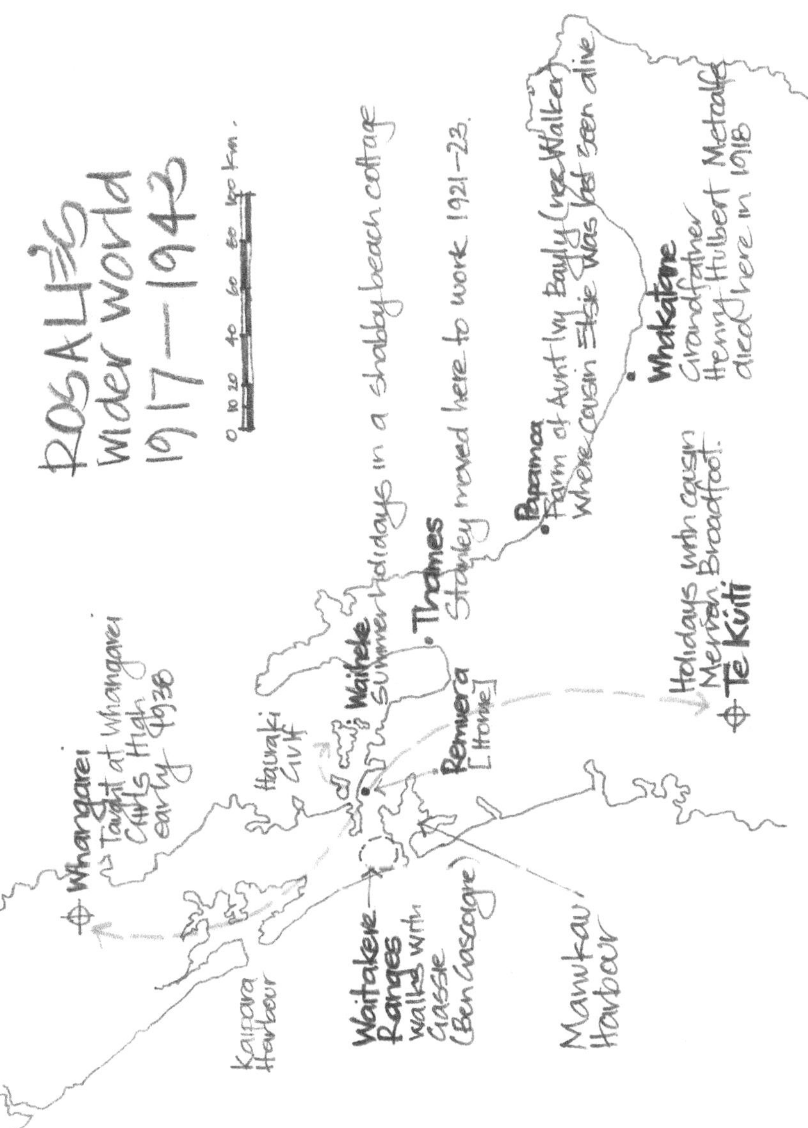

Map 2: Rosalie's wider world, 1917–43.

Source: Map drawn by Kerry Francis, architect and academic, Tāmaki Makaurau Auckland, Aotearoa New Zealand. Courtesy of Kerry Francis.

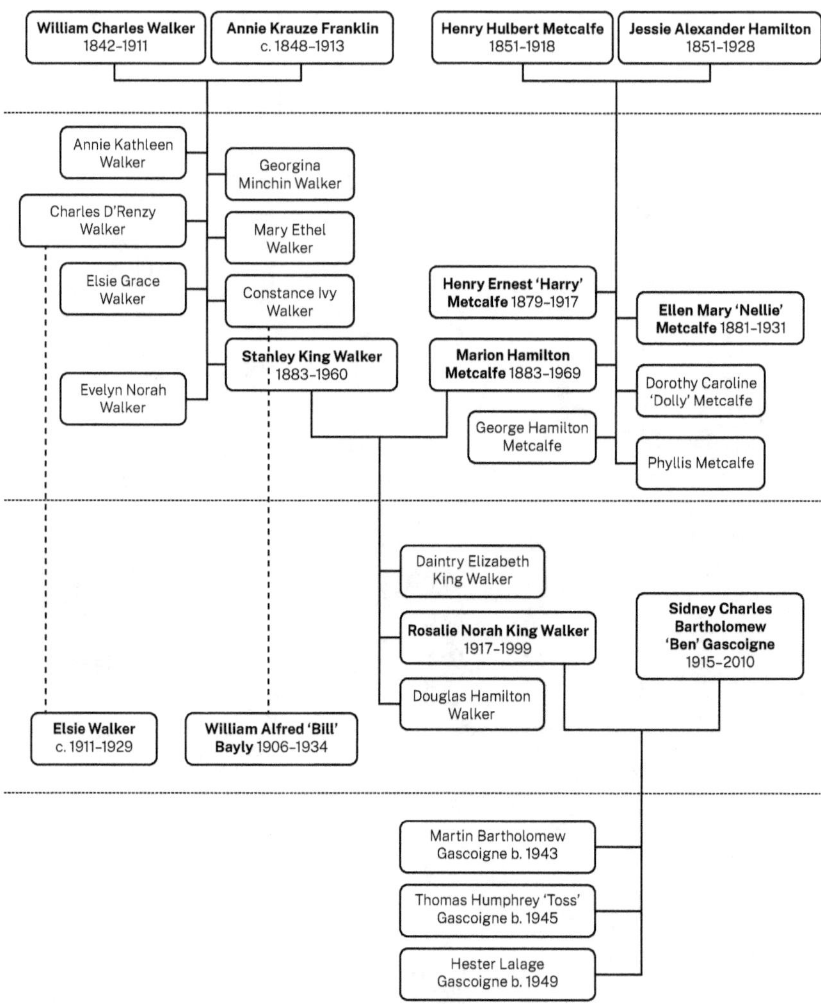

Figure 1.1: Rosalie's family tree.

Source: Author's research.

1

1917–22: 'Happiness didn't enter into it'

Beginnings

The *Auckland Star* recorded sunny, calm conditions on 25 January 1917, the day Rosalie was born in her family home at 8 MacMurray Road, Remuera, an exclusive suburb near Auckland's centre (see Figure 1.2). MacMurray Road lies at the foot of Ōhinerau (Mt Hobson), a pre-European Māori pā (fortified village site).[1] Ōhinerau's slopes were to become Rosalie's playground, a place with the power to shape a sensibility. From the time of her birth until she left for Canberra in 1943, she lived at the base of this maunga (mountain) in three houses within two blocks and four hundred metres of each other.

Marion (née Metcalfe) and Stanley Walker already had one child—Daintry, born in December 1915. The couple's third child, Douglas, would be born the year following Rosalie's birth. Marion gave birth to all three children in the family home at MacMurray Road. Then, as now, MacMurray Road was a broad, tree-lined avenue with wide grass verges and substantial single-storey residences set well back behind hedges or elegant fences. The Walkers' neighbours were well-to-do managers, accountants and merchants, most of whom owned their homes.[2]

1 Auckland Council, 'Ōhinerau / Mt Hobson Path'.
2 Auckland Council, 'Lot 84, MacMurray Road'.

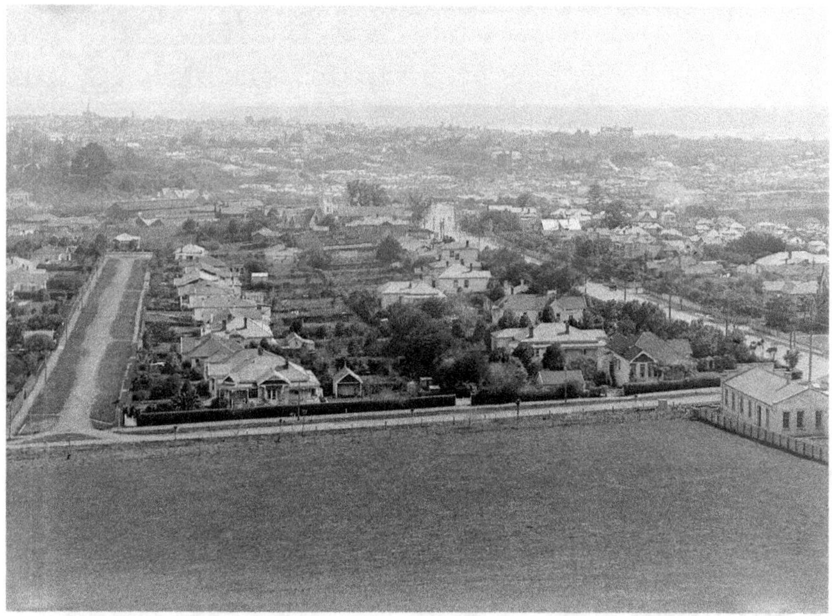

Figure 1.2: MacMurray Road, Remuera (left of picture) and Remuera Road on the right, looking north-west from Mt Hobson, 1920.

Note: Eight MacMurray Road is on the right-hand side of the street, the fourth house from the far end with the lighter coloured roof. The Walker's second house, on Remuera Road, was one of the single-storeyed houses that backed on to MacMurray Road. The steeple of St Marks Anglican Church, where Rosalie was baptised on 20 September 1917 and her grandfather's funeral was held in May 1918, can be seen centre left. Robert Hall Avenue, where Marion and the children moved with Jessie and Nellie in late 1922, is to the left of the far end of MacMurray Road, just out of the picture.

Source: Courtesy of Auckland Libraries Heritages Collections, 4-4603.
Photograph: James D. Richardson.

On 14 August 1916, Marion Walker, four months pregnant with Rosalie, sought home help through an advertisement in the *Auckland Star*: 'Girl or Lady Help wanted to assist—Mrs S. K. Walker, MacMurray Road, Remuera. Phone A749.'[3] Rosalie's daughter, Hester Gascoigne, recalls her mother telling her stories of childhood adventures on Ōhinerau's slopes:

> They roamed wild up there a bit when they were kids … I remember Mum talking about … being chased by draught horses and sitting in the bottom of a hole and this great big horses head … in a sort of friendly enquiring way … peering down.[4]

3 'Domestics Wanted', *Auckland Star*, 14 August 1916, 1.

4 Hester Gascoigne, interview by author, 20 February 2011.

One of Auckland's many volcanic cones, known in te reo Māori as maunga and considered tupuna (ancestors) of Māori, Ōhinerau was scarred by a quarry on its northern slopes. A reservoir topped the cone and cows grazed among the terraces, ditch defences, storage pits and middens that, even today, remain as evidence of the earlier fortified Māori pā.

During childhood Rosalie climbed the green slopes and stood on the summit, her gaze switching between the harbours on both sides of the isthmus that is Auckland. The view provided the training ground for her sense of far perspective, minute attention to detail and layered pasts in the Māori and colonial history of the land on which she stood.

Here were the birthplaces of her visual acuity, which led to her art making, and to her finding her own sort of heaven. She later recalled how she noticed shapes and colours, shadows and light as a young child. In 1980, she told Australian National Gallery curator and friend Ian North, 'I always noticed natural things.'[5] In 1998, during an interview for the *Australian Biography* series, she spoke of strong visual memories from her early years.[6] The earliest were of the tall puka tree, with its large, glossy green leaves, in the garden of her second house in Remuera Road.[7] Rosalie remembered how she and her sister Daintry would seesaw 'up and through the Michaelmas daisies'.[8]

These memories, from Rosalie's first five years, are harbingers of the visual awareness that saw her develop into an artist who produced works that Ian North described as possessing 'lyricism, grace and sense of place … delighted luminous celebrations of the here and how'.[9]

The art of which North spoke was many years in the future. The here and now is the harbour city of Auckland, later referred to by its te reo Māori name, Tāmaki Makaurau. As already described, Marion Walker gave birth to her second daughter in the family home at the foot of a green hill in a pleasant suburb inhabited by the affluent. Rosalie said of her birth: 'I just rushed out—I've always rushed out of things.'[10] She rushed out into a complex family during a traumatic time in Aotearoa New Zealand history.

5 Gascoigne, interview by North, 11.
6 Hughes et al., 'Rosalie Gascoigne Artist'.
7 Meryta sinclairii, the *puka* or *pukanui*, is a large-leaved evergreen tree endemic to Aotearoa New Zealand that grows to about eight metres tall. See Auckland Botanic Gardens, 'Meryta sinclairii'.
8 Hughes et al., 'Rosalie Gascoigne Artist'.
9 North and Catalano, *Australia, Venice Biennale 1982*, 54.
10 Frost, 'Rosalie Gascoigne', 21.

The name of the hill at the end of the street, Ōhinerau, means the place of Hinerau, the goddess of whirlwinds.[11] The world into which Rosalie was born was in a whirlwind. In contrast with the sunny calm reported by the *Auckland Star*, news stories surrounding the day's weather report were dark with the turmoil and destruction of war, including fighting on the Western Front, fears of a renewed German offensive at Verdun and despair that President of the United States Woodrow Wilson's dream for peace without victory seemed impossible. War would soon impact directly on the new baby's family, but on the day of her birth, it was only one of several shadows looming. Although she grew up in a comfortable environment, with green lawns and space to play, Rosalie's childhood was shaped by her parents' difficult marriage and tensions created, at least in part, by their differing social backgrounds.

Grandparents: The Metcalfes and the Walkers[12]

Rosalie's maternal grandparents, Henry Hulbert Metcalfe (see Figure 1.3) and Jessie Alexander Metcalfe (née Hamilton) (see Figure 1.4), met as young people in England. Henry attended Cheltenham College in Gloucestershire at the same time as Jessie's brothers. The school prepared well-to-do young men for life in the service of the British Empire, including the Indian Army, which Jessie's brothers joined. Henry's sisters, Mary Georgina, Clare and Constance, attended the equally exclusive Cheltenham Ladies' College, which aimed to create wives, mothers and teachers to further the interests of the empire.[13]

The Hamiltons and the Metcalfes had lived in the same neighbourhood and moved in the same privileged social circles, so Henry and Jessie's marriage was based on similarity—on social and cultural cohesion—in marked contrast to the disparities between Marion and Stanley, Rosalie's parents.

11 Auckland Council, 'Ōhinerau / Mt Hobson Path'.

12 See Figures 1.3–1.6.

13 Isabel Laing, archivist, Cheltenham Ladies' College, UK, email to author, 27 June 2013. Martin Gascoigne wrote in his family history that Jessie Hamilton attended 'Cheltenham Girls' School'; however, Cheltenham Ladies' College has no record of her attending the exclusive school. It is possible she attended one of the 'number of small private girls' schools in Cheltenham around that time' (Laing to author).

Jessie was born in Glasgow to a comfortable merchant family who moved to Cheltenham when Jessie was thirteen years old. Jessie's Scottish birth was the source of Rosalie's later comments that her siblings, Daintry and Douglas, were Scottish and 'dour', traits that she felt stood in stark opposition to her own Irish and 'silly' nature, traits that she believed she inherited from her father.[14]

The eldest son of southern English gentry, Henry was an engineer spawned by the Industrial Revolution. He practised his profession in England before travelling to South Africa, Brazil and eventually Australia, arriving there in 1878.[15] Jessie joined him in Adelaide in 1879. They married and Jessie gave birth to their first two children, Henry Ernest 'Harry' and Ellen Mary 'Nellie', who was to be significant in Rosalie's childhood. Jessie gave birth to Rosalie's mother, Marion, near Sydney in 1882, and the following year the family moved across the Tasman Sea to New Zealand, where Henry established a successful engineering practice in Auckland.

The Metcalfe family was once 'well connected' and this remained part of their sense of family identity. Their relationship to English royalty is documented in William the Conqueror's genealogy and in the Plantagenet *Roll of the Blood Royal*, a complete table of the descendants of King Edward III of England who were living at the time of the roll's publication in 1911.[16] Once in Auckland, the family found its 'place': family members frequently appeared in the social pages with descriptions of their attire at Auckland society's balls, dances and parties.

In 1917, when Rosalie was born, Henry and Jessie lived in style in *Tararua*, their substantial twelve-roomed home set among large old pōhutukawa trees on two and three-quarter acres in Judges Bay, a pocket of exclusive housing in Parnell, a short distance up Parnell Rise from Auckland city. From *Tararua* they enjoyed panoramic views over Waitematā Harbour and Hauraki Gulf. Henry, a highly respected engineer, ran a successful family engineering consultancy. The Metcalfe's elder son Harry, Henry's business partner, was fighting on the Western Front in France, serving with the specialist New Zealand Tunnelling Company.

14 Hughes et al., 'Rosalie Gascoigne Artist', tape 1.

15 Gascoigne, *Rosalie Gascoigne: Her New Zealand Origins*, 82–113.

16 Marquis of Ruvigny and Raineval, *The Plantagenet Roll of the Blood Royal.*

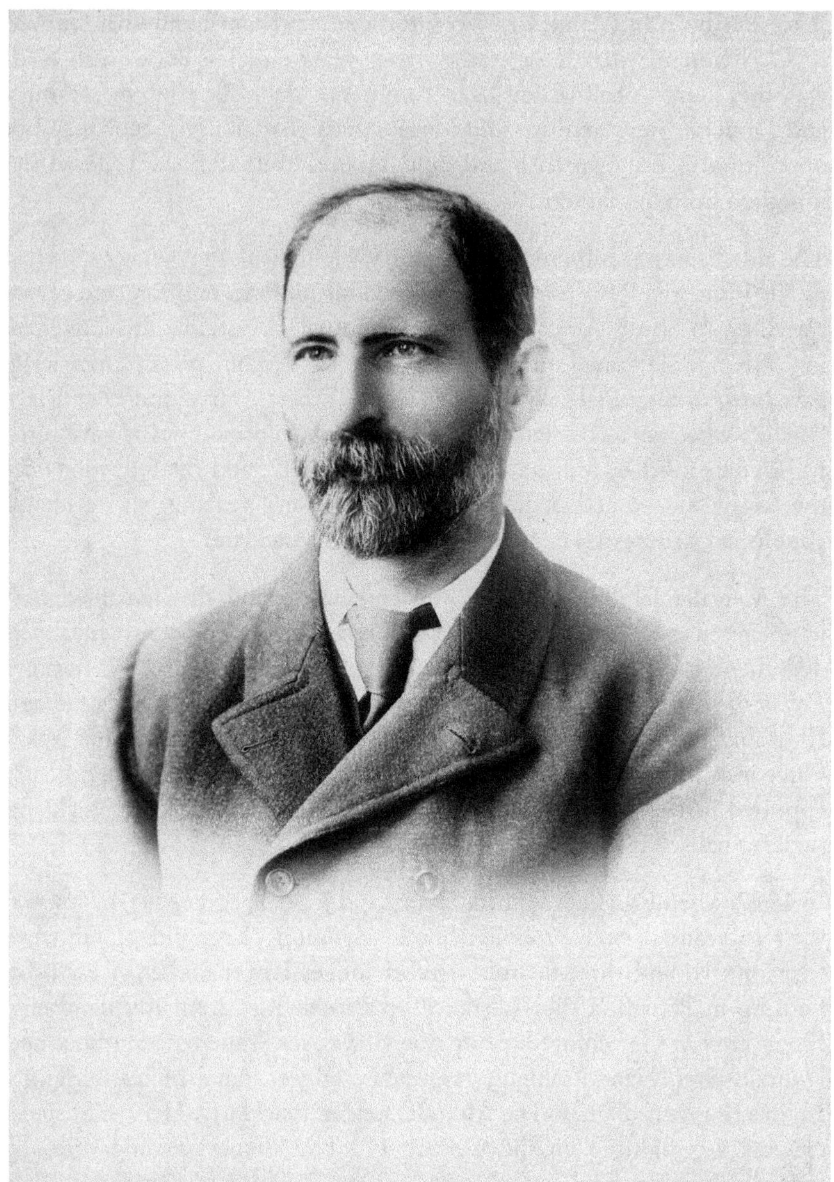

Figure 1.3: Henry Hulbert Metcalfe, Rosalie's maternal grandfather.
Source: Courtesy of the Gascoigne family.

Rosalie's Metcalfe grandparents were a central part of her young life. Her Walker grandparents had both died by the time of her birth. William Charles Walker and Annie Krauze Franklin (see Figures 1.5 and 1.6), both Anglo-Irish and Protestant, emigrated separately from Ireland to New

Zealand in the mid-1860s. William took a partnership in King, Walker & Co., successful commission merchants whose main line was in wines and spirits. William and Annie enjoyed prosperity and high regard in Auckland society. Their names appeared in the social pages among those attending Government House's Queen's Birthday Ball in 1896 and Birthday Reception in 1900.[17] William Walker was a justice of the peace and sat on the Police Court Bench.

Stanley, born in 1883, was William and Annie's second youngest child. He had two half-brothers from his mother's first marriage, six sisters and an elder brother. By all accounts, the family doted on him as the youngest son.[18]

Both grandfathers, then, were well known in Auckland society. Grandfather Metcalfe was respected for his contribution to civil engineering works throughout New Zealand, including the construction of the main trunk railway line, bridges, ports and waterworks. Grandfather Walker was known as 'Whiskey Walker', a well-known, well-liked character. According to the *Observer* newspaper, he was popular in social circles, 'his social qualities making him a favourite everywhere'.[19]

With this mixed inheritance, Rosalie grew up in the context of both an awareness of 'standing' but also an increasing sense of status anxiety. Stanley's family status had already slipped due to his father's death and the resulting loss of income from King, Walker & Co., income on which his family had depended as their major asset. Marion's family status started slipping when Rosalie was a toddler due to the deaths of grandfather Metcalfe and Uncle Harry and the consequent demise of the engineering business. The different social statuses of her parents' families combined with the complexity involved in the Metcalfe family's social slippage during Rosalie's early years, comprised part of the difficult context of Rosalie's early years and contributed to her sense of being out of step. The family in which she grew up, accustomed to high social standing, now struggled to find its footing in the changing Auckland society.

As was usual at this time, the women of both families fulfilled the roles of wife and mother. Later, Marion was to break this pattern, adding another layer of difference to Rosalie's childhood situation.

17 'Govt House Ball', *New Zealand Graphic and Ladies Journal*, 6 June 1896; 'Govt House Reception', *New Zealand Graphic and Ladies Journal*, 16 June 1900.

18 Gascoigne, *Rosalie Gascoigne: Her New Zealand Origins*, 185.

19 *Observer*, 14 May 1887, 11, cited in Gascoigne, *Rosalie Gascoigne: Her New Zealand Origins*, 147.

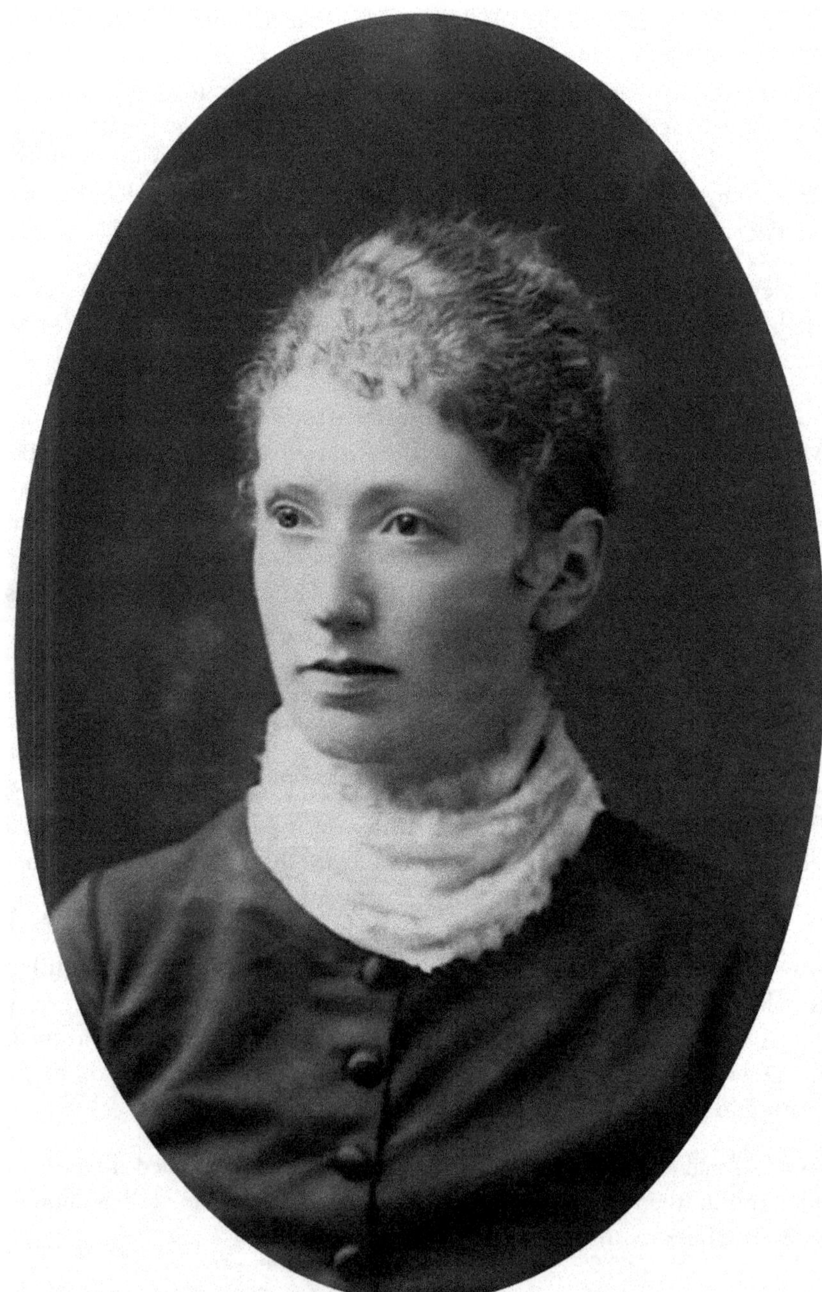

Figure 1.4: Rosalie's grandmother Jessie Alexander Metcalfe (née Hamilton) as a young woman.

Source: Courtesy of the Gascoigne family.

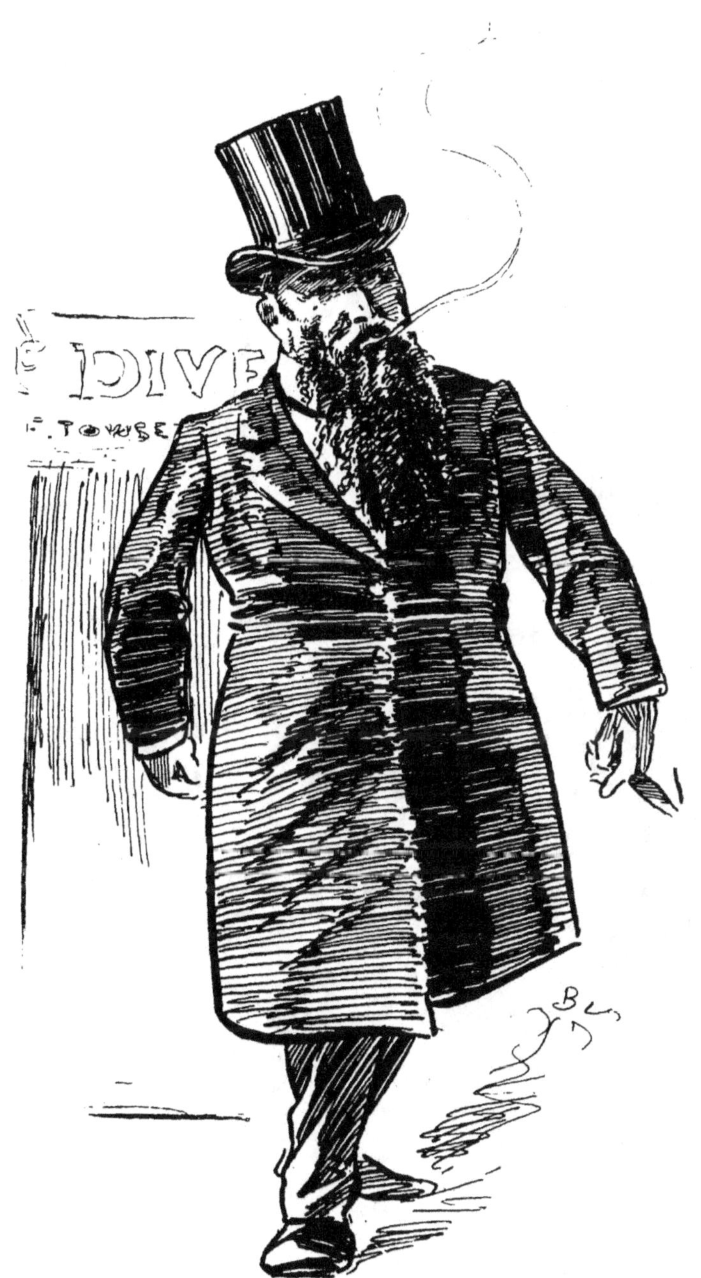

Figure 1.5: William Charles 'Whiskey' Walker, Rosalie's paternal grandfather.

Source: 'Pars about People', Observer, 3 January 1903, 4.

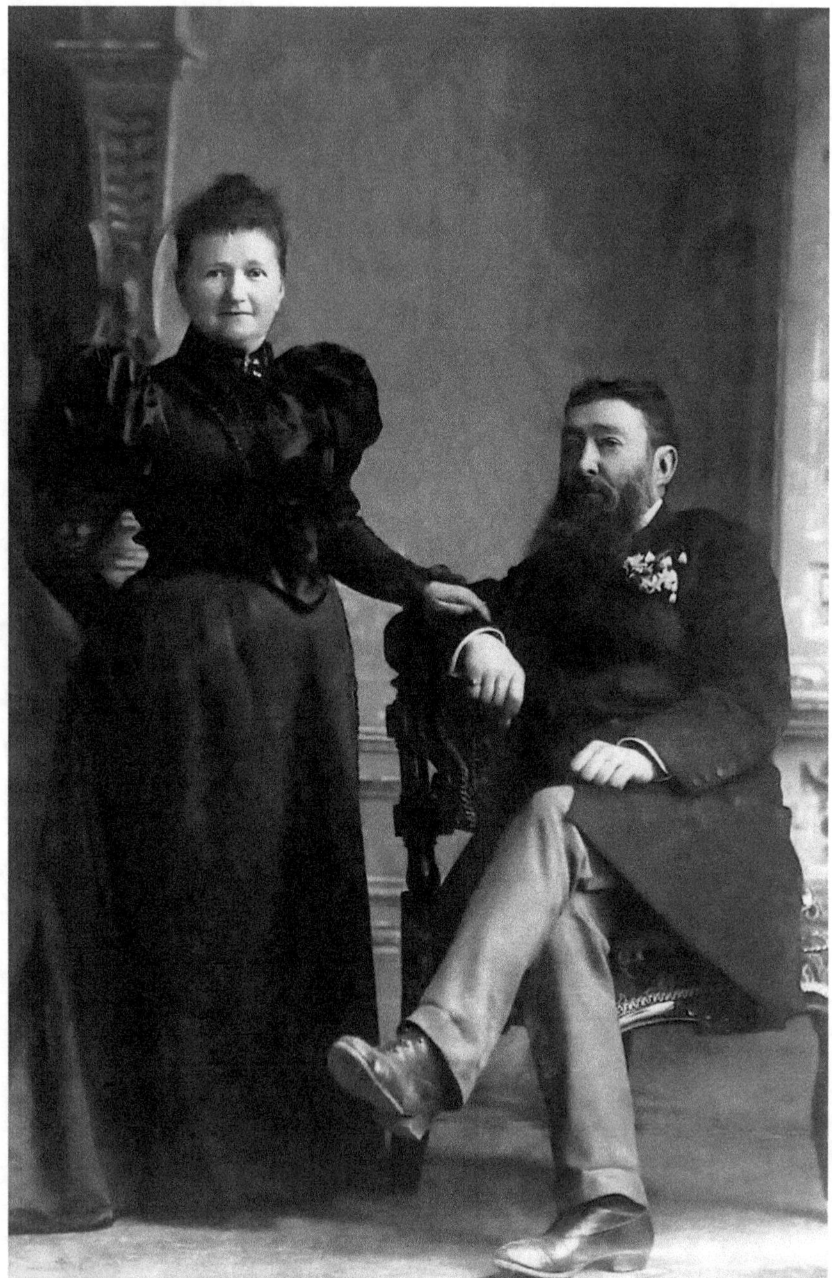

Figure 1.6: William Charles 'Whiskey' Walker and Annie Krauze Walker (née Franklin), Rosalie's paternal grandparents.

Note: Both died before Rosalie was born.

Source: Courtesy of the Gascoigne family.

Parents: Marion and Stanley

Coming from different backgrounds, how Marion and Stanley met remains a mystery. Although Auckland city's population was only around seventy thousand in 1916, and Marion and Stanley lived in the same area, it is likely they moved in different circles.[20] The other Metcalfe sisters who married chose a lawyer and an accountant, respectively, keeping to the professions as was expected of them. Their brother George was a lawyer, and Harry a civil engineer like his father. By the time Marion and Stanley married in March 1915, it was still early days in World War I, but some of the young men Marion had studied with at Auckland University College had already joined the New Zealand Expeditionary Force and left for the battlefront with countless of the young and fit of their generation.

The wedding took place at St Mary's Cathedral, a bastion of the establishment, up the hill from the Metcalfe family home in Parnell (see Figure 1.7).[21] Just half of the wedding photo exists in Rosalie's children's archive of family photographs, a torn strip in which Stanley remains intact, but only fragments of Marion are visible—a lacy white sleeve, a gloved hand clutching a flower basket, a skirt hem just shy of the ground, and a sliver of stockinged leg (see Figure 1.8).[22] Stanley neither smiles nor frowns. He looks directly at the camera, his head tilted slightly towards his bride who is largely hidden beyond the torn edge. Stanley is thirty-one years old. Many of his age group were already in France, Belgium, the Dardanelles and the Middle East with the New Zealand Expeditionary Force, or in training at the camps at Tauherenikau, Trentham or Awapuni racecourses.[23] But he stands instead with a shiny silk top hat clutched between the thumb and fingers of his right hand, dun gloves in his left hand. His dark shoes gleam below frock coat, wing collar and light Windsor-knotted tie. Parted on the left, his wavy hair frames a high forehead and pale eyes, his lips set in a straight line, his features thin pencilled lines.

---

20 'The New Zealand Official Year-Book 1916' gives Auckland city's population as 68,820 and Greater Auckland as 119,336, see Statistics New Zealand, 'The New Zealand Official Year-Book, 1916'.

21 Marriage certificate from Auckland Anglican Archives, Register 1027, St Mary's, Parnell.

22 The photograph appears in Gascoigne, *New Zealand Lives*, 273; Gascoigne, *Rosalie Gascoigne: Her New Zealand Origins*, 184.

23 Tauherenikau was then, and is still, a racecourse in the Wairarapa, north of Wellington. It was used as a training camp before it became too small for the numbers and Featherston was opened in January 1916. Awapuni was the training camp for the first unit of New Zealand Engineers. In September 1915, a training camp was established at Avondale Racecourse in Auckland for the New Zealand Tunnelling Company in which Marion Metcalfe's older brother Henry Ernest Metcalfe served as an officer.

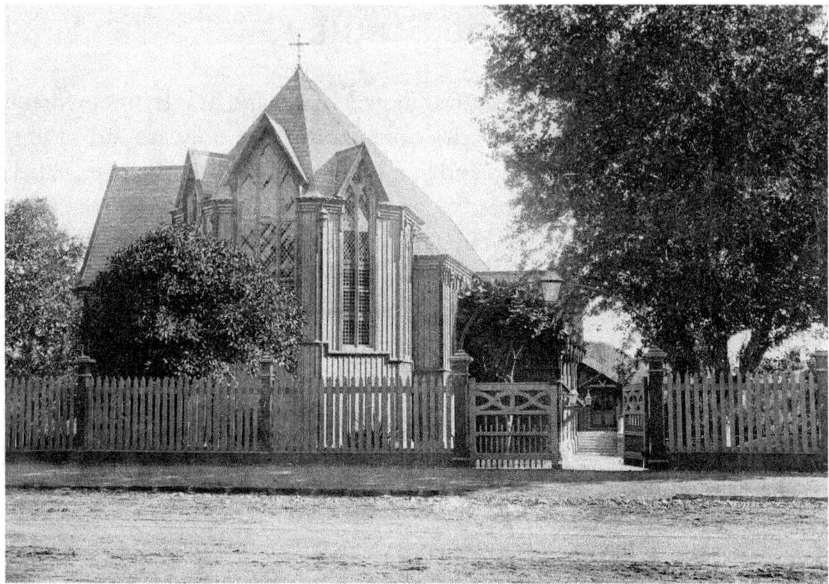

Figure 1.7: St Mary's Cathedral, Parnell, where Marion and Stanley were married in 1915.

Source: The *New Zealand Graphic and Ladies Journal*, 30 May 1903, 1520. Courtesy of Auckland Libraries Heritage Collections, NZG-19030530-1530-1520-01.

According to Martin Gascoigne, Marion removed herself from the photograph.[24] The tear line is neat, as if she took a ruler and carefully tore along its straight edge, suggesting it was not done in a fit of anger. Perhaps she kept the half of the photograph with her image, and it has since been lost. The severed image—and its survival as presumably the discarded half—is indicative of the couple's troubled relationship. It begs the question of why only one-half of the photo survives and why the surviving image is of Stanley.

Her parents' difficult relationship clouded Rosalie's childhood. She found herself caught between Marion and Stanley and their disparate families of origin. The pronounced differences in education, class, status and values inflamed tensions between Marion and Stanley, and even seemed to affect the ways in which Rosalie placed herself in the middle of the family, between her sister, with whom she compared herself unfavourably, and a younger brother to whom she seldom referred. Presumably there was something in

24 Gascoigne, *Rosalie Gascoigne: Her New Zealand Origins*, 185.

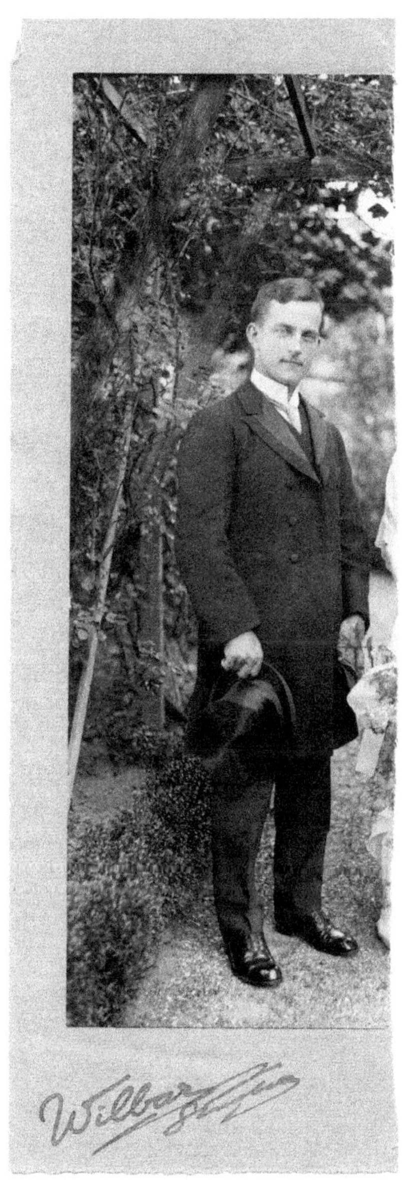

Figure 1.8: Rosalie's father, Stanley Walker, in the remainder of his and Marion Metcalfe's wedding photo, 1915.

Source: Courtesy of the Gascoigne family.

Stanley that Marion initially loved but that wore thin. Passion misspent might have been an undertone in the family in which Rosalie was a watchful child.

Four core aspects impacted Stanley and Marion's marriage and, as a result, Rosalie's childhood: educational difference and Stanley's sensitivity towards it; Stanley's unfitness for service during World War I and the contrast this struck with New Zealand values generally and the Metcalfe family's loss in particular; Stanley's unsteady, unsuccessful career in contrast to Metcalfe professional steadfastness; and the challenges that Stanley's character, including his alcoholism, posed for Marion's values. A sensitive and watchful child, Rosalie was acutely aware of her parents' differences. These characteristics—sensitivity and watchfulness—were key factors in her later artistic development.

Education

Education proved to be a point of tension between Marion and Stanley. Rosalie said her parents' relationship was never equal; her mother had the upper hand and a stronger personality.[25] Whether Rosalie made sense of the unequal relationship in terms of education or her parents framed their difficulties in terms of educational differences is not known, but Rosalie remembered that Stanley 'used to talk about intellectual snobbery … he wasn't of the same scholastic standing as she was'.[26]

Whereas the Metcalfe family had provided equal educational opportunities for daughters and sons, it seems that education may not have held the same importance for the Walkers. Rosalie's Metcalfe great-aunts were educated as well as their brothers, and Marion's parents continued this tradition in New Zealand with their children. In Auckland, Marion attended Miss Edgar's Ponsonby College, a girls' school that taught English, history, geography, French, Latin, arithmetic, algebra, Euclidean geometry, trigonometry and science in addition to the expected and usual feminine accomplishments of the time, sewing, music and drawing.[27] Thus, together with other daughters of Auckland's establishment, she was privileged with a rounded education. From Miss Edgar's, Marion graduated to Auckland Grammar School and then Auckland University College (later the University of Auckland).[28] By the time she graduated with a bachelor of arts in 1905, Auckland Grammar had split into separate girls' and boys' schools in response to Auckland's growing population and changes in legislation that made secondary schooling more widely available.[29]

25 Hughes et al., 'Rosalie Gascoigne Artist', tape 9.

26 Ibid.

27 'Ponsonby College', *Auckland Star*, 16 December 1894: 'The excellence of the tuition given at Miss Edgar's Ponsonby College is manifested by the nature of the work done by pupils.'

28 Northey, Asher and Asher, *Auckland Girls' Grammar School*, 11–74. From 1888 to 1906, girls attended Auckland Grammar School, although classes were strictly single sex. Increasing rolls led to the establishment of a separate Auckland Girls' Grammar School in 1907, although the Howe Street school buildings were not ready until 1909. Marion attended the original Auckland Grammar School in Symonds Street and later taught at Auckland Girls' Grammar School in Howe Street during 1913 and 1914. Rosalie taught there during 1941 and 1942.

29 The chancellor of the University of New Zealand, Sir Robert Stout, former premier and chief justice of New Zealand, conferred Marion Metcalfe's degree on 2 June 1905. Of the twenty-six graduates at the ceremony, seven were women and nineteen were men. 'Auckland University College. Annual Capping Ceremony', *New Zealand Herald*, 3 June 1905, 3.

Little is known about Stanley's schooling. He apparently did not proceed past primary school, completing only the compulsory minimum of education under the Education Act 1877, from the age of seven to fourteen.[30] While in 1900 fewer than 10 per cent (or 2,792) of New Zealand children of secondary age attended secondary school, it is remarkable that the then comfortably off Walkers apparently did not take advantage of secondary schooling for their youngest son.[31] Having not enjoyed educational privileges themselves, Stanley's parents did not share the Metcalfe's educational ethos, and timing did not favour him.

Wider access to secondary school was only encouraged with the introduction of the Education Act 1903, but this was too late for Stanley, who by that time was working as an automobile engineer in New Zealand's growing car business. In this field, however, ambition, curiosity or restlessness seems to have prompted a certain drive in him. He travelled to San Francisco in 1905 where he lived through the earthquake that struck the city in April 1906.[32] The 1910 United States census records that he was working as a machinist at the Union Iron Works, a major shipyard.[33] By the time of the publication of the 1914 New Zealand electoral roll, Stanley was back in New Zealand, an automobile engineer living at St George's Bay Road, Parnell, near to the Metcalfe home.[34] He had served five years of an engineer's apprenticeship but had no certificate, and ten years as a journeyman engineer before establishing his own business in 1914.[35]

War

Marion's brothers Harry and George both served overseas with the New Zealand Expeditionary Force during World War I, while Stanley and his brother D'Renzy remained at home, possibly creating another point of tension. During a period when New Zealand, like other countries in the British Empire, was preoccupied with notions of bold and vigorous manhood, Stanley had been rejected by the recruiting office and categorised

30 Information about compulsory minimum education from Stephenson, 'Thinking Historically', 9.

31 Statistics for 1900 from Butchers, *Education in New Zealand*, 345.

32 Gascoigne, *New Zealand Lives*, 186.

33 United States Census Bureau, '1910 Census: Volume 1. Population, General Report and Analysis'.

34 New Zealand Electoral Roll, 1914, Parnell Roll, 172, no. 8503 on roll.

35 Statement by Stanley K. Walker in Official Assignee, 'Walker, Stanley King'.

as 'fit for home service only' because of 'Defects of the Upper Extremities'.[36] While there is no official recorded description of the defects, Martin Gascoigne suggests the defect was a permanent hand injury that meant Stanley had trouble holding equipment, whether tools or weapons.[37] His exclusion on medical grounds provided physical safety and kept him from the horrors of war, but it exposed him to the moral judgement of people on the home front and saw him marginalised in society given his failure to live up to prevailing ideas of heroic manliness. New Zealand historian James Belich describes anti-'shirker' feeling as so strong that men who had been rejected on medical grounds or were exempted from conscription found themselves obliged to wear badges to prove it.[38] Whether Stanley wore such a badge is not known; however, in a judgemental environment in which women, in particular, demanded 'equality of sacrifice', it is likely that, as a young man at home and not in uniform, he would have been challenged.[39]

When Rosalie was just three months old, on 13 April 1917, the Metcalfes lost their elder son Harry, an officer with the New Zealand Tunnelling Company, on the Western Front (see Figure 1.9). Killed instantly by a shell fragment while on duty, Harry was unlucky. The tunnellers lost surprisingly few soldiers.[40]

The Metcalfes' other son, George, served with the New Zealand Rifle Brigade in Egypt and on the Western Front in France where he was admitted to hospital on five occasions during June 1917 for gas poisoning.[41] He survived the war, but for the rest of his life he suffered nightmares about being buried alive in the trenches.[42] Jessie never recovered from the grief of Harry's death, or perhaps from the trauma that stayed with George.[43]

---

36 *Numerical List of Reservists—Alphabetical Index*, entry number 137078, register number [AD 25 8/8] at Archives New Zealand Te Rua Mahara o te Kāwanatanga, Wellington, New Zealand. For detail about perceptions of manhood in New Zealand during this period, see Phillips, *A Man's Country*; Phillips, 'War and National Identity'.

37 Gascoigne, *New Zealand Lives*, 276.

38 Belich, *Paradise Reforged*, 99.

39 Ibid.

40 Neill, *The New Zealand Tunnelling Company*, 83.

41 George Hamilton Metcalfe—WW1 13056—Army, R107880509, 18805, Archives New Zealand Te Rua Mahara o te Kāwanatanga, Wellington.

42 Gascoigne, *Rosalie Gascoigne: Her New Zealand Origins*, 49.

43 Ibid., 77.

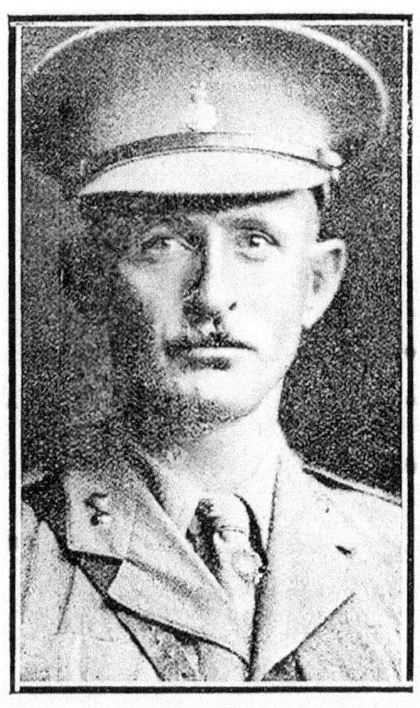

LIEUTENANT H. E. METCALFE,
OF AUCKLAND,
KILLED IN ACTION.

Figure 1.9: Rosalie's uncle Harry, Henry Ernest 'Harry' Metcalfe.

Source: 'New Zealand's Roll of Honour', *Auckland Weekly News*, 10 May 1917, 44. Courtesy of Auckland Libraries Heritage Collections AWNS-19170510-44-04.

In his family history, Martin Gascoigne wonders whether Stanley's non-participation in World War I may have been a cause of tension between husband and wife, as with other wartime marriages in which women were torn by conflicting emotions—anxiety about absent brothers and guilt because husbands were safe.[44] The militaristic atmosphere of male sacrifice perpetuated such raw feelings.[45] It is likely that it would have been a bone of contention for Jessie who lost one son and saw her other one emotionally damaged, while Stanley remained at home only to hurt his family with his alcoholism.

Loss and grief

Just over a year after Harry's death, when Rosalie was fifteen months old, grandfather Henry Metcalfe died suddenly while inspecting harbour works at Whakatane nearly two hundred miles south-east of Auckland (see Figure 1.10). Such was his renown and universal respect that newspapers the length and breadth of New Zealand reported his death.[46] Family legend tells that

44 Gascoigne, *New Zealand Lives*, 276.

45 Ibid.

46 'The Te Puke Times', *Te Puke Times*, 7 May 1918, 2; 'Personal', *Colonist*, 6 May 1918, 4; 'Death of Mr H. Metcalfe, *Poverty Bay Herald*, 4 May 1918, 3; 'Sudden Death of an Engineer, *Wairarapa Daily Times*, 4 May 1918, 4; 'Engineer's Death', *Ashburton Guardian*, 6 May 1918, 5; 'Civil Engineer Drops Dead', *Evening Post*, 4 May 1918, 8; 'Sudden Death', *Northern Advocate*, 4 May 1918, 2; 'Personal', *Wanganui Chronicle*, 6 May 1918, 4; 'Personal', *Waikato Times*, 4 May 1918, 4; 'Casualties', *Christchurch Press*, 6 May 1918, 7; 'Engineer Drops Dead', *Nelson Evening Mail*, 4 May 1918, 1; [Untitled], *North Otago Times*, 6 May 1918, 4; 'Local and General', *Thames Star*, 4 May 1918, 2; 'Personal', *Taranaki Daily News*, 6 May 1918, 4.

when the boat carrying Henry's body arrived at Auckland Harbour, fireboat crews sprayed their hoses in the air as a mark of respect.[47] Coming so soon after Harry's death, Henry's passing dealt a severe blow to the Metcalfes. Apart from raw grief, his death spelled the end of the family engineering consultancy that had enabled them to live in comfort and privilege.

Rosalie's life may have been different on various fronts if her grandfather had lived longer. Apart from the impact of his death on the family's financial situation and social standing, Henry was an outgoing nature lover. It is likely he would have been attentive to his granddaughter who shared much with him. Rosalie remembered complaining that nobody would talk to her, 'because they all read books … all the time' and her mother saying: 'it's a pity your grandfather isn't alive. He would have talked to you'.[48]

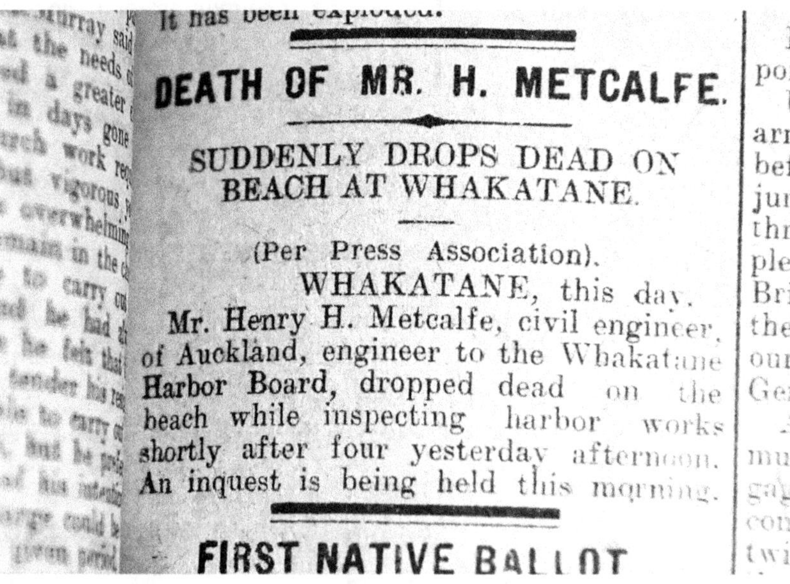

DEATH OF MR. H. METCALFE.

SUDDENLY DROPS DEAD ON BEACH AT WHAKATANE.

(Per Press Association).

WHAKATANE, this day.

Mr. Henry H. Metcalfe, civil engineer, of Auckland, engineer to the Whakatane Harbor Board, dropped dead on the beach while inspecting harbor works shortly after four yesterday afternoon. An inquest is being held this morning.

FIRST NATIVE BALLOT

Figure 1.10: 'Death of Mr H. H. Metcalfe'.

Source: *Gisborne Times*, XLIX, no. 4861, 6 May 1918, 2. Courtesy of the Gisborne Herald/Poverty Bay Herald.

47 Gascoigne, *Rosalie Gascoigne: Her New Zealand Origins*, 102.

48 Hughes et al., 'Rosalie Gascoigne Artist', tape 1.

Henry's books of watercolour paintings, made during the early 1900s when sailing one of his yachts, the *Bluebell*, *Pandora* or *Galatea*, in Auckland Harbour and around the islands of the Hauraki Gulf or as far afield as Tonga, attest to his eye for fine detail.[49] He captured colour and pattern, the movement of clouds, the sweep of the sky and the ballooning of a sail in the wind. Like his granddaughter, observing was not enough for him. He felt called to respond with the work of his hands.[50] His legacy to Rosalie was his eye—his visual acuity and his love for nature; his absence was perhaps a perennial reminder of the losses that shadowed her childhood.

***

The year 1918 was bittersweet and busy for Marion with her father's death, two toddler daughters and the birth in October of her son, Douglas Hamilton Walker. On top of all that, the Walkers moved house shortly after Douglas's birth, seeking more room for their expanded family.[51] It appeared that Stanley's auto-engineering and car sales business flourished in its prime central Auckland location. But he had already overextended himself with the purchase of Velie cars from the United States and his financial situation was to worsen.[52]

For Rosalie's grandmother Jessie, the loss of her husband within a year of her son's death dealt a cruel blow. Most grieving families were unable to travel to their loved ones' graves; however, in 1920, Jessie journeyed to England from where she crossed the Channel with her daughter Nellie to visit Harry's grave in Arras, France (see Figure 1.11). Others who visited Western Front war cemeteries at the same time described the desolation and ravages of war still visible beneath carpets of red poppies.[53]

---

49 See Gascoigne, *New Zealand Lives*, 109–13. Martin Gascoigne included a selection of Henry Hulbert Metcalfe's paintings in his family history.

50 Ibid., 108.

51 They moved to 19 (now 103) Remuera Road, virtually over the back of 8 MacMurray Road. It is interesting to note that New Zealand painter Patricia France, who also came to art later in life, lived just up the road at 214 Remuera Road after returning to New Zealand from Europe in 1931 until about 1959. She and her mother bought a piece of land and had a 'small, beautifully appointed' house designed and built, also at the foot of Mt Hobson. See Donald, *Painting out the Past*, 19.

52 Official Assignee, 'Walker, Stanley King'.

53 *British Australian*, 22 July 1920, 13, cited in Gascoigne, *Rosalie Gascoigne: Her New Zealand Origins*, 77. International travel, especially as far afield as Europe and the Middle East, was the domain of the rich in New Zealand until World War II. The vast distances between New Zealand and the battlefields of Europe and the Middle East, where around 18,500 New Zealanders died, and the cost involved in getting there, precluded most families from visiting the graves of their dead. Historians of New Zealand and of war do not appear to have written about this: Pugsley, McLean, McKinnon, Gentry, King, Belich and Mein Smith make no specific mention of this point.

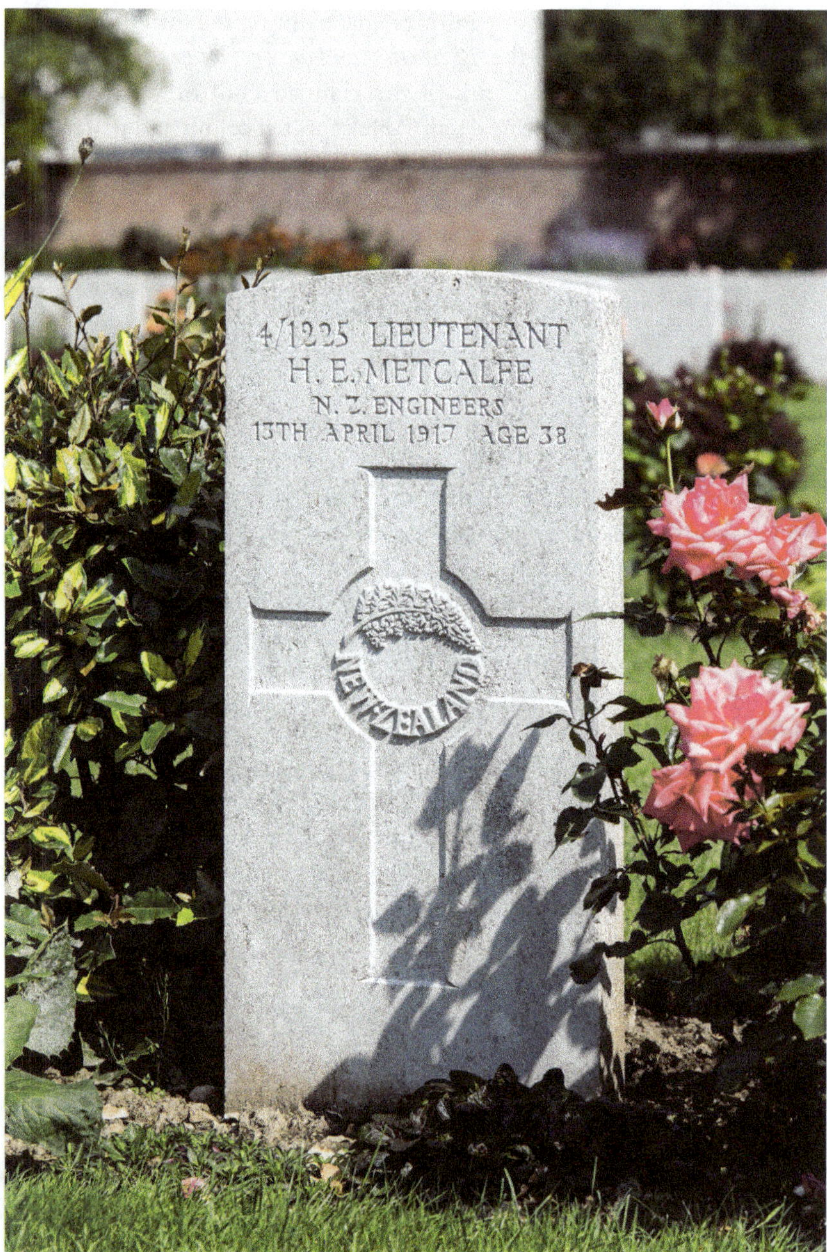

Figure 1.11: Headstone of Lieutenant Henry 'Harry' Ernest Metcalfe (4/1225), Faubourg D'Amiens Cemetery, France.

Note: Harry's mother Jessie Metcalfe and his sister Nellie Metcalfe visited the grave in 1920.

Source: Courtesy of the New Zealand War Graves Trust.

On her return, economic circumstances as a result of Henry and Harry's deaths and the resulting closure of the family business forced Jessie to sell her elegant family home *Tararua* with its extensive gardens and panoramic views. She bought a more modest house in Remuera, near Marion and Stanley and the children.

Marion and Stanley's social status was still such that Marion appeared in Auckland newspapers' social pages. During this period, the Walkers incorporated Stanley's middle name of King into their surname, and the *New Zealand Observer* reported on 1 May 1920 that Mrs King Walker had attended the Royal Race Meeting for the visit of Prince Edward, the Prince of Wales, in 'a biscuit costume, velour hat with apricot plumes'.[54] Again on 13 October, the *Observer* reported that she attended the opening day of the Auckland Racing Club's Spring Meeting in 'claret and biscuit plaid, hat en suite'.[55] The *Auckland Star* reported on 31 August 1921 that Mrs King Walker was 'upon the platform' in 'grey and vieux rose brocade' for the Auckland Grammar School Old Boys' and Old Girls' Association annual ball, attended by six hundred.[56] Marion's sister Nellie was also present, as was their sister-in-law, 'Mrs George Metcalfe'. Marion remained visible in terms of her own social standing, even amid the slips in fortune.

More dark clouds

Two years after Marion's appearance in the social pages for her attendance at the Grammar Old Boys' ball, Auckland's morning paper, the *New Zealand Herald*, on 9 August 1922 featured an incident that suggests all was not well in the Walker household.[57] By this time, Rosalie was five-and-a-half and enjoying the seesaw amid the Michaelmas daisies with Daintry in the garden at Remuera Road.

According to court reports, in May 1922 Stanley had welcomed one Alexander Ellis as a guest to the family's home in Remuera Road, where Ellis took Marion's ring from the mantelpiece and secreted it in his trouser cuff. On departing, he placed the ring on a ledge above the door and later told Stanley where it was on the understanding that the matter would go

54 Dolores, 'The Social Sphere', *New Zealand Observer*, 1 May 1920, 10.
55 Dolores, 'The Social Sphere', *New Zealand Observer*, 13 November 1920, 10.
56 'Women's World: Social Jottings', *Auckland Star*, 31 August 1921, 10.
57 'Breach of Hospitality: Theft of Ring', *New Zealand Herald*, 9 August 1922, 11.

no further. Ellis described the ring incident as a practical joke, but Stanley reported the matter to the police and, on 9 August, Ellis was found guilty of theft.[58] Events of that night raise alarm bells about Stanley's taste in friends and judgement about whom he would invite into his home with a wife and three young children. Such behaviour from two grown men raises questions about other events that evening, the nature of the conversation to which Marion, with her education and cultured background, was subjected, how the children felt about the visitor to their home and what else he may have got up to.

It is unlikely that this disturbing incident was a one-off event. Historians suspect that evidence survives not because it is random but because it reflects a pattern, especially in terms of the records kept or actions taken. That the matter went to court even though Marion received her ring back raises questions about why Stanley took this course of action. It seems unlikely that Marion, from a proud respectable family, would have pressed Stanley to take the matter further given the unwelcome publicity it was likely to generate. Why would Stanley put Marion through the public humiliation of exposing his questionable judgement in inviting into his home a man like Ellis, who admitted to the court that he had previously been before the Wellington court on four charges of false pretences? If we set this story alongside one that Martin Gascoigne told about Stanley inviting the Salvation Army into the garden to play hymns purely to spite Marion, the two stories present a picture of a difficult, teasing, even acrimonious and provocative relationship.[59]

Martin described his grandfather Stanley as an aggressive man.[60] Stanley found ways to belittle and punish Marion for what he considered her intellectual snobbery. Rosalie later noted that Marion's brother George, solicitor and former sergeant with the New Zealand Rifle Brigade during World War I, was terrified of Stanley.[61]

Within a few months of the ring incident, Marion decided that enough was enough. One night in late 1922 a disagreement with an inebriated Stanley pushed her to the limit of her endurance. Marion pulled her children from

58 Ibid.
59 Gascoigne, *New Zealand Lives*, 163.
60 Ibid.
61 Hughes et al., 'Rosalie Gascoigne Artist', tape 1.

their beds and took them to her mother's house three hundred metres around the corner at 2 Halls Avenue where Jessie lived with her unmarried daughter Nellie.[62] The trauma of the night fixed itself in Rosalie's memory:

> There was a nasty altercation, which I needn't go into, and he [Stanley] left the house again, drunk I think he was. And mother got us in a taxi and took us down to grandmother, and we never left.[63]

Even nearly eighty years on, Rosalie did not want to talk in detail about the events of that night. They still held the power to cause her pain or shame. She said he left 'again', suggesting there was a pattern in his behaviour and that Rosalie and her siblings were exposed to the ugliness of Stanley's alcohol-infused behaviour, arguments between their parents and his departures, which until this point had been temporary. Rosalie's life changed on the night she described. She lived at Halls Avenue until she left for Stromlo in 1943.

Marion's departure with the children occurred around the time of Stanley's bankruptcy. Rosalie told how her father 'had a business, which had to be declared bankrupt. He drank it all.'[64] This was in stark contrast with Marion's late father, Henry, who had a reputation as highly intelligent and a successful businessman. Marion adored her father, so Stanley had a difficult role model to live up to. He had failed in business where Henry had been highly successful. Stanley attributed his unfortunate position to 'the slump in the automobile business' and the location of his garage.[65] In contrast, the official assignee reported: 'Creditors … expressed the opinion that the position had largely been brought about owing to the bankrupt drinking to excess.'[66]

The *New Zealand Herald* reported the bankruptcy on 19 October 1922. On 2 December 1922, the newspaper carried an advertisement for the Walkers' house at 19 Remuera Road.[67] In a small city such as Auckland, privacy was a luxury. The bankruptcy and events surrounding it, including

62 None of Rosalie's three houses exist now. The Remuera Road house was demolished in the 1970s and replaced with apartments. Halls Avenue is now Robert Hall Avenue; Jessie Metcalfe's home at 2 Halls Avenue was demolished along with some adjacent houses in the 1960s to make way for the Auckland Southern Motorway. Number 8 MacMurray Road was demolished in the 1960s and replaced with a string of brick and tile home units. All are unusual for an area that virtually remains intact from the time most of the houses were built in the early twentieth century.

63 Hughes et al., 'Rosalie Gascoigne Artist', tape 1.

64 Ibid., tape 1.

65 Official Assignee, 'Walker, Stanley King'.

66 Ibid.

67 'Sales by Auction', *New Zealand Herald*, 2 December 1922, 7; 'Bankrupt Motor Agent', *Auckland Star*, 19 October 1922, 8.

the sale of the house, appeared in the daily newspapers for all to read. For Marion, a member of Auckland's social elite, there would have been no escaping the shame and humiliation. On top of the public humiliation, Marion's family suffered further financial loss. Having been refused a loan by the bank to expand his business in 1916, Stanley financed the deal with a bank overdraft of £1,000 guaranteed by his father-in-law and his sister Georgina's husband, Arnold Barter. Disastrously for Stanley, the bank had called in the loan after Henry died in May 1918. Despite this, Stanley increased his risk and continued importing Velie cars.[68] When the Auckland Supreme Court declared Stanley bankrupt on 17 October 1922, the list of sixty-two unsecured creditors, to whom he owed a total of £1,358 18s 6d, included a debt of nearly £500 to his late father-in-law's estate.[69]

***

Alcohol continued to feature in the family's life throughout Rosalie's childhood and was likely to have been a factor in the outsider feelings she frequently expressed in interviews later in life when she had achieved renown as an artist. Children of parents who misuse alcohol often feel different or out of step, commonly experience low self-esteem, guilt and loneliness, and perform poorly at school.[70] Rosalie did well at school, although she compared herself unfavourably with her sister. It is possible that her apparent lack of confidence was in large part linked to low self-esteem brought about by her father's alcohol misuse.

Stanley fitted the profile of the 'boozer', described by New Zealand historian Jock Phillips in *A Man's Country? The Image of the Pakeha Male—A History*. The 'boozer', perceived as a threat to New Zealand society's morality and economy due to his lack of restraint and productivity, represented the opposite of the temperance movement's ideal man who cared for his family. The temperance movement fought a fierce campaign for prohibition the year of Stanley's bankruptcy and lost by a mere 3,263 votes.[71] All the evidence suggests that Stanley's drinking destroyed his business and caused trauma and shame to his family.

68 The Velie Motors Corporation in Moline, Illinois, manufactured Velie cars from 1908 to 1928.

69 Official Assignee, 'Walker, Stanley King'. According to the Reserve Bank of New Zealand website, this was equivalent to NZD127,302 on 23 September 2013.

70 Gruenert and Tsantefski, 'Responding to the Needs'.

71 Phillips, *A Man's Country*, 64, 74. Alcohol consumption was a significant public issue in New Zealand from the late nineteenth century until well into the twentieth century. Jock Phillips asserts that two masculine ideals coexisted during the early years of the twentieth century—one early frontier model where feats of alcohol consumption were admired and the other, promoted by the temperance movement, involved self-control, moderation, discipline and care for the family.

With his physical 'defects' as identified by the army recruiting office, Stanley fell short of the ideal of heroic, fit masculinity. With his drinking habits, he fell into that careless, derided group that was perceived to seek instant gratification before tending to their family's needs. Stanley's inadequacies pushed his family outside the bounds of respectability and his resulting bankruptcy brought on the Walker family's collapse. At the tender age of five, Rosalie's life changed dramatically.

Living in such a dysfunctional environment would have been stressful for Rosalie and her siblings. A childhood photograph of Rosalie from around 1922 resonates with her words: 'I don't know whether I was terribly happy. We had a broken home … And this was uneasy' (see Figure 1.12).[72] In the photograph, her gaze meets the viewer directly but tentatively. Crookedly parted fair hair falls haphazardly on her forehead, loose curls frame her cheeks, and the merest suggestion of a smile stretches her lips. Someone outside the frame has directed her to hold her hands in front of her chest, fingertips pressed together, palms apart, forming a steeple. She stands in white socks and dark button-strap shoes, knees just touching, feet slightly apart, the right sock corkscrews down her calf. Her pale dress, embroidered along elbow-length sleeves, falls in gathers below her posed hands. The background is bare. She looks like the child she later told stories about—the child who felt neglected or overlooked by the adults in her life.[73] She said her mother was busy and that the people in her life 'didn't have time for children'.[74]

Untidy hair and slipping socks in a formal portrait suggests a careless family or a relaxed one. The adult Rosalie's stories, combined with official records of Stanley's bankruptcy and drink driving charges, belie a relaxed environment. Rosalie's slightly unkempt look fits the pattern of stories she told of non-attentive adults. Her tentative smile and posed appearance may indicate she was camera shy; it could also be evidence of her distress in the face of her parents' tempestuous relationship and life in an abrasive household in which 'nobody said nice things to anybody ever'.[75]

72 Hughes et al., 'Rosalie Gascoigne Artist', tape 1.
73 Ibid., tape 1.
74 Ibid.
75 Ibid., tape 9: 'it was a difficult relationship … And … it was an abrasive household. Nobody said nice things to anybody ever.'

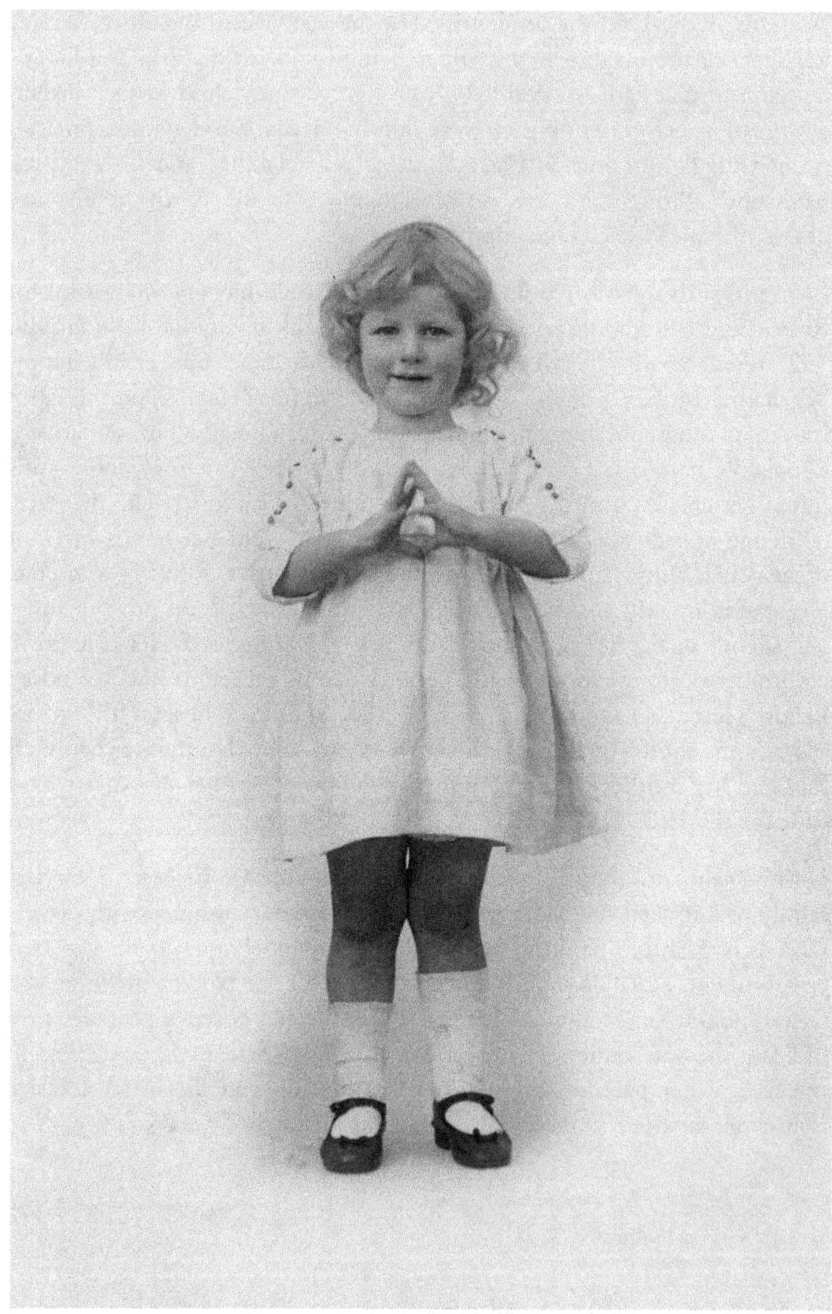

Figure 1.12: Rosalie as a young child, c. 1922.

Source: Courtesy of the Gascoigne family.

Caught between two worlds

Light and shadow played over Rosalie's early years. In the shadow, Rosalie was caught in between her warring parents and their disparate family social statuses. She identified with her shamed and exiled father, telling North: 'I had a bit of that unacceptable Irish from my father.'[76] She juxtaposed herself with her siblings, clarifying her understanding of the 'unacceptable Irish':

> I was a bit silly … I suppose I was more like my father, who had Irish blood in him … my brother and my sister were both more Scottish, British, I think … they were worthy, you see and perhaps dour.[77]

Grief enveloped her family at a time before she had the language to understand events around her or put words to her feelings. There seemed little respite from the maelstrom of death and change. The deaths of her grandfather and uncle, and her brother's birth twenty months after her own were followed by a house move, her parents' acrimonious separation and another move. All this, on top of a slippage in status for a family that had previously enjoyed privilege and prestige, made for a traumatic introduction to life. These turbulent formative years formed the foundation of the shame she said she felt early in life, and contributed to her sense of being out of step. Rosalie's early visual awareness, her memories of Michaelmas daisies and the green puka tree, weave bright threads through these harrowing years and suggest the foundations of her artist identity. Her narrative tells her listeners of the in-betweenness and difficulties of these formative years that shaped her life. She would always struggle with feeling different.

76 Gascoigne, interview by North, 3.

77 Hughes et al., 'Rosalie Gascoigne Artist', tape 1.

2

1923–29: 'I early on got a sense of shame'

The years from Rosalie's sixth birthday until her thirteenth were difficult, with the family adapting to the breakdown of Marion and Stanley's marriage and the move to Jessie Metcalfe's home. Rosalie started school and her mother returned to work as a high school teacher. Rosalie flagged how her feelings of shame textured these years when she told Annabel Frost in 1997: 'I early on got a sense of shame.'[1] The story Rosalie told later of these times features adults with little time for her and her siblings, her grandmother's strictness, the family's abrasiveness and her differentness from her sister and brother. Her narrative evokes bleak loneliness. She wished for a 'normal' family with a resident father; she longed for creative activities and compared herself unfavourably with her older sister.

When she told her story to interviewers decades later, her narrative was silent on significant publicised traumatic events that occurred in her family that might have carried other associations she did not want to own—associations with further slippages of class, status and respectability. While making general mention of her father's drinking, she chose not to speak of the several drink driving charges that were publicised in the court pages of the *Auckland Star*, and his committal for treatment as an alcoholic in 1924 when she was seven. Nor did she mention the highly publicised story of her first cousin, Elsie Walker, who died a mysterious death in 1929, aged seventeen.

1 Frost, 'Rosalie Gascoigne', 20.

Rosalie was a highly resilient child and woman, and the trauma of these events was part of what had shaped her, but she chose to leave such stories in the past. It is likely she was aware of her father's convictions and committal, and Elsie's death, as she was herself becoming a more visible actor in the society that noted such matters, with whatever discretions and euphemisms. She may have consciously omitted such details from her self-narrative, considering them external factors in a story of self-realisation that was, by the time she recounted it, attuned to the more internal dynamics of her identity. But external factors and internal identity dynamics are never so easily separated—they are part of the historical contexts that define us.

The family moved from a household tense with the uncertainty of Stanley's behaviour to a house redolent with grief. In 1998, Rosalie said of the move: 'My mother had arrived on my grandmother, who had lost a son in the war … and there's mother with three children arriving.'[2] It was only five years after Harry's death at Arras on the Western Front and four years after Jessie's husband Henry's sudden death on the beach at Whakatane. Given the double grief, it is unsurprising that Jessie still felt bereft. Added to the load of grief and loss, Jessie had experienced a significant diminution of her resources after her husband and son's deaths and the collapse of the family business. She had been forced from the family's stylish home at Judges Bay. Her daughter's public humiliation would have been a bitter pill, compounded when Marion and the children moved in with her, filling her space and further stretching her resources.

Jessie Metcalfe was around seventy-one years old when Marion and the children moved in with her and her daughter, Nellie. Rosalie's stories, and those of her cousins, depict Jessie as a difficult woman. She had been born to a fine life, with large houses, beautiful clothes, high-class socialising and trips to France. Her father, Mathew Hamilton (1800–1877), achieved elevated social status with a successful business exporting muslins to the West Indies and loading the returning ships with sugar and rum.[3] Jessie was known for her contempt towards relatives in the wider Hamilton family who had not achieved the same success as her father.[4] She discounted people she considered of lesser social importance. It seems unlikely that Stanley would have ever measured up to her high expectations; indeed, this may have been a factor in Stanley and Marion's fractured relationship. Their estrangement would have confirmed Jessie's low regard for him.

2 Hughes et al., 'Rosalie Gascoigne Artist', tape 1.
3 Gascoigne, *New Zealand Lives*, 65.
4 Ibid., 66.

In 1997, Rosalie recalled that, by the time they moved in with Jessie, her grandmother was 'unable to do much for herself', cynically adding 'or so she liked to believe. She needed to be catered to'.[5] One of Jessie's grandsons remembered feeling afraid of her, describing her as 'a bit of a tyrant'.[6] He gave no reason for his fear or judgement, but Rosalie recalled her grandmother's forbidding influence:

> You did not speak until you were spoken to … I remember sitting with plates of vegetables and saying to my grandmother, 'Is it compulsory?'—'yes, it's compulsory.' … You ate the slimy vegetable marrow and … everything because it was compulsory … you just did it.[7]

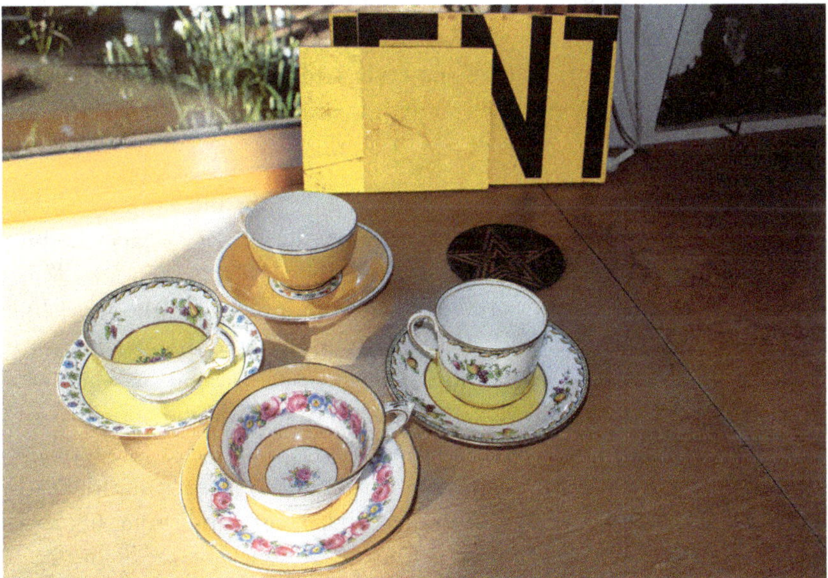

Figure 2.1: Some of Rosalie's collection of yellow bone china cups and saucers and pieces of retro-reflective road signs left in her studio when she died.

Source: Courtesy of Hester Gascoigne and Sally Colahan Griffin. Photograph: Sally Colahan Griffin.

5 Frost, 'Rosalie Gascoigne', 19.

6 Gascoigne, *New Zealand Lives*, 78.

7 Ibid.

On a brighter note, Jessie shared her love of the colour yellow with her granddaughter. Rosalie later incorporated yellow into her art (see Figure 2.1). She acknowledged that her passion for the colour went back a long way—to Jessie in Halls Avenue, recalling: 'My grandmother was very fond of yellow. She had yellow curtains. She used to buy a lot of yellow china.'[8]

With four bedrooms and a maid's room, a sitting room, a dining room and a conservatory, the members of the newly established household enjoyed reasonable space.[9] But Rosalie described the new living arrangement as uneasy and recalled the burden of high expectations: 'people had high standards for you. You had good table manners and you spoke correctly.'[10] The children were seen and not heard 'because people didn't have time for you'.[11] According to Rosalie, the household lacked warmth. There was little sense of fun. Although the move to Jessie's house provided some relief to Marion and the children from the upsets caused by Stanley's alcoholism and bankruptcy, the atmosphere was tense. It was an uneasy sanctuary to which they had escaped.

Jessie frequently visited her daughter Dolly Broadfoot in Te Kuiti, making the 120-mile journey south-west of Auckland to escape the busy Halls Avenue household.[12] She probably enjoyed her son-in-law Walter Broadfoot's success and importance. Broadfoot, a solicitor who specialised in leases for the alienation of Māori land to European settlers, was mayor of Te Kuiti and, in 1928, became the member of parliament for Waitomo.[13] Jessie missed his election by three months. In August 1928, the year Rosalie turned eleven, Jessie died aged seventy-six, at Te Kuiti, after a long illness. Two days after Jessie's death, her funeral cortege left 2 Halls Avenue for nearby Purewa Cemetery where she was buried with Henry. Indicating her social status, the *Auckland Star* reported her death the same day (see Figure 2.2).

8 MacDonald and Gascoigne, *Rosalie Gascoigne*, 12.

9 Auckland City Council, 'Lot 92, Robert Hall Avenue'. Note this property appears in the name of Jessie's son-in-law Walter Broadfoot until 1939 when it was transferred to Marion Walker.

10 Gascoigne, *New Zealand Lives*, 78.

11 Hughes et al., 'Rosalie Gascoigne Artist', tape 1.

12 One visit is recorded in the *King Country Chronicle* XXII, no. 2558 (3 April 1928): 5: 'Mrs Metcalfe, of Auckland, is at present the guest of her daughter, Mrs W. J. Broadfoot.'

13 Walter Broadfoot was deputy mayor then mayor of Te Kuiti from 1923 to 1935. He was elected to parliament in 1928 as a member of the United Party, moved to the newly established conservative National Party in 1936 and remained in parliament until his retirement in 1954. He was junior party whip from 1936, senior whip for the National Party from 1941 to 1949, a cabinet minister from 1942 and postmaster-general in 1949–52. He was knighted in 1955 and died in 1965. See Gustafson, *The First 50 Years*.

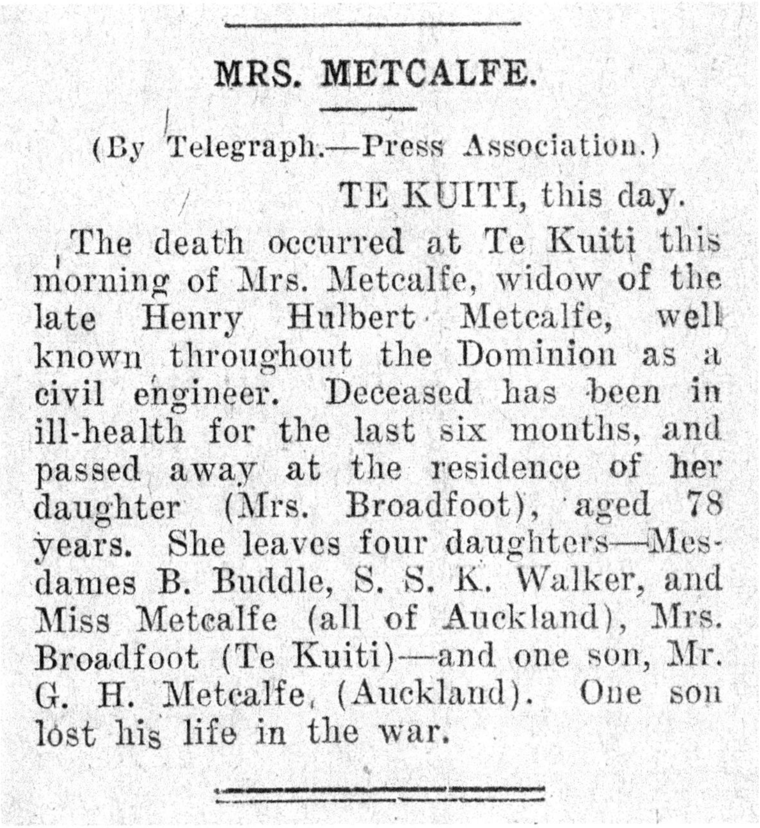

MRS. METCALFE.

(By Telegraph.—Press Association.)

TE KUITI, this day.

The death occurred at Te Kuiti this morning of Mrs. Metcalfe, widow of the late Henry Hulbert Metcalfe, well known throughout the Dominion as a civil engineer. Deceased has been in ill-health for the last six months, and passed away at the residence of her daughter (Mrs. Broadfoot), aged 78 years. She leaves four daughters—Mesdames B. Buddle, S. S. K. Walker, and Miss Metcalfe (all of Auckland), Mrs. Broadfoot (Te Kuiti)—and one son, Mr. G. H. Metcalfe, (Auckland). One son lost his life in the war.

Figure 2.2: Jessie Metcalfe's death notice.

Source: *Auckland Star* LIX, no. 190, 13 August 1928, 3. Courtesy of Stuff Limited, Aotearoa New Zealand.

Aunt Nellie Metcalfe

The other family member in Jessie's household was Ellen Mary Metcalfe, known as Nellie, Jessie's eldest daughter and second child (see Figure 2.3). Nellie had toured Europe from 1905 to 1909 before serving as a Voluntary Aid Detachment (VAD) nurse during World War I in India, where she connected with some of her Hamilton cousins. Very much part of the British Empire, they had joined the Indian Army from Cheltenham College. An unmarried daughter, Nellie fulfilled social expectations when she returned to New Zealand to care for her grieving widowed mother.

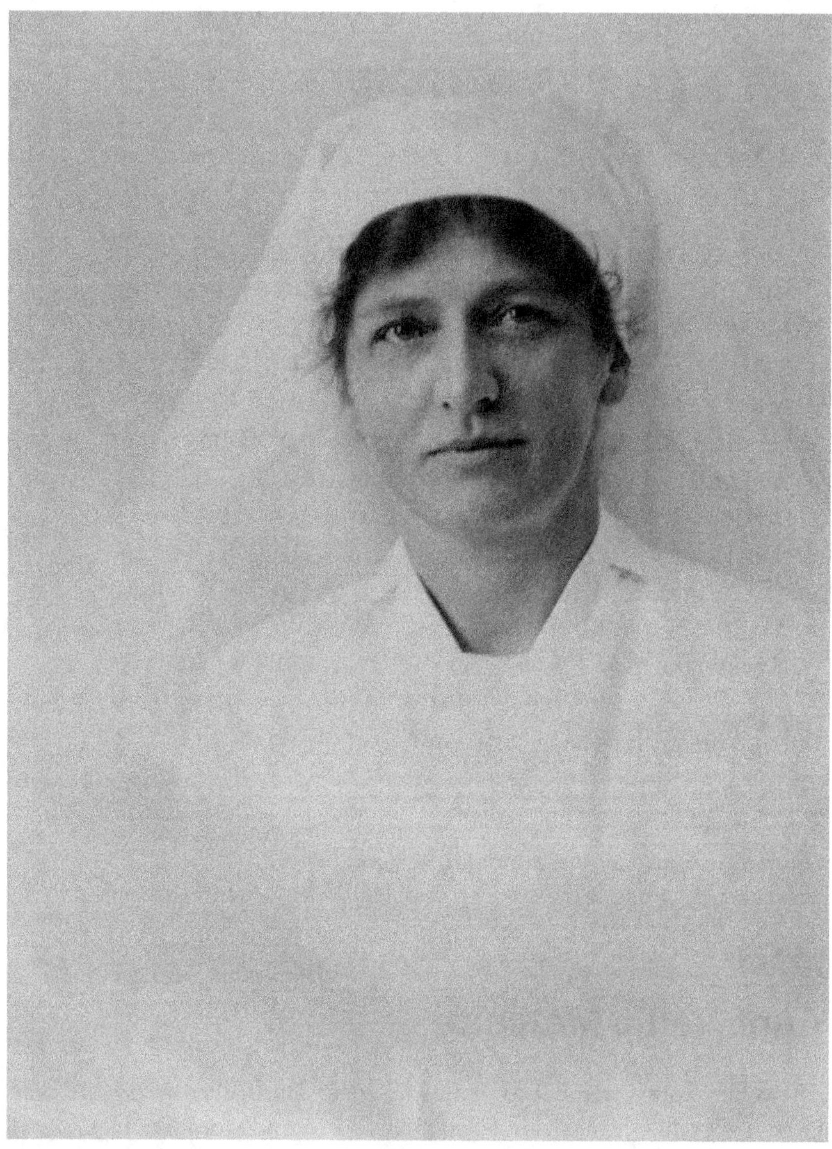

Figure 2.3: Rosalie's Aunt Nellie (Ellen Mary Metcalfe) as a VAD nurse during World War I.

Source: Courtesy of the Gascoigne family.

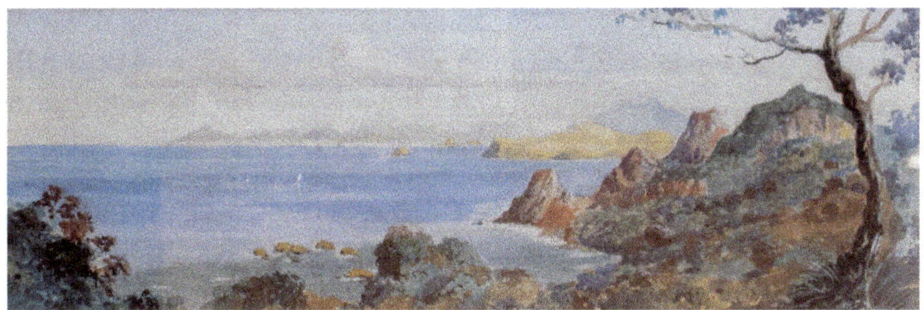

Figure 2.4: A watercolour of a coastal scene near Auckland, painted by Nellie Metcalfe who may have learned to paint from her father.

Source: Courtesy of the Gascoigne family.

Rosalie remembered Nellie as her 'aunt who hadn't married and seemed to be the dog's body'.[14] But Nellie alone responded to Rosalie's childhood longings for creative activities, coming up with inventive ideas for activities like painting flower pots, making a small garden and arranging flowers when her siblings Daintry and Douglas had their heads in books.[15] A watercolour of a coastal scene near Auckland, depicted in Martin Gascoigne's family history, shows that Nellie had been a skilled watercolourist, probably having learned at her father's knee (see Figure 2.4).[16] The arrival of Marion and her children at Halls Avenue added to the demands of caring for her elderly mother, and Nellie had no time to paint. Instead, Rosalie remembered, Nellie was always on the go, polishing tables, painting garden barrels green and raising chickens and ducks.[17]

Apart from Nellie's attempts to provide activity for Rosalie's restless hands, Rosalie told Hughes in 1998 that her childhood was empty of art. One day she won a shiny new paintbox in a game of pass the parcel at a birthday party, but, invoking a picture of a woeful childhood, she told Frost: 'I knew that paint boxes had to be kept clean and neat, not used.'[18] There was, she told Hughes, 'absolutely zilch' art in her childhood. Art had been part

14 Gascoigne, interview by North, 3.

15 Nellie's creativity rated a mention in the *New Zealand Observer* on the occasion of her sister Dolly's wedding to Walter Broadfoot in December 1910. Nellie had made, from white flowers, 'a beautiful white wedding bell' for Dolly's going away party. The Rev. Canon MacMurray performed the wedding ceremony at St Mary's Cathedral under the same wedding bell. See Myra, 'The Social Sphere', *New Zealand Observer*, 24 December 1910.

16 Gascoigne, *New Zealand Lives*, 43. An illustration of a watercolour painting by Nellie and Marion's sister, Phyllis, shown on page 56 of *New Zealand Lives*, is further evidence that the practice of painting, and competency at it, ran in the Metcalfe family.

17 Gascoigne, *Rosalie Gascoigne: Her New Zealand Origins*, 44.

18 Frost, 'Rosalie Gascoigne', 20.

of her extended family life, but it had receded to the background during her early childhood.[19] She remembered feeling stuck in a bookish family and longing to make things. Although she was later familiar with Henry Metcalfe's sketchbooks, during her childhood she thought art was not something people did in her family. The paintings by her Metcalfe great-aunts that hung on the walls at Halls Avenue were from the past, well before her birth.[20] One of her grandfather Henry's sisters, Florence Metcalfe, was an accomplished artist.[21] Martin Gascoigne writes of Florence: 'She was a serious practitioner ... whose work was informed by the English Arts and Crafts movement, Art Nouveau, and stylish book illustration.'[22] Apparently a stickler for the rules of social convention and etiquette who 'made more enemies than friends', Florence travelled around Europe and North Africa, painting and sketching; her subjects were those favoured by English-born Australian painter Ethel Carrick Fox (1872–1952).[23]

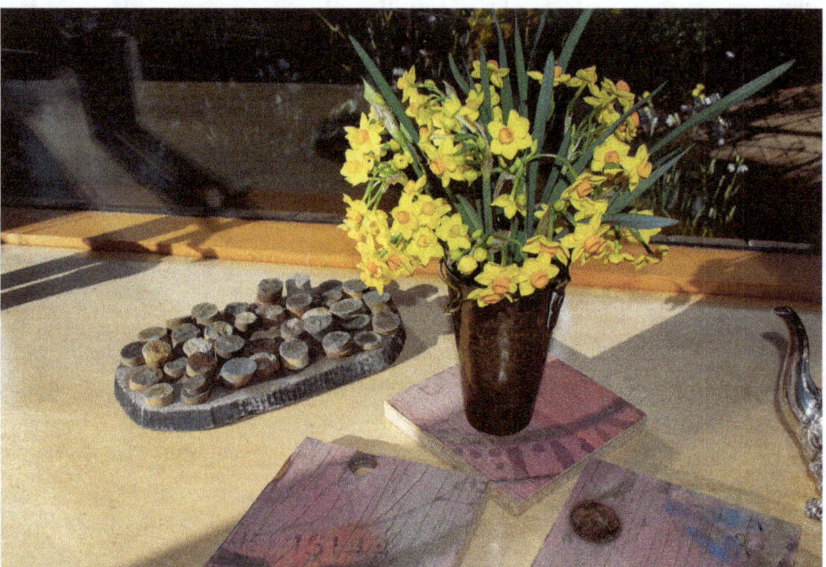

Figure 2.5: The brass container with which Rosalie won a prize at the Remuera Primary School fete in 1929 for an arrangement of buttercups with yellow ribbon, inspired by Aunt Nellie.

Source: Courtesy of Sally Colahan Griffin and Hester Gascoigne. Photograph: Sally Colahan Griffin.

19 Hughes et al., 'Rosalie Gascoigne Artist', tape 1.

20 Gascoigne, *New Zealand Lives*, 133.

21 Gascoigne, *Rosalie Gascoigne: Her New Zealand Origins*, 133–6.

22 Gascoigne, *New Zealand Lives*, 135.

23 Ibid., 133–6.

But neither Florence, her sisters nor Henry were part of Rosalie's childhood. Household management consumed Nellie's time. It allowed her no time to exercise her artistic creativity and, although Nellie encouraged Rosalie, she herself no longer painted watercolours. Rosalie had no shoulders to look over and watch how paintings were made.

Nellie's encouragement did, however, lead to Rosalie's first artistic success. During her final year at Remuera Primary School in 1929, Rosalie won a prize at the school fete for a flower arrangement. Nellie came up with the idea for Rosalie's 'yellow and bright' arrangement of buttercups with yellow ribbon. Rosalie, perhaps with more than a hint of her socially aware grandmother in her, and being, as she described herself, 'a frightful little snob', was concerned buttercups were too common.[24] But, reassured by her teachers, she went ahead with Nellie's idea and won the prize. The win was a harbinger of things to come in the child's ability at form and composition (see Figure 2.5).

By Rosalie's own admission, she, Daintry and Douglas were hard on Nellie: 'We were awful. We ganged up on her.'[25] Rosalie's description of the household paints a picture of difficult and abrasive relationships: 'Nobody said nice things to anybody ever … the siblings sniped … [at] each other' and 'the adults were practically our enemies'.[26] Rosalie was sufficiently aware of these interactions to notice that other families were different: 'you sort of used to look at other people being amiable to each other, other families. Nothing like that in our house.'[27] The household may have been easier after Jessie's death, without her demanding presence and the cloud of shame and disapproval she felt about Marion and Stanley's marriage.

Marion as mother

Despite the uneasy household at Halls Avenue, Marion was fortunate to have somewhere to go. Stanley's bankruptcy left her with nothing. In 1912, she had purchased, through the legal practice of her brother-in-law, a thirty-acre Māori land lease in the King Country—part of the rapid alienation of Māori land facilitated by the New Zealand government through the legal

24 Hughes et al., 'Rosalie Gascoigne Artist', tape 1.
25 Gascoigne, *Rosalie Gascoigne: Her New Zealand Origins*, 44.
26 Ibid.; Hughes et al., 'Rosalie Gascoigne Artist', tape 9.
27 Hughes et al., 'Rosalie Gascoigne Artist', tape 9.

system.[28] But she sold it in December 1916, possibly to finance Stanley's overambitious purchase of four Velie cars from the United States. This enterprise had been instrumental in the collapse of his car repair and sales business.[29]

Having married and left her parents' home to set up her own, Marion may have found it difficult and demeaning to return to live with her mother. Although the Walker children were not unusual living in a fatherless home in the aftermath of World War I, they were very unusual having a mother capable of gaining the type of full-time employment Marion secured on the strength of her education. In 1926, only 3.5 per cent of married Pākehā women were in paid employment outside the home, most of them part-time.[30] Ten years later this had risen only slightly, to 3.7 per cent.[31] Married women were not usually permitted to teach in New Zealand; however, in 1924, just over a year after leaving Stanley and moving in with Jessie, Marion had a job teaching English, history and languages at Epsom Girls' Grammar School, a public school close to home (see Figures 2.6 and 2.7). For many other single parent families, children were boarded out, informally adopted or placed in orphanages.[32] Marion's education gave her access to work in a profession that was attractive as a career prospect, especially in comparison with factory or shop work, and enabled her to keep her family together. Earlier, before she had married Stanley, when she had begun work as a high school teacher after graduation in 1905, salaries, appointment and grading of teachers, and a superannuation fund, were all in place, although equal pay for equal work remained a concept for well into the future.[33] The fact of Marion's full-time employment marked the family as different; intelligent, sociable Rosalie would have been aware that her mother's situation was unusual.

---

28 'Alienation' was the euphemistic legal term used to remove land from Māori. Interestingly, in the case of the land deal in which Marion Metcalfe was involved, all three parties were women—the Māori owner Wikitoria Tahuata, Marion and the woman she eventually sold the lease to, Mrs Bertha Caroline Johnston of Waitomo. The ownership of land by women was apparently not unusual.

29 Official Assignee, 'Walker, Stanley King'; Gascoigne, *Rosalie Gascoigne: Her New Zealand Origins*.

30 Pākehā is the Māori language term for New Zealanders of European descent.

31 Nolan, *Breadwinning*, 124.

32 According to the New Zealand Year-Book, 'the number of homes for destitute children peaked at seventy five in 1935. Most of the children in these homes had at least one living parent; in 1949, only four per cent were true orphans.' See Goodger, 'Maintaining Sole Parent Families', 2.

33 Formed in 1914, the year before Marion got married, the New Zealand Women Teachers' Association lobbied for equal pay, promotion of women and inclusion of women in the team of school inspectors. See Swarbrick, 'Primary and Secondary Education'. By 1930, a male high school teacher still earned up to 25 per cent more than his female colleague with the same qualifications and experience and, in addition, a married man received forty pounds per year allowance. See Butchers, *Education in New Zealand*, 611. Marion's salary would have been between 20 and 25 per cent less than that of man with equal qualifications and experience.

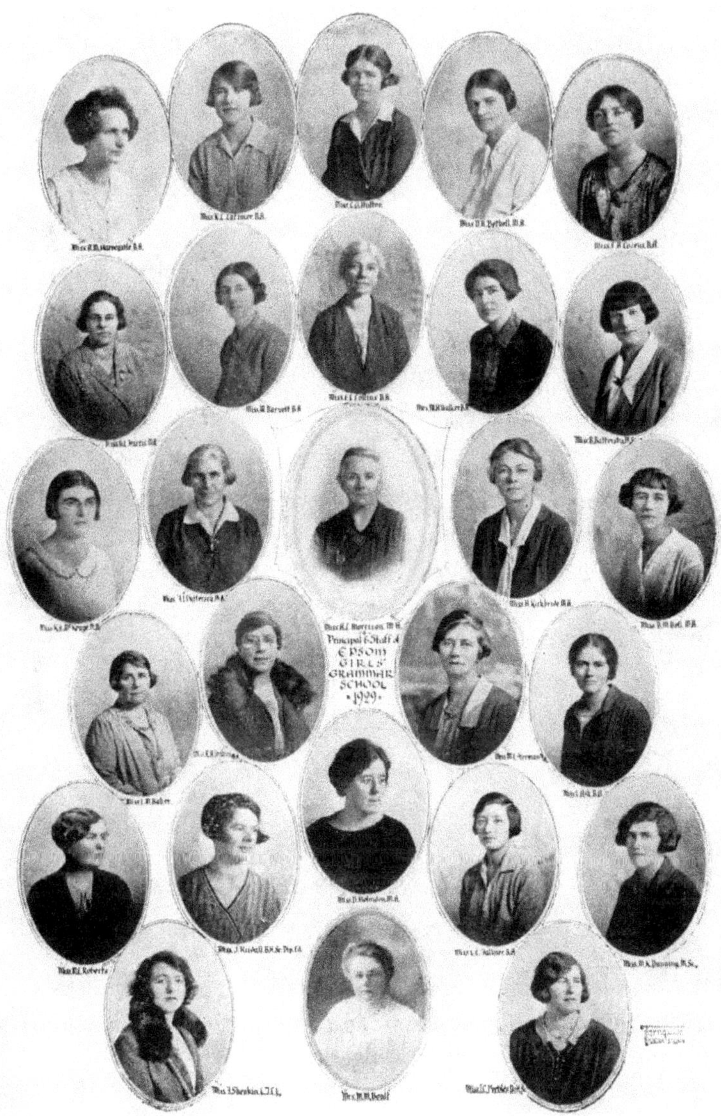

Principal and Staff of the Epsom Girls' Grammar School, 1929.

Figure 2.6: Principal and staff of Epsom Girls' Grammar School, 1929, showing Marion Walker second from the right in the second row from the top.

Notes: One of few photographs of Marion from this time, it exemplifies the unusual world in which she worked—one of educated, professional women. Note that only one of the other staff members is identified as a 'Mrs'.

Source: *Te Korero* (EGGS school magazine), no. 13, September 1929, 40. Courtesy of Epsom Girls' Grammar School.

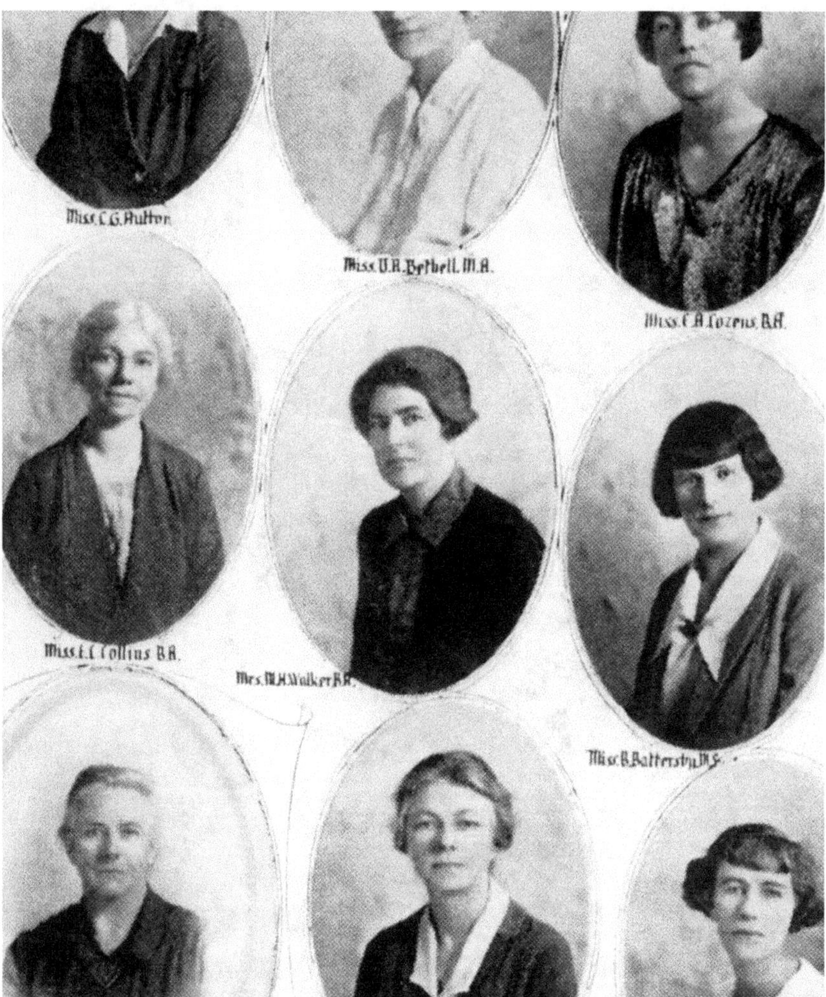

Figure 2.7: Close-up of Marion Walker (centre).

Source: *Te Korero*, no. 13, September 1929, 40. Courtesy of Epsom Girls' Grammar School.

'I went to primary school, which was a horrible shock'[34]

In 1924, when Marion started teaching at Epsom Girls' Grammar, she sent her three children to Remuera Primary School. Daintry was eight, Rosalie seven and Douglas five. It was a late start at school for the two girls given that New Zealand children generally attended school from age five. Having started school two years later than the usual age, Rosalie found herself floundering in comparison with her peers. She had gone to 'the local kindergarten [pre-school]', when she was about four.[35] Perhaps, amid all the ructions of her marriage breaking down and moving house, Marion had found it easier to get the children to the nearby kindergarten, a short walk down the road to Newmarket, than to get them on the tram to Remuera Primary. The shame of her separation from Stanley and the public nature of the bankruptcy and house sale might have been additional reasons behind her keeping the children away from school.

Placed in a class with children of her age who had already been at school for two years, Rosalie found school 'a horrible shock' because 'of course I hadn't learnt the things that the other children had learnt'.[36] In 1998, Rosalie recalled an occasion when the teacher asked the class to 'write a composition about an apple'.[37] She had no idea what a composition was; however, her description of her response to the challenge illustrates her creativity:

> So I looked at … [another child's story], and she said 'An apple is round, an apple is red.' So I thought, oh that's all right … And then I remember I wrote … 'Some apples are brown, and they are called Russet apples.' I remember writing that because we had russet apples growing in the garden. And I thought hers was frightfully boring anyway.[38]

34 Hughes et al., 'Rosalie Gascoigne Artist', tape 1.

35 Ibid. Four was not early for a child to start kindergarten in New Zealand. The Kindergarten Association, founded in 1889 in Dunedin, rapidly spread throughout New Zealand. The Auckland Free Kindergarten Association was formed in 1908 with several kindergartens opening soon after, including one in Newmarket, which would have been the closest one to the Walker homes. See Downer and the New Zealand Free Kindergarten Union, *Seventy-Five Years*.

36 Hughes et al., 'Rosalie Gascoigne Artist', tape 1.

37 Ibid.

38 Ibid.

This description of her composition demonstrates her early eye for detail and colour, and perhaps a certain independence and impatience in the forms imposed upon her. That the memory stayed with her indicates its power in that moment. Already feeling different because of her family circumstances and the disparities between her and her siblings, the comments she made in 1998 suggest that the discomfort and anxiety of the new school environment plummeted her further into insecurity. She said she lived on her wits: 'I was terrified of authority. And … good at games. That's about it.'[39]

Stanley

Rosalie felt the separation from her father deeply. She recalled that Stanley's absence:

> did [have a big effect], but of course you don't analyse when you are young … my school friends' families … had fathers in them—that was awfully nice … there's something missing in your life … I always thought it would be very nice to have a mother and a father and perhaps be normal.[40]

Stanley was not completely absent: he left Auckland and 'went down to Thames … [and] got a job', but he returned from time to time on business and to visit his family.[41] There is no evidence of how frequently he visited or what shape the visits took: his intermittent presence, however, might have compounded Rosalie's sense of alienation from him.

As already noted, Rosalie and her siblings were not unusual in living in a fatherless home.[42] There was, though, a difference between a father who had died and one who had left the family. Some in society might have perceived the Walker family situation in an even dimmer light had Stanley

39 Ibid.

40 Ibid., tape 9.

41 Ibid., tape 1.

42 Gordon Carmichael's demographics, which represent the period from ten years before Rosalie's birth through her childhood years, indicate this, cited in Goodger, 'Maintaining Sole Parent Families'. Wife desertion was common, especially during the economic depression that began in the early 1920s when many men, seeking work, crossed the Tasman to Australia or moved to remote parts of New Zealand unsuited to family life.

and Marion divorced.[43] Although the government had introduced no-fault divorce in 1920, it was still socially unacceptable in the genteel, educated professional elite to which Marion and her family belonged. Marion and Stanley may have felt they were protecting themselves and their children from the censure that often accompanied divorce by remaining married, at least in name. Even so, as a sensitive child with a nascent artist's eye for detail, Rosalie was all too aware of how her family situation differed from others, especially once she attended school and, being gregarious, was invited into other people's homes, experiencing their family situations.[44]

Sadly, Stanley's absence did not prevent him from creating distress in the family. A week after Rosalie's seventh birthday, and probably a week or so into her first school term, Stanley featured in the *Auckland Star* court pages on 6 February 1924 under the headline 'A Little Shaky':

> Stanley King Walker (40), a well-dressed man, snapped his fingers and showed other signs of nervousness when charged with having been found in a state of helpless drunkenness. The police … were called out to Walker at 12.30 a.m. to-day, his condition having attracted the attention of passers-by. A week's remand was granted, so that Walker might be medically attended.[45]

The medical attention Stanley received led to his committal to the Rotoroa Inebriates' Home for twelve months.[46] The Salvation Army had established the home on Rotoroa Island in Auckland's Hauraki Gulf in 1911 for the compulsory committal and treatment of alcoholics under the Inebriates and Drunkards Act 1906. It is unlikely the Walker children would have seen anything of their father that year because the island's isolation was considered crucial for treatment.

---

43 Brown, 'Loosening the Marriage Bond', 230. According to Brown, divorce was frowned on. New Zealand's no fault divorce laws, based on three years' mutual separation and enacted in 1920, were designed 'to avoid the painful scrutiny, the embarrassment, the gossip, and the ostracism which might be visited upon the couple that used other grounds to petition for divorce'. Despite such liberal legislation, divorce remained rare—primarily the domain of the working class.

44 See Hughes et al., 'Rosalie Gascoigne Artist', tape 1. Rosalie described herself in relation to her sister: 'She wasn't sensitive like I was.'

45 'A Little Shaky', *Auckland Star*, 6 February 1924, 8. Reports of this incident also appeared in a number of other New Zealand newspapers.

46 Stanley's 1924 committal to Rotoroa was reported twelve years later in 'Intoxicated', *Auckland Star*, 15 July 1936, 8.

utter travesty is understandable when the whole scheme is subjected to careful analysis.

The four finalists, in each instance appeared nightly in the various centres at the theatre controlled by N.Z Entertainers, Ltd., and were actually part of the performance inasmuch as they were used as a draw for the crowd.

The public were cordially invited, as they are being invited in Auckland at present, to pay 6/-, 4/-, and 2/- plus tax for the privilege of voting for a girl who may ultimately represent the Dominion as the national ideal.

It matters not to either the hypocritical daily press, who have

Ltd., have boosted its prices up from 6/8 during the week to 11/- plus tax on the last two nights of the competition November 19 and 20.

The "N.Z. Herald" seemed rather surprised that the "novelty" had not appealed more to the Auckland public.

Is it any wonder?—eleven shillings a seat!

Far better to exclude the public altogether for the final selection rather than permit such objectionable profiteering.

As "Truth" has already stated, it joins issues with the thousands of well wishers of the competitors, but at the same time it deplores the palpably unfair methods of selection and the business of using the girls as pawns in a particularly sordid publicity stunt.

WHEN WALKER MADE THE PACE

(From "N.Z. Truth's" Special Auckland Representative.)

A light meal at half past six—no lunch—four or five spots, at an average cost of four or five pounds a spot—truly a hectic day.

When Stanley King Walker came up from his Hauraki Plains garage to Auckland to buy a motor-car for a client, he little dreamt that his day in town would be so costly.

His boat arrived in the misty dawn and, with the exception of breakfast at the very early hour mentioned, he had nothing to eat all day.

Consequently, not having lined his inside with the necessary "blotting paper" to absorb the four or five spots he had during the course of his day's bargain driving, their collective kick was more potent then he anticipated.

He managed somehow to drive his lately acquired purchase down Queen Street, but his course was erratic and he just succeeded in missing the traffic cop at the Quay Street intersection.

Walker was fined £20 and was ordered to have his driving license suspended for two months.

Figure 2.8: Stanley's drink driving exploits exposed his family to shame through the publicity he attracted in newspapers around the country.

Source: 'When Walker Made the Pace', *New Zealand Truth*, 18 November 1926, 7. Courtesy of Auckland War Memorial Museum Tāmaki Paenga Hira, AP7.5 NZT.

Rosalie did not refer to this period in later interviews. The emotional abandonment that is common in children with parents who abuse alcohol, as well as in children whose parents leave them or die, is well documented.[47] Nearly three years later, in November 1926, Stanley appeared again in the

47 Angus Bancroft et al., *Parental Drug and Alcohol Misuse*.

Auckland Star and also in the *New Zealand Truth* (see Figure 2.8).[48] The *Star* reported his second conviction for drunken driving for which 'he pleaded guilty to a charge of being in a state of intoxication while in charge of a motor car in Quay Street'.[49] Despite the magistrate's talk of imprisonment, Stanley was fortunate to only be fined, even though it was a substantial amount—twenty pounds. He was suspended from driving for two months, with the magistrate warning that 'he must now realise the serious position he is in if he offends again'.[50] Rosalie was nine years old.

The newspapers that reported Stanley's convictions also featured Rosalie's early search for expression through her activity in the children's pages. This makes it scarcely conceivable that she could have been unaware of her father's notoriety. Rosalie enjoyed the children's pages of the *Auckland Star* and *New Zealand Herald*, which reported her successes in their competitions. Her wins included riddles, wise sayings and identifying missing items from lists. Her March 1929 prize-winning riddle provides an early glimpse of her wit:

> If a soldier and a sailor were locked in a car, which would get out first?
>
> The soldier, because he has the khaki (car key).[51]

In an unfortunate conjunction, the same edition of the *Auckland Star* that reported Rosalie's win with this riddle also recorded Stanley's third offence for drink driving: 'Stanley King Walker, a motor mechanic was today fined £10 for drunkenness while in charge of a motor car. His licence was cancelled for two years.'[52] Rosalie was twelve years old and in her final year at Remuera Primary School.

Rosalie's passing mention of Stanley's alcohol problems in the life narrative she told in the 1990s suggests she may have known about some of his drink driving charges at the time, or was at the very least aware that something was amiss. It is likely Rosalie, Daintry and Douglas experienced shame—either the shame of confusion on feeling they were responsible for the

---

48 'Missed His Lunch but Had Some Drinks. Intoxicated in a Car. Country Motorist Fined £20', *Auckland Star*, 10 November 1926, 8; 'When Walker Made the Pace', *New Zealand Truth*, 18 November 1926, 7.

49 'Missed His Lunch but Had Some Drinks'. Quay Street is in central Auckland.

50 Ibid. According to the Reserve Bank of New Zealand's inflation calculator, twenty pounds in 1926 was equivalent to NZD2,400 on 21 June 2024.

51 'Results of Competition of March 13', *Auckland Star*, 27 March 1929, 24.

52 'Drunken Motorist Fined', *Auckland Star*, 27 March 1929, 11.

unspoken, or shame at their father's behaviour and his convictions and committal to Rotoroa. In her book, *Family Secrets: Shame and Privacy in Modern Britain*, which examines the difference between secrecy and privacy in British families from Victorian times to the modern day, Deborah Cohen asserts: 'that families instil shame is a commonplace'.[53] Rosalie's absorption of shame is unsurprising in the context of her family story. Her parents' broken marriage at a time when separation and divorce were deemed socially unacceptable in genteel society, and Stanley's publicised drink driving exploits, devolved pain and pressures onto Rosalie at an age when she lacked the ability or skills to manage it.

A snapshot taken around 1929 provides a telling perspective on Stanley's relationship with his children: in suit, collar and tie and presumably on a visit to Halls Avenue, he grips the handle of a push mower on a daisy-studded lawn (see Figure 2.9). The long shadows tell us it is late afternoon, the sun low in the sky. Douglas, around ten years old, leans into his father, his head just short of Stanley's shoulder. Stanley's gaze is directed down to the lawnmower. Only Douglas looks at the camera, unsmiling. Daintry, in her Epsom Girls' Grammar gymslip and a large-collared white blouse, hovers in the background, as does Rosalie, their eyes also cast down towards the mower. Rosalie and Douglas both balance with one foot resting on the other. Daintry alone smiles, although barely. The viewer's gaze is drawn to Douglas's solemn face. It is a self-conscious shot in which the children and their father appear disengaged, unwilling participants in the making of the image. Rosalie, her left hand across her abdomen, stands opposite the triptych of her father and siblings. She looks uncomfortable. Douglas seems to be the only one of the children attempting to make some connection with his father, but Stanley appears unresponsive as he continues to push the mower. If this were to be a tableau of suburban paternal domesticity, it remains infused with awkwardness. It is a snapshot in which the subjects seem unwilling and uncomfortable, reflecting their relationships with each other, providing a glimpse of the abrasive family relationships described by Rosalie in a 1998 interview.[54]

53 Cohen, *Family Secrets*, 266.

54 Hughes et al., 'Rosalie Gascoigne Artist'.

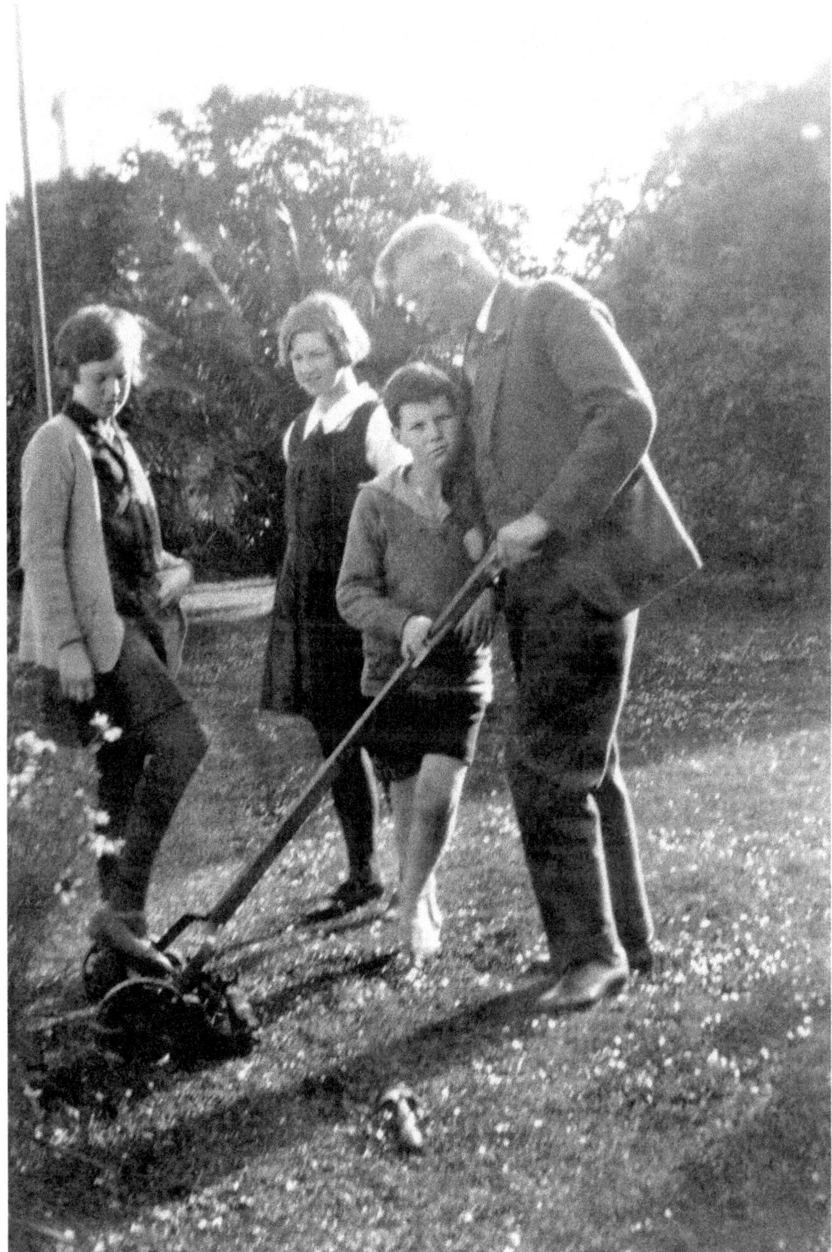

Figure 2.9: From left, Rosalie, Daintry, Douglas and Stanley at 8 Halls Avenue, c. 1929.

Source: Courtesy of the Gascoigne family.

Rosalie: A gregarious outsider?

In adulthood, Rosalie told stories about how she differed from her siblings and how she found them poor company. They were 'bookish'; she enjoyed the outdoors, making things, being active. She was, she said, more emotional than Daintry and Douglas. She described herself as the most gregarious of the three children; she had friends and would be invited away with their families.[55] Perhaps at home with her bookish siblings and busy working mother, Rosalie could not find the space to allow her outgoing nature to flourish. Away from the family, she was able to relax, liberate her easygoing nature and find the affirmation she craved.

Rosalie later described herself during childhood as being an outsider who did not fit in with her siblings and as being more emotional than them, and, at the same time, as being popular with other children and adults. The latter is confirmed by her schoolfriends' memories of her. Given that we respond differently according to circumstances, it makes sense that Rosalie may have felt an outsider in some situations and fitted in comfortably in others.

In interviews given once she had achieved fame as an artist, Rosalie seldom mentioned her younger brother Douglas, but frequently compared herself with her elder sister and found herself wanting. In the 1990s, Rosalie told a story of having lived in her elder sister's shadow. She described Daintry as a 'heavyweight' who was 'trusted at an early age to … go to the grocer across the road where you weren't allowed to cross'.[56]

Seventy years after the three siblings started school at Remuera Primary, Rosalie recalled feeling inadequate in comparison with Daintry. She said she struggled to catch up with her classmates, while 'my sister, of course, swam through it, being frightfully, frightfully clever'.[57] One cannot help wondering how it might have been for Daintry who was four years behind her peers, and must have coped with that strain in her own way.

Rosalie's frequent unfavourable comparison of herself with Daintry is a central part of her self-narrative. Time and death have obscured any 'truth', in Passerini's terms, that this may reveal. When Rosalie told her self-narrative for the first time—to Ian North in 1982—she included a brief version of

---

55 Ibid.: 'I was always good company for other children, you know. I used to get asked away on holidays and things. And both my brother and sister were fairly solitary'.

56 Ibid., tape 1.

57 Ibid.

her sense that she was less intelligent, more emotional and more solitary than her sister; that she was interested in looking rather than doing. She built on this in Hughes's interview. Perhaps this was how she remembered childhood, or perhaps it fitted with her developing story as having taken decades to discover her 'true' identity as an artist.

She enjoyed a friendship with her cousin Merron, daughter of Marion's sister Dolly and her husband Walter Broadfoot in Te Kuiti.[58] Rosalie described Merron as: 'more of my persuasion … than my brother and my sister'.[59] She enjoyed the space and freedom of country holidays spent in Te Kuiti: 'it was always the paddocks … not much adult supervision. It was always with the children' and, presaging her later art, 'you made something out of nothing'.[60] Her connection with Merron indicates that Rosalie was not completely isolated or lacking a sense of common feelings, although the 120 miles between Te Kuiti and Remuera meant that their visits with one another were infrequent.

While she enjoyed time spent with Merron at Te Kuiti, the annual summer holiday on Waiheke Island near Auckland delivered bliss.

Waiheke: 'I used to watch the tides and wander along the rocks'[61]

Each summer for about five years, Marion took Rosalie, Daintry and Douglas to Waiheke Island, a popular seaside resort in the Hauraki Gulf, about thirty kilometres by ferry from Auckland (see Figure 2.10). Marion and her children spent six weeks in the same 'shabby little beach cottage' at 'the same lonely beach every Christmas'.[62] In a reflection of the pressures of living with her grandmother's Victorian attitudes towards children, Rosalie assumed they were taken away to give Jessie a rest.[63]

58 Walter and Dolly Broadfoot had two daughters, Beverley and Merron.
59 Gascoigne, interview by North, 4.
60 Ibid.
61 Ibid.
62 Hughes et al., 'Rosalie Gascoigne Artist', tape 4.
63 Frost, 'Rosalie Gascoigne', 20: 'I think the reason why we went to Waiheke each year was to give my grandmother a rest.'

Rosalie, Daintry and Douglas colonised the beach in front of the holiday house, resentful when others 'invaded' their space:

> We loved the house and deserted beach. If by chance someone did wander onto our territory—and the shoreline was public of course, people had every right to share it with us—we resented their presence.[64]

This account, combined with the fact that she told only one story about having visitors as a child, raises questions about the family's insularity. In his book about ethical and practical issues in the therapeutic management of family secrets, Mark Karpel writes that when all family members know what is happening, a secret can strengthen the boundary between the family and the outside world.[65] In later life, Rosalie was a private person. She was evasive about personal questions in interviews (including about the reasons for her marriage to Ben as discussed in Chapter 4); it is understandable the family would have valued privacy in the face of the demeaning nature of Stanley's public convictions for drinking. Rosalie's family may have sealed their lips, closed ranks and erected the 'stout walls' Cohen identified as necessary for privacy.[66]

Rosalie enjoyed the freedom of beach walks, swims and collecting shells on Waiheke. Daintry and Douglas liked to spend their time differently:

> I used to be a shell collector and my brother and sister were much more basic and they would … build a boring old raft … and they'd spend all this time with hammers and things. Oh it was a terrible raft—it sank … I used to watch the tides and wander along in the rocks … and spend a lot of time by myself.[67]

She enjoyed the solitariness of beach walking, where she developed the collecting habit that was to form the basis of her later art making. During these holidays Rosalie began to love weathered things. The unpretentious 'shabby beach cottage' where they stayed provided a powerful contrast to the genteel Victorianisms of home. She said the cottage formed her love of objects carrying the marks of time and use, the faded colours that have been out in the sun and the wind; these were the materials that she came to value in her art.[68]

64 Ibid.
65 Karpel, 'Family Secrets', 2.
66 Cohen, *Family Secrets*, 267.
67 Gascoigne, interview by North, 4.
68 Hughes et al., 'Rosalie Gascoigne Artist', tape 4.

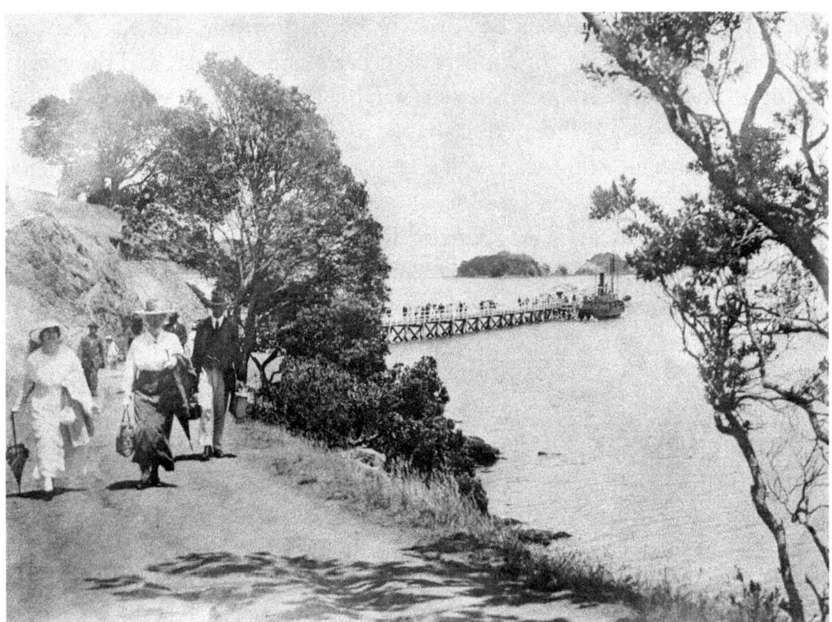

Figure 2.10: Picnickers and holidaymakers arriving at Waiheke Island, with the steamer ferry at the wharf, 1922.

Note: The Walker family would have travelled by ferry from Auckland to Waiheke.

Source: Courtesy of Auckland Library Heritage Collections, Auckland Libraries, 7-A9476.

Waiheke holidays also fostered Rosalie's relationship with nature. Some of the happiest childhood memories she related were of Waiheke Island summers where the days were 'as golden as the ripened plums that grew wild on the island's hillsides'.[69] She nodded off to sleep at night in the salt air and woke each morning to the sound of waves lapping the sand.

People who knew Rosalie during her childhood recalled that she loved looking at nature. Back in Auckland, her school friend Ruth Evans remembered they would enjoy walks around Remuera admiring 'the beautiful houses and gardens … Sometimes we climbed Mt Hobson and observed the Waitematā Harbour in all its moods.'[70] Evans's comment prefigures Rosalie's later love of gardening and flower arranging.

69 Frost, 'Rosalie Gascoigne', 19.

70 Ruth Evans to Ben Gascoigne and family, 28 October 1999, Papers of Ben Gascoigne 1938–2007, National Library of Australia (hereafter Papers of Ben Gascoigne), box 3.

Even if Rosalie seldom felt accepted in her family, she looked at nature and felt accepted by it.[71] In concert with her misfit identity, and the family relationships by which she defined herself, her love of nature weaves through her story as a constant thread that shaped and formed her, texturing her life. She told North in 1982 that Waiheke was a significant influence on her art making: 'I think when I look back on it that would be one of my great influences, that island.'[72] Apart from Daintry and Douglas, there is little mention of others in her Waiheke summer stories. Fortunate to be in a position to enjoy holidays away, they returned just in time for the start-of-term school bell.

Elsie Walker

Less than two months after Jessie's death, Rosalie's first cousin, Elsie Walker, was found dead in a disused Auckland quarry on 5 October 1928. Seventeen-year-old Elsie was the second eldest of Stanley's brother D'Renzy Walker and his wife Mereana's seven children.[73] Elsie's dream had been to move to Auckland and train as a dressmaker, but instead her father sent her to live with her aunt and uncle at Papamoa to 'get her into a better environment', away from Māori who had been her main companions in the remote east coast settlement of Raukokore, near Cape Runaway, this despite the fact that Elsie's mother was Māori and D'Renzy had been estranged from his father after marrying Mereana.[74] Elsie lived with Stanley's sister Ivy, her husband Frank Bayly and their five children on their farm at Papamoa, in the Bay of Plenty south-east of Auckland. The Baylys paid her a small wage in return for household duties and she slept on the verandah.[75]

One night Elsie mysteriously disappeared from the Bayly farm. Five days later and around 188 miles away from the farm, two boys out rabbiting found her body, hidden in scrub and gnawed by rodents. Elsie's mysterious death aroused the prurient interest of newspapers throughout New Zealand and across the Tasman in Australia.

---

71 Frost, 'Rosalie Gascoigne', 19–21.

72 Gascoigne, interview by North, 4.

73 Mereana Walker does not rate a mention in any of the newspaper reports about Elsie's death and the inquest; neither is she mentioned on the death certificate nor Elsie's gravestone at Purewa Cemetery in Auckland.

74 'Elsie Walker Mystery, Further Evidence', *Wairarapa Daily Times*, 15 January 1929, 5.

75 'Some More Mysterious Circumstances about Elsie Walker's Death', *New Zealand Truth*, 24 January 1929, 7.

Leading the salacious charge was *New Zealand Truth*, a tabloid newspaper established in Sydney before being brought across the Tasman to New Zealand by Australian owner John Norton in 1905.[76] A populist newspaper, *Truth* offered a heady mix of sex, crime and initially radical politics that, by the 1920s, had become reactionary, aimed at working-class New Zealanders. The complexity and mystery of Elsie Walker's death, combined with a long-running inquest, opened the way for *Truth* to devote a sensationalist half page to it each day (see Figure 2.11). Redmer Yska described how *Truth* handled the story:

> In the pages of *Truth,* one of the biggest crime stories of the interwar period unfolded week by week like the plot of a cheap novel, with a cast of suspects, heroes and villains.[77]

Around the time of the Elsie Walker case, *Truth* was selling 100,000 copies a week. This was in a population of just under 1.5 million.[78]

In 'The Cultural Remains of Elsie Walker', New Zealand historian Bronwyn Dalley attributes the interest in Elsie's case to a number of factors, including:

> the unsolved, perennially open nature of the case; its seemingly bizarre aspects; and the imaginative possibilities provided by the death of a healthy, seventeen-year-old female virgin with seminal stains on her underwear.[79]

Newspapers reported in great detail on each stage of the police inquiry, including, in the context of conjecture about the causes of her death, details of semen on Elsie's underwear. The chief person of interest, William 'Bill' Bayly, was Ivy and Frank's son, and Elsie's (and Rosalie's) first cousin. Bill had a reputation as a seducer who the police considered 'sexually weak'. He had been charged with carnal knowledge of a local girl in 1926 and, even though he was not convicted, his reputation was such that his name was usually associated with any scandal involving young women in the district.[80]

76 Yska, *Truth*, 8, 9.

77 Ibid., 77.

78 Statistics New Zealand, 'The New Zealand Official Year-Book, 1928'.

79 Dalley, 'The Cultural Remains of Elsie Walker', 140–62.

80 Superintendent W. G. Wohlmann, Auckland, to commissioner of police, Wellington, 13 November 1928; Report of Constable Rimmer, Waihi, 3 November 1928; and statement of Bill Bayly, 27 October 1928, cited in ibid., 142–3.

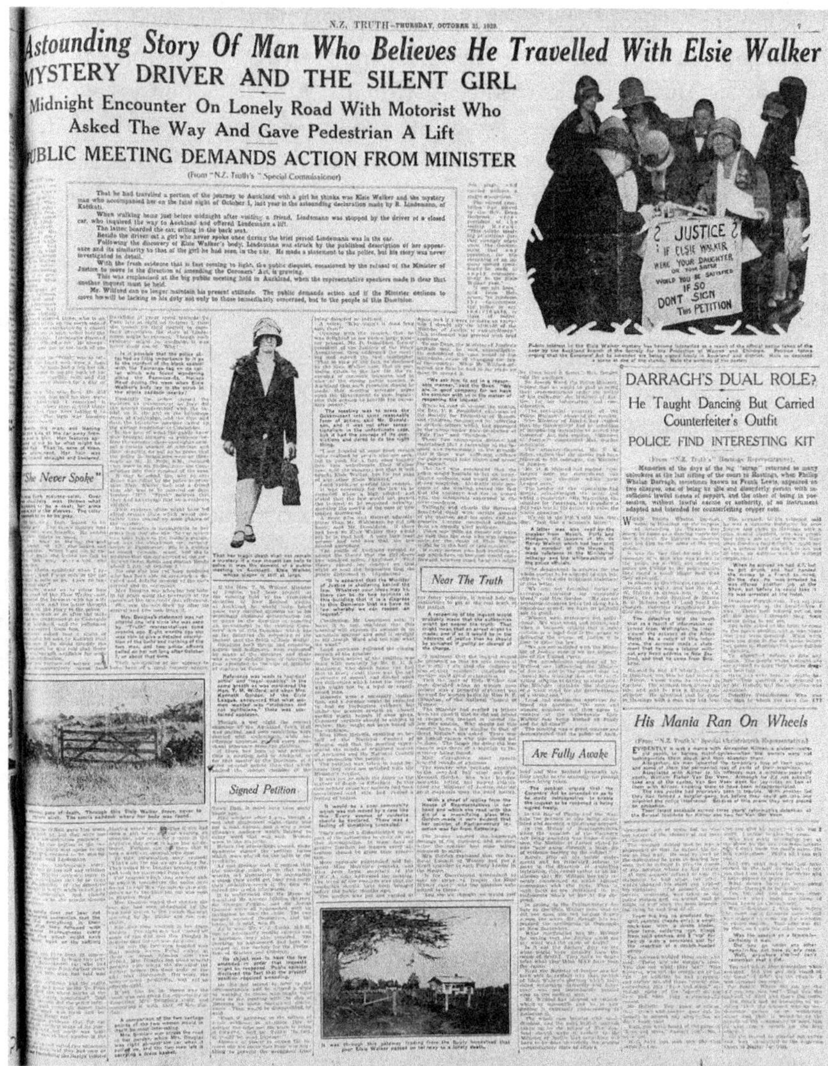

N.Z. TRUTH—THURSDAY, OCTOBER 31, 1929.

Astounding Story Of Man Who Believes He Travelled With Elsie Walker

MYSTERY DRIVER AND THE SILENT GIRL

Midnight Encounter On Lonely Road With Motorist Who Asked The Way And Gave Pedestrian A Lift

PUBLIC MEETING DEMANDS ACTION FROM MINISTER

(From "N.Z. Truth's" Special Commissioner)

"She Never Spoke"

Near The Truth

Signed Petition

Are Fully Awake

DARRAGH'S DUAL ROLE?

He Taught Dancing But Carried Counterfeiter's Outfit

POLICE FIND INTERESTING KIT

His Mania Ran On Wheels

Figure 2.11: Sensationalist newspaper coverage of the Elise Walker case.

Notes: Australian-owned populist newspaper the *New Zealand Truth* led the salacious charge with coverage of the Elsie Walker case, devoting a half page to the sad story each day. Note the photograph at top right of the page. There was public outrage over police handling of the case. The Society for the Protection of Women and Children launched a petition for changes to the Coroners Act enabling inquests to be reopened.

Source: 'Astounding Story of Man Who Believes He Travelled with Elsie Walker', *New Zealand Truth*, 31 October 1929, 7. Courtesy of Auckland War Memorial Museum Tāmaki Paenga Hira, AP7.5 NZT.

Rosalie did not speak of Elsie in her later interviews; neither did she speak of her to her own children. Yet it seems unlikely she would not have known Elsie's sad story. Rosalie's son Martin suggests that, given her age at the time, she would have been aware of Elsie's death and the surrounding publicity.[81] Rosalie herself said of Auckland that 'everyone knew everyone else or at least knew about everyone else'.[82] In addition, Marion taught Elsie's elder sister Annie, who lived with Stanley's sister in Auckland, at Epsom Girls' Grammar and the two formed a friendship that lasted until Marion's death, so it is likely that Rosalie knew Elsie's sister and would have been aware of the tragedy.[83]

For a young, literate, astutely aware girl, the very public sexual undertones would have been deeply embarrassing, even more so because another cousin was the chief person of interest in the case. The publicity would have distressed Marion who probably offered Annie some comfort in her grief, and Rosalie is likely to have witnessed Annie's grief close at hand. Grief and shame constitute a powerful combination and generate confusion. That Rosalie never talked about her cousin suggests that she may have practised what pastoral care theologian Professor Robert H. Albers termed 'discretionary shame', protecting her privacy and wellbeing.[84]

The mystery of Elsie's death remained in the public domain all during the following year. On Rosalie's twelfth birthday, 25 January 1929, the coroner delivered his verdict that there was no conclusive evidence as to whether Elsie's death had been murder or an accident. Criticising the police's handling of the case, he called for a commission of inquiry. After the commission exonerated the police, the Society for Protection of Women and Children, still dissatisfied with police management of the case, including the manner in which Elsie's body was handled and the fact that there was no trial, took up Elsie's case as a cause célèbre. It presented a petition containing over fifteen thousand signatures to parliament, urging that the Coroners Act be amended to allow for inquests to be reopened. Although the coroner supported the proposal, in November 1929, Minister of Justice Thomas Wilford announced his refusal to amend the Coroners Act 1908 to enable a second inquest.[85] Such was the strength of interest in the case, Wilford was

81 Gascoigne, *Rosalie Gascoigne: Her New Zealand Origins*, 177.

82 Frost, 'Rosalie Gascoigne', 19. When I asked them in 2012, my uncle (b. 1916) and aunt (1919–2013), who were born and raised in Auckland, recalled the case from their childhoods, including the drama and considerable speculation associated with it.

83 Gascoigne, *New Zealand Lives*, 191.

84 Albers, 'Shame: A Dynamic'; Schneider, *Shame, Exposure and Privacy*, 254–6.

85 Wilford, 'Elsie Walker Case', 3.

relocated to the New Zealand High Commission in London because his decision was so unpopular with the New Zealand public. The new minister of justice, Sir Thomas Sidey, allowed for new inquests or the reopening of inquests, but not retrospectively. The case was closed and remains unsolved to this day.[86]

Rosalie's later practice of collecting and making art from objects discarded in the countryside evokes for me the image of her cousin's body abandoned in the quarry. Her *Pale Landscape* (1977), a massive mat of newspapers around four metres by seven metres softened to a creamy yellow and threaded with hundreds of swan feathers, brings to mind the newspaper stories about her father and her cousins Elsie Walker and Bill Bayly. In *Pale Landscape*, the feathers interrupt the words, breaking down the stories, silencing them. She replaced daily news with something beautiful that spoke of the landscape she had made her own, far from the setting of difficult childhood stories and likely ensuing shame.

Sunlight, sand, shells and shame

Her parents' fractured relationship, caused by tensions over educational differences and Stanley's failure to live up to the male ideals of the time because of his drinking and his bankrupted business clouded Rosalie's life from 1923 until 1929. So too did Elsie's death in 1928 and the attendant publicity the following year.

A central thread from these times is Rosalie's sense of feeling different—from her siblings, from the children at school, from her Scottish grandmother. She did not speak of Elsie's death in interviews, nor to her family. She chose which aspects to reveal and which to remain silent on. This was her way of claiming some of the agency she lacked at the time. She spoke of shame and difference, weaving the two threads through her story. Interwoven with the coarseness of these are finer threads about her love of nature and her awareness of visual things like shadows on the wall, flowers, shells or leaves (see Figure 2.12). She used strong imagery, demonstrating her visual acuity. Nellie's encouragement and family holidays at Waiheke were key influences on the development of Rosalie's creativity during this period. Her self-narrative covering these years, in her omissions as well as her inclusions, laid the groundwork for the influences on her later art practice.

86 For a full account of the case, see Bainbridge, 'The Death of Elsie Walker'.

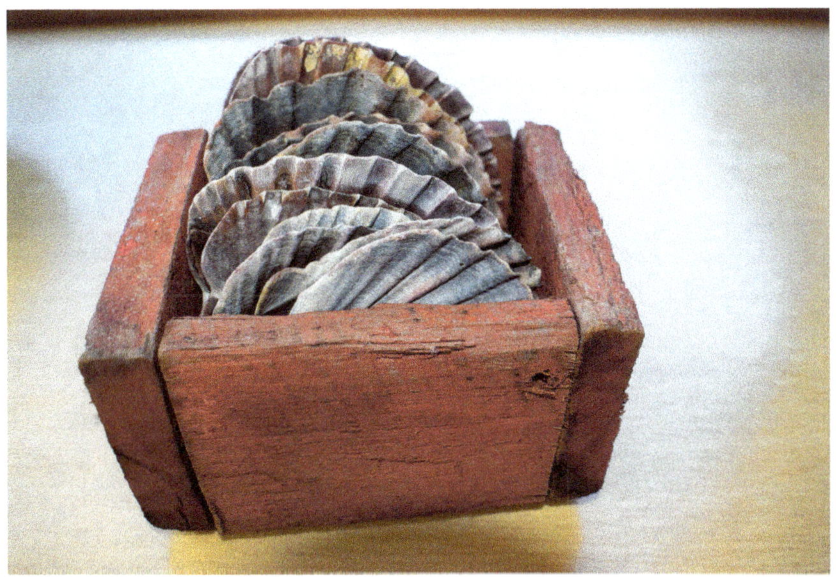

Figure 2.12: Scallop shells collected by Rosalie.

Source: Courtesy of Sally Colahan Griffin and Hester Gascoigne. Photograph: Sally Colahan Griffin.

3

1930–34: 'I went to the school my mother taught at which was a bad thing'

Soon after her thirteenth birthday, in January 1930, Rosalie commenced the first of five years at Epsom Girls' Grammar School (EGGS), the local public high school where her mother taught (see Figures 3.1–3.4).

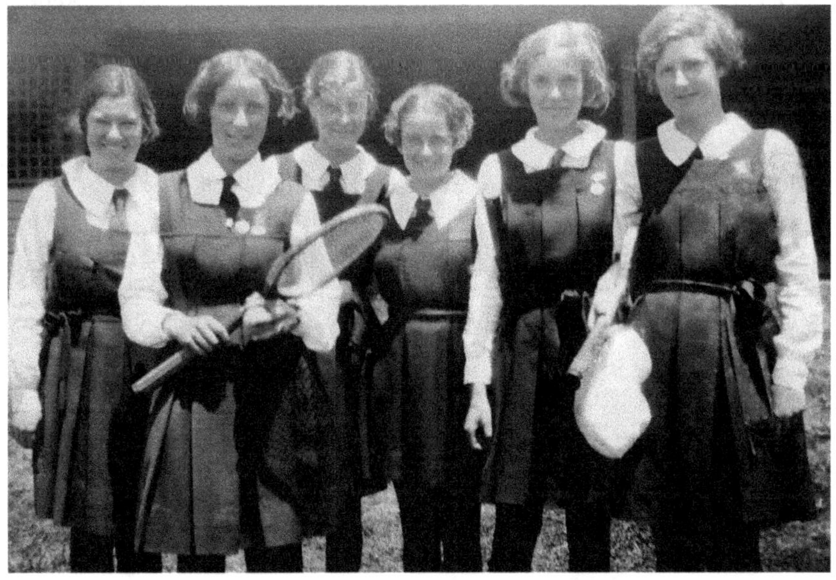

Figure 3.1: Rosalie (far right) with friends at Epsom Girls' Grammar School.
Source: Courtesy of the Gascoigne family.

Schoolgirl

During these formative years, education was central to this part of Rosalie's life on two counts. School provided her with the stability and structure that may have been lacking at home. Also, New Zealand's policies and practices on domestic education for girls, based as they were on an idealised family, may have contributed to the feelings of being different, a misfit, an outsider, which she later talked about. Her family fell short of the ideal family promoted by the government and women's organisations such as the Women's Christian Temperance Union. In the longer term, the same policies shaped her thinking about a woman's role in home and family.

When Rosalie set off for her first day at EGGS in early 1930, she was one of a fortunate although slender majority. Of the 23,022 pupils (12,059 boys and 10,963 girls) who, with Rosalie, left public primary schools at the end of 1929, only 53 per cent of girls and 51 per cent of boys proceeded to secondary school. The remainder went into trades, other occupations or remained at home.[1] In 1930, only 55 per cent of children (33,868) of secondary school age enjoyed the privilege of an education.[2] Free secondary education was available to those who passed the Proficiency Examination at the end of primary school, around the age of twelve or thirteen, but taking up this opportunity depended on familial attitudes and finances. Many families saw little point in educating their daughters past primary school as they believed that almost inevitable marriage and motherhood required no schooling beyond that which was compulsory. Even if girls did proceed to secondary school, a large proportion of them left in their first two years. Melanie Nolan states that, 'in 1917, 20% of girls left during or at the end of their first year, and 35% of the remainder left during or at the end of their second year'.[3] These figures remained high during the years of Rosalie's schooling, the Great Depression a major factor, with Nolan reporting that the figures in 1939 were 22 per cent and 32 per cent, respectively.[4] Rosalie's family believed in the value of education and had the financial means to provide it for her.

1 Statistics New Zealand, 'The New Zealand Official Year-Book, 1931'.

2 Butchers, *Education in New Zealand*, 344–5; Nolan, *Breadwinning*, 124. Nolan states that 55 per cent of primary pupils went on to secondary school in 1932; Butchers cites 2 per cent of the total population.

3 Nolan, *Breadwinning*, 124.

4 Ibid.

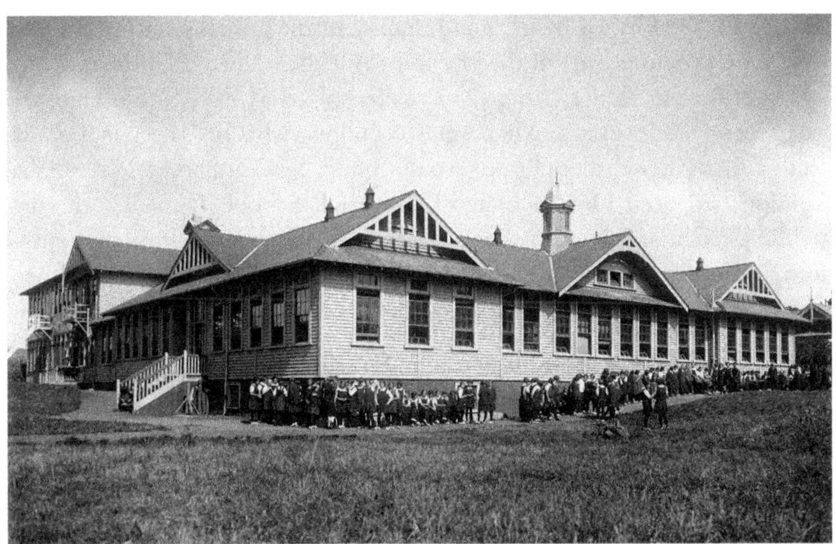

Figure 3.2: Pupils outside Epsom Girls' Grammar School, 1926.

Note: Built during World War I when funds were tight, EGGS lacked the imposing buildings enjoyed by other schools governed by the Auckland Grammar Schools' Board.

Source: Courtesy of Auckland Libraries Heritage Collections 1-W0605. Photograph: Henry Winkelmann (1860–1931).

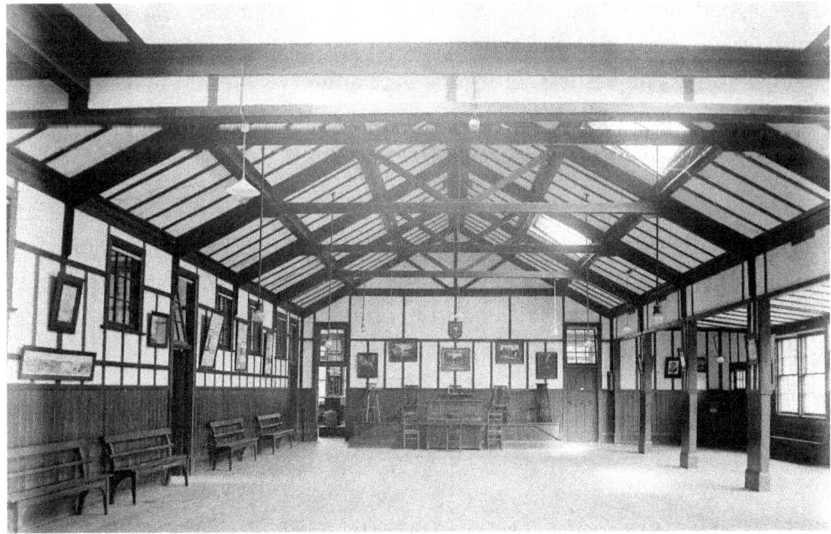

Figure 3.3: Epsom Girls' Grammar School hall, 1930.

Note: Rosalie would have attended daily school assemblies here and had lessons in the classrooms opening off it.

Source: Courtesy of Auckland Library Heritage Collections, Auckland Libraries, 4-2876. Photograph: James D. Richardson.

EGGS was established in 1917 in response to the growing need for a girls' school on the other side of the city from Auckland Girls' Grammar, which was overflowing as the city grew. Rosalie started at EGGS the same year as its new headmistress, Miss Agnes Loudon, who had been appointed from a field of twelve applicants from around New Zealand and Australia. Loudon had been Dux of Otago Girls' High School, Dunedin, the first public girls' high school in the southern hemisphere, which offered girls a formal education to prepare them for tertiary studies.[5] Loudon herself, then, was a product of New Zealand's government-funded education system.

EGGS was a ten-minute walk from 2 Halls Avenue via St Marks and Manukau Roads: no more rushing for the tram up Remuera Road to primary school. Rosalie did not like the fact that her mother taught at EGGS and her sister was already a pupil there:

> I went to the school my mother taught at which was a bad thing … [because] you don't want to be identified with a staff member. And of course, anything you did got relegated back to the staff room. And you had an older sister who was different, so it wasn't really good. You felt you were overlooked all the time.[6]

Here, Rosalie contradicts herself, in one breath claiming that nothing she did escaped notice, and in the next lamenting that she was overlooked. Told decades later, Rosalie's story presents her as stuck between her mother and her sister. This restless sense of being at once visible and invisible would feature often in her life, perhaps shaping an aesthetic that sought to reclaim meaning from discarded objects.

Pupil numbers during Rosalie's EGGS years—ranging from 642 in 1930 to 631 in 1934—were large enough for her to merge with the crowd, but small enough for the wider school community of teachers and students to know her mother was a teacher and her older sister another pupil.[7] Escape was impossible, individuation a challenge.

---

5 'Epsom Girls' Grammar, New Headmistress Appointed, Miss A. N. Loudon, of Otago', *Auckland Star*, 31 October 1929, 11.

6 Hughes et al., 'Rosalie Gascoigne Artist', tape 1.

7 Christine Black, EGGS archivist, email message to the author, 31 July 2013: 'School numbers: 1930–642; 1931-588; 1932-574; 1933-605; 1934-631. The drop in numbers is attributed to the opening of Otahuhu Technical High School, now Otahuhu College in the south of Auckland and the withdrawal of pupils as a result of the Great Depression.'

Rosalie's relationship to Daintry is a central feature in her later descriptions of her EGGS years. While she did not explain what she meant by describing her sister as 'different', she spoke of Daintry as an almost superhero figure, impossible to live up to. Daintry was 'very much cleverer', trusted more, 'very authoritative' even at a young age; she was 'frightfully, frightfully clever' and 'knew everything' about the 'ordinary things of life' whereas Rosalie said she knew nothing.[8] The image she painted of her sister was one of relentless competence; by contrast, persistent self-deprecation lay at the heart of the image she painted of herself: 'I always knew she [Daintry] was better. And she was better. She was sensible. She was adult.'[9] Her sister, she recalled, could do things 'properly, but I couldn't'.[10] The truth of this self-narrative lies, perhaps, as much in the protections Rosalie sought from academic and family expectations as in any objective comparison. According to her classmate Ruth Evans, Rosalie was 'extremely clever but not overly academic' or ambitious: 'She was able to perform well in English, Mathematics and Science but was reluctant to do homework so didn't perform well in subjects that required learning [like] French vocabulary.'[11] Daintry seemed to define a work ethic that Rosalie felt alienated from and did not seek to emulate.

Contemporary evidence, in particular, academic results, contests Rosalie's stories about her sister's superiority. EGGS' annual class lists, showing the girls in order of their overall place in class, indicate that the sisters were similar in academic ability and school social status; both were prefects in their senior years.[12] Nevertheless, Rosalie continued to tell the story of Daintry as more intelligent, more mature, more responsible and less sensitive than her: 'There was no doubt about the scholastic prowess of my sister. She was old for her age … and she was responsible. And she

8 Hughes et al., 'Rosalie Gascoigne Artist', tape 1.

9 Ibid.

10 Ibid., tape 2.

11 Gascoigne, *Rosalie Gascoigne: Her New Zealand Origins*, 209.

12 All information from Epsom Girls' Grammar School class lists 1930–34 courtesy of Epsom Girls' Grammar School Archives, Auckland, New Zealand. According to these, Daintry did no better at school than Rosalie and neither girl's name appears in scholarship or prize lists. In 1930, in Class 3A, Rosalie came nineteenth in languages and twenty-first in sciences out of a class of thirty-three. Daintry was fifteenth out of thirty in Class 4A. In 1931, Rosalie was sixteenth out of thirty-one in Class 4A and Daintry was fifteenth out of thirty in Class 5A; in 1932, Rosalie was twenty-second out of thirty-two in Class 5A and Daintry was twentieth out of twenty-three in Class 6B Modern; in 1933, Daintry was bottom of her class of ten Upper Sixth pupils, and Rosalie was seventh out of eleven in the Lower Sixth. For her Upper Sixth year, Rosalie came seventh out of a class of eleven. Both girls were prefects in 1933 when Daintry was in the Upper Sixth and Rosalie in 6B; Rosalie was again a prefect in her Upper Sixth and final year at school.

wasn't sensitive like I was.'[13] Despite the similarity in their academic results, Rosalie's story of their difference justified her more associative, intuitive self-image. Her family valued academic success: 'Oh, they *liked* brains in my family', so she used academia as her point of comparison.[14] Although she expressed affection for her sister in later life and made an artwork in memory of her, Daintry is more evident in Rosalie's self-narrative as a device against which Rosalie defines herself, rather than a person who experienced her own insecurities living in the dysfunctional Walker household.[15]

Much later in life Rosalie acknowledged her surprise when Daintry told her: 'Oh I always felt I could do no right, and you always could do right.'[16] Rosalie chose to ignore Daintry's words, telling her interviewer: 'But I didn't ever think that. Because she was clever, and the family hope certainly rested on her.'[17] Rosalie adhered to the narrative she had created—Daintry's confessed feelings of inadequacy did not sway Rosalie from her own story. It is feasible both sisters felt inadequate as a result of family dynamics, such as the abrasiveness Rosalie described, or their mother's lack of availability to them as she juggled the demands of being a single parent in full-time employment. Perhaps each felt an 'outsider' in relation to the other. Such alienation might occur as a result of family strain.

Just as she later spoke to Hughes of the need for 'a selfish eye' in art making and the necessity to 'recreate the world that you love and admire as best you can', Rosalie recreated a story that suited her purpose.[18] Having actively constructed a personality that was essentially disengaged and excluded empathy, she sought surrogate connections in other domains, specifically nature, poetry and, later, art.

The shame of the previous chapter is here coupled, at least in Rosalie's reflections, to a defensive but resilient absence of empathy towards her sister. Again, the self-image jars a little with others' recollections of Rosalie.

---

13 Hughes et al., 'Rosalie Gascoigne Artist', tape 1.

14 Ibid.

15 The artwork was *Hill Station* 1989, see Gascoigne, *Rosalie Gascoigne: Her New Zealand Origins*, 243–5.

16 Hughes et al., 'Rosalie Gascoigne Artist', tape 3.

17 Ibid.

18 Ibid., tape 6.

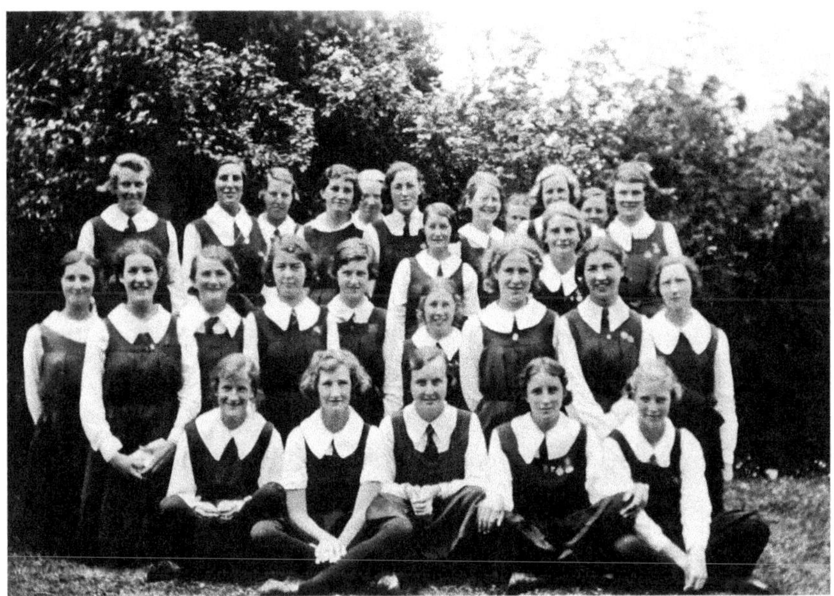

Figure 3.4: Rosalie is in the centre row, fifth from the left in this class photo from Epsom Girls' Grammar School, c. 1932.

Photograph: Courtesy Gascoigne family archive.

Schoolfriend Ruth Evans recalled Rosalie as 'confident and well-liked by pupils and teachers', remembering her for her 'kindness, originality and wry humour … She was compassionate and would feel sorry when her friends endured bad luck. She could be patient too, with those in sore trouble.'[19] Another friend from Remuera Primary and EGGS contradicted Rosalie's self-representation as a loner who lacked confidence. In a condolence letter to Ben Gascoigne after Rosalie's death in 1999, Dorothy Gifford remembered 'happy parties at the Walker home in Remuera in our teen ages, where she [Rosalie] was always so bright, witty, full of fun'.[20] Such recollections, no doubt, were coloured by time and by the occasions of their expression: it is not so much a question of which accounts are true, but of the truths they convey about these formative aspects of Rosalie's later childhood.

19 Ruth Evans to Ben Gascoigne and family, 28 October 1999, Papers of Ben Gascoigne, box 3.

20 Dorothy Gifford (née Buchanan) to Ben Gascoigne, 25 October 1999, Papers of Ben Gascoigne, box 3.

'I was the middle of three'

A central thread of Rosalie's narrative relates to her place as the middle child. Daintry, Rosalie and Douglas were born within the short space of three years, with Daintry born thirteen months before Rosalie and Douglas twenty-one months after. She repetitively recited her middle place to Hughes, defining herself by the absence of qualities of her sister and brother on either side of her:

> Well I was the middle of three … Being the middle one is a bit—I had a younger brother, and an older sister who was very much cleverer than I was … And I was the one in the middle.[21]

Rosalie identified with common beliefs that middle children are neglected and overlooked—in-between children who lack adult attention. To North, who asked how her family regarded her, she replied: 'The middle child who wasn't as bright as the first child and who was too emotional.'[22] Again she made no mention of Douglas but compared herself with Daintry, this time bringing emotion into the story. Yet, talking to Annabel Frost in 1997, she described herself as the sensible one when her siblings became upset as their mother left their home for work: 'I remember not understanding what the fuss was about and holding up a hand in front of them to try and stop the clamour.'[23] All were truths in the assemblage of her life story, and reflect the place of context and contingency in all lives.

Douglas seldom rates a mention in Rosalie's stories. She alludes to her resentment of him because he did not have to do anything around the house: 'we girls had to do everything. And this was a rather sore point.'[24] According to Rosalie, Douglas was spared the household tasks expected of the girls. She experienced the gendered allocation of tasks in a household where the absence of a father might have made them more striking.[25] But her image of rising above the emotionality of these circumstances also speaks volumes for the role she found, or was given, in coping.

21 Hughes et al., 'Rosalie Gascoigne Artist', tape 1.
22 Gascoigne, interview by North, 3.
23 Frost, 'Rosalie Gascoigne', 20.
24 Hughes et al., 'Rosalie Gascoigne Artist', tape 9.
25 See, for instance, Salmon and Schumann, *The Secret Power*.

We have neither Daintry's nor Douglas's perspectives on their childhoods. In adulthood, Douglas, an accountant, was clearly a troubled man who did not reconcile himself with his father. His own marriage was unhappy and he tragically ended his own life by taking arsenic in 1977.[26] Daintry had a successful career as an agricultural scientist and, at the age of fifty, married a colleague. After her husband drowned while sailing with Douglas in 1972, a friend asked Daintry if she would be lonely living on their farm on her own. Daintry replied: 'I've been lonely all my life.'[27] Rosalie expressed surprise to Hughes about this remark 'because she [Daintry] … was a real adult to me. I always felt I was a little ignorant type girl … she bore everything, you see. She was very strong.'[28] And again, that concession—of endurance now coupled to being adult and clever—reveals another dimension to the silent transactions over role and responsibility among the Walker children.

Despite her feelings of not measuring up as a child, evidence suggests that Rosalie enjoyed the happiest, most constant adulthood of the three Walker children. Perhaps all three felt inadequate, but it seems they were not able to support each other emotionally, remaining disengaged, and, in Douglas's case, possibly even estranged. Douglas never visited Rosalie in Canberra. Daintry visited at least once—in 1985 when she attended Rosalie's granddaughter's christening.[29] Rosalie made three visits to New Zealand with her young children while her parents were still alive: in 1946, 1948 and 1957.[30] In late 1988, Rosalie visited her sister on her Waikato farm. Daintry was ill then and died a few months later, in February 1989.[31] All this was far in the future from the sisters' EGGS school days; however, it offers glimpses of relationships shaped during their formative years at 2 Halls Avenue.

Whatever Rosalie's unhappiness, the school's green fields, tennis courts, her friends and poetry probably provided a welcome respite from the oppressive weight of illness and discord at home. During much of Rosalie's third- and fourth-form years, Aunt Nellie Metcalfe, who had managed the household,

26 Douglas Hamilton Walker, New Zealand death registration printout number 3528/1977.

27 Hughes et al., 'Rosalie Gascoigne Artist', tape 9.

28 Ibid.

29 Martin Gascoigne, interview by author, Canberra, 9 December 2014.

30 Gascoigne, *Rosalie Gascoigne: Her New Zealand Origins*, 236. In 1946 and 1948, Rosalie took Martin and Toss with her; in 1957, Hester accompanied her.

31 Martin Gascoigne, interview by author.

was chronically ill with debilitating heart disease.[32] Rosalie's comment that, 'well, you just knew to be quiet. And you were quiet', may have related to memories from the time of Nellie's illness.[33]

The one person who appreciated and encouraged Rosalie's artistic inclination now suffered chronic pain and depleted energy; yet, surprisingly, Rosalie made no mention of Nellie's illness in her later interviews. Nellie died at home at 2 Halls Avenue aged only fifty on 15 July 1931, mid-way through Rosalie's second year at EGGS. She had been ill for fourteen months. Nellie was dispatched as she appears to have lived—with little fanfare. She was cremated at Waikumete Crematorium in West Auckland the following day.[34] Underscoring the Metcalfes' carefully marshalled residual wealth, Nellie bequeathed the bulk of her estate to Rosalie and Daintry, which helped towards their university costs.[35] She left nothing to Douglas, perhaps recognising from her own life that, despite equal education opportunities in her family, women needed more support than men to make independent lives. She had affirmed Rosalie's artistic sensibilities, and the manner of her life both alerted Rosalie to the risks of gendered expectations of women giving up everything for others and reinforced her later resolve to prioritise her art ahead of all else once her children were grown and independent. But her example figures hardly at all in Rosalie's later self-narrative.

Stanley's return and the idealisation of the family in contemporary New Zealand

After Nellie's death, Rosalie got her wish 'to have a mother and father and … be normal' when Stanley returned to Marion and the children.[36] She told Hughes: 'He [Stanley] came back, and mother let him stay …

32 Nellie's death certificate records that she had been ill for fourteen months with chronic nephritis (Coma syncope or degeneration of the cardiac muscle) and heart disease.

33 Hughes et al., 'Rosalie Gascoigne Artist', tape 2. It could equally have referred to the time when her grandmother was alive and demanded quiet or after her father returned to the family home and the children may have needed to remain quiet in the sense of not being provocative, potentially angering their father and mother.

34 Ellen Mary Metcalfe, New Zealand death registration, Auckland District, no. 955, quarter ending 31 September 1931.

35 Gascoigne, *Rosalie Gascoigne: Her New Zealand Origins*, 44; Probate for METCALFE, Ellen Mary, Archives New Zealand Auckland: BBAE 1570 153 570/1931. Apart from a small bequest to her goddaughter, Nellie bequeathed her estate to Rosalie and Daintry. The probate documents list the estate's value as 'under the value of £1300', which at 21 June 2024 equated to around NZD179,000 according to the Reserve Bank of New Zealand inflation calculator.

36 Hughes et al., 'Rosalie Gascoigne Artist', tape 9.

My grandmother and my aunt were both dead by then.'[37] The increased space at 2 Halls Avenue as a result of Nellie's and Jessie's deaths, and the fact that it was now Marion's family home, enabled her to accommodate Stanley without her family's opprobrium. Love, pity or convenience may have been factors in her decision. The Great Depression was biting deep in New Zealand society; Stanley was out of work.

Marion was trying to keep a roof over her family's head and mother them during a period when the nuclear family was being idealised. Aotearoa New Zealand historian Jock Phillips explains that much focus in culture and social attitude then was on the woman as provider of a healthy and wholesome environment for children, to which husbands would happily return after a hard day's work.[38] The Walker household did not fit this ideal with a busy working mother and a father who was absent for many years and unemployed when he eventually returned. The nuclear family ideal continued to be promoted well into the 1930s by three major agencies—the prohibition movement, the government and the Society for the Protection of the Health of Women and Children (SPHWC)—and, as Patricia Grimshaw argues, by the prevalent forces of evangelical Protestantism.[39] The pressure of such normative scrutiny can only be guessed at, especially in the proud, strict, Walker home. Marion might have felt deficient as mother and wife and thereby obliged to take Stanley back. She may also have felt that having a husband in the home would improve her status, as separated and divorced women were frowned upon. In either case, Stanley's return was at best only a partial answer to these challenges.

The pressures on Marion as a wife had their counterpart for Rosalie whose education added its own gloss to the idealising of nuclear family life. By the time Rosalie began at EGGS, the movement advocating domestic education for girls and women had achieved its aim: the state had acknowledged

37 Ibid., tape 1.

38 Phillips, *A Man's Country*, 223. The prohibition campaign elevated women as moral guardians who protected their hardworking husbands and kept their children pure by making good clean homes and cooking healthy wholesome food provided by their breadwinner husbands. These notions were reinforced by the government's Old Age Pension Bill 1898, which protected nuclear families from the demands of aged relatives, and the Workers' Dwelling Bill 1905, which was to provide spacious comfortable homes to encourage the wage-earner to spend his evenings at home with his family rather than out pleasure seeking in pubs and other unsavoury places. Truby King and the SPHWC were concerned with the evolution of the Anglo-Saxon race and considered mothers pre-eminently responsible for ensuring this evolution through providing healthy and wholesome environments in which their children could grow to good health, and to which their husbands would happily return after a hard day's work.

39 Grimshaw, *Colonialism, Gender and Representations of Race*, 3.

its duty to teach girls to be housewives.[40] Domestic science was firmly established in the curriculum. The cult of domesticity and the propaganda surrounding it were integral parts of Rosalie's formative years, and likely factors in her belief that she must have children: 'I had to have children, I knew I had to have children … I just needed them … It was unthinkable for me not to have children.'[41] Her education was designed to entice her into a domestic role, yet her own family remained remote from this ideal. For a sensitive child such as Rosalie, this situation was likely a heavy burden.

Her father's return to the family home was problematic. Rosalie recalled that Stanley's habits did not change and the family had 'royal battles', now perhaps uninhibited by the presence of other judging adults since Jessie and Nellie had died.[42] Martin Gascoigne described the new two-parent family as an uneasy household, recounting his understanding that Stanley retreated 'down the coast' at least once, to 'dry out' at the home of his niece.[43] At Halls Avenue, Stanley had a room of his own. He worked from a shed in the garden, although what he worked at is not known.[44] Rosalie said she never got to know her father well or to understand him.[45]

Even after Stanley's return, Marion remained the family's sole breadwinner. Although she was ahead of her time as a woman in full-time employment and with a recognised status as a teacher, she was also caught in her time by expectations on women as wives and mothers. Rosalie had her own experience of this tension. An interview with Hughes in 1998 includes her sense of neglect because her mother worked outside the home:

> People used to say to us, 'Your mother's a wonderful woman.' And we all knew she was wonderful … [but] at one stage … in my teenage years, I was saying 'Oh you're so busy racing up the stairs to heaven that you don't care about any of us.'[46]

40 Nolan, *Breadwinning*, 104–36.

41 Hughes et al., 'Rosalie Gascoigne Artist', tape 1.

42 Ibid., tape 9: 'My father's habits didn't change'; tape 1: 'My father didn't give up his ways. And so we had royal battles.' It is unclear whether the 'royal battles' were between Marion and Stanley, the children and Stanley or both.

43 Gascoigne, *Rosalie Gascoigne: Her New Zealand Origins*, 194.

44 Ibid., 25.

45 Hughes et al., 'Rosalie Gascoigne Artist', tape 8.

46 Ibid., tape 9.

In adulthood Rosalie grew close to Marion but during childhood she felt abandoned by her busy mother and her physically or emotionally absent father.

Nature

Rosalie's love of nature was profoundly important in her childhood. She looked to nature and its beauty in Auckland's harbour and on its hills for some relief and comfort during the dark times of Nellie's illness and death and the battles after Stanley's return. With friends she walked Remuera streets and climbed Ōhinerau (Mt Hobson) to enjoy the views across Auckland's two harbours (see Figure 3.5). Evans recalled that Rosalie possessed an eye for nature and beauty during childhood: 'Even then she was observing very closely all the beauty around her.'[47]Rosalie enjoyed the feelings nature awoke in her and related them to the poetry she learned in English classes that profoundly affected her; she claimed an affinity with nature and 'a rapport with some sorts of poetry'.[48] Her love of nature, and description of it as her friend recur in her autobiographical narrative and are important bases of her later art: 'I always noticed natural things, beaches and collecting, finding, happening upon, being favoured because this and this was lying there when you happened to be walking. That's the stuff.'[49]

The poetry she learned at EGGS by writers such as Keats and Wordsworth taught her about the 'echoes of emotions' and the magnificence of nature that one could feel from art.[50] Yet, all the time, while visualising poetry and developing her habit of looking at the world, she believed she could neither paint nor draw.[51] She would look at art displayed in the EGGS hall and dream of being able to make work good enough to be included: 'I thought it would be heaven to get a drawing on the wall.'[52] She never achieved that particular heaven at EGGS but more than made up for it later in life.

47 Ruth Evans to Ben Gascoigne and family, 28 October 1999, Papers of Ben Gascoigne, box 3.
48 Hughes et al., 'Rosalie Gascoigne Artist', tape 8.
49 Gascoigne, interview by North, 5.
50 Ibid., tape 5.
51 Ibid., tape 8.
52 MacDonald and Gascoigne, *Rosalie Gascoigne*, 12.

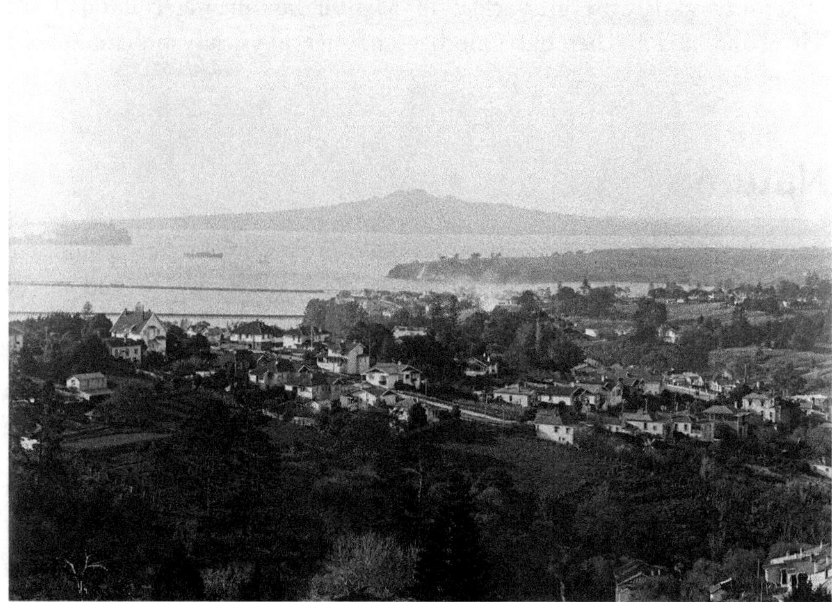

Figure 3.5: Tāmaki Makaurau Auckland's Waitematā Harbour, including Rangitoto Island (centre distance) from Ōhinerau (Mt Hobson), May 1927.

Notes: Rosalie was born and brought up at the foot of Ōhinerau Mt Hobson. In her early years on Mt Stromlo, she said she missed the familiar on her new horizon: 'no harbour, no Rangitoto, no nothing. All the things that were built into you had disappeared.'[53]

Source: Courtesy of Auckland Libraries Heritage Collections, 1-W0826. Photograph: Henry Winkelmann (1860–1931).

If she believed she was unable to paint or draw, Rosalie knew she could write. When North interviewed her in 1982, she remembered that her interest in literature inspired her to write for the school magazine: 'Wrote things for the school magazine. That sort of stuff.'[54] In the 1930s EGGS did not give individual credit to writers published in the annual school magazine *Te Korero*, so it is not possible to identify her work.[55] However, given her childhood love of shell collecting and the fact that she said she wrote for the magazine, it is possible that the following poem about a seashell is hers. It is ascribed to IVA (i.e. Four A, the top fourth-form stream), her class that year (see Figure 3.6).

53 Hughes et al., 'Rosalie Gascoigne Artist', tape 1.

54 Gascoigne, interview by North, 16.

55 The magazine's name, *Te Korero,* is te reo Māori for to tell, say, speak, read, talk, address.

TE KORERO. 43

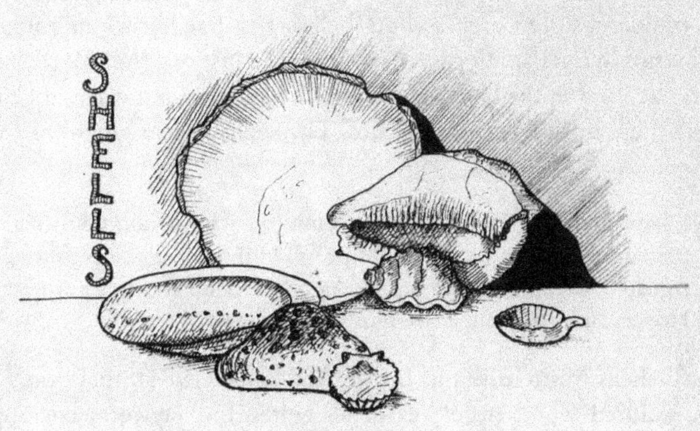

The Shell.

Upon the shining sands it lay,
  A fragile thing of beauty rare,
Of palest pink and softest grey,
  A gem to please a maiden fair.

I picked it up and to my ear
  I held the dainty fluted shell,
And from its murm'ring I could hear
  The wondrous tales it had to tell.

It sang of scenes where breakers curl
  And toss white heads upon the sea,
Of coral pink and gleaming pearl—
  All this and more it told to me.

It sang of caves and hollows where
  Are monsters smaller creatures dread,
And mermaids combing golden hair
  Upon the rocks with seaweeds spread.

It sang of wonders far below,
  Of scenes in calm and storm,
Of clefts where wondrous sea-plants grow
  In all their bright and varied form.

A wave crept up and at my feet
  Itself it spread in frothing foam.
I left the shell and saw it meet
  The tide, then wandered on alone.

—IV.a.

Figure 3.6: *The Shell*, a poem possibly written by Rosalie.

Source: *Te Korero* (EGGS school magazine), no. 15, September 1931, 43. Courtesy of Epsom Girls' Grammar School archive.

The Shell is sister in sensibility to three of Rosalie's works from the 1980s.[56] Each work evokes her childhood summers, particularly her times on Waiheke Island. In *Untitled (25 Scallop Shells)*, Rosalie arranged twenty-five 'palest pink and softest grey' scallop shells across five horizontal rough sawn timber strips in a grid pattern of five times five, just one short of the number of years she lived in the harbour city where Hauraki Gulf waves rolled shells just like these onto its sandy beaches. The shells were a gift from Rosalie's son Toss:

> I have a son in Hobart and he came up with a non-Christmas present, which was a cardboard box full of those magnificent shells. Apparently you can pick up stacks of them on the beaches near Hobart and I find them absolutely fascinating.[57]

She used shells from Toss's gift box in *Red Beach* (1984), shells on wooden blocks, painted wood from soft drink crates and plywood backing, and *Yellow Beach* (1984), a diptych of scallop shells on plywood framed with yellow painted wood from soft drink boxes.

A photograph of Rosalie in Auckland before she left for Mt Stromlo shows her wearing a necklace made of small shells, and, in 1999, when she had returned for an exhibition of her work at Toi o Tāmaki Auckland Art Gallery, photographs show her wearing silver shell-shaped earrings. Her love of shells endured throughout her life.

Cousin Bill and the Ruawaro murders

In 1933, towards the end of Rosalie's penultimate year at EGGS, her Walker cousin William 'Bill' Bayly, son of Stanley's sister Constance Ivy and her husband Frank, was charged with the murders of his farming neighbours Christobel and Samuel Lakey at Ruawaro near Huntly in the Waikato, south of Auckland. The prosecution proposed that one motive for the murder included Christobel Lakey's accusation, during one of their many arguments, that Bayly had murdered his cousin Elsie.

56 All three works feature in Gascoigne, *Rosalie Gascoigne: A Catalogue Raisonné*.

57 Gascoigne, *Rosalie Gascoigne: A Catalogue Raisonné*, 2

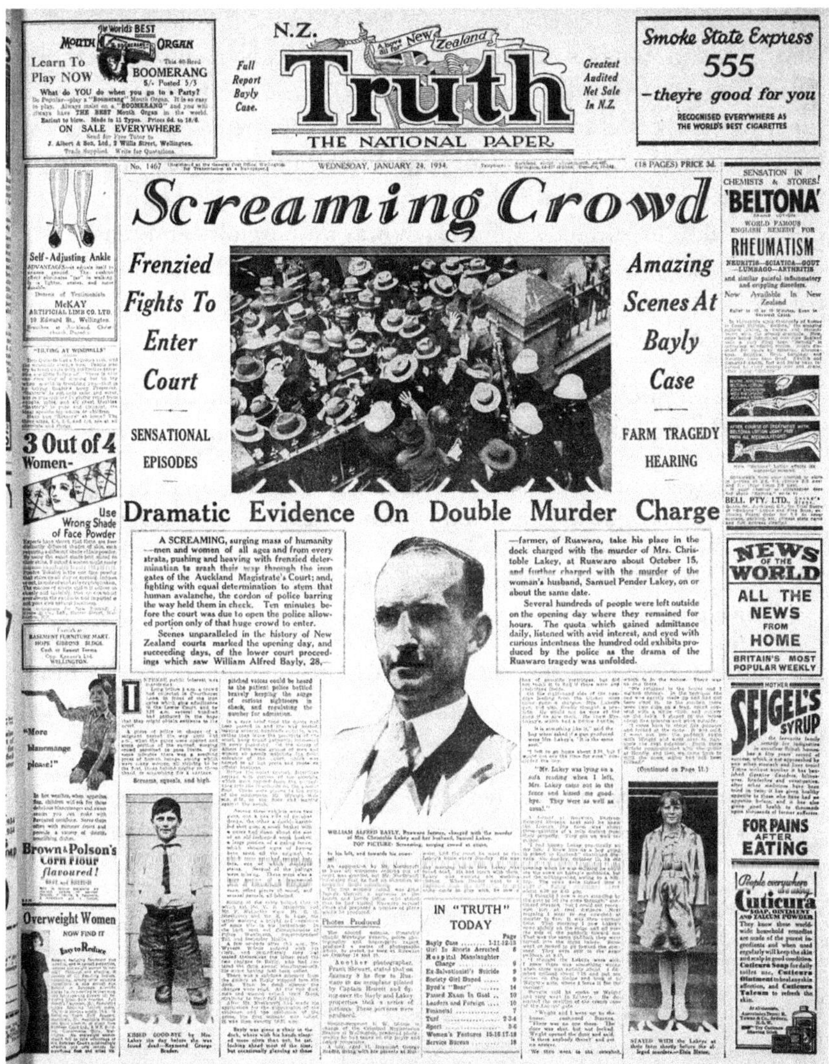

N.Z. Truth

A Paper all for New Zealand

THE NATIONAL PAPER

Full Report Bayly Case.

Greatest Audited Net Sale In N.Z.

No. 1467 WEDNESDAY, JANUARY 24, 1934. (18 PAGES) PRICE 3d.

Screaming Crowd

Frenzied Fights To Enter Court

SENSATIONAL EPISODES

Amazing Scenes At Bayly Case

FARM TRAGEDY HEARING

Dramatic Evidence On Double Murder Charge

A SCREAMING, surging mass of humanity—men and women of all ages and from every strata, pushing and heaving with frenzied determination to crash their way through the iron gates of the Auckland Magistrate's Court; and, fighting with equal determination to stem that human avalanche, the cordon of police barring the way held them in check. Ten minutes before the court was due to open the police allowed portion only of that huge crowd to enter.

Scenes unparalleled in the history of New Zealand courts marked the opening day, and succeeding days, of the lower court proceedings which saw William Alfred Bayly, 28,—farmer, of Ruawaro, take his place in the dock charged with the murder of Mrs. Christobel Lakey, at Ruawaro about October 15, and further charged with the murder of the woman's husband, Samuel Pender Lakey, on or about the same date.

Several hundreds of people were left outside on the opening day where they remained for hours. The quota which gained admittance daily, listened with avid interest, and eyed with curious intentness the hundred odd exhibits produced by the police as the drama of the Ruawaro tragedy was unfolded.

WILLIAM ALFRED BAYLY, Ruawaro farmer, charged with the murder of Mrs. Christobel Lakey and her husband, Samuel Lakey.

Photos Produced

IN "TRUTH" TODAY

	Page
Bayly Case	1-11-12-13
Girl In Shorts Arrested	8
Hospital Manslaughter Charge	9
Ex-Salvationist's Suicide	9
Society Girl Duped	9
Byrd's "Bear"	14
Passed Exam In Gaol	10
Leaders and Foreign	10
Financial	7
Turf	2-3-4
Sport	5-6
Women's Features	15-16-17-18
Service Bureau	18

(Continued on Page 11.)

Figure 3.7: Newspaper coverage of Bill Bayly's case, 1934.

Note: This front page of the *New Zealand Truth* illustrates the huge public interest in Bill Bayly's case. The newspaper coverage was relentless. Source: 'Screaming Crowd', *New Zealand Truth*, 24 January 1934, 1.

Courtesy of Auckland War Memorial Museum Tāmaki Paenga Hira, AP7.5 NZT.

As with the earlier tragedy of cousin Elsie's death, the case captured the New Zealand public's interest and received wide newspaper coverage beneath dramatic headlines (see Figure 3.7). From January to the end of June, newspapers throughout New Zealand reported daily on the case. Crowds queued each morning for seats in the Auckland Magistrates' Court where the case was heard. Police used a gun cartridge as a key piece of slim evidence and, in late June 1933, Bayly was found guilty and sentenced to death. On 20 July 1934, mid-way through Rosalie's final school year, her cousin was hanged at Mt Eden Prison just one mile from EGGS where she probably sat in class.[58]

There was no hiding from it. A few days after the hanging, the *Auckland Star* highlighted the significance of the case and the publicity it achieved:

> The way in which the crime was committed, the long and laborious search for evidence, the nature of that evidence, and especially the experts' portion of it—all of these not only have invested the Bayly case with a public interest never equalled in our history, but place it in a position of its own in the annals of crime.[59]

As Martin Gascoigne concedes in his 2012 revision of the family history in *Rosalie Gascoigne: Her New Zealand Origins*, Rosalie knew Stanley's siblings and:

> they were very different from her Metcalfe aunts and uncle … she was certainly old enough to remember the turmoil that hit the Walkers in the 1920s and early 1930s, even if she never spoke about it.[60]

Rosalie's silence on both cases may indicate that, as an adolescent, she internalised the shame.

Developmental psychologist and psychoanalyst Erik Erikson was known for his lifespan theory of psychosocial development that included five stages up to the age of eighteen years and three further stages beyond.[61] Erikson described identity development as a critical task of adolescence.[62] Pastoral care theologian Professor Robert H. Albers explained that the pain of shame increases with the greater social awareness of the maturing

58 The prison is directly next door to Auckland Grammar School, where Douglas Walker was then a pupil.

59 'Lessons of the Case', *Auckland Star*, 25 June 1934, 6.

60 Gascoigne, *Rosalie Gascoigne: Her New Zealand Origins*, 159.

61 Seligman, *Theories of Counseling and Psychotherapy*, 51–5.

62 Ibid., 53; Erikson, *Childhood and Society*, 262–3.

adolescent.[63] Rosalie was engaged in the critical task of developing her identity at a time when compelling family shame intersected with her increasing social awareness. Significantly for Rosalie's outsider narrative, a person experiencing shame may experience a split or incongruity between their public and personal selves.[64] This notion of a 'split' resonates with Rosalie's descriptions of her feelings of inadequacy and identifying as a misfit. A double murder and resultant hanging in the family that featured as major national news for nine months would be enough for all but the most resilient person to induce shame or acute embarrassment. This, on top of the publicity around Elsie's death and Stanley's drunken driving charges and bankruptcy, would have been a significant burden for a child to shoulder and are likely to have caused or exacerbated her sense of feeling out of step.

A widening world

School figured large during these years. Whatever Rosalie's reservations at being associated with her teacher mother, and however much she distanced herself from her sister, the school probably provided structure and relief from her complicated home life. In 1934, despite all she had to contend with, Rosalie achieved the necessary marks to be awarded a university bursary. She was one of only 214 New Zealand school pupils who gained around eight pounds per year (the equivalent of $2720 in June 2024) to undertake academic study.[65] The previous year Daintry had won an equivalent bursary; five of Daintry's classmates won more prestigious scholarships.[66] Rosalie was about to launch into adult life where she would enjoy increasing agency.

63 Albers, *Shame: A Faith Perspective*, 58.

64 Pattison, *Shame: Theory, Therapy, Theology*, 39.

65 Total secondary school pupils in New Zealand in 1934 were 31,829. See Statistics New Zealand, 'The New Zealand Official Year-Book, 1936'. The successful recipients were listed, in order of merit, in Wellington's *Evening Post*. Rosalie features 125th on the list with a mark of 1,186 (out of 2,000). See 'The University. National Bursaries. Dominion List. Order of Merit', *Evening Post*, 1 February 1935, 10. Her friend Joyce Hewitson was 97th with 1,292 marks, and noted New Zealand theologian and academic, Sir Lloyd Geering, who was tried for heresy by the Presbyterian Church of New Zealand in 1966 because of his denial of the physical resurrection of Jesus, was 16th on this list with 1,593 marks. A quick search of the names of the young men reveals that a number of them died in World War II.

66 Note that S. C. B. Gascoigne won a national scholarship in 1932 with 1,757 marks.

4

1935–43: 'English, French, Latin, maths and Greek … I got my BA'

From 1935 to 1943, Rosalie matured from an eighteen-year-old, first-year university student into a twenty-six-year-old on the verge of departing Auckland for Mount Stromlo, near Canberra, and marriage. Most of the previous few years' tumult passed as she moved towards independence. An image emerges from available sources that accords with aspects of her later self-narrative: a young woman riven with uncertainty, surprised at her popularity with men but unsure about how to develop relationships with them. Gascoigne family history tells that a number of young men courted Rosalie at university, but apart from a reference to these other suitors in a letter Ben wrote to Hannah Fink in 2001, the only contemporary sources available are letters Rosalie wrote to the man she eventually married—Ben Gascoigne, then known as 'Gassy'.[1] This slender collection offers impressions of their growing relationship, as it does of Rosalie's changing relationship with Marion, as mother and daughter found common ground in their shared experiences as high school teachers. Her family life retained some of the tensions and silences of her childhood. Apart from six weeks when she taught at a high school north of Auckland, she continued to live at home with her mother and father, yet Stanley is absent from Rosalie's letters and barely features in her later narrative for this period. The comfort of nature remained one point of certainty in her life as she grew to adulthood.

1 Rosalie variously spelt this 'Gassie' or 'Gassy' in her letters. I have used 'Gassy' for consistency. In letters among Ben Gascoigne's papers in the National Library of Australia, most of his Auckland friends addressed him as 'Gassy' until his death.

1935: Auckland University College

Thanks to her university bursary and Aunt Nellie's bequest, in 1935 Rosalie commenced study towards a bachelor of arts in English, pure mathematics, Greek and Latin at Auckland University College, established in 1883 as part of the University of New Zealand (see Figures 4.1 and 4.2). Mary Eagle and Martin Gascoigne suggest that Rosalie's university education was significant for her art career on several counts, including her study of literature and poetry. They propose that Professor Arthur Sewell's emotional performances of the English Romantic poets may have opened her mind to the power of rhythm in the natural world; and that pure mathematics, with its sculptural idea of tetrahedrons or quadric forms, might have engaged Rosalie's imagination.[2] However, in her own recollections, Rosalie made little of her university education, centring instead on her growing relationship with her future husband and fun times in the bush with the university Field Club.

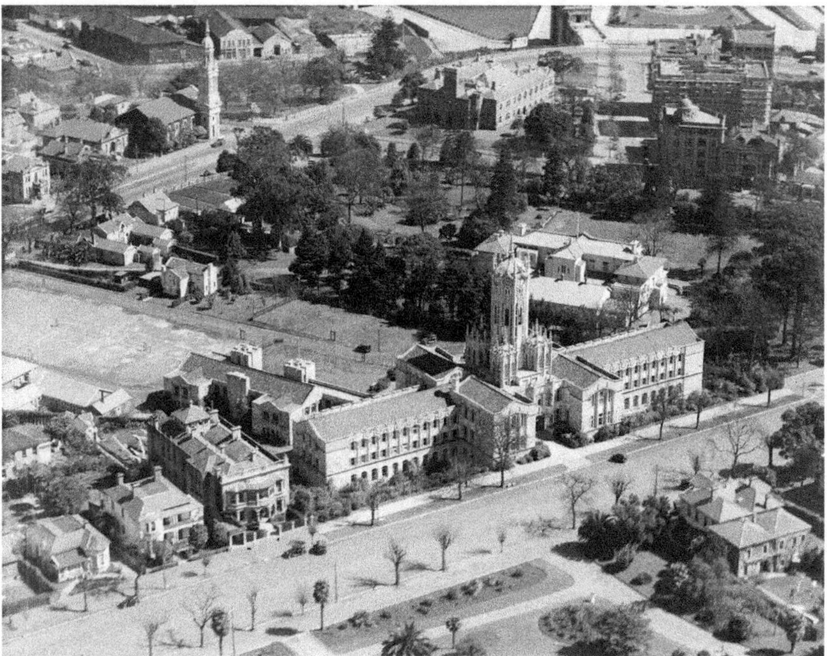

Figure 4.1: Auckland University College buildings, including clock tower and Princes Street in foreground, c. 1939–46.

Source: Whites Aviation Ltd. Photographs: WA-05320-F. Courtesy of Alexander Turnbull Library, Wellington, New Zealand, natlib.govt.nz/records/30651991.

2 Gascoigne, *Rosalie Gascoigne: Her New Zealand Origins*, 214–15.

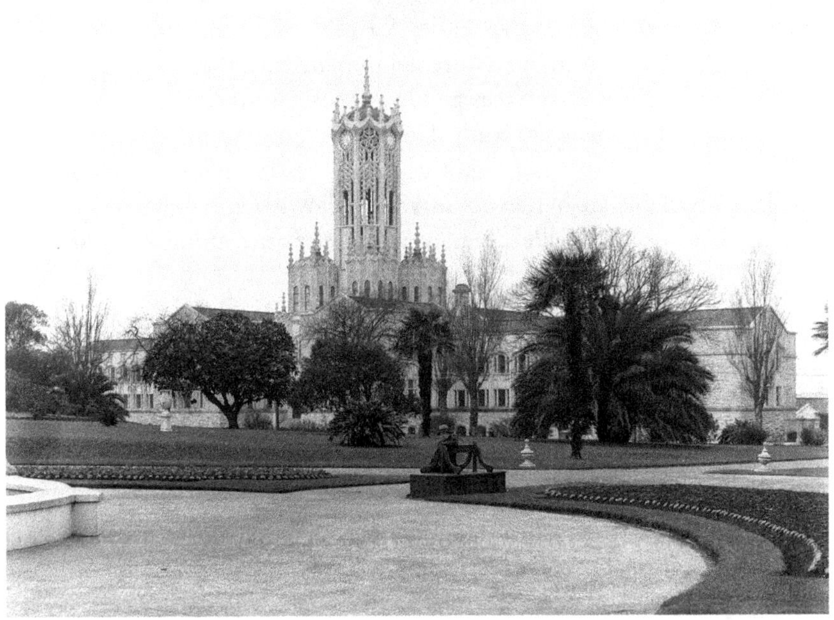

Figure 4.2: Arts Building, Auckland University College, viewed from Albert Park, c. 1930.

Notes: The building has a Canberra connection in that it was designed by the American-born architect Roy Alston Lippincott. Lippincott was married to the Canberra designer Walter Burley Griffin's sister Genevieve and had been working on the design of Canberra in Australia prior to the Auckland University College commission.[3]

Source: *Auckland Star*. Courtesy of Stuff Limited, Ōtautahi Christchurch, Aotearoa New Zealand. Negative: 1/1-002884-G. Courtesy of Alexander Turnbull Library, Wellington, New Zealand, natlib.govt.nz/records/22346662.

Rosalie would concede her good fortune of birth into a class that made university study a possibility: 'you were lucky that you could go on having an education and going to university, because other people didn't, they worked in factories and things'.[4] At that time the New Zealand University Act 1870 fell short of its aim for inclusive, open access and education for all. In the years between Marion's attendance and Rosalie's graduation, the university came under fire from the Trades and Labour Council for being a 'class institution' that 'represented a small and egotistical class'.[5] In Auckland, a high proportion of the students came from the grammar schools, and from at least moderately well-to-do, middle-class families,

3 Tyler, 'Mcdonald, Mullions and Smith Architects'.

4 Hughes et al., 'Rosalie Gascoigne Artist', tape 1.

5 Sinclair and McNaughton, *A History of the University of Auckland*, 105.

as did Rosalie and her friends.[6] Attendance depended on a number of factors apart from intelligence and aptitude. A family that could afford to keep a child at school during the years needed to matriculate was essential, as was the ability to pay university fees and living costs for the minimum of three years required for university study. Despite the personal insecurities Rosalie and her family had experienced, access to education remained among the privileges available to her in these years following the Great Depression through her bursary, Nellie's bequest and the relative affluence enjoyed by the family as a result of Marion's secure job.

In 1998, Rosalie told Hughes that she attended university for the practical purpose of gaining a qualification to earn a living: 'I had to earn my living, and that was the only thing.'[7] While she emphasised that there was no other opportunity open to her, she was also following in her mother's footsteps, and most of her close school friends also attended.

Rosalie confessed to Hughes that 'boys, men!' were what interested her during her university years, exclaiming 'what else?'[8] She played tennis and enjoyed being part of a social circle. Characteristically, Rosalie would later emphasise the deficit of that time, reflecting in 1997 that if she had been around creative people she might have chosen another path.[9] It is true that those years saw the university at a low ebb: historian Keith Sinclair noted its lack of lively intellectual and literary activity during these years, still in the shadow of the Great Depression but before the 'second literary movement of note' in the years immediately following World War II.[10] However, whether from a lack of confidence, a desire to be free of the constraints of school and family, or simply reflecting her personality, her narrative suggests little desire for the company of creative people; she remained chiefly interested in dancing, tennis and field clubs.

6 Ibid.

7 Hughes et al., 'Rosalie Gascoigne Artist', tape 1.

8 Ibid.

9 'I think now that if I'd been put amongst creative people it would be a different story', in MacDonald and Gascoigne, *Rosalie Gascoigne*, 12.

10 Sinclair and McNaughton, *A History of the University of Auckland*, 183. Those in the 'second literary movement of note' included writers and poets such as Kendrick Smithyman, Mary Stanley, James K. Baxter and Maurice Duggan.

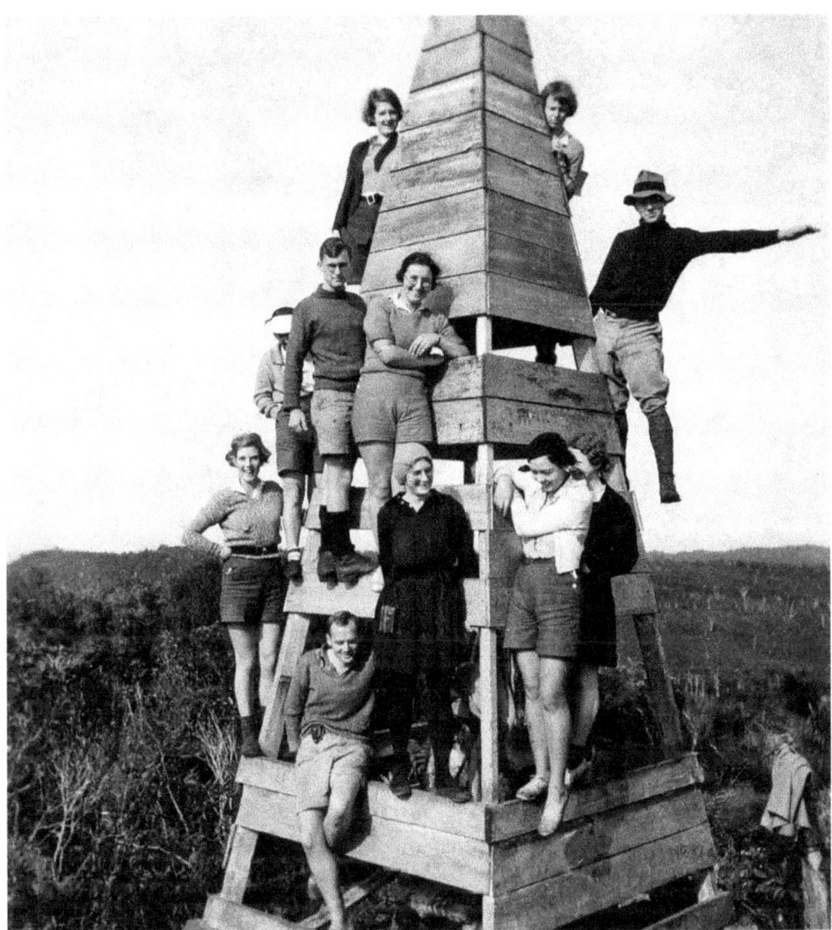

Figure 4.3: Auckland University College Field Club, c. 1935–38.

Notes: Rosalie is standing top left, her close friend Marie Best is bottom left, and one of her suitors, Charles Fleming (who became a leading ornithologist and environmentalist) is on her right, wearing a hat.

Source: Courtesy of the Gascoigne family.

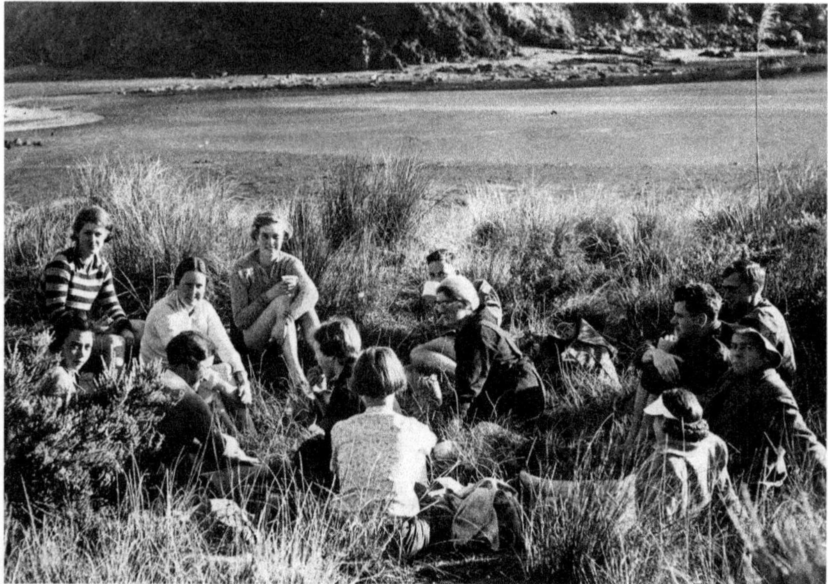

Figure 4.4: Auckland University College Field Club, c. 1935–38.

Notes: Rosalie is on the left in a striped jumper. Mary Best and Charles Fleming are present again. Rosalie loved nature and the outdoors. The Field Club provided her with opportunities to enjoy the outdoors with friends.

Source: Courtesy of the Gascoigne family.

Rosalie wove her love of nature into the university narrative. She joined the university Field Club, which provided the opportunity to combine outdoor activities, such as tramping (bushwalking) and camping, with the study of natural history.[11] It also gave her the opportunity to socialise with boys amid what she recalled as the 'back-to-nature way of life'—walking for miles and having meals in old bush huts.[12] By the mid-1930s, when Rosalie participated, the club had moved towards the promotion of a serious scientific atmosphere.[13] She told Hughes that 'scientific women were pretty earnest', so a friend invited her and her old school friend Marie Best, both humanities students, along for 'a bit of light relief' (see Figures 4.3 and 4.4).[14] Rosalie and Best enjoyed themselves. The science students 'wanted to know the scientific name of everything' but she was not interested.[15]

11 Tramping is the New Zealand equivalent of bushwalking in Australia and rambling or hiking in the UK.

12 Hughes et al., 'Rosalie Gascoigne Artist', tape 1.

13 McCallum, 'A Review of Field Club Research', 223.

14 Hughes et al., 'Rosalie Gascoigne Artist', tape 1. The friend Rosalie refers to was from Epsom Girls' Grammar, Marie Best.

15 Ibid., tape 1.

Rosalie also enjoyed dancing. Newspaper reports of her presence at dances and balls provide evidence that she was in the social swim. New Zealand writer and museum curator Georgina White wrote that dances varied in formality and exclusivity at this time. The ideal was to wear a new dress to each dance or ball, as this was evidence of financial standing. A newspaper reporter was positioned at the door and every woman dancer gave her name and a description of her dress.[16] Unless they were dignitaries or special guests, the men remained nameless shadows. Newspaper reports indicate that Rosalie attended many dances, conforming to the model of a different dress for each occasion.[17] And each dance perhaps led to invitations to the next. In Figure 4.5, Rosalie's attendance is recorded at the 'coming-out' dance for Betty Sloman, her neighbour around the corner in MacMurray Road.[18]

Rosalie also attended University Rowing Club dances, graduation balls and the commerce students' ball.[19] Her confidence grew as she discovered that boys liked her. Having attended a girls' school for five years from the age of thirteen, she may not have been accustomed to day-to-day contact with boys, apart from her younger brother and perhaps his friends. She described her surprise at her popularity:

> There were boys who … singled you out for attention, this was a revelation to me … it was a bolstering effect to me that in spite of this girl being prettier and this girl being this sort, somebody singled you out.[20]

---

16 White, *Light Fantastic*, 121.

17 In March 1935, Rosalie attended the university's reception dance for freshers, wearing white and orange floral georgette. Her friend Marie Best wore rose pink organdie. In August 1936, she attended the Insurance Officers' Benevolent Ball in bronze and gold floral ninon. Multiple newspaper reports—see footnote below.

18 'Debutantes' Dance', *Auckland Star*, 7 May 1936, 12.

19 'University Students. Reception for Freshers', *Auckland Star*, 18 March 1935, 10; 'Insurance Ball. Tenth Annual Function. Gay Cabaret Scene', *Auckland Star*, 2 August 1935, 11; 'Graduation Ball. Unique Decorations. Gay Scenes at University', *Auckland Star*, 16 May 1936, 20; 'College Rowing Club. A University Function', *Auckland Star*, 30 March 1936, 10; 'Rowing Club Dance. A University Function', *Auckland Star*, 15 March 1937, 10; 'Graduation Ball. Function at University. A Scene of Gaiety', *Auckland Star*, 15 March 1937, 17; 'Varsity Dance. Novel Decorations. After-Degree Function', *Auckland Star*, 20 November 1937, 17; 'University Ball. Capping Day. Well Attended Function', *Auckland Star*, 14 May 1938, 14; 'Flannel Dance. University College. Rowing Club Function', *Auckland Star*, 4 April 1938, 11; 'Commerce Ball. Enjoyable Dance. Function at University', *Auckland Star*, 20 June 1938, 12.

20 Hughes et al., 'Rosalie Gascoigne Artist', tape 9.

DEBUTANTES' DANCE.

The Rialto ballroom was gay with multicoloured streamers and rows of coloured balloons last evening when the joint hostesses, Mrs. R. Abbott, of Dilworth Avenue, Remuera, and Mrs. A. E. Sloman, of MacMurray Road, Remuera, held a particularly enjoyable debutante dance in honour of their daughters, Miss Noelene Abbott and Miss Betty Sloman. The supper tables were beautifully arranged. Down the centre were rows of Sheffield candelabra, lighted with gold candles, while numerous large silver bowls filled with yellow African marigolds and trails of maiden hair fern, made a charming setting.

Mrs. Abbott and Mrs. Sloman received the guests, the former wearing a gown of black panne velvet with a plaited silver and velvet collar, and the latter in a frock of black mirror velvet, with two diamante clasps at the neck. Miss Noelene Abbott wore a beautifully cut frock of ice white and silver thread diagonal striped cloque. The crossed-over bodice was finished with a corded girdle, and silver threaded roses were placed on one shoulder. The full skirt was made with a small train. A lovely frock of pearl-toned crepe satin, gathered from a hip yoke, and forming a full skirt, was worn by Miss Betty Sloman. Two bands of lace were arranged over the shoulders, and a silver rose was placed on the front of the bodice. They carried Early Victorian posies of pink rosebuds and forget-me-nots set in silver holders. Miss Helen Sloman wore frilled cameo pink georgette and satin; Miss May Sloman, black georgette and spray of gold roses; Mrs. M. Guthrie, deep blue georgette and silver clasps.

Among those present were: Mrs H. Goldie, Misses Elaine Court, Alison Bell, Barbara Nolan, Peggy Chambers, Helen MacCormick, Mary Ellis, Mary Tibbs, Rosalie Walker, Mavis Brown, Pat Finch, Jocelyn Patterson, Evelyn Asmuss, Margery Chatfield, Jocelyn Hesketh, Enid Kelly, Peggy Cawkwell, Joan Crouch, Peggy Scott-Young, Marjory Clarke, Maud Bailey, Phyllis Keith, Elizabeth Frater, Jocelyn Archey, Alison Milsom, Joan St. George, Betty Griffiths, Gwen Darling, Joan Charlton, Barbara Forte, Joan Duthie, Nance Andrews, Maureen Abbott, Audrey Pentz, Betty Goldie, Beryl Christian, Dorothy Badeley, Kathleen Sellars, June Hillary, Gwenyth Lorie, Joan McChesney, Gracie McFlynn, Eileen Laurie, Peggy Schofield, Jean Wright, Gypsy Spedding, Margaret Gilmour, Valerie Pope, Shirley Law, June Vickerman and Jean Goudie.

Figure 4.5: 'Debutantes' Dance', *Auckland Star*, 7 May 1936, 12.

Note: Rosalie's name appears in the fifth line of the final paragraph.

Source: Courtesy of Stuff Limited, Ōtautahi Christchurch, Aotearoa New Zealand and the Alexander Turnbull Library, Te Whanganui-ā-Tara Wellington.

One of the men who singled her out was Sidney (Ben) Gascoigne, then known as 'Gassy' or 'Gassie'. The Gascoigne family legend is that Ben was one of a number of Rosalie's suitors at university.[21] Rosalie said: 'he was a big man on campus. My mother said I always had a "bump of reverence". I was reverent for popularity, because I was offbeat even then.'[22] Rosalie was evidently drawn to Gassy's popularity. Association with someone of such status on campus boosted her confidence. He represented the university as an oarsman and was extremely bright. Deciding between arts and science, he chose to enrol in a BSc in maths and science because of the severe stammer that plagued him from an early age. He considered the stammer would be less of an obstacle when seeking employment in science and mathematics, so regretfully forsook history for which he had a passion and had excelled at.[23] Successful at anything to which he turned his hand, Gassy

21 Gascoigne, *Rosalie Gascoigne: Her New Zealand Origins*, 292.

22 MacDonald and Gascoigne, *Rosalie Gascoigne*, 13. The 'bump of reverence' refers to phrenology, the pseudoscience popular in the nineteenth century that claimed to divine personality characteristics from skull structure.

23 Crompton, 'Professor Ben Gascoigne'.

won a raft of scholarships.[24] He was also popular around campus. When he won the Michael Hiatt Baker Scholarship and left Auckland in 1938 to begin his PhD in physics (geometrical optics) at the University of Bristol, England, the Auckland University newspaper *Craccum* demonstrated the esteem in which he was held:

> We say 'goodbye' to Mr S. C. B. Gascoigne, MSc, sports editor for *Craccum*, Aunt Alice in private life [as the author of *Craccum*'s agony column], holder of more scholarships than any space will record, an enthusiastic footballer and oarsman, past member of the Students' Executive, and one of the kindest-hearted and most generous of men that the Editor of this little journal has ever been privileged to meet.[25]

Whether 'Aunt Alice' offered Rosalie any advice we do not know, but *Craccum*'s picture presents a contrast with Rosalie's father Stanley: it is a picture of a man who promised kindness and generosity, while knowing how to enjoy himself in healthy ways. His friends included Edmund Hillary who in 1953 with Nepalese Indian mountaineer Sherpa Tenzing Norgay was one of the first two people to have reached the summit of Mt Everest. Rosalie often quoted Hillary's well-known comment after conquering Everest, 'Well, we knocked the bastard off!', as a contrast with art where, she said, 'you never knock the bastard off … It's like a bottomless pit.'[26] Rosalie was drawn to Gassy as a man who appeared to promise her much that her father lacked.

In 1998, Hughes asked her: 'So while you were an undergraduate and you were seeing lots of boys, was there one in particular that emerged eventually?' Rosalie responded evasively: 'It was a long time ago.'[27] For Ben, however, there was no question. He described how quickly Rosalie won his heart:

> In no time at all, I was overwhelmed and enchanted, and I knew there would never be anyone else for me. And there never was. One time I was walking out of the Physics building, down some stone steps, and I looked up and there she was, and she said to me afterwards 'and when I saw the way your face lit up, I knew at once you loved me'.[28]

24 Hughes et al., 'Rosalie Gascoigne Artist', tape 1. Ben won the Senior Scholar (University of NZ) in Pure Maths and Physics, and the Shirtcliffe Graduate Bursary in 1935; he earned a double first in maths and physics for his MSc in 1937; and he won the Michael Hiatt Baker Scholarship for his PhD in 1938.

25 'S. C. B. Gascoigne, M.Sc', *Craccum* 12, no. 9 (28 July 1938): 3. Also cited in Gascoigne, *Rosalie Gascoigne: Her New Zealand Origins*, 218.

26 Hilary, *Nothing Venture, Nothing Win*, ch. 10; Hughes et al., 'Rosalie Gascoigne Artist', tape 3.

27 Hughes et al., 'Rosalie Gascoigne Artist', tape 9.

28 Ben Gascoigne to Hannah Fink, 7 June 2001, Papers of Ben Gascoigne, box 5.

While Ben spoke of his love for Rosalie, she never mentioned love in her later interviews, characteristically protecting her privacy. Neither did she speak of it in contemporary sources, although she signed her letters to Gassy with love. Ben's description of Rosalie's observation contrasts with her descriptions of adults during her childhood having little time for her. She clearly had his attention. It is notable that Rosalie later took the initiative and proposed marriage to Ben when he was focused on his career.

The two met over a bridge table in 1933, during Rosalie's lower sixth-form year. A mutual friend, Bob Foster (see Figure 4.6), had roped Gassy into a game to make up a four with Rosalie. Although they had both been at Remuera Primary School at the same time, and Gassy had been in Daintry's class, neither remembered having met earlier. They did not have much to do with each other until 1935.[29]

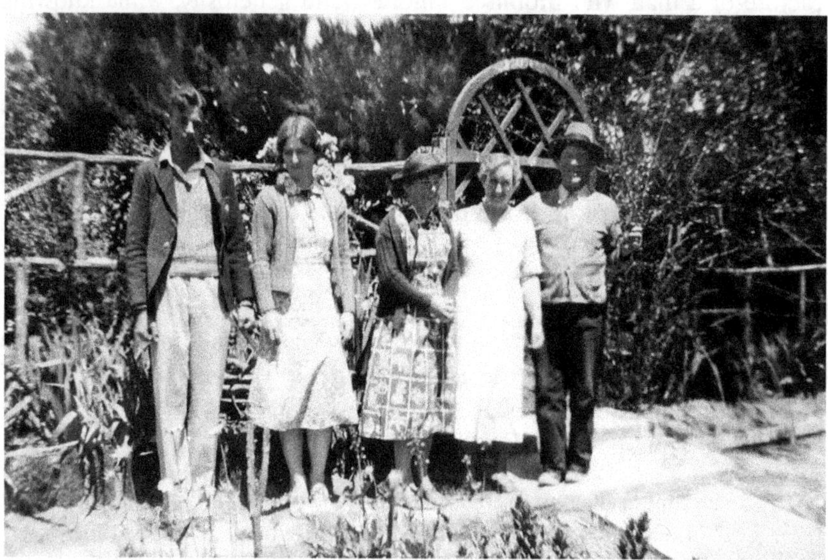

Figure 4.6: Rosalie with her mother Marion Walker, Bob Foster and friends, Blenheim, 1934.

Note: Bob Foster, a friend from Remuera and Auckland University, introduced Rosalie to Ben Gascoigne over a bridge table at his Remuera home in 1933.

Source: Courtesy of the Gascoigne family.

29 Ibid.

Once they got to know each other, Rosalie and Gassy caught the train to Henderson in west Auckland some weekends. From there they walked through pristine native forest full of birdlife over the Waitakere Ranges to the wild west coast where the Tasman Sea thunders onto black iron sand beaches such as Piha, Karekare and Whatipu. They also enjoyed the theatre and saved to go several times a year to performances at His Majesty's Theatre in Queen Street in the centre of Auckland.

A small collection of Rosalie's letters to Gassy from 1938 to 1941 yield glimpses of their relationship. One of her letters suggests they were just 'platonic' friends:

> Sometimes at dances I've felt it might be a good idea to go a little mad with someone slightly less platonic. After all, dances are rather an artificial kind of enjoyment and shouldn't be taken too soberly.[30]

Or perhaps she was expressing frustration at the nature of their relationship. Maybe she wanted more from Gassy but struggled to express her need in the absence of a role model for male–female relationships in her own family. Whatever she felt, Rosalie was not, at that stage, going to be hurried into making a decision about her life. She had several suitors and, Ben said, 'she never committed herself, not to me nor to any of the others, and there were three or four of them'.[31] He remembered 'a remarkable letter, written in red ink and unlike any other she ever wrote'.[32] The letter from Rosalie survives in Ben's archive in the National Library of Australia. An excerpt alludes to her consideration of the aforementioned suitors:

> Your chief fear seems to be that I'll take you too seriously. There is neither hope nor fear of that. I'm not taking anyone seriously. I'm having a good look around and finding out what I really want and when, about four years hence, I've made up my mind, I'll start in being ingratiating. Then if it's you, look out![33]

Despite all of Gassy's impressive attributes, Rosalie's experience of growing up in the shadow of Stanley and Marion's relationship had probably made her acutely aware of how relationships could go wrong; she wanted to be entirely sure before she committed herself to someone.

30 Rosalie Walker to 'Gassy', postmarked 15 March 1938, Papers of Ben Gascoigne, box 3.

31 Ben Gascoigne to Hannah Fink, 7 June 2001, Papers of Ben Gascoigne, box 5.

32 Ibid.

33 Rosalie Walker to 'Gassy', 15 March 1938, Papers of Ben Gascoigne, box 3.

'My father's habits didn't change'

Stanley had not changed his ways.[34] In July 1936, the *Auckland Star* and Wellington's *Evening Post* reported on Stanley's third drink driving charge.[35] Rosalie was nineteen years old and in her second year at university. The numbers of students at university might have provided her with some anonymity and protection from embarrassment, although by that time Stanley had been living with the family for five years and was presumably known to her friends.

In a prominent position on page eight, the *Auckland Star* reporter regaled readers with a detailed account of the events, depicting Stanley as a drunken buffoon (see Figure 4.7).[36]

Stanley's lawyer pleaded for leniency on the basis that it was his first offence in seven years. The magistrate noted that Stanley had been 'addicted to liquor for a number of years' and considered sending him to prison, but decided instead to fine him and cancel his licence for five years.[37]

As a car owner, Stanley was one of a privileged minority; in 1929, only one New Zealander in ten owned a motor vehicle.[38] He was lucky to escape a prison sentence. No doubt Marion and her adult children were relieved to be spared that shame. The report referred to earlier charges—in 1926 and 1929—and that he had been committed to the Rotoroa Inebriates' Home for twelve months in 1924.[39] It was all out in the open in the small community that was Auckland.

A gap appears in Rosalie's academic record from this time until the second half of the 1937 academic year. She completed parts of Greek I, Latin II and English II in the first half of 1936, but did not complete the full units until the second half of 1937. A year later, in December 1937, her name was included in the passes for Latin II, English II and Greek I in the newspaper listings.[40] This was in the days when a unit equalled a full year of study in each subject.

34 Hughes et al., 'Rosalie Gascoigne Artist', tape 9: 'my father's habits didn't change'.

35 'Drunken Drivers Cases at Auckland', *Evening Post*, 15 July 1936, 13; Hughes et al., 'Rosalie Gascoigne Artist', tape 1.

36 'Intoxicated', *Auckland Star*, 15 July 1936, 8.

37 Ibid.

38 Pawson, 'Cars and the Motor Industry'.

39 'Intoxicated'.

40 Her name is included in the passes for Latin II in the *Auckland Star*, 24 December 1937, 15, and English II and Greek I in the *Auckland Star*, 13 December 1937, 13.

8 FINAL EDITION.

INTOXICATED.

TWO MOTORISTS.

LICENSES SUSPENDED.

ONE A THIRD OFFENDER.

CAR DAMAGES HOUSE.

Two men appeared on summons before Mr. W. R. McKean, S.M., in the Police Court this morning for being in a state of intoxication while in charge of a motor car. In each case a fine of £10 was imposed and the license cancelled, one for five years and the other for three years. Both cases were the result of mishaps on the road.

Addicted to Liquor.

The first case was that of Stanley King Walker, a middle-aged man, who admitted that he was in a state of intoxication while in charge of a car in Randolph Street, Newton, on June 6. He also pleaded guilty to a further charge of negligent driving. Mr. Allan Moody appeared for the accused.

Sub-Inspector Fox said Walker's car backed into a shop and the shopkeeper was unable to open his front door. He saw Walker, the driver of the car, staggering, but Walker entered his car and drove off. A little later on Walker's car crashed on to the verandah of another house in the same street, causing considerable damage to the house. This had been repaired by Walker. The occupier of the house looked out and saw Walker walking up the street in a drunken condition. Walker fell and injured his head and was taken to hospital. His excuse was that his car was in gear when he started it. In 1926 Walker was fined £20 for being in a state of intoxication while in charge of a car, and in 1929 he had been fined £10 on a similar charge and his license cancelled for two years. In 1924 Walker was committed to the Roto Roa inebriates' home for twelve months.

The fact that Randolph Street had a particularly steep grade and that Walker experienced engine trouble was stressed by Mr. Moody. The repairs to the house had cost him £11, while Walker had worked on two or three Saturdays repairing the damage. It was seven years since Walker's last offence. "As no doubt your Worship will be dealing with his license, I would ask you to give him another opportunity and not impose a penalty other than a fine," said counsel.

"Apparently this man has been addicted to liquor for a number of years," said the magistrate. "I am not so sure that I should not send him to prison for this offence, but I suppose the chief thing is to see that he is kept off the road for a considerable period."

Walker was fined £10 on the first charge and on the second he was convicted and ordered to pay the costs. His driver's license was cancelled for five years, the magistrate directing that no other license should be issued until that period had expired.

DRIVER UNCONSCIOUS.

EXILE ENDS.

MR. NELSON SAILS.

LIKES DOMINION, BUT —.

MAU STRONG IN SAMOA.

(By Telegraph.—"Star" Special Reporter.)

WELLINGTON, this day.

Accompanied by three of his daughters, Mr. O. F. Nelson leaves by the Maui Pomare this afternoon for Samoa. He is not coming back. "I like New Zealand, I like its people," he smilingly said, "but—."

Mr. Nelson is going back to take over the leadership of the Mau. "It is not a question of reinstatement," he said. "My people have had full confidence in me all the time I have been away, and I have been acting for them here."

Mr. Nelson was not anxious to discuss the relationship between the New Zealand authorities and the Samoan people. "At present," he said, "things are at a critical stage, and the position will have to be handled with tact and diplomacy. I am anxious to do everything to assist in a settlement for the happiness of my own people and to the credit of the new Government. I do not wish to elaborate on the matters at issue, but developments depend on how far the Government will grant concessions to the Samoans. The less that is said to create any doubt in the minds of either side, the better it will be for all concerned. I am very anxious to assist, without prejudice, to the claims of my people.

New Policy Wanted.

Mr. Nelson pointed out that the big difficulty was the difference between the viewpoint of the European and the viewpoint of the native. The two, he emphasised, would have to be reconciled. The Government had every intention of arriving at a conciliation and was trying to get the Samoans to forget the past. "The trouble, of course, is to do that," he added. He thought that a new policy of administration of the Samoans' affairs might go a long way towards helping the native to forget the past, and to restore confidence. "Indeed, I feel that a distinct change of policy and outlook is very essential."

He thought that there would be a better understanding in the future, and he believed that the present negotiations would result in an amicable settlement of the long-standing controversy. It might be necessary for both sides to give and take a little, as conditions in Samoa and New Zealand were so different that what might be applicable in this country might not be applicable in Samoa. The civil servants in Samoa, for instance, were executive officers, who had to carry out the policy of the Government of the day. They might find it hard to carry out an absolutely new policy to the satisfaction of the Samoans and the Government.

The previous Government had regarded the Mau as rebellious, Mr. Nelson continued, but by a change of outlook a more reasonable interpretation of the native point of view had been obtained. The Mau flag had been converted into a flag of conciliation and that and other changes made the prospects more hopeful for better understanding. He added that with the exception of the paid officials, who, he thought, were sympathetic, the Mau

Figure 4.7: 'Intoxicated', ***Auckland Star*****, 15 July 1936, 8.**

Source: Courtesy of Stuff Limited, Ōtautahi Christchurch, Aotearoa New Zealand and Auckland War Memorial Museum Tāmaki Paenga Hira, AP7.5 AUC.

The silence hovers with other gaps in her story. We can only speculate as to what kept her from her studies that year.[41] Failures were routinely recorded on the back of student record cards, but there is no such record on hers. We can surmise that the public nature of her father's behaviour may have been too much to bear and she took leave from her studies. There is no record of her having done anything else during that time apart from attending two balls in the first half of 1937.

1938: Teaching at Whangārei Girls' High School

In early 1938, her final year at university, Rosalie travelled one hundred miles north to Whangārei Girls' High School (WGHS) where she taught English, history and Latin for six weeks. In a number of letters preserved by Ben, she described her working days at the school and her leisure time. In her acerbic fashion, she described the school staff as 'not particularly competent … [but] v. nice—a jovial crowd and seem to find life v. amusing, and they make it so, for me at least'. She found the school 'a terrific muddle … with a most unsettled atmosphere pervading the whole place'.[42] While criticising the school, its teachers and pupils in one of her English classes—'the girls for the most part seem rather uncouth. Typical backblocks, I should say'—she was also self-deprecating:

> I was determined that whatever my shortcomings as a teacher might be, at least I wld. be respected as a keeper of order. So my classes are orderly if uninformed, poor things.[43]

Yet, implicitly, Rosalie's letter conveys confidence and self-assuredness. It was her first experience of work and being paid. With all the confidence of youth, her descriptions romp through the day, pronouncing on all she saw and did. A comment in the same letter conveyed her love of dances and presaged her future years as a stranger in a new country:

41 Stephen Innes, archivist, Auckland University library, email to author, 8 August 2013: 'There does appear to be something odd about 1936 and 1937 and it is possible she enrolled at the beginning of 1936 but for some reason did not complete them that year and didn't sit the exams until 1937.'

42 Rosalie Walker to Gassy, 15 March 1938.

43 Ibid.

> Gosh, I'm looking forward to that Rowing Club Dance. It's all very well being learned and independent for a while but one does long to be young again sometimes. Oh, for irresponsible Varsity life! Not but what I'm getting a decided kick out of this. It's only that there's not much escape when one's a stranger in a strange town.[44]

She sounded in control, and happy to be so, when talking about the school and her work. It was another story when she broached the matter of relationships.

The letters, as so often is the case, are a one-way communication, since Rosalie did not retain Ben's letters. In another letter, we glimpse Rosalie's insecurities about personal relationships in her allusion to the fact that she was shy and ill-at-ease in Gassy's company:

> You say that I'm often distant. Would you ever chance to think that I might be ill at ease or embarrassed or shy[?] … And you don't know what I'm thinking? Well, most times that I'm gazing profoundly into space I'm thinking, 'O, hell, isn't this terrible … What on earth can I say?' … Disappointed? I'm afraid, dear heart, that you've been crediting me with an intellect.[45]

Rosalie's sensitivity and unease echo through her words. Despite stories of her popularity with men, she was short on confidence in her relationship with Gassy. Evidence is lacking as to whether she found it easier with other men. In her next letter, her lack of confidence shows again as she rails against the unfairness of people blaming her when they feel they do not function well in her presence:

> And, again, you say you're never at your intelligent best when you're with me. Et tu, Brute? There must be something wrong with me. Other people have told me [the same thing] … and I'm getting a bit fed up. Have I got a hyper-critical nature or a superior air or something? I must have. But surely that's for me to worry about, not you. After all, it's my loss.[46]

Her comments suggest that the superiority implied in her attitude towards WGHS staff and pupils from 'the backblocks' carried over to other relationships and that other people did not appreciate it or were offended. She possibly learned a sense of superiority from her grandmother Jessie

44 Ibid.

45 Rosalie Walker to Gassy, 3 March 1938, Papers of Ben Gascoigne, box 3.

46 Rosalie Walker to Gassy, postmarked 15 March 1938, Papers of Ben Gascoigne, box 3.

Metcalfe. Some of it may have been self-protection, as mentioned in the previous chapter, but her apparent tendency to superiority and directness became part of her personality and continued to irk some people in her orbit throughout her life.

Rosalie might have felt inadequate in some circumstances, but she impressed the school's headmistress.[47] Miss Himmel offered her more relief teaching but Rosalie turned the offer down because of her dissatisfaction with her pay, which barely covered living costs.[48] At the end of March she returned to Auckland and was again able to attend lectures, but more to her preference were the dances, including the Rowing Club Flannel Dance in April, the graduation ball in May with a 'large and happy throng of students', and the commerce students' ball in June at which the *Auckland Star* recorded she wore forest green and black brocade.[49]

Back in Auckland, Rosalie was able to spend more time with Gassy, who eventually took his talents and intellect further afield. In August 1938, he sailed on the RMS *Rangitata* to begin his doctoral studies in Bristol, England. Rosalie remained in Auckland studying. She does not appear in the dockside photographs with Gassy, his father, brother and two sisters on the day of his departure but they corresponded while he was away.

1939: University graduation and Auckland Teachers' Training College

Despite all the disruptions in her life, including her father's conviction and Gassy's departure for Bristol, Rosalie graduated in May 1939 with a bachelor of arts. On graduation day she processed with the other graduands down the Wellesley Street hill from the university to the splendid wedge-shaped Italian Renaissance Revival–style town hall in the central city (see Figures 4.8 and 4.9). The women wore white frocks with gowns and mortarboards.[50] Her aunt, Phyllis Buddle (née Metcalfe), Marion Walker's youngest sibling, was an official guest, as was Agnes Loudon, her headmistress from EGGS.[51]

47 Rosalie Walker to Gassy, postmarked 23 February 1938, Papers of Ben Gascoigne, box 3.
48 Rosalie Walker to Gassy, 3 March 1938.
49 'Commerce Ball—Enjoyable dance—Function at University', *Auckland Star*, 20 June 1938, 12.
50 'Capping Day', *Auckland Star*, 6 May 1939, 17.
51 'Capping Day'.

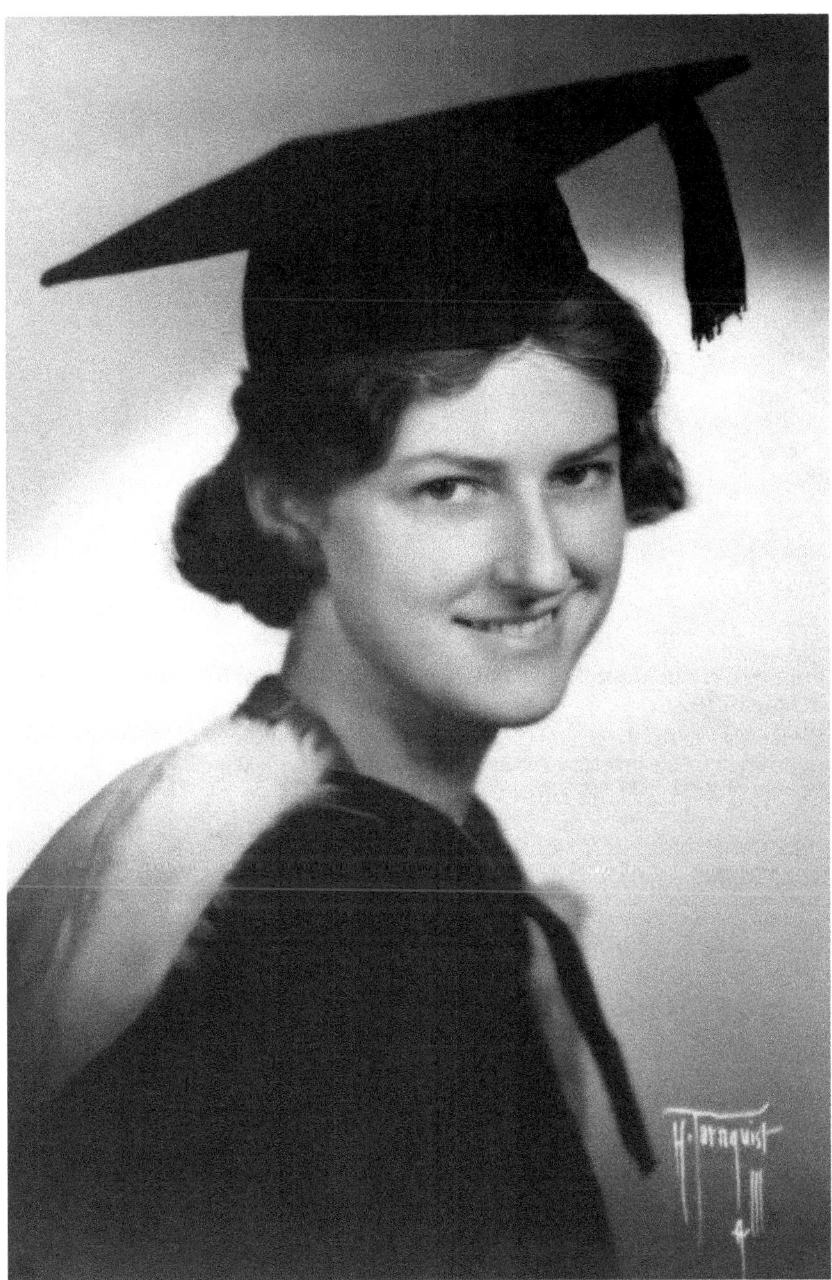

Figure 4.8: Rosalie on her graduation from Auckland University College, May 1939.

Source: Courtesy of the Gascoigne family.

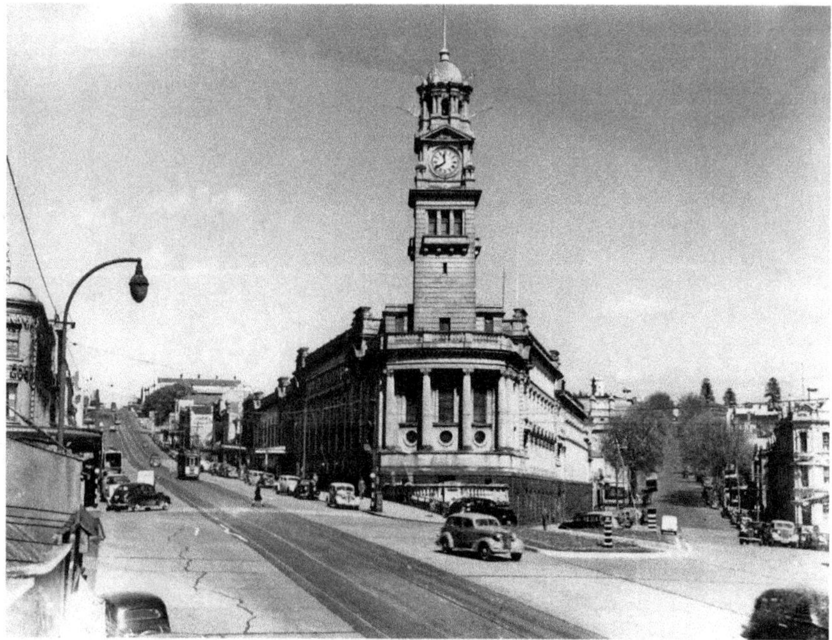

Figure 4.9: Auckland Town Hall, c. 1940, the scene of Rosalie's graduation in May 1939.

Source: *New Zealand Herald*, n.d. Courtesy of New Zealand Media and Entertainment Holdings Ltd, Aotearoa New Zealand and the Auckland War Memorial Museum Tāmaki Paenga Hira, PH-NEG-C33727.

As was the tradition, the university student association's annual publication listed each graduand with literary quotes chosen to reflect their personality. Those for Rosalie reflect her later comments about an abrasiveness, which she inherited or learned. Her quick wit also rates a mention:

> Rosalie Norah Walker
> You have a nimble wit;
> I think 'twas made of Atlanta's heels.
>
> —Shakespeare
>
> Like the prick of a needle,
> Duly sharp.
>
> —Carlyle[52]

52 *Kiwi*, official organ of the Auckland University College, see vol. 34 (1939): 49.

Taking her sharp wit, Rosalie set off for Auckland Teachers' Training College, just down the road from her old school in Epsom. Although she spent a year at the college in 1939, followed by three years teaching, she made little comment in her later autobiographical narrative about this time, perhaps because her heart was not in it. To Hughes she expressed a lack of any sense of agency about the direction she took: 'I didn't decide what to do … I got my BA and that was it, and then I went teaching.'[53]

Miss Walker, schoolteacher: 'I liked it when I knew the answers'[54]

Rosalie expressed her ambivalence about teaching to Hughes:

> I enjoyed [teaching] when I knew the subject, and I was good with children. I could teach English and Latin but when it came to history or geography I was just hopeless. I hadn't read the books.[55]

She spent at least part of 1940 teaching at Kowhai Intermediate School near central Auckland before moving to Auckland Girls' Grammar School the following year.[56] Rosalie was twenty-four years old. Daintry was studying away from Auckland; World War II had begun and Douglas had joined the New Zealand Army, which deployed him in the Pacific the following year.

Meanwhile, the war in Europe accelerated and Gassy's PhD scholarship at Bristol University was running out. In 2000, when Professor Bob Crompton interviewed Ben Gascoigne for the Australian Academy of Science, Ben told him that prior to leaving Auckland for Bristol he had decided Rosalie was the girl he wanted to marry.[57] After war broke out when he was about halfway through his time in Bristol, he said he thought that if he 'stayed in England I would never be able to get back and might never see her again'.[58] He was fortunate to get a passage back to New Zealand during the war years

53 Hughes et al., 'Rosalie Gascoigne Artist', tape 1.

54 Gascoigne, interview by North, 5.

55 Hughes et al., 'Rosalie Gascoigne Artist', tape 1.

56 A progressive public school that attempted to better bridge the gap between primary and secondary schooling, Kowhai had been inspired by the American progressive New Education movement of the 1920s. Hinchco, 'A History of Middle Schooling in New Zealand'.

57 Beeby, *The Biography of an Idea*, 124.

58 Crompton, 'Professor Ben Gascoigne'.

when personal travel was restricted as well as risky. With her characteristic lack of confidence, Rosalie had not expected his return, and felt incapable of living up to his expectations:

> I'm afraid you think I'm a lot of things I'm not, and when you come back (when you write that I just smile gently, bec. I can't imagine you coming back—really I can't) you'll probably find my feet are clayier than ever. Alas—I'll never be able to live up to you and your ideas of what I am.[59]

But Ben did return, sailing from England on the SS *Orcades*, making a friend on board who was to have significance for Rosalie's art career.[60] Perth-born abstract painter Carl Plate was returning to Australia after spending several years in Europe studying in London at the St Martin's School of Art and the Central School of Arts and Crafts. Plate and Ben became firm friends.

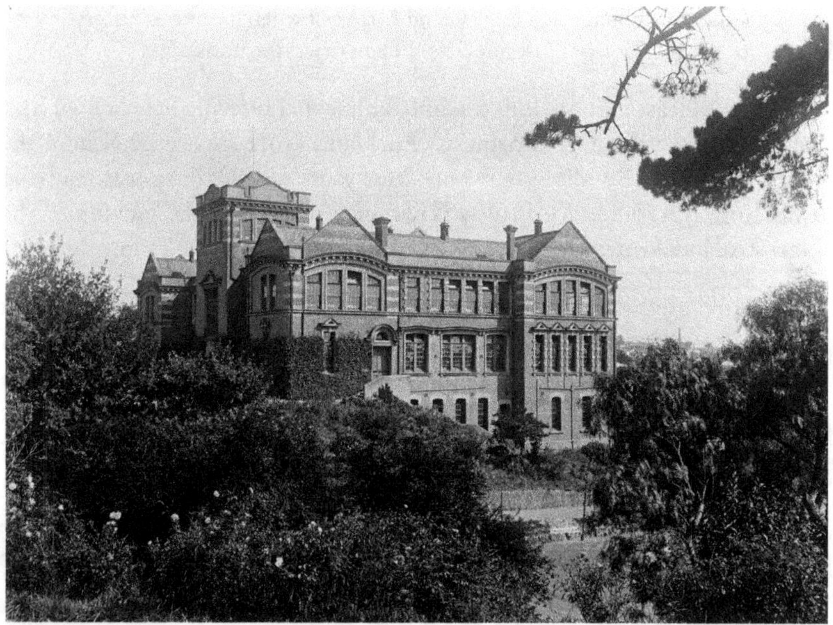

Figure 4.10: Auckland Girls' Grammar School, 1926.

Note: Rosalie taught here in 1941 and 1942.

Source: Courtesy Auckland Library Heritage Collection, Auckland Libraries, 1-W0602. Photograph: Henry Winkelmann (1860–1931).

59 Rosalie Walker to Gassy, c. May 1940, Papers of Ben Gascoigne, box 3.

60 Crompton, 'Professor Ben Gascoigne'.

Ben said he had returned to New Zealand for Rosalie but the wedding bells remained silent. First he felt he had to find employment. He was deemed unfit for active service because of his stammer and poor eyesight.[61] No work opportunities presented themselves in New Zealand apart from electrician's mate at the freezing works.[62] He completed his thesis in New Zealand and, in 1941, the University of Bristol awarded him a PhD. By August that year he had taken a job more suited to his considerable skills and education designing telescope optics at the wartime optical munitions plant that had been established at the Commonwealth Observatory on Mt Stromlo near Canberra in the Australian Capital Territory.[63] So he left again, without Rosalie.

At the time Ben departed for Australia, Rosalie had been teaching at Auckland Girls' Grammar School for seven months, having gained employment through the Department of Education (see Figure 4.10). She said little about the two years she taught there: 'I taught Latin, English, French, some abominable history—dreadful.'[64] In 1942, 'Miss Walker', as the girls would have called her, was busy as a staff representative on the School War Effort Committee, a tradition begun during World War I and re-established during World War II. In addition to girls knitting balaclavas, mittens and scarves by the hundreds for soldiers, each class made a patchwork quilt to be sold for the war effort. In 1941 and 1942, Rosalie supervised the construction of her classes' patchwork quilts.[65] These possibly inspired her later to make her own quilt, an activity that sustained her during the isolation and loneliness on Stromlo.[66]

In a letter to Gassy on Stromlo, the reader is treated to a glimpse of Rosalie's daily life—a busy one involving work, friends and family.[67] Inspired by Carl Plate, Gassy had sent her a framed art print, which she much appreciated:

61 Gascoigne, *Rosalie Gascoigne: Her New Zealand Origins*, 220–3.

62 Hughes et al., 'Rosalie Gascoigne Artist', tape 2.

63 Gascoigne, *Rosalie Gascoigne: Her New Zealand Origins*, 227; Bhathal, Sutherland and Butcher, *Mt Stromlo Observatory*, 64–6.

64 MacDonald and Gascoigne, *Rosalie Gascoigne*, 13.

65 Northey, Asher and Asher, *Auckland Girls' Grammar School*, 134.

66 Hughes et al., 'Rosalie Gascoigne Artist', tape 2.

67 The letter is dated 'Sun Feb 20th' with no year but it is undoubtedly 1942 because she mentioned the death of Bob Foster's brother, Athol, who died in an RNZAF plane crash in July 1941, and by February 1943 she was married to Ben and living on Stromlo, Papers of Ben Gascoigne, box 3.

> I like the picture very much espec the sky and I like the general blueness … The only other pictures I have are my Madonna and an oil. So thank you very much.[68]

Gassy had begun encouraging Rosalie's interest in art. Her letters illustrate a life without the hallmarks of a misfit or outsider. Perhaps the discrepancy with her later narrative can be explained by different behaviour within the stifling stuffiness of her family, with whom she still lived. This, however, is contradicted by contemporary references to parties at her home that depict her as sociable and popular. She met with friends, visited them in their homes, entertained them in hers, went to the cinema, window-shopped, played tennis, holidayed in the country where she rode horses, picked wild cherries and swam. She described clothes she was making, friends' engagements, and her fury at being virtually snubbed on a visit to a friend's house. Full of abbreviations, the letters reflect her love of density, a love she later applied to her art making. They carry the reader along at a breathless pace, as if she lived life with urgency and a momentum that left no space for self-doubt. She ended her letter of 24 February 1942: 'My bath is now overflowing.' The letter is as jam-packed with anecdote as some of her later works are with materials. She later said: 'I like things crammed up, like a pomegranate's seeds, thick, thick.'[69] She led a busy life full of family, friends, work and a vigorous social life. This was all about to change.

Rosalie tired of waiting for Gassy. When Hughes asked her, 'so how was it that Ben was the one … that you eventually married?', Rosalie evaded a direct reply: 'Life, dear, I suppose. Life.'[70] She continued: 'He was clever. And of course, I wasn't.'[71] Hughes pressed on, determined to get an answer that told the story, but Rosalie continued her evasions:

> Well, avenues of escape of course, narrowed. You might say that. And I knew I was always meant to get married, and that was my thing. I felt that various people had gone off to war, various people had been killed, and it was possible, you see. And he had a good job in Australia, away from NZ—which wasn't a good idea, because I found it very hard to leave. Just that.[72]

---

68 Rosalie Walker to Gassy, 20 February 1942, Papers of Ben Gascoigne, box 3. Ben Gascoigne had purchased the framed print with its 'general blueness' from Plate's shop Notanda in Rowe Street in Sydney and sent it to Rosalie for Christmas. See Fink, 'Rosalie Gascoigne (1917–1999): Sunflowers 1991'.

69 MacDonald and Gascoigne, *Rosalie Gascoigne*, 68.

70 Hughes et al., 'Rosalie Gascoigne Artist', tape 1.

71 Ibid.

72 MacDonald and Gascoigne, *Rosalie Gascoigne*, 14, 15.

Despite it being hard for her to leave New Zealand, Rosalie proposed marriage to Gassy by telegram and, receiving the answer she hoped for, prepared to move across the Tasman.[73] Because of Gassy's involvement in defence matters, he could not leave Australia. Like many brides during the war years, Rosalie was about to leave her family and marry among strangers, describing the situation as inevitable: 'War is a different time—bare days, bare days. People got terribly factual. So I came over. Right into the middle of wartime Stromlo.'[74]

Rosalie flew to Australia in January 1943, travelling by flying boat from Auckland to Sydney. She took a gift for Ben—a chess set carved by Crimean prisoners of war that she had purchased in an Auckland antique shop (see Figure 4.11).[75] The fine carved detail of the chess pieces appealed to her nascent artist's eye. The makers were, like she was to become, strangers in a foreign land. The set's board prefigured her latter grid-pattern pieces, in particular *Checkerboard*.[76]

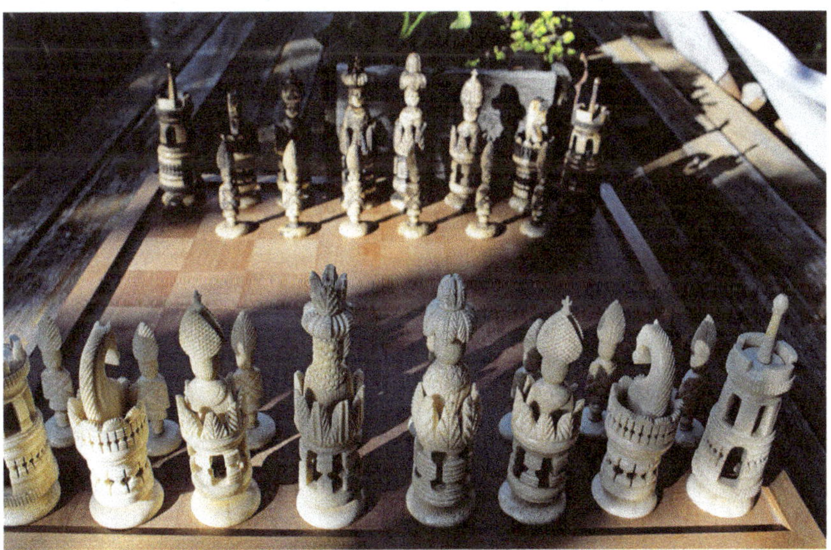

Figure 4.11: The chess set carved by Crimean prisoners of war in England that Rosalie bought in an Auckland antique shop as a wedding present for Ben.

Source: Courtesy of Hester Gascoigne and Sally Colahan Griffin. Photograph: Sally Colahan Griffin.

73 Hughes et al., 'Rosalie Gascoigne Artist', tape 2; MacDonald and Gascoigne, *Rosalie Gascoigne*, 68.

74 Gascoigne, *New Zealand Lives*, 228.

75 Hester Gascoigne, interview by author, 20 March 2010.

76 *Checkerboard* can be seen in Gascoigne, *Rosalie Gascoigne: A Catalogue Raisonné*, 241.

In-between years

Rosalie's self-narrative presents this period as a hiatus: she was studying out of necessity rather than interest in order to fulfil family expectations and get a job. She suggests she did the minimum required to pass at university and that she enjoyed dances and Field Club trips more than academic study.

The environment was not conducive to developing her latent artistic talents. She believed she could not draw or paint, prerequisites for an art career at that time, and there was no real literary culture at university in which to immerse herself had she felt so inclined. She drifted into teaching but was not inspired to continue.[77]

In her narrative, she presents herself as discontentedly going with the flow of family expectations and the need to earn a living, as if she lacked agency. Yet, tired of waiting for Gassy, and uninhibited by gender stereotypes, having grown up with a mother who was the family breadwinner, Rosalie took the initiative and proposed marriage to him. She omitted this fact from her self-narrative, possibly because that degree of personal agency did not fit with the story she wished to tell, or possibly because it might have embarrassed Ben. She described her marriage as an escape, presumably because it gave her a way out of teaching, while at the same time saying she found it very hard to leave New Zealand, expressing some of life's complexity and ambiguity.[78]

Rosalie's references to not fitting in are supported by her letters from this period that tell of her tendency to be judgemental and patronising in her circle of young adults; some people found her superior and hypercritical and felt demeaned or belittled by her. She would later describe herself as 'difficult', and others evidently found her so during these early years of her adulthood. On the other hand, she was well-liked—by her friends and certain boys she met. In her story of herself as a young woman, she was not focused on her studies, which she saw merely as a means to end, and felt out of place as a school teacher. She further developed a picture of herself as an outsider, continuing this theme from her childhood and setting the scene for the story of her move to Australia.

77 Gascoigne, *Rosalie Gascoigne: Her New Zealand Origins*, 228.

78 Hughes et al., 'Rosalie Gascoigne Artist', tape 1.

PART II

1943–69

STROMLO AND DEAKIN

‘The long littleness of female life’

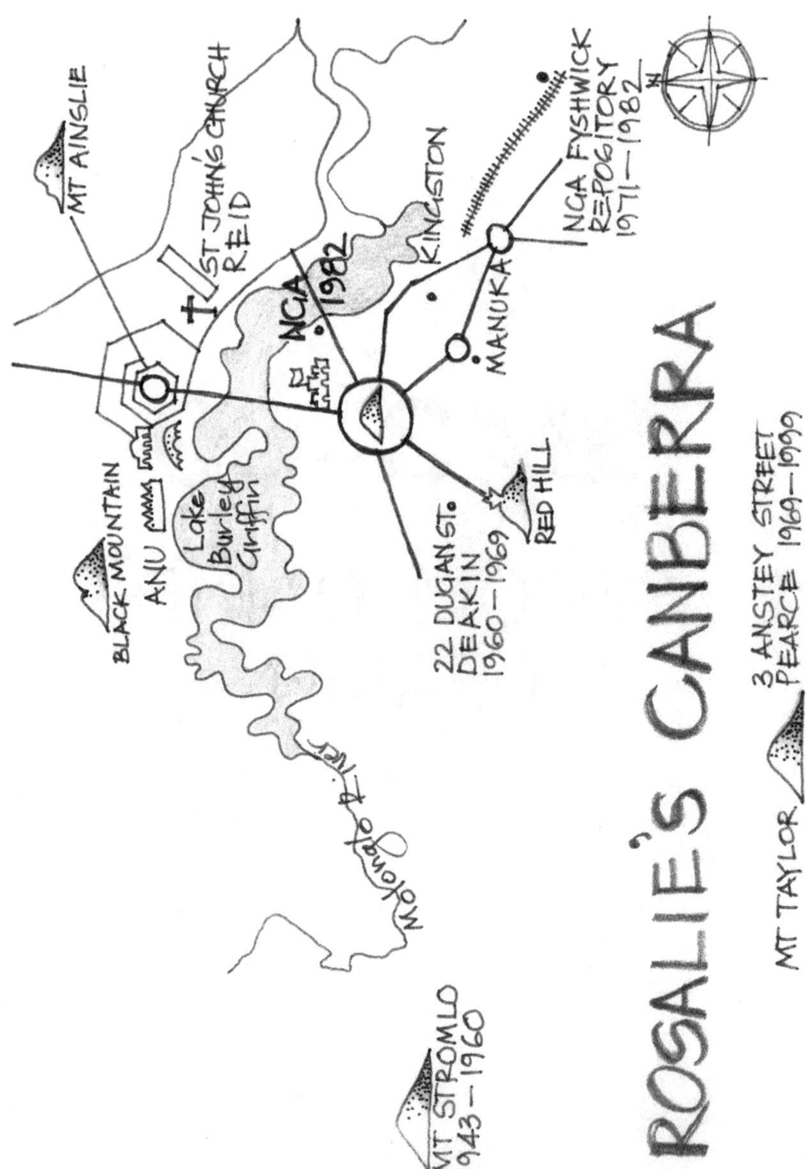

Map 3: Rosalie's Canberra.

Source: Map drawn by Kerry Francis, architect and academic, Tāmaki Makaurau Auckland, Aotearoa New Zealand. Courtesy of Kerry Francis.

5

1943: 'Fate set me down, a bride'

Rosalie arrived on Mt Stromlo in January 1943. Within three days of her arrival she was married; within ten months she was a mother. As with other periods in her life, sources about her first year on Stromlo are scant. They include interviews she did thirty to forty years later, a *New Zealand Herald* report of the wedding and Stromlo scientist Clabon Allen's diary.

In this one year, 1943, Rosalie's life turned upside down. She who was used to being an independent professional woman in a busy city found herself a wife then a mother in a small scientific community. She knew the anxiety and heartbreak of having a seriously ill baby when she gave birth to her first child, Martin, in November 1943. This introduction to motherhood was not what Rosalie had expected or hoped for. She said she grew older through the trauma of that experience and felt that it set her apart from other women on the mountain.

Having described her feeling that she was an outsider in her family during childhood, in later interviews she deepened that self-narrative to incorporate nationality and work. As a New Zealander in Australia she felt different. As a full-time wife and mother with an arts and humanities background, she felt she did not fit with the scientists who were her new husband's colleagues on Stromlo.

The different landscape of Canberra and the Monaro, a great sunburnt limestone plain with flocks of big colourful, noisy birds, shocked Rosalie and, at the same time, continued her trope of visual awareness. The move away from all that was familiar, from friends and family, shook her at the core of her being, but her resilience and affinity with nature saw her through.

Rosalie turned to the natural environment in desperation and loneliness. Nature had been important to her since early childhood, and it became crucial on Stromlo, as it offered its own affirmation:

> I didn't need it as much in New Zealand, because I had friends ... and when you're in a scientific community you don't have friends of your own choosing. See, if you're a university person, you naturally can choose your friends ... I was fairly desperate for something that I could associate with. And well, nature was my friend.[1]

Marriage: 'She carried a bouquet of white roses and daisies'

> Fate set me down, a bride, in a small scientific community on a hill-top covered with pine trees, and in the next eighteen years proceeded to teach me a lot I didn't know about nature, both human and otherwise.[2]

With her white lace wedding dress and the carved Crimean chess set for her bridegroom packed in her bag, Rosalie flew across the Tasman Sea in a Short S-30 flying boat operated by Tasman Empire Airways Ltd, the forerunner to Air New Zealand. The flight took nine hours, delivering Rosalie to her new life a few weeks short of her twenty-sixth birthday. It was wartime, so arranging travel was complex; safety considerations and rationed fuel meant she had to apply for permission to travel.[3] Within twenty-four hours of waving farewell to her family and friends at the flying boat base at Auckland's Mechanics Bay, she arrived on Mt Stromlo, an isolated hill observatory with a tiny community

---

1 Hughes et al., 'Rosalie Gascoigne Artist', tape 1.

2 Rosalie Gascoigne, 'Too Many Pine Trees', Papers of Rosalie Gascoigne, 1930–2011, National Library of Australia (hereafter Papers of Rosalie Gascoigne), box 3.

3 Gordon Carmichael notes that preferential arrangements where passports were not required for British subjects travelling between Australia and New Zealand were suspended during World War II when all travellers required exit permits and travel documents. My extensive search of Archives New Zealand Te Rua Mahara o te Kawanatanga for files on civilian travel permits turned up only files for applications related to commercial travel directly related to war work. A search for New Zealand government policy on travel permits also failed to turn up any relevant information. I know, however, that permits were required. Apart from Carmichael's comment, in 1944 my mother, Aylsa Vahry, was preparing to travel from Auckland to England to marry my father. In August 1944, she wrote to my father, Captain Basil Francis: 'I have just completed the application forms for my permit to leave NZ so the only thing now is to await the reply from Wellington and I believe that takes some time.' It was to be some months before the permit came through and a ship's passage was made available. She arrived in England (Liverpool) in February 1945. Rosalie would have been subject to similar, if not identical, requirements.

of around eighteen people near Australia's fledgling national capital, which itself was only four years older than Rosalie.[4] Canberra's population was around twelve thousand in 1943; by contrast, Auckland's population was 223,000 (see Figures 5.1–5.4).[5] She had left behind her family, friends and profession in the bustling harbour city where she had enjoyed the independence of a working woman, the sophistication of theatre, cinema and dances as well as bushwalking and beaches.

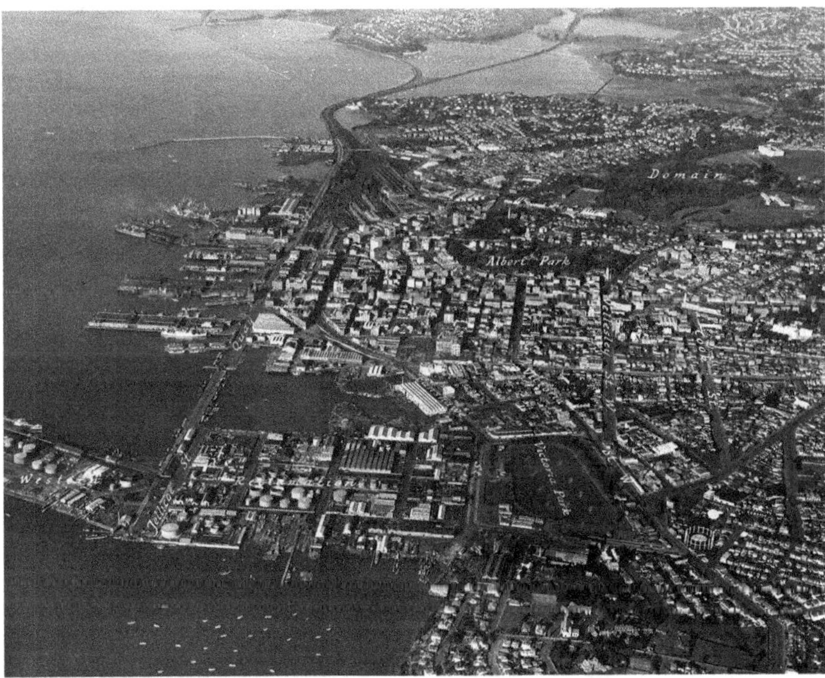

Figure 5.1: Auckland city and waterfront, 1947.

Note: This image shows the contrast between the city Rosalie left behind and the small community to which she moved on Mt Stromlo.

Source: Courtesy of Auckland Libraries Heritage Collections 580-ALB22-054. Photograph: Whites Aviation Collection, Alexander Turnbull Library.

4 Tasman Empire Airways Limited (TEAL), the forerunner of Air New Zealand, had been operating the flying boats from Mechanics Bay in Auckland since 30 April 1940. The trans-Tasman flight, for those who could afford this ultra-modern form of travel, took about nine hours, in contrast with the three days by ship. Carmichael, ed., *Trans-Tasman Migration*, 7.

5 Canberra's population was 15,146 in 1947. According to the New Zealand Official Year-Book, the population of Auckland city and surrounding boroughs was 223,700 on 1 April 1941. The wider Auckland region had a population of 582,513. See Statistics New Zealand, 'The New Zealand Official Year-Book, 1943'.

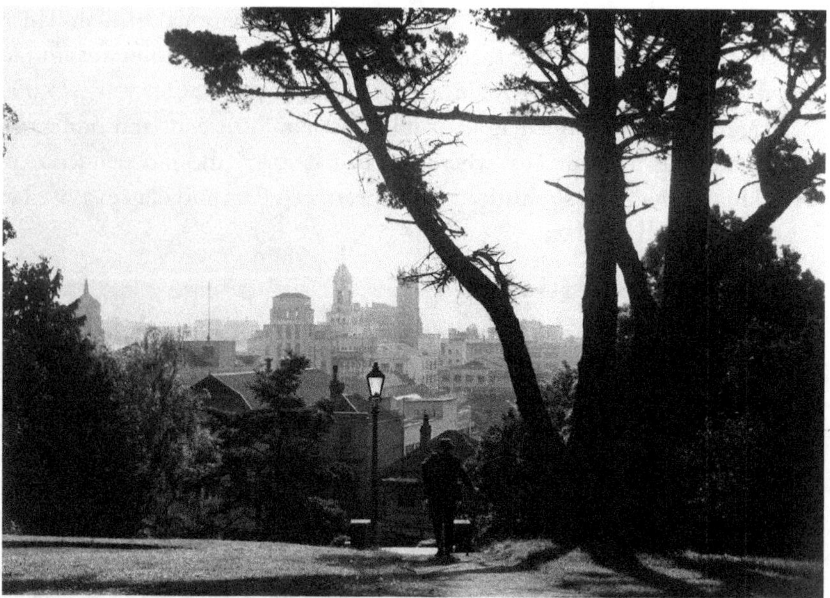

Figure 5.2: Albert Park, 1940s, opposite Auckland University College.

Source: Courtesy of Auckland Libraries Heritage Collection Footprints 02492. Photograph: Francis Alton (1926–1997).

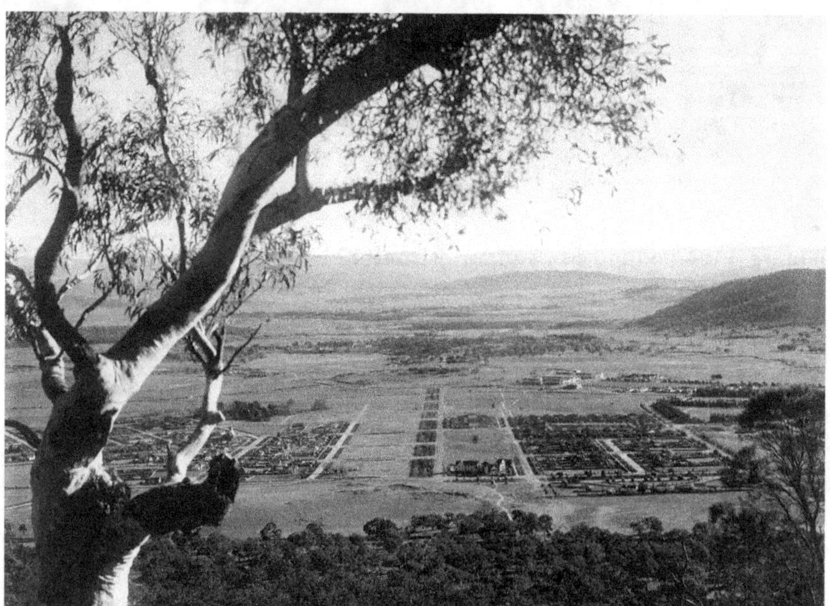

Figure 5.3: View from Mt Ainslie, Canberra, showing the subdivisions of Reid, Braddon, City Shops, Acton and Mt Stromlo.

Source: NAA: A1200, L11508.

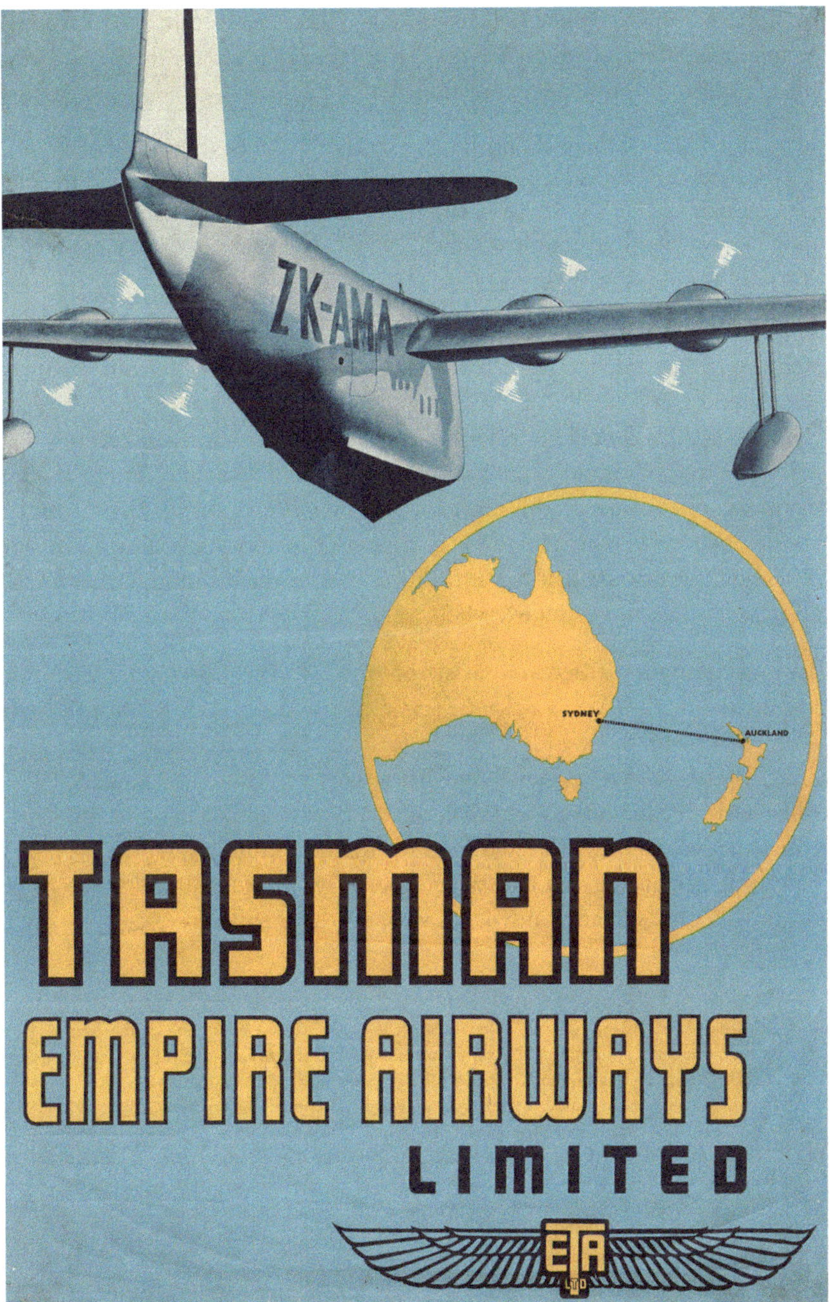

Figure 5.4: A poster, c. 1940, advertising the flying boat service on which Rosalie flew from Auckland to Sydney.

Source: Courtesy of Alexander Turnbull Library, Wellington, New Zealand, natlib.govt.nz/records/23113739.

In sloping handwriting, Dr Clabon 'Cla' Allen, a Stromlo staff member, recorded Rosalie's arrival on Wednesday 6 January in the diaries he had kept since 1922 to improve his expression:[6]

> Sid [Ben Gascoigne] and Rosalie arrived in Canberra in the early afternoon and came practically straight out. I came down to meet them and we talked over a cup of tea. She is rather tall and slight, rather nice looking when dressed to suit. She seems to fit into our household very easily.[7]

Rosalie stayed with Cla Allen and his wife Rose for the days before the wedding. Rose Allen was a New Zealander, but Rosalie did not warm to her, later describing her as 'screamingly tactless'.[8] Rosalie's first days on the mountain were taken up with wedding arrangements and meeting her bridegroom's colleagues in the bachelors' quarters.[9] Years later, after Rosalie's death in 1999, one of the bachelors, Francis Lord, wrote Ben a tender condolence letter, which included a snippet of memory revealing a soft side to Rosalie: 'From the day you introduced her to the Stromlo bachelors she always charmed me—and everybody else.'[10]

Two contemporary records exist of the Walker–Gascoigne wedding. In Auckland, the *New Zealand Herald* reported on it. On Stromlo, Cla Allen described the wedding in his journal. His description conjures an image of the Allen house bustling with activity on Saturday 9 January 1943. Allen and his two young sons, Clabon and Bryden, drove to town (probably Kingston) where they collected food for the reception.[11] Wartime rationing had limited clothing, tea and sugar since 1942, but meat and butter were freely available, so ham sandwiches were on the menu.[12]

---

6 See Gascoigne, 'Allen, Clabon Walter (Cla) (1904–1987)'. Allen was one of the four original staff physicists at the Commonwealth Solar Observatory when it was first established in 1924 and he remained there until he was appointed to a position in England in 1951.

7 Clabon Walter Allen, 'Diaries', 6 January 1943, vol. 18, Papers of Clabon Walter Allan, 1922–1953, National Library of Australia (hereafter Papers of Clabon Walter Allan), box 2.

8 'Screamingly tactless' from Hughes et al., 'Rosalie Gascoigne Artist', tape 2. Allen's mother, Alice Hooper Aitken, was also a New Zealander who had married his South Australian father. Allen's wife, Rose McKenzie née Smellie (often referred to as Vick by her husband in his diaries), was a New Zealander whom he married in Gisborne, New Zealand, in 1937.

9 Allen, 'Diaries', 7 January 1943, vol. 18, Papers of Clabon Walter Allan, box 2: 'Sid and Rosalie spent the day in Canberra and visited the bachelors in the evening.' 'The bachelors' referred to the shared dormitory style accommodation on Mt Stromlo where most of the single men lived.

10 Francis Lord to Ben Gascoigne, c. 1999, Papers of Ben Gascoigne, box 3.

11 Allen, 'Diaries', 9 January 1943, vol. 18, Papers of Clabon Walter Allan, box 2.

12 Australian War Memorial, 'Rationing of Food and Clothing'; Commonwealth Rationing Commission, *Departmental History*, 7–9; Butlin and Schedvin, *War Economy*, 286–309, 785.

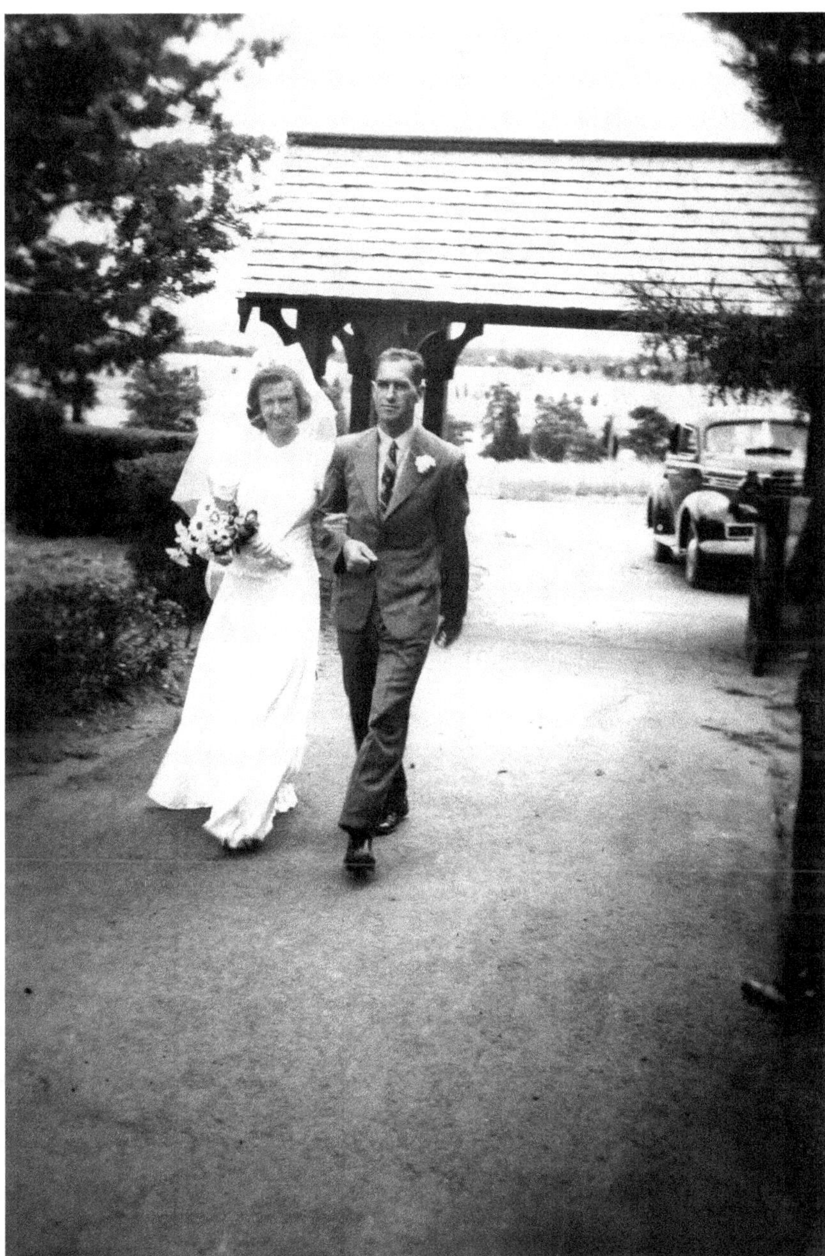

Figure 5.5: Rosalie arrives at St John the Baptist Anglican Church with Clabon 'Cla' Allen who, in the absence of her family, had been asked to 'give her away'.

Source: Courtesy of the Gascoigne family.

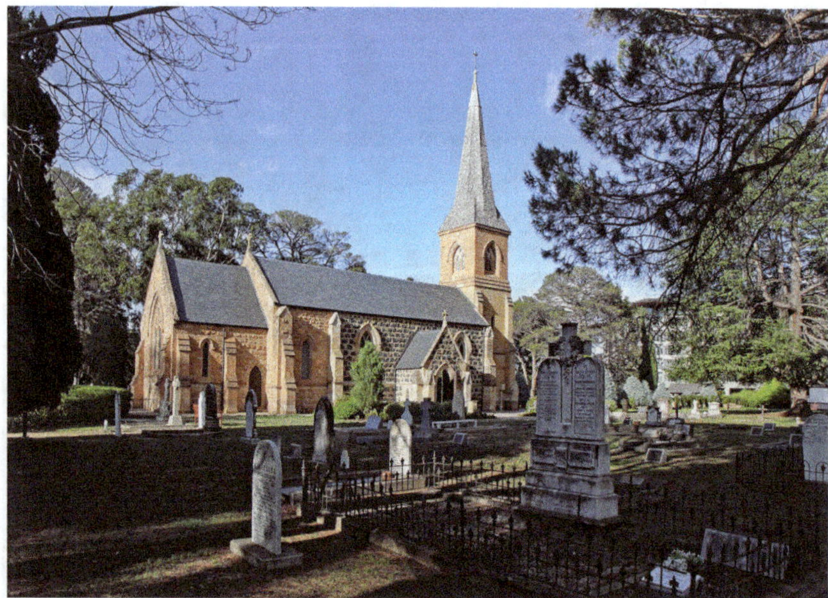

Figure 5.6: St John the Baptist Anglican Church, Reid, the oldest church in Canberra, where Rosalie and Ben were married.

Source: Courtesy of Randall Wilson. Photograph: Randall Wilson.

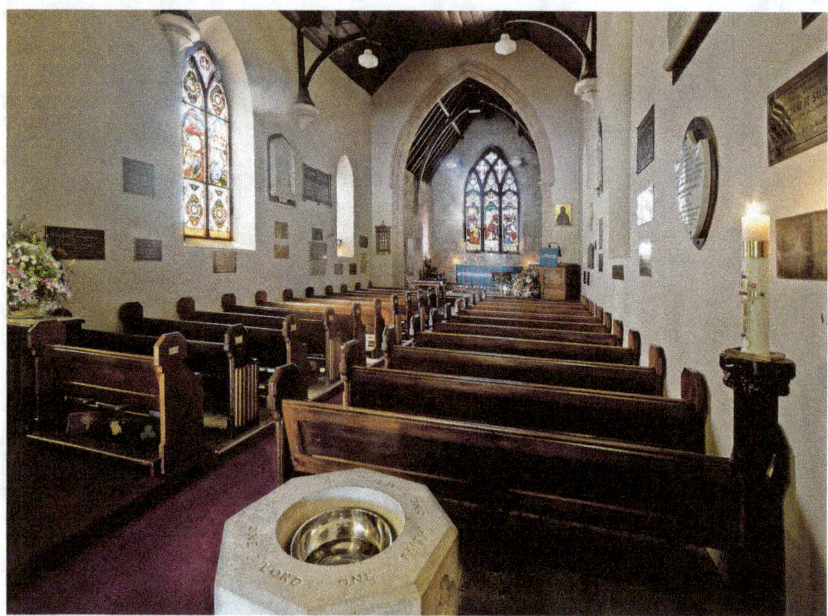

Figure 5.7: Interior of St John the Baptist Church.

Source: Courtesy of Rodney Garnett. Photograph: Rodney Garnett.

Back at the Allen house it was all hands on deck, Rosalie included, to make the sandwiches before the drive down the mountain for the wedding at Canberra's oldest church, St John the Baptist Anglican Church in Reid. Once the bride was garbed in her wedding finery, she travelled the eleven-and-a-half miles in a taxi with Allen who, in the absence of Rosalie's family, had been asked to 'give her away' in the traditional Anglican wedding service (see Figures 5.5–5.7).

In a perfunctory description of the ceremony, Allen wrote of their perfectly timed arrival at the church 'by stopping the car for a few minutes':

> The two of us marched up the aisle. Sid took some time over the responses [because of his stammer] but didn't miss a word. Then Vick [Rose Allen] and I acted as witnesses in the Vestry. There were some more photographs taken and then I drove home fairly fast to be ready for the guests … The spread looked most attractive and we all ate and drank well. There was some sherry and champagne for the toast. Dr Woolley [director of the observatory] proposed the toast to the Bride and Bridegroom to which Sid answered appropriately. Rosalie changed about 6.30 and we watched them go off before the party broke up.[13]

The wedding guest list of thirty comprised Stromlo staff. Allen summarised the day as busy and satisfying: 'All were enthusiastic about the success of the wedding and reception.' After helping with the clean-up he returned to his work on the six-pounder gun sight—the observatory's wartime business encompassed the research, design and production of such equipment.[14]

In Auckland, the Walker and Gascoigne families and friends celebrated at a party hosted by Marion Walker. A family photograph shows the guests lined up in the garden with the two mothers, Rene Gascoigne and Marion Walker, in the middle of the front row flanked by their respective daughters. Assorted aunts and friends stand behind them against a leafy hedge in the Auckland sunshine. Clothing rationing may have constrained the elegance of the occasion, but the women were all smartly turned out in print or plain frocks, most with hats at jaunty angles and smiles on their faces. When the *New Zealand Herald* reported the wedding nearly three months later, the reader was left with no doubt as to the significance of the occasion given the importance of scientific work at the observatory and Ben's special wartime role (see Figures 5.8 and 5.9).

13 Allen, 'Diaries', 9 January 1943.

14 Ibid.; Bhathal, Sutherland and Butcher, *Mt Stromlo Observatory*, 63–75.

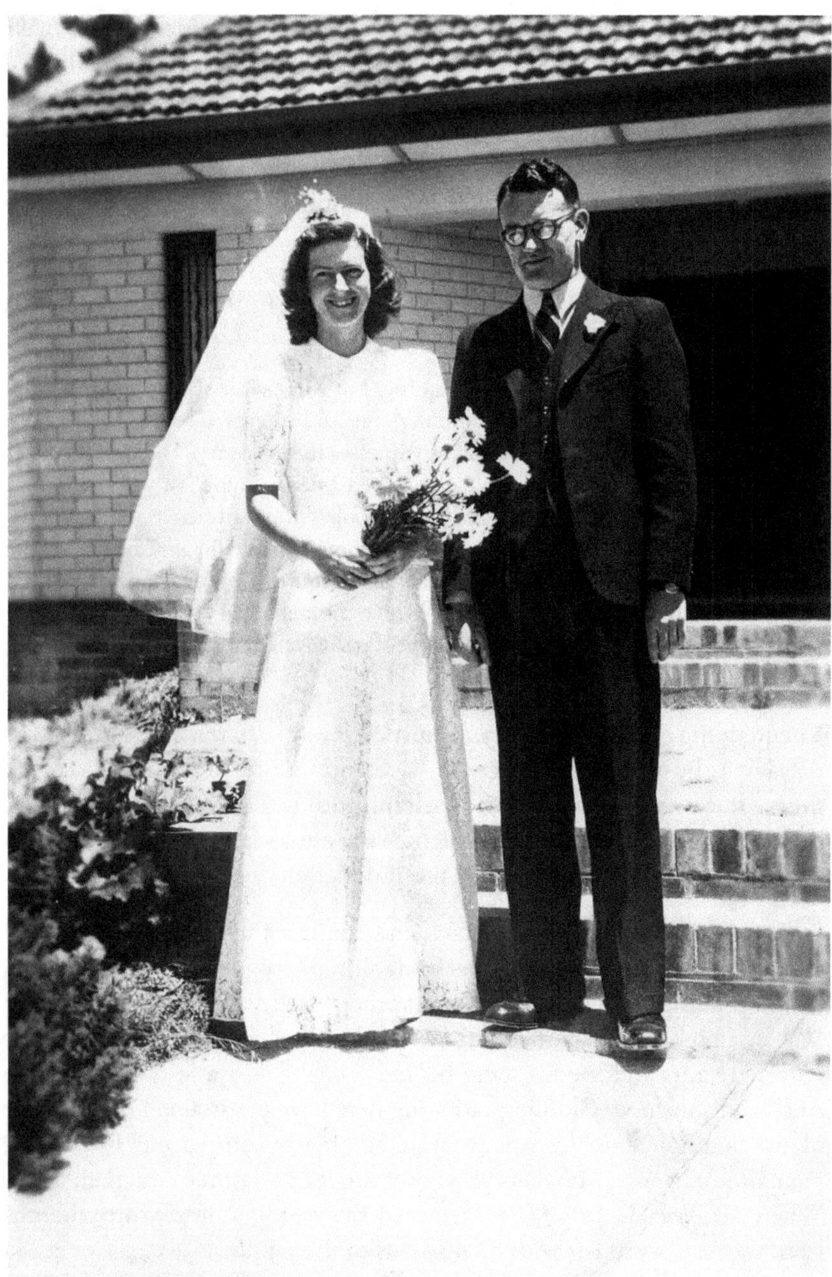

Figure 5.8: Rosalie and Ben Gascoigne on their wedding day, 9 January 1943, outside the Allens' house on Mt Stromlo where their reception was held.

Source: Courtesy Gascoigne family archive.

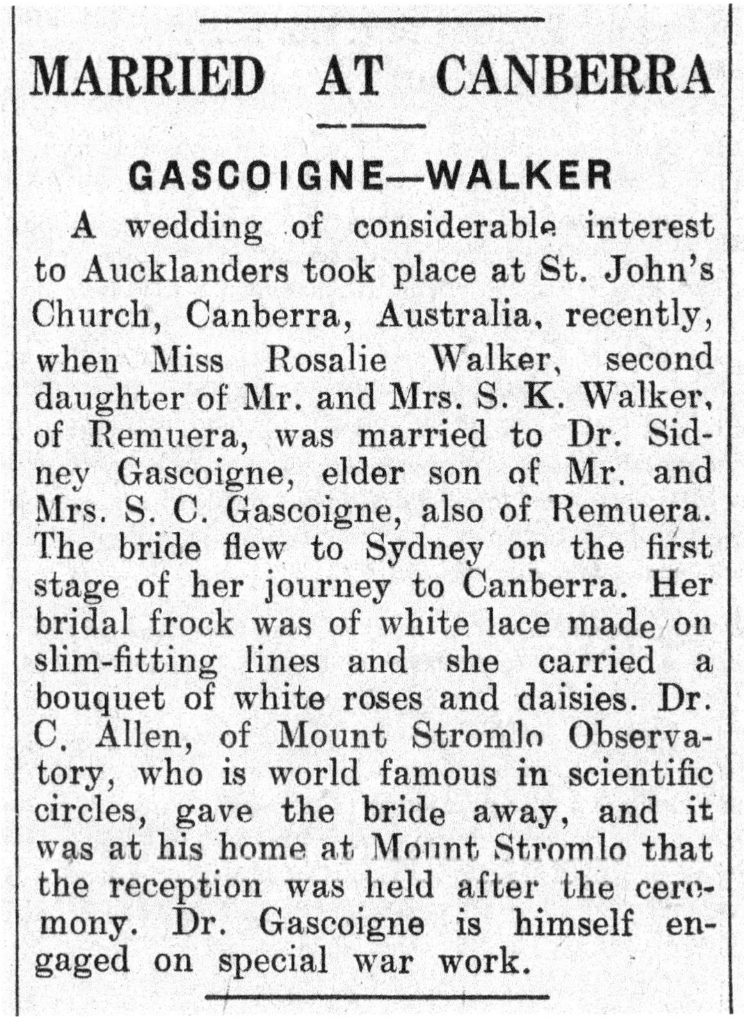

MARRIED AT CANBERRA

GASCOIGNE—WALKER

A wedding of considerable interest to Aucklanders took place at St. John's Church, Canberra, Australia, recently, when Miss Rosalie Walker, second daughter of Mr. and Mrs. S. K. Walker, of Remuera, was married to Dr. Sidney Gascoigne, elder son of Mr. and Mrs. S. C. Gascoigne, also of Remuera. The bride flew to Sydney on the first stage of her journey to Canberra. Her bridal frock was of white lace made on slim-fitting lines and she carried a bouquet of white roses and daisies. Dr. C. Allen, of Mount Stromlo Observatory, who is world famous in scientific circles, gave the bride away, and it was at his home at Mount Stromlo that the reception was held after the ceremony. Dr. Gascoigne is himself engaged on special war work.

Figure 5.9: 'Married at Canberra, Gascoigne–Walker', *New Zealand Herald*, 31 March 1943, 5.

Source: Courtesy of New Zealand Media and Entertainment Holdings Ltd, Aotearoa New Zealand and Auckland War Memorial Museum Tāmaki Paenga Hira.

Honeymoon: Sydney and Hordern's New Palace Emporium

From the reception, the newlyweds again travelled the dirt road down the mountain to Canberra's best hotel, the Hotel Canberra (now the Hyatt) where they spent the night. They set off for Sydney the following morning. Legend has it that the new bride renamed her husband 'Ben' the morning after their wedding, but if there was any rationale for this, it has been lost.[15] Maybe Rosalie decided 'Gassy' was no longer appropriate for a married man carrying out important war work for the Australian government. As his given name was Sidney, he was known as Sid on Stromlo. Perhaps Rosalie felt that neither 'Sid' nor 'Gassy' lent themselves to sweet murmurings; or maybe she thought that since she was taking on a new name in marriage, it was only fair that he did too? Rosalie had said that her mother was the stronger personality of her parents; implicitly, perhaps, she was making her own mark on her new marriage.

Whatever the reason, both sporting new names, the Gascoignes shopped in Sydney for household items at Anthony Hordern & Sons' smart New Palace Emporium at Brickfield Hill. Rosalie said 'people didn't have any money to buy anything'; however, in Hordern's elegant environment, the Gascoignes purchased a house-load of furniture, at least on hire purchase: bedroom and dining furniture, a three-piece lounge suite, bedding, card table, stools, pine safe, a rug and two druggets (rugs) to the value of £136 14s 3d with an initial deposit of £100.[16] Ben earned around £350 in 1943 when the average male wage was £299 per year, and presumably, Rosalie brought savings from her three years' work as a high school teacher in Auckland.[17]

15 Hannah Fink to Ben Gascoigne, 10 April 2006, Papers of Ben Gascoigne, box 5. Fink mentions the name change. Ben was known by various names at different times in his life: 'Gassy' in Auckland, S. C. B or Steve or Sid on Stromlo, and Ben. A letter addressed to him on Rosalie's death in 1999 started 'Dear S.C.B, Ben/Steve'. See 'Terry' (in Bowral) to Ben, November 1999, Papers of Ben Gascoigne, box 3.

16 Hordern's hire purchase document, Papers of Ben Gascoigne, box 3; Hughes et al., 'Rosalie Gascoigne Artist', tape 2: 'People didn't have any money to buy anything.'

17 Average male wage (£5/15/8 per week), see John Curtin Prime Ministerial Library, 'Austerity, Liberty and Victory'.

Stromlo and difference: The colours, the sky, the people

On Monday 18 January 1943, Allen recorded that the Gascoignes returned from their honeymoon and occupied their new home. With the rush of the wedding and honeymoon over, Rosalie found herself having to settle into day-to-day life. The prosaically named 'Residence 19', where the Gascoignes were to live for the next seventeen years, lay in close proximity to the homes of other married observatory staff and their families (see Figure 5.10).[18] It was one of about seven houses on Mt Stromlo's southern slope, built for staff accommodation because of the relative isolation of the observatory. With big eaves, the house seemed to provide a haven from the heat, but it was another story in winter:

> It was cold. And the air hung purple … in the passages … To go down to the bedroom and get a handkerchief was more than you could bear. Stayed in the kitchen by the fuel fire. It was very, very cold in winter. It was hot in summer of course.[19]

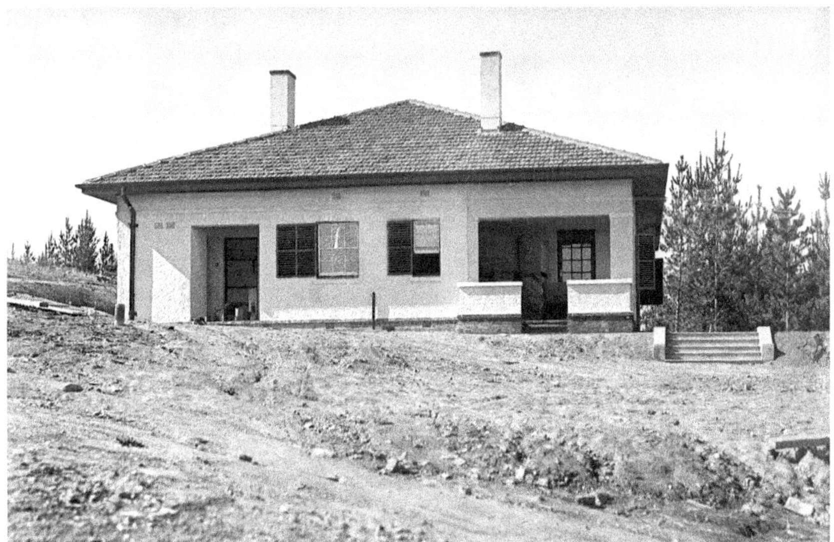

Figure 5.10: Residence 19, Mt Stromlo Observatory, Rosalie and Ben's home from January 1943 to 1960.

Source: Courtesy of the National Archives of Australia, Image No. A3560, 1820, Item ID 3130562.

18 Allen, 'Diaries', 18 January 1943, vol. 18, Papers of Clabon Walter Allan, box 2.

19 Hughes et al., 'Rosalie Gascoigne Artist', tape 2.

Stromlo confronted Rosalie with two significant differences from Auckland: physical and social. The physical features of the place—landscape, flora, fauna and climate—were radically different from Auckland. The social character of the tiny hilltop community was also a far cry from Auckland's more cosmopolitan city. Rosalie was accustomed to being an independent young woman with a job, male and female friends, and an active social life. In Auckland she enjoyed easy access to cinemas, theatres, dances and libraries, all either a walk or short tram ride from Halls Avenue. On Stromlo, she was isolated; her new husband was preoccupied with the stars, she had no close friends or family nearby, and the only escape route was a rattly bus 'like a very old, low flying aircraft' that left the mountain at nine and returned at noon, leaving little time to shop.[20]

Rosalie told Hughes that marriage meant a lot of hard work that she was not very good at and also 'a lot of solitude. It meant leaving behind everything I'd known in New Zealand.'[21] She refused to say much more, responding further to Hughes's question about her marriage: 'does one have to spell everything out?'[22]

Ben

Ben offered Rosalie constancy without pressure. He was focused on his wartime work, and later on the stars. A general discussion about the astronomers' absorption in their work in Vici MacDonald's monograph *Rosalie Gascoigne* includes a sentence that might refer to Rosalie: 'An attractive young bride cried that, far from admiring her, her new husband spent all his time in the bedroom staring at the night sky.'[23] Rosalie told MacDonald: 'the astronomers were ruled by the clouds. They were allocated a certain number of nights each month on the telescope but if visibility was poor, their turn was lost.'[24] Providing some insight into Ben's personality and their relationship, she said:

20 MacDonald and Gascoigne, *Rosalie Gascoigne*, 15.

21 Hughes et al., 'Rosalie Gascoigne Artist', tape 2.

22 Ibid., tape 2.

23 MacDonald and Gascoigne, *Rosalie Gascoigne*, 15. When Ben joined the Mt Stromlo Observatory in 1941, it was an optical munitions factory and remained so for the duration of World War II, after which Director Richard Woolley changed the direction to stellar astronomy. It is not clear whether Rosalie's comments relate only to the period after WWII or include the war years when the telescopes may have been used for some astronomy. See Bhathal, Sutherland and Butcher, *Mt Stromlo Observatory*, 66–78.

24 Ibid., 15.

> You wouldn't want to be married to an astronomer when his nights were cloudy … Ben was obsessed, absolutely obsessed. But you can't be an astronomer unless you're dedicated to your work. Wives had to make the best of it.[25]

Rosalie frequently deflected, as she did here in her generalised reference to 'wives', but she was one of them. Her sense of privacy and propriety protected both her and Ben. She alluded to his possible moodiness on cloudy nights, and broadly referred to his 'obsession' but went no further. She was a private person and with his gaze on the stars, Ben offered her personal space. He was highly intelligent but she had the upper hand with speech. Ben's stammer sometimes restricted him from quick repartees; Rosalie, by contrast, was quick with sharp judgements of people and situations.

Of the most intimate aspects of their life I have nothing to say nor do I wish to speculate, nursing no desire to be one of those biographers who, as described by Janet Malcolm, '[tiptoe] down the corridor together [with the reader] to stand in front of the bedroom door and try to peep through the keyhole.'[26] Rosalie's story, however, does suggest she was at times dissatisfied with aspects of the marriage, in particular, with Ben's focus on his work, which left little time for her. Living in his shadow irked her.

For Ben, Mt Stromlo was the place where he finally had a decent job and where he saw his future. He was professionally satisfied, having moved from a small optical munitions workshop in New Zealand to optical munitions on a far bigger scale than anything New Zealand could offer him.[27] A letter he wrote to art writer Hannah Fink in 2000 acknowledges how isolated Rosalie felt in her early years on Stromlo:

> It took me too long to realise how profoundly she [Rosalie] was affected by those totally new surroundings, and by the small and not particularly congenial group of people in which she … found herself. I could have done more about it, though I sometimes wonder … just how.[28]

Rosalie might have found constancy in their relationship, but she had again been thrown onto her own devices in seeking her own purpose.

25 Ibid.

26 Malcolm, *The Silent Woman*.

27 See Bhathal, Sutherland and Butcher, *Mt Stromlo Observatory*, 66–78; Crompton, 'Professor Ben Gascoigne'.

28 Hannah Fink to Ben Gascoigne, 3 January 2000, Papers of Ben Gascoigne, box 5.

Difference

War brought disruption and mobility to many people, placing them in communities where urgency and impermanence shaped daily life and obscured a vision of the future. Rosalie was far from alone in the isolation she felt at Stromlo, but that did not diminish its impact or discount the particular forms it took for her. Decades later, Rosalie related to interviewers her sense of displacement in the new land when she talked about the shock of difference.[29] As a new migrant, this was almost inevitable. Migration studies show that a rift occurs, a displacement, a dissonance, between the migrant's previous life and the one in the new place.[30] However, because Rosalie's weekly letters to Marion during this period were lost in one of Marion's moves, Rosalie's later reflections on this time are the sole source of her feelings about her new home.[31]

Just as she had felt she did not fit in with her family during childhood, she now felt an outsider on Stromlo, although for different reasons. She attributed her differentness on Stromlo to the fact that she was a New Zealander in Australia, a humanities person in a community of scientists, and a tertiary-educated woman among less well-educated spouses. She said she was 'bored to screams' amid women who took seriously only their domestic tasks.[32]

She longed for conversation with men because 'being university trained you were used to men', but she felt that was socially unacceptable: 'It looked as if you were a man-eater; other women thought you were after their husbands.'[33] She told how she envied the men their lives. Her reflections convey a sense of longing for her old life in Auckland: 'the husbands, of course, all went up to the observatory, and they had a life up there that was forbidden to women on the mountain, who were mainly housewives'.[34]

29 Ibid.; Gascoigne, interview by Topliss; Gascoigne, interview by North.

30 See C. K. Steedman in Leese, Piatek and Curyllo-Klag, eds., *The British Migrant Experience*, xxi; Thapan, ed., *Transnational Migration*; Gabrielle Fortune, 'Mr Jones' Wives'; Ossman, ed., *The Places We Share*; Poot, 'Trans-Tasman Migration, Transnationalism'.

31 Martin Gascoigne, interview by author, Canberra, 9 December 2014. Martin told me the letters had 'disappeared' in one of Marion's house moves. Given that Marion died in 1969 before Rosalie had made a name for herself as an artist, it is unsurprising that the letters were not then identified as important sources.

32 Gascoigne, interview by Topliss, 32. Recent biographies of other women in Canberra, including Eilean Giblin by Patricia Clarke, show that many women in Canberra were in the same position, but found it difficult to break out of the situation to reach each other. See Clarke, *Eileen Giblin*.

33 Hughes et al., 'Rosalie Gascoigne Artist', tape 2.

34 Ibid., tape 1.

Her remembered loneliness echoes through her reflections that the men had luxuries like morning tea, 'and they know people, and they walk along corridors and they say good morning to them'.[35]

Several aspects of Rosalie's sense of 'differentness' coalesced under the watchful eyes of her new neighbours. Her behaviour was scrutinised in ways that were more direct and more impossible to evade than that which had hemmed the edges of her life in New Zealand due to family scandals. Her nationality, her class and her lack of domesticity were exaggerated in even the simplest task such as laundry:

> People even said 'she's got no idea, she hangs the tea towels there and the pyjama pants there and what are you, and then the pyjama jacket right on there' and I thought, 'what does that matter'? But that's the way they thought, they were trained. And also I was New Zealand trained and I think New Zealanders were very different from Australians at that stage.[36]

A sense of failure dogged her for years until fame offered its own affirmation:

> Oh I was really stupid, yes I think I was really stupid because I think I was concerned with all the ways I was a failure because I certainly didn't win a lot of marks for the most elegant lunch party or the tidiest house or hanging out the washing in a regular form.[37]

Apart from the laundry references, Rosalie was never specific about how these alleged differences manifested themselves, but the feeling was pervasive, and she framed it in the most absolute terms—the irreducibility of her nationality:

> I think being a New Zealander made me an outsider. I think per se it does. We're different people you know. We were—well especially in those times, and you wanted your own people around you.[38]

Her neighbour Rose Allen was also a New Zealander. That Rosalie did not feel Rose was 'one of her people' suggests she was probably feeling the difference of class and education and even region rather than the broad sweep of nationality. Her narrative moved swiftly forward with the beat of her felt difference:

35 Ibid.

36 Feneley and Gascoigne, 'Express Highlights'.

37 Ibid.

38 Hughes et al., 'Rosalie Gascoigne Artist', tape 2.

> I didn't fit in. I always was slightly out of step, because I thought differently and I said things differently. And I think with the woman next door, well the fact that I had had an education was bad news. I read books too, that was the end of me.[39]

Her relationship with the other wives on Stromlo will be discussed in the next chapter; suffice to say, in later life, she spoke condescendingly of them and told a story of their rejection of her. Some found Rosalie bossy, abrasive and argumentative, which may have explained some of her sense of social isolation.[40] A woman who played tennis with Ben at Stromlo on Saturdays prior to Rosalie's arrival spoke of her and her friends' surprise on meeting the new bride: 'She was bossy. We were expecting a more compliant woman. Ben was very pleasant. She was very definite—she was abrupt.'[41] These responses to her manner may have been behind her sense of being out step.

Notwithstanding Rosalie's claim to difference, in reality, she was not alone. The small community on Stromlo was genuinely polyglot in its make-up. Most people on the mountain were newcomers to Stromlo or Australia. World War II was in its fourth bloody year and the Stromlo community included refugees from the horrors of Nazi-dominated Europe, along with scientists from all over Australia, New Zealand and Europe. Crucial gun sights promised from the United Kingdom had not eventuated, so Australia needed to create its own precision optical industry; the Australian government turned the Commonwealth Solar Observatory at Mt Stromlo over to wartime optics.[42]

Rosalie herself said there were 'assorted people, different degrees of education. Different backgrounds.'[43] Because of such differences, 'you've got to try very hard'.[44] She described feeling different and an outsider while in the midst of a community comprising difference and full of outsiders. Her narrative of difficulty in adapting to her new home sits alongside that of a group on Stromlo who faced significant challenges in Australia.

39 Ibid.
40 'Bossiness, abrasiveness, argumentativeness', from anonymous sources—friends of Rosalie.
41 Anonymous source—friend of Rosalie.
42 Bhathal, Sutherland and Butcher, *Mt Stromlo Observatory*.
43 Gascoigne, interview by North, 8.
44 Hughes et al., 'Rosalie Gascoigne Artist', tape 1.

Francis Lord had moved to Stromlo from Sydney because of the suspicion and anger directed at him as an 'enemy alien'.[45] Hans Meyer, Gustav Krentler, Kurt Gottlieb, Ernst Freye, Ernst Fröhlich and Georg Frohlich were German and Austrian Jews who had escaped Nazi tyranny in Europe to Britain only to be rounded up and put on the SS *Dunera* in July 1940 and sent to Australia where they were interned.[46] In his search for staff with precision optical experience, Richard Woolley located these men in internment camps and arranged for their release to Stromlo where their skills were needed.[47] Despite the significant contribution they were making to the war effort, distrust of German and Austrian nationals, even if they were Jewish, meant they were not permitted to travel more than a mile from the observatory.[48]

Life was difficult for these men who had escaped Nazi persecution only to experience severe limitations on their freedom in Australia.[49] However, the men on Stromlo were more fortunate than most of their fellow '*Dunera* boys' who remained in internment camps. Rosalie's experiences, on the other hand, were of a different order. She enjoyed the right to freedom of movement limited only by remoteness and transport availability.

Visual difference: Light, colour, birds

Rosalie's sense of difference may have been grounded in her visual sensitivity. The Monaro's colours, dry landscape, huge skies and big birds amazed her. In 1998, she recalled her first reaction to Stromlo fifty-four years earlier:

45 Born in what is now the Czech Republic, Lord escaped Nazi occupation and made his way to Australia where he worked for the British Optical Co. in Sydney. He was eventually, according to Bhathal, Sutherland and Butcher, dismissed as an 'enemy alien'. Woolley employed him on Stromlo. Bhathal, Sutherland and Butcher, *Mt Stromlo Observatory*, 67.

46 Sherratt, 'A Wartime Observatory Observed'. Another internee, Georg Frohlich, died in Canberra Hospital in 1942; Hans Meyer later formed an optical business in Sydney with Francis Lord; Gus Krentler died accidentally by cyanide poisoning in a Sydney hotel in 1944; Kurt Gottlieb died in 1996, and Ernst Freye, toolmaker, disappeared without trace after the war.

47 It was only after strong representations to UK authorities and the Australian War Cabinet that they were finally released under Woolley's supervision but with restrictions on their movement.

48 Sherratt tells that, on some bicycle rides, they made a point of reaching their foot across the border and touched a toe in New South Wales. Sherratt, 'A Wartime Observatory Observed'.

49 These outsiders were blamed for taking Australian jobs and found themselves under suspicion when flashing lights were reported on Mt Stromlo.

> I remember the first impression I got of Mount Stromlo was the colour actually. It was a different colour scheme from New Zealand and it was all orange roofs and really deep green pine trees and blue sky. And I remember saying to somebody 'the colour, the colour'.[50]

Rosalie found the heat on Stromlo overwhelming: 'The first summer, walking outside the kitchen door … the sun hit you like a hammer … that was a shock, because Auckland isn't like that.'[51] The dry landscape, heavy with dark pines on the mountain, contrasted with Auckland's lush greenness. Everything was different: 'There wasn't much in the way of flowers, really that grew indigenously. There was more in New Zealand than that.'[52] The sky struck her as huge with 'a lot of air'.[53] She said of the birds: 'they were all big and they toppled the branches like the biblical birds … and as for the parrots … it was like living in a zoo for a while'.[54]

The big 'biblical birds' accentuated the difference between Auckland and Stromlo. As New Zealand poet, artist and curator Gregory O'Brien wrote:

> A small child growing up in the Auckland suburb of Remuera in the 1920s would have heard a lot of birdsong: native and exotic, the ample trees of the suburb providing an ideal platform for such a chorus.[55]

Perhaps Stromlo's big, bright, raucous birds crowded out some of the difficulties of Rosalie's early years. It may be that the 'huge sky [and] lots of air' diminished the shame or humiliation she may have felt at her family history.[56] The big skies towered over her past, reducing unpleasant memories to dots on the vast horizon.

A new place enabled her to start afresh, discarding the pain of her broken family and alcoholic father, Elsie's tragic story and Bill Bayly's shameful one. At the very least, she could keep it to herself. Her feeling of difference may now be explained, at least in part, by the silenced stories. The towering skies, vivid colours, hot sun and birds of biblical proportions hushed and shrank Rosalie's family story.

---

50 Feneley and Gascoigne, 'Express Highlights'.
51 Hughes et al., 'Rosalie Gascoigne Artist', tape 2.
52 Feneley and Gascoigne, 'Express Highlights'.
53 Ibid.
54 Ibid.
55 O'Brien, 'Plain Air / Plain Song', 21.
56 'Huge sky and lots of air', in Hughes et al., 'Rosalie Gascoigne Artist', tape 2.

In her sense of isolation and her amazement at the new environment, Rosalie turned to her old friend nature, the constant in her life.[57] She enjoyed a rapport with nature.[58] She used her eyes to make sense of the new land, and began to develop a relationship with the Canberra hinterland—the Monaro—and a sensibility for its great blonde paddocks and colour:

> I was just homeless. And having given away the New Zealand countryside which I was so keen on … it was vital to my [consciousness] that I should be received here by nature which … is my permanent friend in this life.[59]

Gone were the puka (*Meryta sinclairii*, puka or pukanui) and pōhutukawa trees of her childhood, along with the melodious tūī and the plump kererū (wood pigeon), with its flash of iridescent green and whooshing wings. Surrounded by exoticism, Rosalie sought acceptance in the strange land. She began to familiarise herself with the extraordinarily different landscape by intense looking, further honing her visual acuity. In so doing she refined a sensibility that Canberra artists and poets who became her friends in the future would affirm. It would ultimately contribute to the making of her as an artist. Perhaps she knew Rilke's words:

> If you trust in nature, in the small things that hardly anyone sees and that can so suddenly become huge, immeasurable; if you have this love for what is humble and try very simply, as someone who serves, to win the confidence of what seems poor: then everything will become easier for you, more coherent and somehow more reconciling, not in your conscious mind perhaps, which stays behind, astonished, but in your innermost awareness, awakeness, and knowledge.[60]

Rosalie looked to nature and trusted it as Rilke exhorted. She saw those 'small things that hardly anyone sees' and developed a fine sensibility for the landscape. Her relationship with it deepened until she began to make art that expressed her sensibility and feelings for the natural environment around Canberra.

Philosopher Vilém Flusser argued that it is only when we are confronted with the unfamiliar, as Rosalie was with the landscape and the birdlife of the Monaro, that we see clearly. In a familiar environment, Flusser asserted, we

57 Gascoigne, interview by North, 7: 'The constant thing, still with me, was nature.'
58 Hughes et al., 'Rosalie Gascoigne Artist', tape 5: 'I've got a rapport with nature, I always have had it.'
59 Gascoigne, interview by North, 7.
60 Rilke, *Letters to a Young Poet.*

generally only see change, so a migrant is both a mirror and window onto the world.[61] Australian art writers and curators Kelly Gellatly and Deborah Clark both assert that Rosalie made art that enabled Australians to see their country through her fresh eyes.[62] But that was later. In the meantime, her isolation and her husband's absorption with his work freed her to spend time in the countryside and consolidate the love and friendship with nature she began as a child. Both the familiarity with the Monaro landscape and the visual acuity she developed during this time were key in the development of her art.

Pregnancy and motherhood

It was not long before Rosalie was contending with dreadful morning sickness on top of her sense of isolation. Her first pregnancy was difficult. Rosalie remembered she was 'as sick as a dog'.[63] She missed her Auckland friends. Her repetition of the word 'hard' in later interviews about this time hammers home just how difficult she found her first pregnancy: 'It was hard, it was hard … not having friends. This was hard. This was really hard.'[64] Her neighbour Rose Allen, having already had three children, was 'immensely useful to her', but the relationship was not easy.[65] Her debilitating sickness during her whole pregnancy created a sense of failure:

> Having babies is a natural thing, you see, very natural. You just have it. You don't have morning sickness, because you're very, very well, you know, in the seventh month or something, you're walking around very jubilant. And if they've known people who were seven months pregnant, that's how you should be right from the start.[66]

Excluded from the ideal of a blossoming pregnant woman, Rosalie decided at the last moment that she could not stay with the Allens while Ben travelled to Sydney on a work trip. In a fearful bout of loneliness, she determined to

61 Flusser, *The Freedom of the Migrant*, 15.

62 Kelly Gellatly wrote: 'Gascoigne's work helps us to see our surroundings a-new'; Deborah Clark said: 'No other Australian artist has sung a song of the Canberra district as sustained and singular as hers.' See Gellatly, 'Rosalie Gascoigne', 19; Clark, 'Standing on the Mountain', 33.

63 Hughes et al., 'Rosalie Gascoigne Artist', tape 2.

64 Ibid., tape 2.

65 Ibid.

66 Ibid.

go with him. Her misery huddles in Cla Allen's record that his wife 'had gone to some trouble getting ready for Rosalie here, but she wasn't a cheerful visitor this afternoon and it was as well she went off to Sydney'.[67]

On Friday 19 November 1943, her labour began and Rosalie travelled to the brand new Canberra Community Hospital on Acton Peninsula where she laboured for three days before her baby was born. Allen records waiting the three long days for news until finally word arrived on Sunday teatime that a boy had been born.[68] The following lunchtime Ben visited the Allens for lunch and announced that the baby was to be called Martin.[69]

All was not well with the new baby. While the rest of the Stromlo community were relaxing at one of their regular summer Sunday picnics at the Cotter Dam, news arrived that the Gascoignes had taken Martin to Sydney by train to be operated on for projectile vomiting.[70] Physically and emotionally ravaged by an arduous pregnancy followed by a long and difficult childbirth, Rosalie was plunged into one of the most vulnerable times in her life. Far from the home she had left less than a year earlier, she lacked the comfort of old friends and her mother. Rosalie felt alone and unsupported by 'hideous' Canberra hospital staff, and fearful for her new baby:

> He had pyloric stenosis, which just means you vomit … I had a hideous doctor and a hideous matron. And it took me three days to have the baby. And immediately I sat up in my hospital bed, 'You've got to take this baby to Sydney, he's got something wrong with it' … I had to go down by train.[71]

The Stromlo community rallied around the Gascoignes. One source suggests Stromlo technician Unity Cunningham, goddaughter of former attorney-general Sir Robert Garran, who had befriended Rosalie, travelled with her to Sydney.[72]

---

67 Allen, 'Diaries', 6 April 1943, vol. 18, Papers of Clabon Walter Allan, box 2.

68 Allen, 'Diaries', 21 November 1943, vol. 19, Papers of Clabon Walter Allan, box 2.

69 Allen, 'Diaries', 24 November 1943, vol. 19, Papers of Clabon Walter Allan, box 2.

70 Allen, 'Diaries', 5 December 1943, vol. 19, Papers of Clabon Walter Allan, box 2. The Cotter Dam, a concrete gravity dam opened in 1912 for the new federal capital, was a favourite picnic spot with a swimming hole.

71 Hughes et al., 'Rosalie Gascoigne Artist', tape 2.

72 A tribute written for Unity's funeral in 1945 by her godfather, former attorney-general Sir Robert Garran, records that 'Rosalie found in Unity Cunningham an intelligent and congenial companion; more than that, she became a dear friend of the family'. See Papers of Rosalie Gascoigne, box 3.

Whatever material support was provided, Martin's period in hospital preceded acknowledgment of the emotional needs of children and their parents, particularly the condition now known as 'separation anxiety', that can occur in children separated from their parents for any length of time.[73] Hospitals limited visiting hours, meaning parents could spend only brief periods each day with their sick child. In the year of Martin's birth and hospitalisation, UK psychiatrist Harry Edelston attempted to draw attention to the risk of psychological damage caused by 'hospitalisation trauma' but met with fierce resistance from his colleagues. It was years before the situation improved for hospitalised children and their parents.[74] At the time of Martin's admission to hospital, Rosalie had been in Australia only eleven months. She lacked the support of family and long-term friends. As if that were not difficult enough, Martin's hospitalisation in Sydney meant not only was she parted from her tiny baby, but also from her new husband. Ben's work commitments meant he could spend little time in Sydney with Rosalie. Martin languished in the Sydney hospital. Rosalie was permitted to visit only briefly at prescribed times. Fifty-five years later, Rosalie remembered the trauma:

> It was really very traumatic. And in the end they operated, because they had to. And he survived it, you see. So that was okay. But … I grew older in those years I can tell you.[75]

Thankfully, Marion Walker was able to take leave from her teaching job at Epsom Girls' Grammar School in Auckland. She joined her daughter in Sydney to provide her with company and support.[76] Rosalie, her mother and baby Martin finally arrived back on Stromlo on Wednesday 2 February 1944 (see Figure 5.11).[77] Whatever the comfort of that return, the challenges of the preceding year were immense, entrenching further a personality wrestling with dislocation and a self-narrative adding the dimensions of wife, misfit and mother.

73 Hendrick, 'Children's Emotional Well-Being', 213.

74 Ibid., 215.

75 Hughes et al., 'Rosalie Gascoigne Artist', tape 2.

76 Headmistress's Report, *Te Korero,* 1944, Epsom Girls' Grammar School.

77 Allen, 'Diaries', 2 February 1944, vol. 19, Papers of Clabon Walter Allan, box 2.

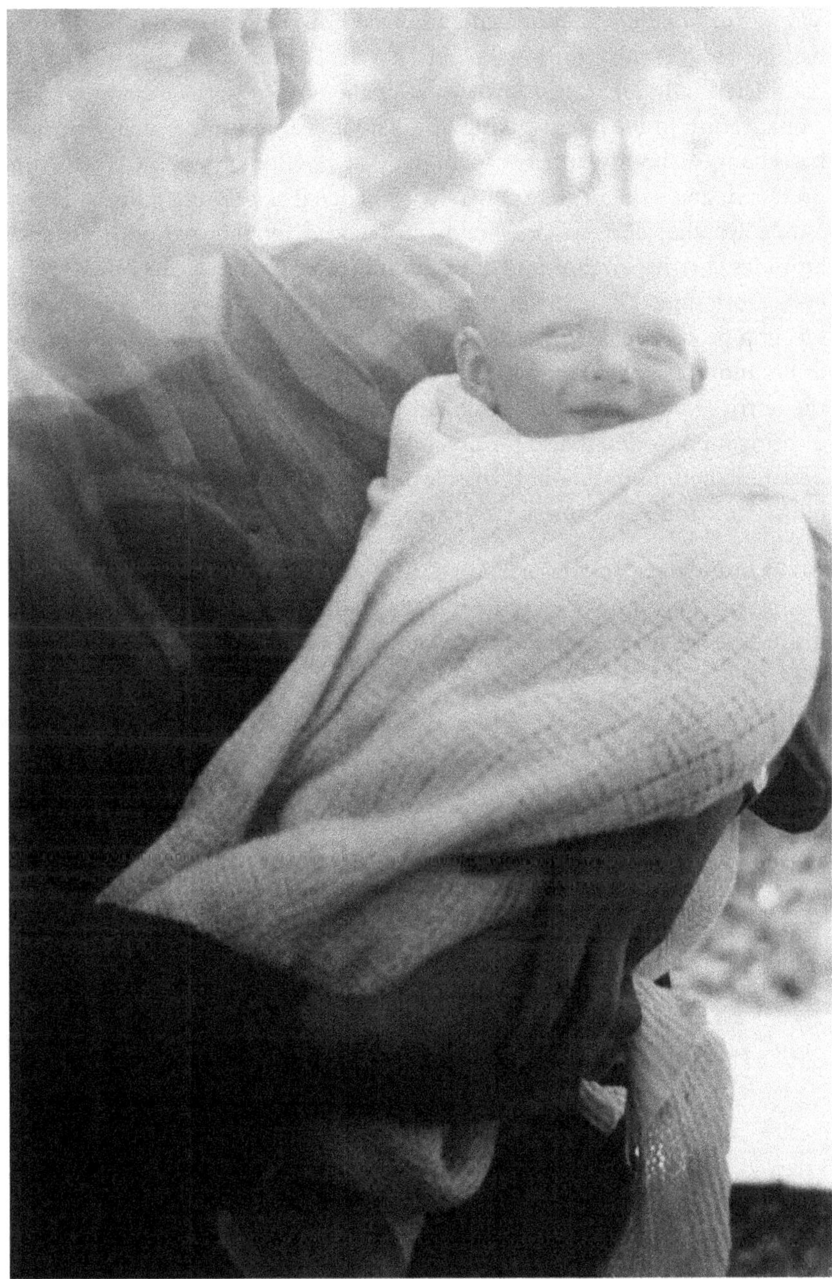

Figure 5.11: Home again. Rosalie with baby Martin back on Mt Stromlo, February 1944.

Source: Courtesy of the Gascoigne family.

Women of Rosalie's class and generation were on the cusp of change. Women had gained visibility during World War II as they filled jobs previously considered only for men. However, after the war, it was assumed that they would return to the home, giving up such jobs for returning men. Attitudes had changed about women's capability; yet, a period of social conservatism prevailed, and women were generally considered as belonging in the home. While Rosalie's life was inevitably influenced by this pattern and such attitudes, her experience and understanding of women's capabilities were even more direct and personal. Not only had she known independence as a young professional woman, but she also had a highly unusual role model in her mother as the family breadwinner. While this put her family outside the norm of New Zealand families and probably contributed to her feeling of being an outsider, it also meant she had firsthand experience of women's potential, compounding her frustration with the domestic requirements of housework and being the shadow behind the man.[78]

At the same time, Rosalie's acclimatisation to her new physical environment was adding crucial elements to the sensibility that would later frame her distinctive eye for the world and its tangle of objects and relationships.

78 Hughes et al., 'Rosalie Gascoigne Artist', tape 8.

6

1944–49: 'You had to make a life out of nothing'

Rosalie arrived home from the hospital in Sydney with baby Martin on 2 February. Her mother stayed to help until late June.[1] Rosalie gave birth to Thomas ('Toss') in 1945, and Hester in 1949.

With three young children, the domestic tasks she so disliked consumed her time. Her life was 'taken up with the fuel stove. Chopping the firewood … What the children can wear. If they're cutting teeth.'[2] Just as she had disliked teaching because she felt totally incompetent, her narrative of this time reveals how much she disliked housework. In 1995, she told Helen Topliss that she was 'a failed housekeeper, absolutely terrible' and 'bored to screams'.[3] In the same way that she compared herself unfavourably to her sister Daintry during childhood, she critically compared herself with the other Stromlo women in relation to household skills: unlike them, she was 'not a born housewife'.[4] Her feelings compounded her isolation. She told Hughes: 'I was cursed with the fact that I was different.'[5]

1 Allen, 'Diaries', 23 June 1944, vol. 19, Papers of Clabon Walter Allan, box 2: 'Mrs Walker and Ben had gone off to Sydney—however Mrs Walker cannot go on her plane and will be returning.'

2 Gascoigne, interview by North, 9.

3 Gascoigne, interview by Topliss, 32.

4 Hughes et al., 'Rosalie Gascoigne Artist', tape 1.

5 Ibid.

Rosalie continued to feel excluded from what she described to North in 1982 as the 'club' of observatory employees.[6] She used her eyes to make the Canberra hinterland her home. She occupied the area with her body—walking across it and around it with her young children, familiarising herself with the land and the grasses and stones and everything that grew or lived or lay on it. She made games for the children out of stones and puddles:

> My afternoons used to be taken up with pushing a pram and one [child] in the hand, and the neighbour's child with me. We'd walk along to the Oddie, which was the telescope there, and there'd be a big mud puddle. Okay, everybody can throw three stones into the big mud puddle, and then we can go home and [have] afternoon tea, which is biscuits with cheese and tomato.[7]

While Ben looked at the stars Rosalie looked across to the horizon and at the ground (see Figure 6.1). She searched longingly for the familiar:

> I used to stand on the top of the hill and look out and [think] surely I'll see Rangitoto … the island in Auckland harbour … there was no sea, [there was] nothing.[8]

Ben was often away. In 1944, he was involved in moving the Commonwealth Time Service from Melbourne to Stromlo, necessitating long periods interstate when Martin was tiny. For Rosalie, this meant: 'You had to make a life out of nothing.' This became her enduring philosophy.[9] As she told Topliss: 'You had to make a life, if you were my persuasion, out of more or less nothing, you sort of boy scouted it up and it's been … the basis of my art.'[10]

Significantly, in that scouting, Rosalie gravitated towards a group of other displaced people on the mountain. The 'bachelor establishment', she recalled, 'really saved my life'.[11] She was referring to the single men living in the bachelor's quarters, mainly professional and technical staff employed at the observatory, many of whom were European refugees (see Chapter 5). She described her interactions with the bachelors as 'good works', suggesting she could and should reach out to these lonely men.

6 Gascoigne, interview by North, 8.
7 Hughes et al., 'Rosalie Gascoigne Artist', tape 2.
8 Ibid., tape 1.
9 Ibid., tape 2.
10 Gascoigne, interview by Topliss, 2.
11 Hughes et al., 'Rosalie Gascoigne Artist', tape 2.

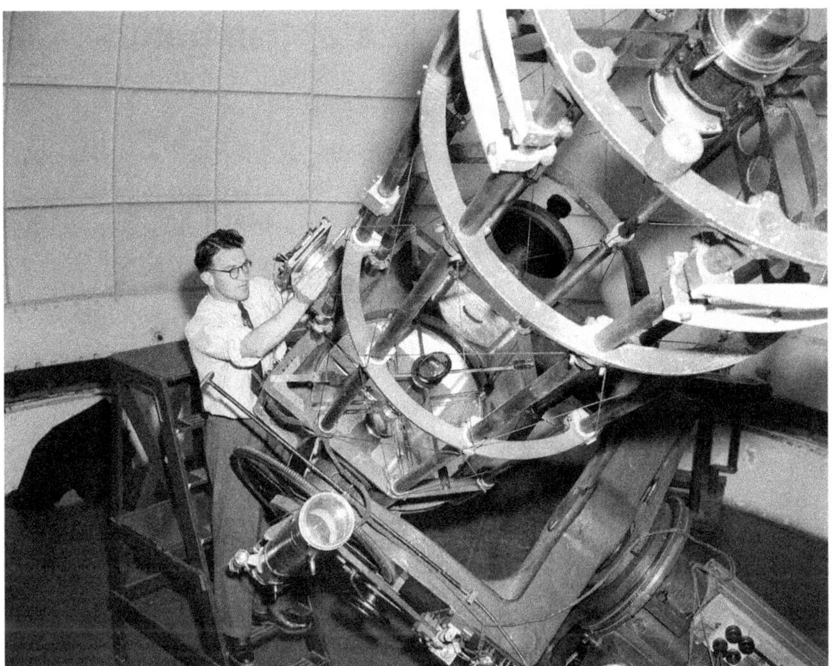

Figure 6.1: Ben at work, Mount Stromlo Observatory, 1948.

Note: Rosalie said: 'He was an astronomer. Astronomy comes first.'[12]

Source: Courtesy of the National Archives of Australia, 11895377. Photograph: F. Fisher.

Rosalie's mountain community was rich with people from all over the world and other parts of Australia. Such was the influx of new Australians to the Canberra region during and after World War II that, by 1949, the general store J. B. Young had installed an interpreter with seven languages for Saturday morning trading.[13] On Stromlo, such diversity was marked, as can be glimpsed in the diary of Ernst Fröhlich, a German Jewish refugee who lived on the mountain at the same time. Like Ben and Rosalie, Fröhlich arrived there as a result of war, although in dramatically different circumstances. Fröhlich was one of the bachelors who Rosalie said made a difference to her on Stromlo.

12 Hughes et al., 'Rosalie Gascoigne Artist', tape 2.

13 Jim Gibbney, *Canberra 1913–1953*, 239. It is not clear from Gibbney's text whether the interpreter worked at J. B. Young's Civic or Kingston shop.

'There was a bachelor establishment which really saved my life'

War had taken Ben and Rosalie to Stromlo. It provided a backdrop to Rosalie's first years there, as it did to many of the so-called bachelors. Rosalie seldom spoke of World War II, but she did so in 1982 when she indicated to Ian North that she had felt fortunate to be in a relatively safe place:

> Oh well, at least you weren't being shot at … This is war time and you were damn lucky that you had … a house and nobody was shooting at you … there's the Japanese coming down to Darwin … we were a wonderful target [on] Stromlo … And Canberra … They could have got the 8,000 [people in Canberra] in one fell swoop.[14]

Here we see Rosalie putting a positive spin on her situation, while also reliving wartime fears, when at the time she felt homesick, isolated and lonely. Perhaps she recalled conversations with the bachelors who had fled Nazi tyranny in Europe. Perhaps she was thinking of her brother Douglas who served with the New Zealand Army in the Pacific during those years. Strangely, Rosalie made no mention of Douglas's wartime service in interviews, suggesting that she may have been disconnected from her brother's experience. It is also possible that, because Douglas had taken his own life by then, Rosalie chose not to talk about him out of sadness or discretionary shame, given the unfortunate stigma often associated with suicide.

The war was ever-present on Stromlo, where the work was devoted to manufacturing optical munitions like gun sights and artillery directors for Australian troops.[15] Cla Allen's diaries provide glimpses into his worries and possibly those of others in the Stromlo community. For example, on 6 June 1944, Allen noted that the Allied entry into Rome had been overshadowed by news of the Allied landings in Normandy: 'Apparently the invasion has started.'[16] The following day he expressed anxiety as people waited for reports of the Normandy invasion.[17] It is not difficult to imagine

14 Gascoigne, interview by North, 9.

15 Bhathal, Sutherland and Butcher, *Mt Stromlo Observatory*, 64.

16 Allen, 'Diaries', 6 June 1944, vol. 19, Papers of Clabon Walter Allan, box 2: 'Yesterday came the news of the Allied entry into Rome but this was overshadowed today by news of the Allied Landings in Normandie [*sic*]. Apparently the invasion has started.'

17 Allen, 'Diaries', 7 June 1944, vol. 19, Papers of Clabon Walter Allan, box 2. 'There was some anxiety during the day for the first progress reports of the invasion—the landings seem to have been established.'

the internee bachelors anxiously awaiting news of the situation in their European homelands. Francis Lord, Hans Meyer, Gustav Krentler, Kurt Gottlieb, Ernst Freye and Ernst Fröhlich all had family and friends back in Europe for whom they feared. However, Rosalie made no reference to discussing the war in Europe with them.

She gave two reasons for the bachelors' importance to her. One was that they provided her with the intellectual stimulation and variety of friends she was accustomed to in Auckland.[18] The other, possibly more significant reason, was that the bachelors fulfilled a need in her to do what she called 'good works', pointing to less articulated aspects of her sense of self and role in the early Stromlo years when she was confronted with existential questions about her identity and purpose in life.

Her narrative suggests that she was willing to offer hospitality and a friendly ear to the bachelors:

> the bachelors … were all rattling round in the big bachelor quarters on the top of the hill [see Figure 6.2]. They had no womenfolk. A lot of them were homeless from Europe … and they used to come wandering down the hill, and you'd be doing the garden … they wanted a cup of tea and a bit of conversation, so you'd say 'Come on, we'll make a cup of tea.'[19]

Her reference to the bachelors' homelessness spotlights two issues in her relationship with them: the difference between her and them, and her own sense of homelessness in the new environment. Just as she described the bachelors as homeless, Rosalie told North she felt homeless in her early Stromlo years.[20] Paradoxically, her sense of similarity through shared homelessness reinforces the differences between her and them. In contrast to the bachelors, Rosalie not only had a home with her husband and children, but also, being a New Zealander, she was 'at home' insofar as she was a British subject living within the British Empire and speaking her native language.

18 Hughes et al., 'Rosalie Gascoigne Artist', tape 2.

19 Ibid., tape 2.

20 Gascoigne, interview by North, 8.

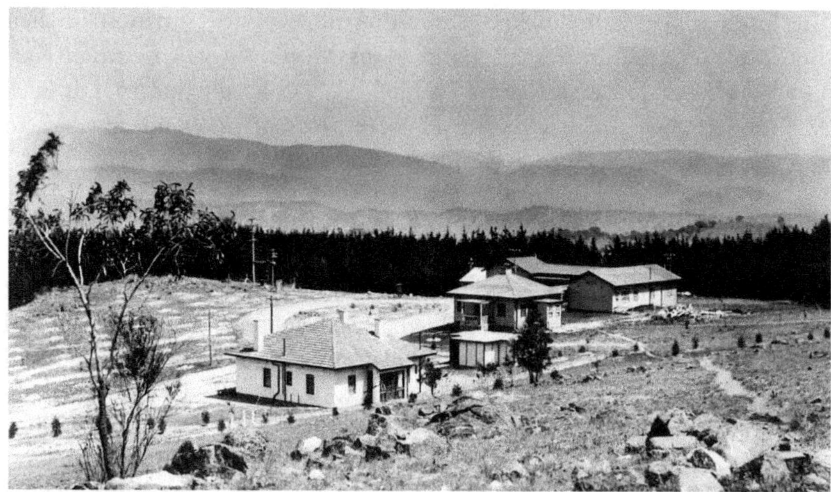

Figure 6.2: New residences and bachelor quarters, Mt Stromlo, 1944.
Source: Mt Stromlo Archives.[21]

Once again, the retrospective nature of her narrative means we do not know her feelings at the time, but it appears she used the bachelors as a framing device for her own sense of displacement. Rosalie was, of course, being interviewed about herself because, as a successful artist, people were interested in her. It is only natural that she would focus on herself and attempt to portray a sense of who she was through distinguishing herself from others. Nonetheless, she used people as framing devices with little apparent empathy. Just as the bachelors had no voice or right of reply when she told her self-narrative, neither did her family members in her stories of childhood, nor the other Stromlo women during the period this chapter covers. Her self-narrative evokes a deepening sense of a woman who, once she achieved recognition and affirmation as a result of her artistic success, felt sufficiently free and confident to use others in the same way she used her materials to construct something that pleased her, in this case her self-narrative.

She may also have been drawn to the bachelors by echoes of her father—the allure of the lonely man separated from his family, perhaps stirred by memories of the years Stanley was cast out. Whatever the reason, interacting with the bachelors gave her a purpose. It was a simple thing but the kindness and hospitality she showed them reflects her mother's generosity during the Great Depression, when Rosalie and her siblings were instructed to give two

21 See The Australian National University, 'A Home on the Hill'.

shillings and as much tea and bread and butter as they could consume to the exhausted, unemployed men who knocked on the door at Halls Avenue seeking work.[22] This fits with her characterisation of her relationship with the bachelors as 'good works':

> I used to be terribly good on good works … it seemed to be … the place where you did something that was needed … You were really … needed … And it was about one of the things you could do. That's the terrible fate if you get to doing good works with your life.[23]

Despite her opinion that doing good works was a terrible fate, she told Hughes in 1998 that she enjoyed it: 'Oh I did, I needed to do it, but it wasn't fulfilling like art is to me.'[24]

Rosalie's fulfilment from art lay in the distant future, but, importantly, her reference to art reminds us that her self-narrative was retrospective—she looked back on the past from the 1990s. As she did so, links, roles, attractions and connections emerged and shaped her story. She was likely drawn to similarities or parallels, such as the one between her outcast father and the solitary bachelors, although she did not appear to consciously make this connection, or at least never talked about it. These connections are as important as the memories themselves. She recalled her own lack of agency and absence of role outside the home in contrast with the 'club' of observatory staff. Rosalie's attraction to nature bridged these times with her girlhood despite the differences in the physical worlds of Auckland and the Canberra hinterland. She was disappointed in the lack of community she found among the women, perhaps seeking something similar to that she had known in Auckland with her old friends and the relationship she formed in adulthood with her mother.

Ernst Fröhlich: 'Enemy alien' and likely kindred spirit

One of the bachelors, Ernst Fröhlich, kept a diary that echoes much of Rosalie's later reminiscences. He was one of around two thousand male German and Austrian Jewish refugees, aged between sixteen and forty-five,

22 Hughes et al., 'Rosalie Gascoigne Artist', tape 1.
23 Ibid.
24 Ibid., tape 2.

who had escaped from the terror of Nazi-occupied Europe only to be arrested as enemy aliens in Britain and shipped in dire conditions on the *Dunera* to Australia for internment in an arrangement between the British and Australian governments.[25]

Fröhlich's diary, now in the National Library of Australia, covers the period from December 1940 to December 1941.[26] From his arrival in Australia until August 1941, Fröhlich was confined in internment camps at Hay, New South Wales, and then Tatura in regional Victoria. From 14 August 1941, his diary covers his arrival and first four months at Stromlo. Rosalie did not arrive on Stromlo until January 1943 so we can only wonder about conversations they may have had. There is no doubt that the two would have met in the small Stromlo community and that Fröhlich was probably one of the bachelors who wandered down the hill to Residence 19, looking for a cup of tea and conversation.

Fröhlich penned his desperation at the Hay internment camp: 'real life stopped at the moment when we were interned'.[27] On the train journey from the *Dunera* in Sydney to the internment camp, he commented on the kangaroos and 'many other exotic animals [and] trees'.[28] Like Rosalie, who said 'the sun hit you like a hammer', he was shocked by the extremes of climate: 'extremely hot in summer and bitterly cold in winter … Hot wind which made one feel it would burn one's hair.'[29] Unlike Rosalie, who was free to go wherever she liked, limited only by distance, transport availability and petrol rationing, Fröhlich, although fortunate to have been released to work at the observatory, had severe restrictions on his movements.

Fröhlich had decided to use his time in the internment camps to continue learning: 'even if I were kept here for years I would not have wasted my time but would have gathered strength for the struggle in real life.'[30] Like Rosalie did later with art, Fröhlich taught himself optics, remarkably, from a book in the Hay camp library and others sent by family friends from Europe.[31]

25 See Pearl, *The Dunera Scandal*; Lewin, *The Dunera Boys*; Patkin, *The Dunera Internees*; Neuman and National Archives of Australia, *In the Interest of National Security*. It was initially regarded as scandalous that the '*Dunera* boys', mainly professionals fleeing for their lives, were shipped to Australia. They were eventually given the option to return to Britain; however, nine hundred, including Fröhlich, decided to remain in Australia where they made major contributions to cultural and intellectual life.

26 Fröhlich, 'Diary of Ernst Fröhlich'.

27 Fröhlich, 'Diary of Ernst Fröhlich', 27 December 1940.

28 Ibid.

29 Ibid.; Hughes et al., 'Rosalie Gascoigne Artist', tape 1: 'The sun hit you like a hammer'.

30 Fröhlich, 'Diary of Ernst Fröhlich', 13 January 1941.

31 Ibid., 18 January 1941, 7 February 1941.

He then wrote to Richard Woolley, director of the Stromlo Observatory, who set him an exam to test his knowledge. Impressed by his grasp of the subject, Woolley gained Fröhlich's release for work at Stromlo.[32] Fröhlich recreated himself as an optics specialist and later as an engineer and physics teacher. As Rosalie changed her name by marriage, Fröhlich anglicised his from Ernst Friedrich Fröhlich to Ernest Frederick Frohlich; and, just as Fröhlich struggled in the camps with low moods, as did many of the internees, and had to persuade himself to exercise and wash each day and to continue learning, Rosalie also grappled with feelings of loneliness and isolation.

Despite anger at his treatment in the camps and on the journey to Stromlo, and at the plight of internees still in the camps, and despite mourning the absence of women and comfort, and his continued lack of freedom, Fröhlich was able to write: 'I sit in the safest possible place on earth and earn nearly a quid a day.'[33] Similarly, Rosalie was able to say: 'oh well, at least you weren't being shot at.'[34] Both saw positive aspects of their situations while they struggled with new identities. Fröhlich's diary includes almost daily reports of the war in Europe, a pressing subject for him because his family and friends were in the thick of it. Fröhlich and Rosalie decided in their respective situations that they would make the most of their lives where they found themselves.

Rosalie recalled for Hughes the emptiness and the isolation and her decision to get used to it:

> Oh, you were just plain isolated. I remember returning from New Zealand once … and standing on the hillside and the air—I remember the air hanging from the heights of heaven down to the earth. Such a lot of air … I remember saying to myself, well nothing's going to happen and you might as well get used to it.[35]

32 Ibid. Fröhlich travelled to Stromlo on 14 August 1941 with a police escort all the way: 'I hated it. Police all over the world are alike. At Canberra one policeman asked me whether I was a member of the Hitler Youth. What do you say to that? I still don't feel like a free man.' Fröhlich was one of the first *Dunera* internees to be released in Australia.

33 Ibid., 21 August 1941, but 'no women, no comfort, no freedom'.

34 Gascoigne, interview by North, 9.

35 Hughes et al., 'Rosalie Gascoigne Artist', tape 2.

Her words are pragmatic and without self-pity. As if she knew this was an artist's lot, she made the isolation work for her. Rosalie expressed frustration at the lack of educated women for company. Likewise, in Hay, Fröhlich bemoaned the fact that 'the people [in Hut 3] are terribly uneducated and common in their way of talk'.[36]

Although Fröhlich's experience was magnified many times in relation to Rosalie's, they were likely kindred spirits; however, accepted social norms around male and female interactions may have made friendship difficult, especially in the small Stromlo community. Did they sit opposite each other at the pine table purchased at Hordern's and drink tea from her favourite floral bone china teacups while discussing their respective experiences of displacement? Did the walls of Residence 19 melt away as they recalled their home countries, family, old friends, and the differences in flora, fauna and climate?

Another European Jew displaced by war, philosopher Vilém Flusser, asserted that the dislocation and loss associated with migration stimulates creativity. Flusser argued that we notice only change in our familiar surroundings, whereas in a new place we see things in sharp focus. This fresh focus stimulates creativity.[37] Rosalie's habit of looking at her environment in an attempt to situate herself in the new landscape, together with the shock of the difference between Auckland and the Monaro, stimulated her visual acuity. The dramatic change in surroundings was just one of the changes she was forced to cope with.

'I was bored to screams'

When Hughes asked how she passed her time during this period, Rosalie responded bleakly:

> Ah, the washing. The clothes-line up on the windy hill. Stoking the fire … Meals. All that sort of stuff. I didn't do anything really. There wasn't time. There was exhaustion at the end of the day. And there wasn't much offering … the only meeting place on the mountain was up at the observatory.[38]

36 Fröhlich, 'Diary of Ernst Fröhlich', Saturday 1 March 1941.

37 Flusser, 'Exile and Creativity', 81–7.

38 Hughes et al., 'Rosalie Gascoigne Artist', tape 2.

Rosalie would walk up to the office in the hope of either mail or a friendly chat:

> You'd see some of those glamorous people who worked. People smiled at them in corridors. I used to say to my husband, 'You don't know what it's like in a house all day, with nobody'. It was real loneliness.[39]

Rosalie had been used to a busy teaching job with chats in the staffroom during breaks and greetings in the corridors. While the men resident on Stromlo worked up at the observatory 'the women all hung around in the houses. And … friendships came and went.'[40]

She described the Stromlo women as 'the housewives, the entrenched people … mostly assorted'.[41] Her narrative gives the impression that she had little insight into their lives or struggles; yet, at other times, she demonstrated solidarity and compassion. On several occasions she acknowledged that she was not alone in her loneliness. While voicing her outsider refrain later, in a 1962 radio talk she acknowledged that other women struggled with small community life:

> From time to time there were women who thought the solution to the problem was to withdraw to their ivory castles and neither see nor be seen. This never worked. They got melancholy and temporarily rather queer, and eventually returned to the fold.[42]

Again, in 1997 she told Hughes: 'everybody got lonely, and everybody was missing their families'.[43] She said you had to be strong to survive; one woman left because she was about to have a nervous breakdown and another woman 'went a bit peculiar'.[44] While claiming she was different from the other women and suffered because of the difference, she acknowledged that other women were challenged by life on Stromlo, too.

However, maintaining her narrative of resilience, Rosalie was always an observer rather than a participant. With a touch of superiority, she asserted her strength of character in comparison to others who succumbed to melancholy. We are left in no doubt of Rosalie's strength. She tells a story of her survival in contrast to other women who gave up. There was much to

39 Ibid.
40 MacDonald and Gascoigne, *Rosalie Gascoigne*, 14.
41 Hughes et al., 'Rosalie Gascoigne Artist', tape 2.
42 Gascoigne, 'Too Many Pine Trees'.
43 Hughes et al., 'Rosalie Gascoigne Artist', tape 2.
44 Ibid.

challenge them. In the small community, feuds developed over such things as children's tricycles 'so then the mothers fall out … because their horrible child has done something to your dear little thing. And then the men fall out.'[45] She did not reveal details of feuds in which she was involved; Rosalie maintained her observer status.

She admitted to Hughes that she could be difficult: 'I don't agree with people a lot … I don't want to do what other people want to do.'[46] She emphasised her difference. Teaching in Auckland had confronted her with the reality that she 'was starting to diverge absolutely, terribly, out of the practical, logical world into this other world'.[47] Her move to Stromlo further eroded her sense of who she was: 'I didn't know what I was. I just knew I was out of step and always looking.'[48] But she nursed a profound need to be liked by the other Stromlo women. In her interview with Hughes in 1998, she smiled then laughed while talking about this need, as if embarrassed to admit it: 'you really want them to like you. You want someone to like you, goodness knows.'[49] Rosalie wanted to fit in and she tried to find ways of doing so:

> you go on trying to establish yourself in a foreign place where people are conditioned differently and I didn't feel that I fitted in terribly well. And I found that I liked things that other people didn't like and I always felt that I was slightly out of step, but I tried hard because one needs to be popular, you see.[50]

It was not that people were not interested in her. In 1962, she told her ABC radio listeners:

> One woman found that my arrival on the mountain provided her with a badly needed new interest in life. This lady was in my house twice a day, thrice a day. Her gate would click loudly and there she would be … bursting into the kitchen and even down the passage if I wasn't immediately on the spot.[51]

45 Ibid.
46 Ibid., tape 8.
47 Gascoigne, interview by North, 5.
48 Ibid.
49 Hughes et al., 'Rosalie Gascoigne Artist', tape 8.
50 Feneley and Gascoigne, 'Express Highlights'.
51 Gascoigne, 'Too Many Pine Trees'.

The image of her neighbour's intense loneliness, and Rosalie's own, grows as Rosalie continues the story:

> She would sit limp in a chair pouring out a vigorous account of what the baby ate and what her husband ate and what he said and did and what the neighbours said and did.[52]

Rosalie knitted while the neighbour talked. Making something was perhaps a compensation for the tedium—a place of retreat.

She longed for good conversation, 'just for something that wasn't about sweeping the clinkers out of the stove, what washing powder you used'.[53] Her descriptions of the community give the impression she was the only educated woman among the Stromlo wives, but there were others. Dr Priscilla Fairfield Bok (1896–1975), wife of Bart Bok, Stromlo's director from 1957 to 1966, was herself an astronomer with a PhD from the University of California, Berkeley, who had taught at distinguished US colleges (Smith, Wellesley and Connecticut). From 1957 to 1960, US author and historian Miriam Phillips Dunham (1899–1990), a graduate of Radcliffe College and author of children's books on astronomy, lived on Stromlo with her astronomer husband Theodore Dunham.[54] Admittedly, Bok and Dunham arrived on Stromlo fourteen years later than Rosalie, but Rosalie did not differentiate between her years on Stromlo, creating the impression that she felt isolated for the whole seventeen years.

Another highly educated woman, Royal Buscombe, moved to Stromlo from Canada in 1952 with her astronomer husband Bill Buscombe. Royal had an undergraduate degree from the University of Toronto and a master's degree from Bryn Mawr College, Pennsylvania.[55] In 1992, after Rosalie's death, Royal wrote a letter of condolence to Ben, which makes it clear that she and Rosalie had some contact, as one would expect in such a small community. In contradiction of the condescending impression Rosalie gave in her narrative, Royal referred to Rosalie's kindness during her own struggle adjusting to life on the mountain: 'She [Rosalie] was a nice person, very kind to me when we first came to Stromlo and I was having a hard time

52 Ibid.
53 Hughes et al., 'Rosalie Gascoigne Artist', tape 2.
54 Helen Bailey Bayly, email to author, 26 August 2014. Bayly was a part-time student working on Mt Stromlo from 1956 to 1960. 'First she was an assistant to Dr. Ben Gascoigne, then for Professor Bart Bok, and also with Dr Alex Rodgers'. See 'Helen Bailey Bayly's Photo Album', specifically www.mso.anu.edu.au/gallery3/index.php/search?album=59&q=Dunham.
55 'Royal Buscombe Obituary', *Chicago Tribune*, 3 June 2012.

adjusting.'[56] A keen archaeologist, Royal was also a collector of baskets, jewellery and tapa cloth from Pacific societies.[57] It would be expected that there was potential for friendship between the two women, but from this distance in time we can have no idea about the chemistry between them. What we do know is that Rosalie was not alone in her struggle. From Buscombe's reference to Rosalie's kindness, it is possible to adduce that, by 1952, Rosalie had settled better and was able to reach out to newcomers, easing their path as she would have liked to have it done for her in the early years. But she did not mention Royal in her self-narrative. Perhaps because to do so would have disrupted her outsider narrative. The women she mentioned are those who rejected her in some way and so upheld her outsider status. She accentuated her disengagement from people in her narrative, preferring instead to highlight her connection with nature.

Both Rosalie and Royal were part of one successful community venture—a sewing circle, in which they found solace and companionship. The women met at each other's houses fortnightly in the evenings: 'Supper, by law, was … tea and biscuits' to avoid meetings becoming yet another domestic burden and ensure the focus remained companionship while undertaking mending chores.[58] In her 1962 radio talk, Rosalie described its success:

> Everyone had her house warmed in turn. Just seeing each other in a group sweetened relationships—a fact that is probably ABC to a psychologist but which was a profound and hard-won truth to us.[59]

In her condolence letter to Ben, Royal recalled the sewing circle:

> … and especially the one when Rosalie told Jean Abraham to just 'cobble it up' as she mended one of Harry's shirts and the 'cobble' turned out to be on the most visible side![60]

Rosalie's later friend, poet Rosemary Dobson, described how 'Rosalie sometimes railed against trivial domesticities.'[61] It is easy to imagine Rosalie, with her total lack of gravitas for domestic matters, frivolously

56 Royal Buscombe to Ben Gascoigne, 2 November 1999, Papers of Ben Gascoigne, box 3.
57 Royal Buscombe, 'Royal Buscombe Collection'.
58 Gascoigne, 'Too Many Pine Trees'.
59 Ibid.
60 Royal Buscombe to Ben Gascoigne, 2 November 1999.
61 Rosemary Dobson, 'Rosalie Gascoigne 1917–1999: A Memoir', Papers of Rosalie Gascoigne, box 1.

tossing off the advice in the relief and lightness of the moment, and the women being so engrossed in 'talking their heads off' that Jean did not notice she was working on the wrong side of the shirt!

Royal's story illustrates in small part that Rosalie's life was not without fun and friendship, contrary to the impression she sometimes gave in her narrative. The sewing circle yielded companionship and laughter while completing practical tasks, if not always efficiently.

Assembling a story

Rosalie made two visits to her parents and friends in Auckland during the period covered in this chapter, 1944–49 (see Figures 6.3 and 6.4). During these years, she characterised herself by differentiation from others: for example, the other women on Stromlo liked housework, she did not; one neighbour did not read books, whereas she enjoyed reading. Her descriptions of the Stromlo women were, at times, disdainful, yet we get no real understanding of them. Rosalie provided glimpses of their loneliness and struggles in the small community. The women were useful narrative devices that enabled Rosalie to differentiate and define who she was. Where some of them did not survive the small, isolated community, Rosalie did because, in the end, the solitude suited her. It allowed her to build on the visual awareness that she developed as a child. A photograph that exists online, although not available to use in this study, shows Rosalie sitting in the Stromlo library with Dr Priscilla Bok sometime between 1957 and 1960.[62] The two women sit side-by-side in between tall shelves of books, apparently relaxed in each other's company. The caption notes that they helped catalogue studies of the southern skies in Mt Stromlo's library.

Rosalie told few positive stories of relationships on Stromlo. To do otherwise would have weakened the picture she created of bleak, isolated loneliness where nature was her only friend. While there is no doubt that Rosalie's early Stromlo years challenged her to the core of her being, she did enjoy light moments and some connection with others.

62 The photograph is located in 'Helen Bailey Bayly's Photo Album'. I was unable to get permission to use the photograph, which can be found here: www.mso.anu.edu.au/gallery3/index.php/before2003/helen_bailey?page=3.

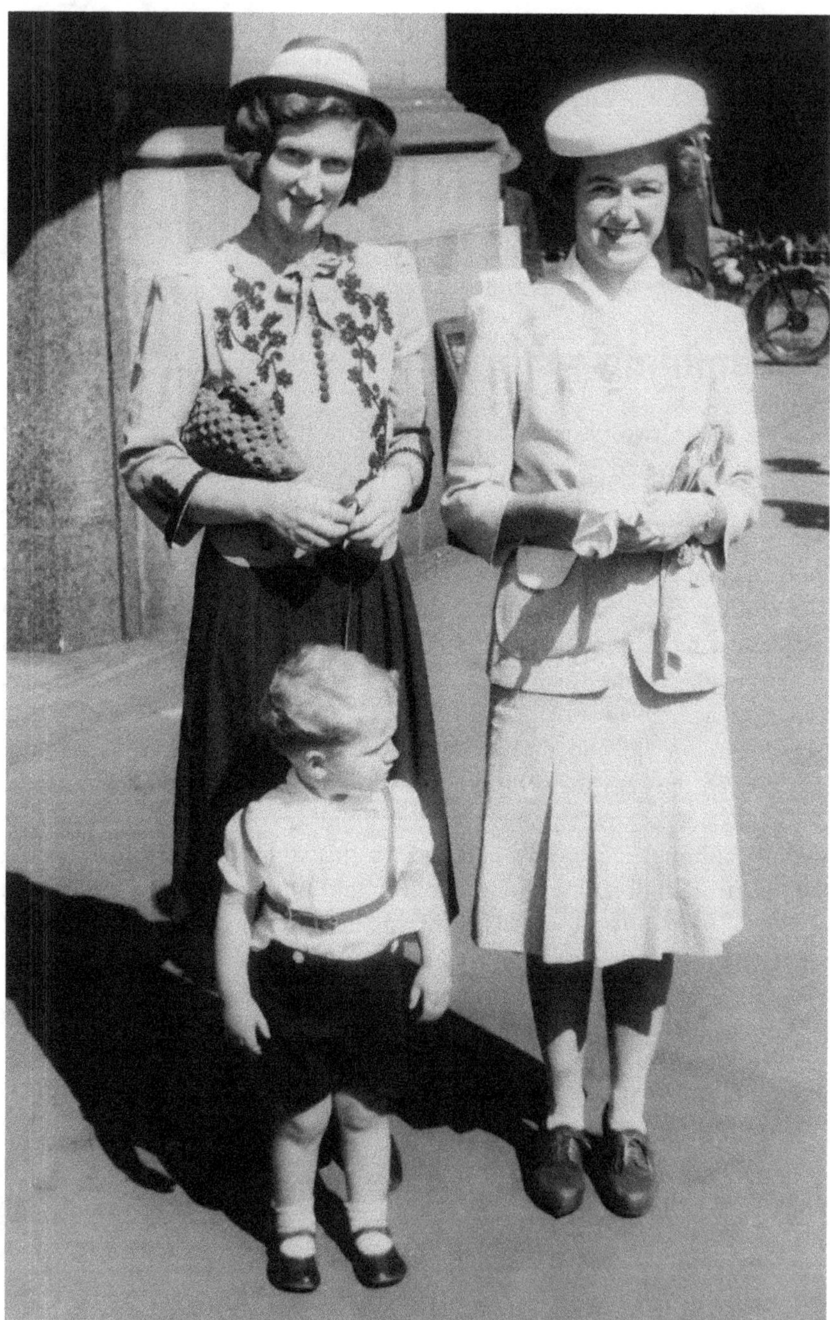

Figure 6.3: Rosalie and Martin, during a visit to Auckland c. 1944, with Rosalie's lifelong friend Marjorie Daniel.

Source: Courtesy of the Gascoigne family.

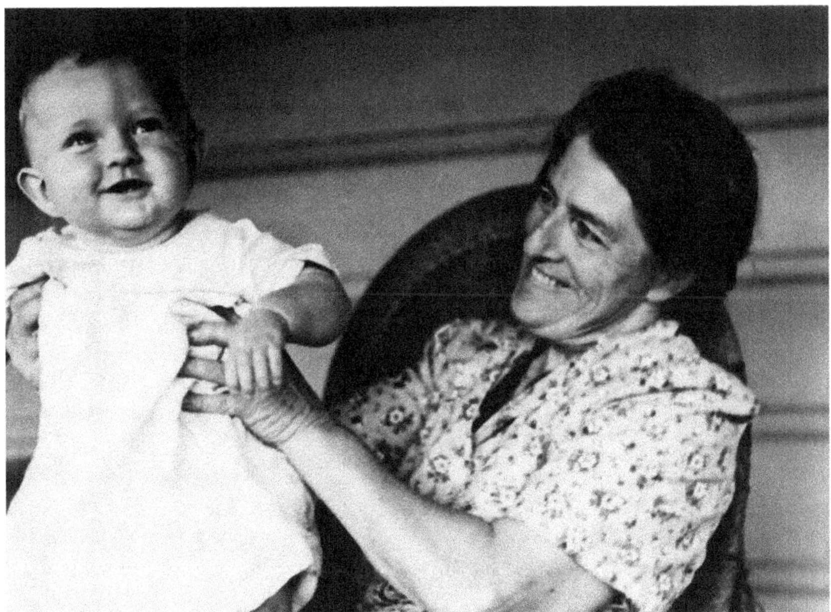

Figure 6.4: Marion Walker with Toss, Auckland, c. 1945.
Source: Courtesy of the Gascoigne family.

When she looked back to the 1940s and 1950s on Stromlo from the perspective of a successful artist, Rosalie saw her experiences during these years as having been vital in shaping her aesthetics and her sensibility through the sense of isolation that drove her to deepen her friendship with nature. My research into some of the other women on the mountain indicates that their situations had many elements in common with Rosalie's, and it is important to balance this against the almost mythic proportions attributed to Rosalie's narrative by some art historians. Accounts of the outsider on a bare, stony mountain tug at heartstrings, but also deflect attention from those aspects of Rosalie's context that were not so much particular to her but part of wider transformations for women in society.[63]

63 Rosalie made two visits to her parents and friends in Auckland during this period. See Figures 6.3 and 6.4.

7

Late 1940s to 1960: 'Glory struck'

Where the previous chapter presented an overview of Rosalie's story of her early years on Stromlo, this chapter uses the interplay between her interview narratives and the limited contemporary sources available to underline the ways in which she survived her loneliness (see Figures 7.1 and 7.2). Her survival strategies proved to be foundational for her art practice.

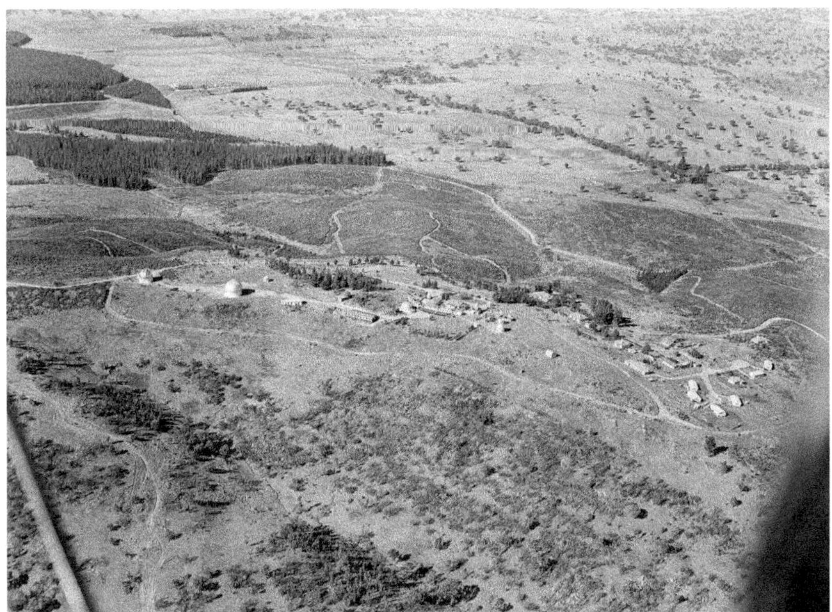

Figure 7.1: Aerial view of Mt Stromlo, 1956.

Source: Courtesy of the National Archives of Australia, A7973, INT487/6, item 7815161.

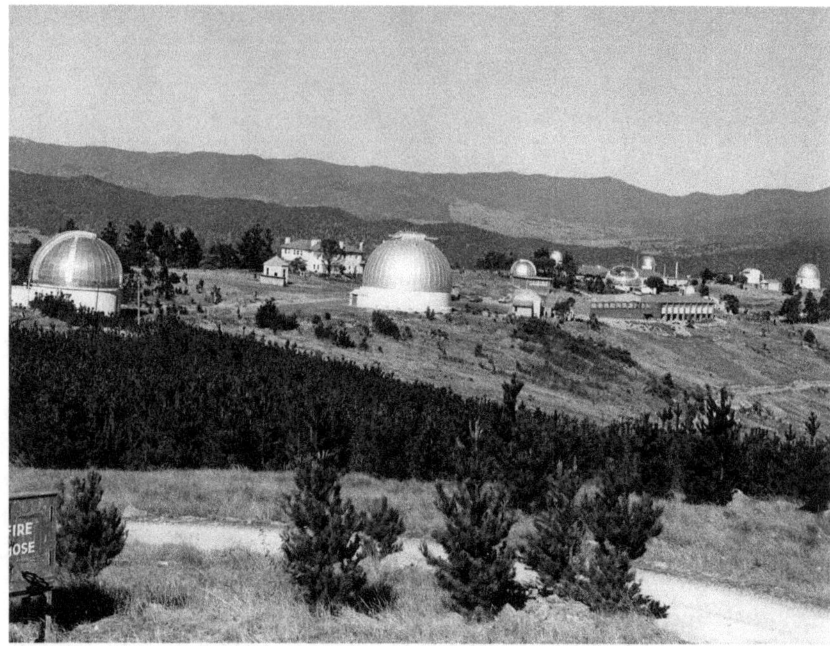

Figure 7.2: View of Mt Stromlo Observatory, c. 1955.

Source: The Australian National University Archives, Records of the Commonwealth Solar Observatory (Mt Stromlo) and Kurt Gottlieb, ANUA 615-387.

When she spoke about this period to North, Hughes and Topliss in the 1980s and 1990s, Rosalie maintained her outsider narrative while introducing threads of resilience and creativity. She spoke of her need for approval and affirmation, exacerbated by her growing interest in an aesthetic based on the discarded, weathered cast-offs she found in the local terrain. Others in her community did not share her perception of beauty in these battered, rusty objects. These jettisoned rejects and a lone marigold growing through rubbish evoke her situation in the small scientific community.[1] The marigold inspired her to grow flowers, which led to arranging them, which led to her making art. In the meantime, she made a patchwork quilt: she spread fabric pieces on the floor in the same way that she later laid out the pieces of soft drink crates, road signs or building debris she carved up, forming grid patterns to make the art that made her famous. These techniques of seeking patterns and reclaiming lost things have an obvious parallel with her circumstances. With the benefit of hindsight, her survival strategies proved to be important steps on the way to her artistic acclaim.

1 Hughes et al., 'Rosalie Gascoigne Artist', tape 2.

Equally, however, she began developing skills that, in the following decade, placed her in a strategic position in terms of art history, art tastes, the growth of dealer galleries and the development of Australia's national gallery. The intersection between these elements—her coping strategies, a parallel story of an expanding art establishment looking for a new vision, and the shape she retrospectively bestowed on her life when seeking meaning in her difficult childhood and dislocation—begin to suggest the kind of 'truth' that Rosalie represented to herself and to others in her narrative. Her success was still in the future, but reflecting on her life during these years shows Rosalie assembling an identity and a frame that prepared that path. She arranged her experiences into a seamless tale that explained and made sense of her life.

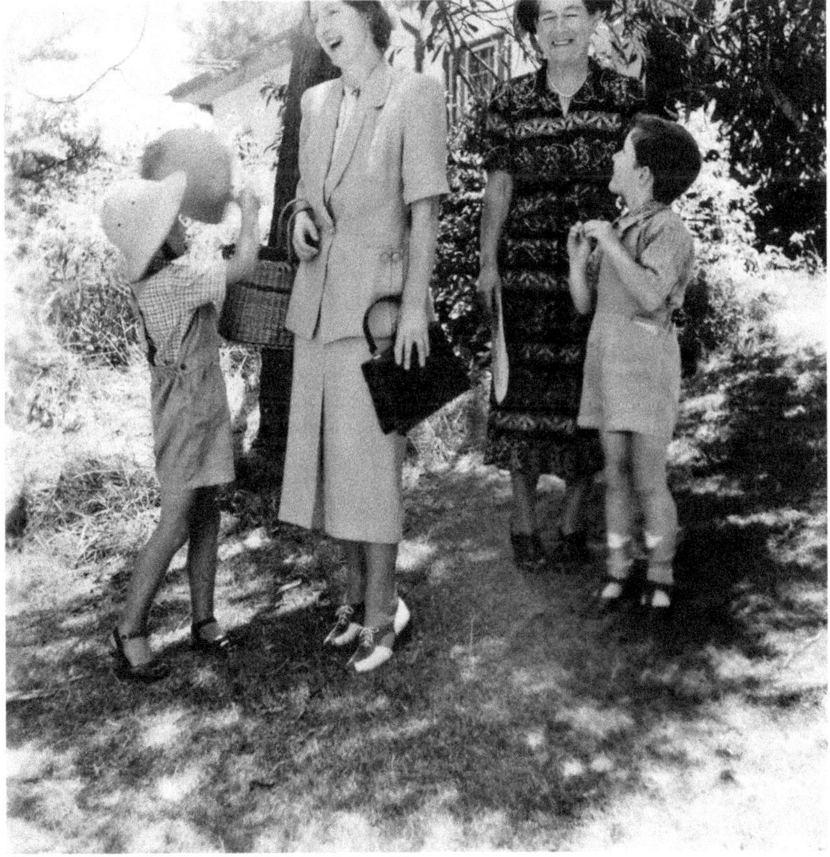

Figure 7.3: Rosalie with Marion Walker, Toss and Martin, c. 1948–49.
Source: Courtesy of the Gascoigne family.

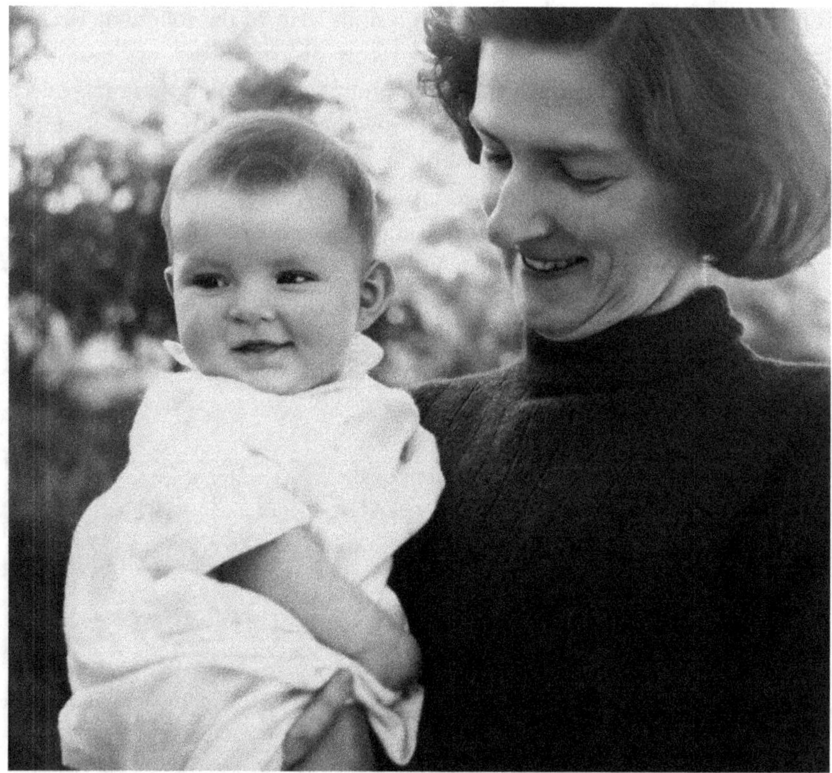

Figure 7.4: Rosalie with Hester, c. late 1949 or early 1950.

Note: In late 1971, when Rosalie was invited to feature in Faye Bottrell and Wesley Stacey's *The Artist Craftsman in Australia* (1972), Ben wrote to Martin: 'I haven't seen her [Rosalie] so elated since Hester turned out to be a daughter and not a third son.'[2]

Source: Courtesy of the Gascoigne family.

During this period, Rosalie was busy with young children. She had visited Auckland in 1944 (see Figures 6.3 and 6.4) and made a further visit home with Martin and Toss in 1948 (see Figure 7.3). The photographs of Rosalie with her children depict a happy and engaged family (see Figures 7.4–7.7). Rosalie began to adapt to isolation through tentative artistic practice when she commenced her patchwork quilt, but moved towards a more resolved practice through gardening and then flower arranging. The latter brought her into a strand of innovative domestic aesthetics that had expanded since the 1930s, gave her space to find a fusion for her own ideas and sensibility, and won her acceptance within a consolidating circle in the particular, privileged world that was Canberra by the late 1950s.

2 Ben Gascoigne to Martin Gascoigne, 16 November 1971, cited in Eagle, *From the Studio of Rosalie Gascoigne*, 34.

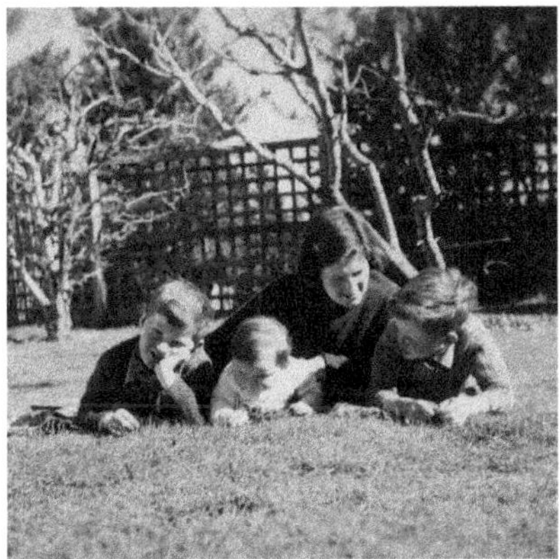

Figure 7.5: Rosalie with Toss, Hester and Martin on the back lawn at home, Mt Stromlo, 1950.

Source: Courtesy of the Gascoigne family.

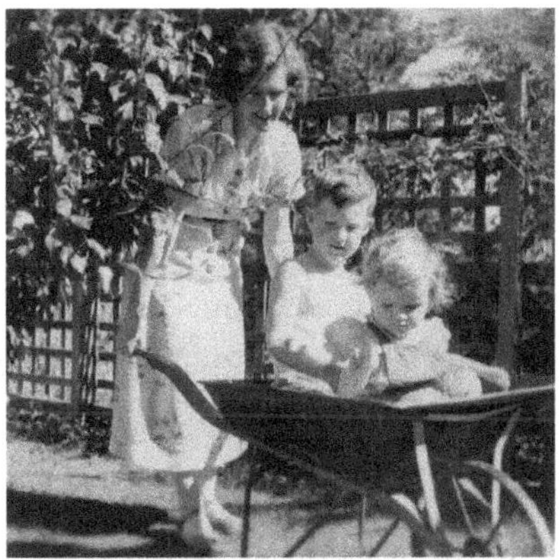

Figure 7.6: Rosalie with Hester and Toss, Mt Stromlo, 1951.

Source: Courtesy of the Gascoigne family.

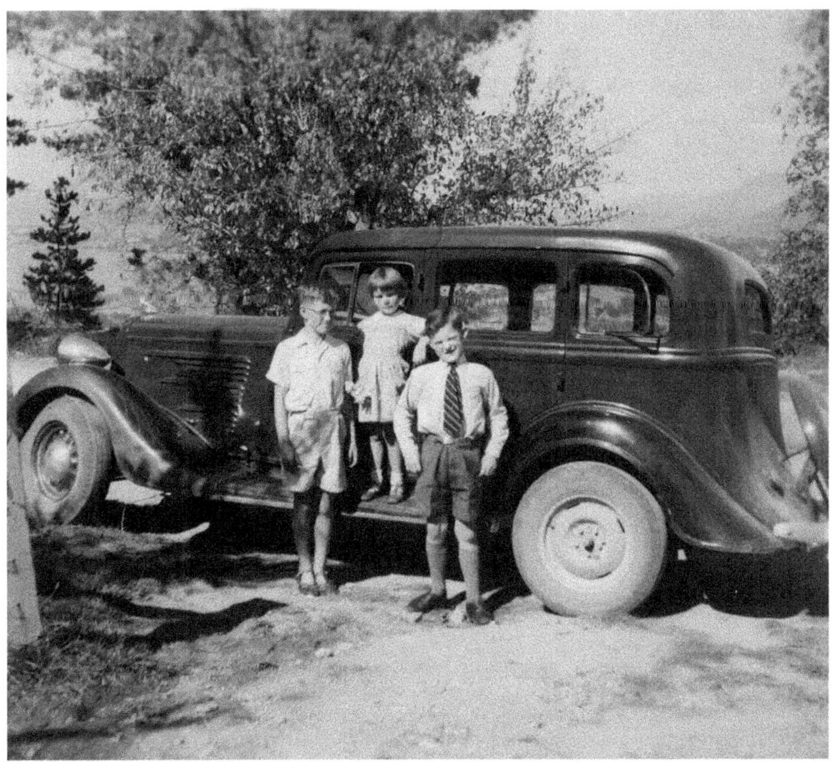

Figure 7.7: Martin, Hester and Toss Gascoigne, c. 1954.

Source: Courtesy of the Gascoigne family.

Survival strategies: Patchwork, books and flowers

During the 1940s and 1950s, Rosalie's creativity manifested itself in the range of survival strategies she developed—patchwork, books and flower growing. Using dressmaking scraps, she started making a quilt that took her seventeen years to complete (see Figures 7.8 and 7.9).[3] The quilt afforded her company at night when the children were in bed and Ben was stargazing. Wartime rationing followed by postwar shortages meant that fabric was scarce, so, just as she later made art from discards, she constructed the quilt from fabric scraps scavenged from neighbours. One woman's refusal stung her:

> I used to spread these coloured patches around the floor and put them together. And beg what scraps of material I could from anybody, because you couldn't even buy it, you see, in those days. And one woman—I will never forget her … I said, 'Could I have a piece of that dress you're making?' and two weeks later, she said, 'Well, when I've finished wearing the dress you can have it.' She wouldn't give it to me.[4]

The story advances her lonely outsider feelings. It is not clear why the woman refused to give Rosalie fabric scraps; it could be that the material was distinctive and the woman did not want it to be seen as part of a quilt until she had stopped wearing the dress, but quilts were usually used within a home and not displayed publicly. Rosalie's making of it represents a gesture of reconciliation with domesticity, but, in openly seeking scraps from others, also a subversion of it. This story reinforces her picture of herself as a friendless outsider. She needed her audience to know the extent of the misery that involved her difficult adaptation to a new place, new roles and a new identity and the way other women on the mountain received her. In her 1962 radio talk *Too Many Pine Trees,* Rosalie's loneliness and isolation are unmistakable in her evocation of how much the patchwork quilt meant to her:

3 Ibid.
4 Ibid.

> One drab winter I was infinitely consoled by a patchwork quilt I started to make. While the wind howled among the pines and hurled itself against the side of the house and my husband went off up to work I used to sit piecing flowery hexagons together, and the colour and the cheerfulness of the materials never failed to bring company into the room for me.[5]

She had begun making quilts with her students from Auckland Girls' Grammar for the war effort. Perhaps this experience was a factor in inspiring her to take up patchwork during that desolate Stromlo winter. Reading was another pattern established in Auckland. Although her narrative of earlier times expressed frustration at her bookish siblings, her educated family of origin had nurtured a culture of reading. Rosalie found comfort in the company of literary characters, sampling a wider imaginative world of possibilities.

Her habit of reading precipitated further rejection when a neighbour commented dismissively: 'You are an educated woman. You read books.'[6] Rosalie said she felt totally 'cut out' by the comment, but she continued reading. Unfortunately, there is no record of what she read during these years; however, 'convinced that too much nature and limited human contact is not good for anyone', she read voraciously, 'books on people and more people' to get the human contact she missed.[7] She recalled that she met:

> the pleasant, the calculating, the good and the bad, the rich and the poor, the stupid, the fascinating, the artistic—hundreds of them, and they all helped, even the ones I didn't believe in.[8]

The characters peopled the gaps in her life. Unlike her real-life companions, they did not judge her. She enjoyed agency in her interactions with them; they transported her to other places and into lives different from her own and those of people in her immediate vicinity.

5 Rosalie Gascoigne, 'Too Many Pine Trees', Papers of Rosalie Gascoigne, box 3.
6 Hughes et al., 'Rosalie Gascoigne Artist', tape 2.
7 Ibid.
8 Gascoigne, 'Too Many Pine Trees'.

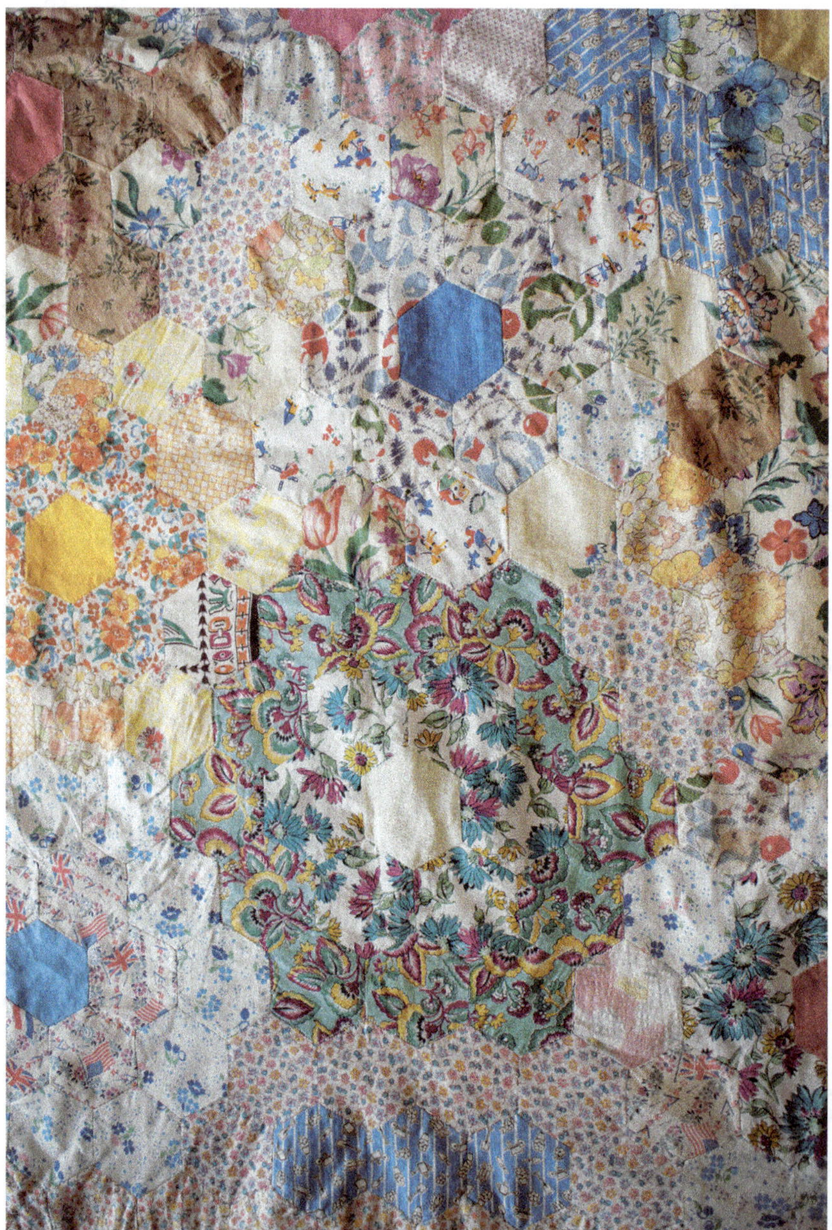

Figure 7.8: Detail of the quilt Rosalie made on Stromlo.

Notes: It took Rosalie many years to finish. Because of fabric shortages during and after World War II, she begged scraps from neighbours, unlike her later art practice where she would only use materials she found herself.

Source: Courtesy of Hester Gascoigne and Sally Colahan Griffin. Photograph: Sally Colahan Griffin.

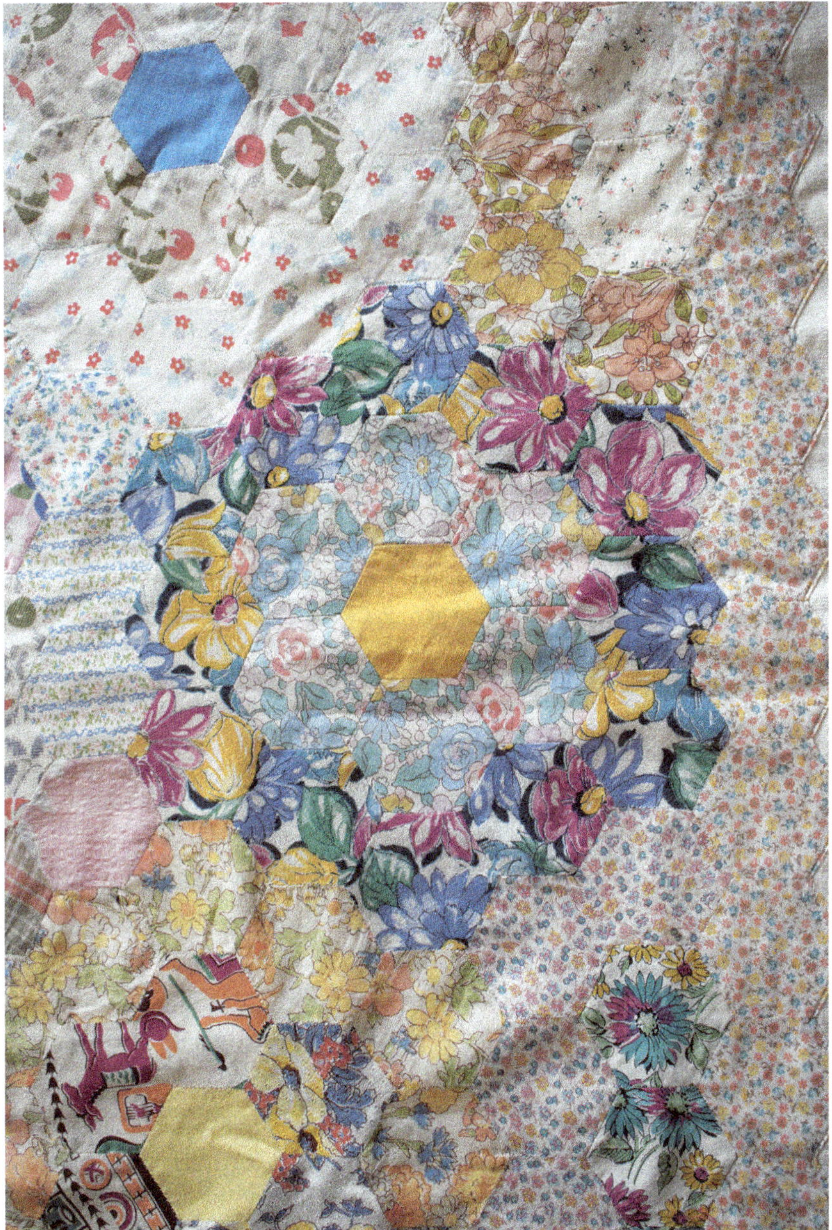

Figure 7.9: Another detail of Rosalie's quilt.

Source: Courtesy of Hester Gascoigne and Sally Colahan Griffin. Photograph: Sally Colahan Griffin.

Nature as friend

While she enjoyed the company of book characters, Rosalie further developed her friendship with nature. Alongside her outsider narrative, her stories of nature as her friend gained momentum as she moved towards an aesthetic that was also a statement of her personal situation. She felt as alien and discarded on Stromlo as the rusty petrol cans and bits of farm iron lying on the stony hillside. She saw a reflection of her own foreignness in the unfamiliar nature of the things that pleased her eye.

She told North:

> I used to walk around the mountain by myself, especially when the children got older and went to school … I'd go way over the hill and … look at everything, absolutely everything, even the snakes.[9]

This recollection speaks of desperation—even the most foreign (to a New Zealander) and dangerous creature received her attention. She described her habit of intense looking and engagement with all aspects of nature on the mountain:

> I interviewed them [natural things]. I liked the look of them, their presence, you see … And sometimes I knew names and sometimes I didn't. But they were foreign to me … I liked them. [I felt] a sort of warmth I suppose … recognition … They do get to be your familiars when there's nothing much else.[10]

The natural world offered her beauty as well as friendship. She personified nature. Her statement that she felt 'a sort of warmth' towards things she found outdoors bolstered her feeling as someone who was different. She liked the foreignness of 'natural things' as she called them. Her 'recognition' of them was that they were as foreign to her as she was to them.

Once the children were older and at school in Canberra all day, Rosalie's isolation was accentuated. She roamed the mountain seeking beauty and familiarity, always ensuring she was back in time for the school bus. She later said that she began 'bringing rather wild things into my house, which rather alarmed the neighbours … great branches, because I thought they

---

9 Gascoigne, interview by North, 11. It was not until the mid-1950s that all three Gascoigne children were at school.

10 Hughes et al., 'Rosalie Gascoigne Artist', tape 3.

were beautiful'.[11] Her neighbours featured in her story as people who were disquieted by her unusual behaviour. Rosalie carried her finds home to Residence 19 and displayed them on the mantelpiece:

> I needed things to look at, you see. And it wasn't much, you see nobody had any money. You didn't get to the shops anyway. And I needed things to look at, I really did. So if I put an old kerosene tin lid on because I thought it was a lovely orange or something, and put it there, well that was something for me to look at.[12]

She enjoyed the branches, stones and discarded weathered things and was aware that others might not see beauty where she did. She revealed herself to be a diffident creator, part scavenger, part curator, not yet confident that others would agree with her notion of beauty or find visual pleasure in the rustic treasures she found outdoors. She felt vulnerable exposing her finds to others' view. Some of this diffidence and vulnerability crept in to one of the earliest filmed interviews, *Survey 2, Rosalie Gascoigne*, made in 1979 on the occasion of the exhibition of the same name at the National Gallery of Victoria.[13] While verbally expressing confidence in her art, her body language and tone of voice slipped back to the early days of uncertainty. As she spoke about how long it took her to find what she was really about, Rosalie's voice dropped, and she looked away from the camera as she told the off-screen interviewer: 'I think I'm really unconvincing. But you know, I learnt how to be conventional—you have to put concrete over what you are.'[14] In her interview with Robin Hughes in 1998, a more confident, self-assured Rosalie maintained direct eye contact with Hughes as she related how she did not show her early finds to anyone, but, in the next breath, said they came in to look:

> I didn't ever show anybody. People came in to look. But they didn't understand mostly … why you liked something or why you didn't like something … It takes decades to get yourself independent of other people's preferences. Especially if you're vulnerable … And I … was plenty vulnerable … In the end, if you go for other people's appreciation, it passes and you change … So you have to go for … whatever you like. And that's what makes you different in the end, because everybody is born different.[15]

11 Ibid., tape 2.
12 Ibid., tape 3.
13 *Survey 2, Rosalie Gascoigne* (television interview with Robert Lindsay).
14 *Survey 2, Rosalie Gascoigne.*
15 Hughes et al., 'Rosalie Gascoigne Artist', tape 3.

With recognition and affirmation, Rosalie's confidence had grown. Meanwhile, the search for beauty in the countryside became a family pastime. At the service of thanksgiving for Rosalie's life on 5 November 1999 in Canberra, Martin told the gathering how his mother had involved the whole family in the hunt: 'Rosalie taught us to look with a discerning eye. Family picnics involved the game of gathering stones, and competing to spot the roundest or the blackest.'[16] She incorporated her love of nature, and need to place herself in the landscape, into her family life; it drew her family together—an affirmation both of herself and of an ideal of parenting. Not only Rosalie, but her whole family traversed the countryside and made it theirs by unwittingly situating themselves in it. For the children, however, the experience would not have contained the urgency it did for Rosalie. The Monaro was their birthplace; they knew no other landscape. For Rosalie, such familiarity was hard-won. She felt vulnerable in the strange environment, yet, at the same, traversing the countryside became a family ritual—a type of family connection she had apparently not known during her childhood.

A marigold growing among the rubbish

Rosalie used a strong visual image to introduce her audience to the trigger that motivated her to start gardening. In 1949, the year she gave birth to Hester, Rosalie spotted a lone marigold growing among the rubbish at the bottom of their Stromlo garden: 'One day I looked down the slope to the back gate, and there was one marigold growing … And I thought, you can make a sloping garden there.'[17]

The image of the lone marigold emerging from the rubbish resonates with some of Rosalie's descriptions of the isolation she felt as a new bride in a strange land. Flowers had previously played a role in her narrative when she told Hughes that one of her earliest memories was seesawing above the Michaelmas daisies with her sister.[18] The story of her winning first prize at primary school with an arrangement of buttercups and brass was another.

16 Martin Gascoigne, 'Rosalie—M.B.G. Eulogy', 1999, Papers of Ben Gascoigne, box 3.

17 Hughes et al., 'Rosalie Gascoigne Artist', tape 2. See also MacDonald and Gascoigne, *Rosalie Gascoigne*, 16.

18 Hughes et al., 'Rosalie Gascoigne Artist', tape 1.

Flowers provide some continuity in her story, together with her theme of nature as a friend. They buoy her motifs of looking at, and awareness of, nature, and link stages of her life to one another.

Rosalie said that flowers made an immense difference to her life; she dreaded the winter 'when all colour vanished from the garden and the hill was bitter with meagre stones', making it necessary to search 'for any sort of visual excitement'.[19] Her description of a colourless garden and bitter hill might have been a metaphor for her life, but her claim that she then searched for visual stimulation assures her audience she was not someone who succumbed to difficult times. The marigold drew her into making her own splashes of colour during bleak winters, symbolising her resilience and creativity.

Growing flowers led to Rosalie arranging them in ways that reflected wider transitions in an aesthetic that mixed changing ideas of domesticity and women's self-expression. The connections here went beyond her own situation: they reflected the shifting contours of home making at the time, the different personalities within the home, and the ambivalences these transitions and personalities brought to women's roles. Rosalie captured a local synthesis of these dynamics.

For Rosalie, the practice helped to break down elements of her isolation. By 1955, her reputation for growing flowers led to an invitation to exhibit at the Horticultural Society of Canberra (HSC) show:

> I toiled night and day and I had one of these gardens with tall delphiniums and lots of stuff. People were rather amazed … I used to work like crazy in it. And then one day somebody came along and said they're short of people for the horticultural show, do put … something in. So I thought, oh how exciting.[20]

When she first entered the HSC's Spring Bulb Show decorative arts section in 1955, Rosalie was overwhelmed to win a prize for 'an arrangement of polyanthus or primroses'.[21] Fellow Stromlo resident and astronomy wife Royal Buscombe, who also won a prize in 1955, probably encouraged her

19 Gascoigne, 'Too Many Pine Trees'.

20 Hughes et al., 'Rosalie Gascoigne Artist', tape 4.

21 'Display of Daffodils Highlight Annual Spring Bulb Show', *Canberra Times*, 19 September 1955, 5; Gascoigne, interview by North, 10.

to enter.[22] Rosalie's joy shone through her reminiscence: 'I got a second prize! Oh, I must say, the distinguished … Win a prize in public!'[23] That her artist's eye was developing is evident. From that point on, Rosalie exhibited regularly, and with considerable success. The *Canberra Times* recorded her regular wins in the decorative section until November 1962.[24]

Rosalie's enthusiasm for flower arranging and competition grew and she looked forward to the Horticultural Society announcing the categories for each competition.[25] Her story continues to reinforce her narrative of difference as she told North that, even at that early stage, she 'was working away from the mob, by myself … and so I didn't find it terribly hard to look different even then'.[26] By now, 'different' had a cache of its own. She recounted just how different she was:

> I used to bring in these great branches and I used to think what a good grey, what a good blonde, and I'd make a great big thing and everybody would rear back. And they had their dahlias in their front halls and I had all this stuff.[27]

22 See 'Display of Daffodils Highlight Annual Spring Bulb Show'; Martin Gascoigne's annotations on Gascoigne, interview by North, 10.

23 Gascoigne, interview by North, 10.

24 'Quality in Flowers Despite Rain', *Canberra Times*, 12 March 1956, 4: 'Arrangement depicting "autumn": Mrs M. Griffiths 1, Mrs R. Gascoigne 2. Breakfast table arrangement: Mrs R. Gascoigne 1, Mrs J. Hurrell 2'; 'Horticultural Society's Spring Bulb Show', *Canberra Times*, 17 September 1956, 14: 'Arrangement of pansies: Mrs R. Gascoigne 1. Arrangement depicting "spring": Mrs R. Gascoigne 1, Miss E. Shumack 2'; 'Horticultural Spring Bulb Show a Success', *Canberra Times*, 18 November 1957, 5: 'Arrangement, all white: Mrs R. N. Gascoigne 2, Mrs C. C. Green 2. Small arrangement for bedside table: Mrs R. N. Gascoigne 1, Mrs E. Riek 2. Simple arrangement for breakfast table: Mrs R. N. Gascoigne 1, Mrs J. Michell 2'; 'Winners of Gowrie Garden Competition Announced', *Canberra Times*, 17 March 1958, 4: 'Arrangement fruit and flowers: Mrs R. Gascoigne 1, Mrs. P. Reynolds 2. Arrangement "autumn": Mrs R. Gascoigne 1, Mrs C. B. Rafferty 2'; 'Early Season Lowers Bulb Standard', *Canberra Times*, 16 September 1958, 9: 'Simple arrangement for breakfast table: Mrs R. Gascoigne 1. Modern arrangement "with driftwood": Mrs R. Gascoigne 1. March 1959 arrangements of roses (modern)'; 'Autumn Show Awards', *Canberra Times*, 23 March 1959, 11: 'Own arrangement, "autumn": Mrs I. Widdowson 1, Mrs H. Reynolds 2; Mrs S. Gascoigne. Low arrangement: Mrs. R. Boardman 1, Mrs. J. Hurrell 2; Mrs S. Gascoigne h.c. (highly commended)'; 'Daffodil Honours to Mr. Riek at Spring Bulb Show', *Canberra Times*, 20 September 1960, 8: 'Mrs S. C. B. Gascoigne's modern arrangement of flowers with driftwood was the outstanding exhibit in the decorative section'; 'Roses Feature Spring Show at Albert Hall', *Canberra Times*, 14 November 1960, 7: 'Simple for breakfast table: Mrs S. C. B. Gascoigne 1'. Possibly she stopped entering at this stage as she spent six months in Europe in 1963 when Ben did an exchange to the Royal Greenwich Observatory then at Herstmonceux, East Sussex, England, and after her return she focused her energies on ikebana.

25 See Martin Gascoigne's annotations on Gascoigne, interview by North, 10, footnote 20.

26 Ibid., 11.

27 Ibid., 10.

Once again, she contrasted herself with her neighbours—her great grey branches shocked them. The image of them 'rearing back' is a potent one of people pulling away from her. Her words 'and they had their dahlias' suggest dahlias were a comfortable, socially acceptable domestic image, contrasted with bare grey branches. But at least Rosalie now elicited responses stronger than simple rejection.

Her different style made an impact now it had a forum of its own. Ben remembered overhearing two farmers in the late 1950s astounded by her use of spiky blue devil, a noxious weed: 'One of them said to the other, "I can remember when we were paid to grub that stuff out!"'[28]

Around 1958, Rosalie was particularly daring when she made *Cotter Road*, an arrangement from a skull, rocks and grass on a sheet of copper with a blue denim backdrop. Named after the then gravel road that had limited movement off the mountain in Rosalie's first years on Stromlo, Ben described the arrangement as 'the first sign she was going off in a different direction … it evoked the Cotter Road in a remarkable way, using the most commonplace of materials'.[29]

But where did flower arranging fit in Australian society at the time, and were there particular factors that led to Rosalie's different style? The high number of articles about flower arranging in Australian newspapers during the 1940s to the 1960s affirms its popularity and influence at the time. It provided an outlet for women in the home. From 1949 to 1960, the *Canberra Times* alone includes 330 mentions of flower arranging, including demonstrations, reviews of books on the art, flower shows and classes.

Most influentially, or iconically, these trends were reflected in the figure of Constance Spry. In Britain during the 1930s, Spry had raised floral arrangements to an art form by discarding rigid Victorian rules and encouraging personal expression and the use of humble materials such as wildflowers, weeds and vegetables.[30] For both Rosalie and Spry, the practice emerged from difficult personal circumstances and a search for expression. Like Rosalie, Spry began gardening when, as a newlywed, she moved to a new city and later, unhappy in her marriage, survived by making a garden from a tangle of weeds in much the same way Rosalie made a garden from

28 MacDonald and Gascoigne, *Rosalie Gascoigne*, 17.

29 Ibid.

30 All information about Spry's life in this paragraph comes from Shephard, *The Surprising Life of Constance Spry*; Coxhead, *Constance Spry*.

a rubbish heap. Spry developed creative and innovative ways to arrange flowers, eventually opening a florist shop from where she taught the socially privileged, making a considerable impact in bringing modernism to Britain's 'high society'. However, Spry believed flowers were for everyone, so, during World War II, she began offering flower-arranging lessons in London to women of all classes. She was determined to introduce beauty into their lives through the simple romance of flowers, whether they were fine roses in crystal vases or roadside buttercups in jam jars. Rosalie's aesthetic mirrors Spry's. Both women saw beauty in the ordinary and the humdrum, the discards and the everyday.

Spry's aesthetic was innovative, but so was her approach to the process of making arrangements: discarding rules, she encouraged women to 'do what you please, follow your own star, be original if you want to be and don't if you don't want to be'.[31] Spry's sentiments, if not her confidence, resonate with Rosalie's later words about making art to please herself rather than anyone else: 'It's all for me; it's not for what the viewer sees.'[32]

Spry's approach to flower arranging took on in the Australian corner of the empire through the books she published in a steady stream from 1934.[33] They were widely circulated in Australia, as were numerous books by local authors like Eleanor Gill and Helen Blaxland, both of whom had adopted Spry's aesthetic.[34] In 1946, Blaxland noted the widespread popularity of flower arranging. She highlighted the importance of enjoying the flowers and developing one's own style.[35] In the foreword to Eleanor Gill's sixteen-page booklet published in 1959, *Decorative Work for the Beginner*, Nancy Nivison emphasised the individuality of flower arranging as well as its status as an art: 'Flower arrangement is an art in which the personality and taste of the individual is expressed as definitely as a painting.'[36] In these terms, Rosalie

---

31 Shephard, *The Surprising Life of Constance Spry*; Coxhead, *Constance Spry*, 6.

32 Quotation from Rosalie in Josephine Humphreys to Rosalie Gascoigne, 14 April 1993, Papers of Rosalie Gascoigne, box 1.

33 The books were: Constance Spry, *Flower Decoration* (London: Dent, 1934); Constance Spry, *Flowers in House and Garden* (London: Dent, 1937); Constance Spry, *Garden Notebook* (London: Dent, 1940); Constance Spry, *Summer and Autumn* (London: Dent, 1951); Constance Spry, *Winter and Spring Flowers*,(London: Dent, 1951); Constance Spry, *How to do the Flowers* (London: Dent, 1952, 1953); Constance Spry, *A Constance Spry Anthology* (London: Dent, 1953); Constance Spry, *Party Flowers* (London: Dent, 1955); Constance Spry, *Simple Flowers: 'A Millionaire for a Few Pence'* (London: Dent, 1957); Constance Spry, *Favourite Flowers*, (London: Dent, 1959).

34 Blaxland and Haxton, *Flower Pieces*; Blaxland, *Flower Pieces: On the Arrangement of Flowers*; Blaxland, *Collected Flower Pieces*; Gill, *Decorative Work*; Rogers and Kloppman, *Australian Flower Arranging*.

35 Blaxland and Haxton, *Flower Pieces*.

36 Gill, *Decorative Work*.

was a successful practising artist decades before she achieved recognition. That the person practising this medium was, typically, a woman, and the space one of domesticity, was an integral part of the transformations reflected in this movement.

Spry's aesthetic informed flower arranging in Australia and its influence can be seen in Rosalie's individual approach and freedom of expression. Art historians such as Mary Eagle, Kelly Gellatly and Daniel Taylor overlook Rosalie's flower arranging, attributing her later interest in the more esoteric discipline of ikebana with greater influence.[37] However, it is important not to overlook the influence, or at least the sense of context, that Spry represented in the rise of flower arranging from a traditionally feminine and domestic art that was not taken seriously. Rosalie knew Spry's work. She mentioned her in the Hughes interview, commenting that Spry's approach taught colour.

That she made little mention of Spry when speaking of her own artistic success is perhaps not surprising given that, until recent years, Spry was sidelined to the domestic and female domains. As recently as 2004, UK design giants Terence Conran and James Dyson denounced Spry's work as 'high society mimsiness' when they objected to her inclusion in an exhibition at London's prestigious design museum.[38] During the 1940s to the 1960s, when Rosalie engaged in flower arranging, the prevalent attitude towards the traditional arts and crafts practised by women in the home was that, as women's domestic practices, they were not 'art'. Spry was captured by a modernism that was considered more decorative than radical by the 1960s. Her initial clientele was dismissed as a social elite. A generation later, and finding her way in very different circumstances, Rosalie captured a different constituency. The transition between these worlds is worth closer attention.

Just as she made only passing mention of Spry, in 1982 Rosalie denied knowledge of the influence of Sydney-based artists Thea Proctor and Margaret Preston on flower arranging. Proctor and Preston reinforced the status of flower arranging as art in Australia. Proctor painted flowers in the modernist style from the 1920s, was in demand for her advice on public flower arrangements and wrote women's magazine articles about flower

37 See Gellatly, 'Rosalie Gascoigne', 10, 11.

38 Joanna Fortnam, 'Society Florist Remembered in Mayfair', *Telegraph*, London, 13 November 2011, www.telegraph.co.uk/gardening/gardenprojects/8884531/Society-florist-Constance-Spry-remembered-in-Mayfair.html.

arranging until her death in 1966.[39] Preston's art influenced a particularly Australian style of flower arranging with her elevation of the native banksia and other native flowers as floral subjects.[40] Like Spry, she used unusual materials in floral displays, something Rosalie later took several steps further in her use of discards from paddocks. Rosalie told North in 1982 that she had not been aware of Preston. She did not mention Proctor: 'I'm not aware of anything. What I was aware of is me and nature, what was there. And what I happen to like.'[41] Perhaps Rosalie downplayed any such influence so as not to seem merely fashionable. She maintained her self-narrative of uniqueness as an artist who had not 'read the book' and made art that was different because she had 'made it up' herself.[42] It seems unlikely Rosalie was not at least attuned to the early stages of this interest: she certainly became closely associated with its later developments.

One of the first recorded instances of Rosalie's work being on public sale was in March 1960 when her dried flower arrangements were for sale at the Pan Pacific and South East Asia Women's Association's garden party on the grounds of the Canadian high commissioner's home. Watercolours by her friend and fellow New Zealander, the prominent artist and zoologist Pamela MacFarlane (née Sinclair) were also on sale.[43]

In the following decade, Rosalie became sought after as a demonstrator and teacher of flower arranging in Canberra. Her four-page script (c. 1960) for talks she gave about dried flower and grass arrangements illustrates the seriousness with which she took the subject, and the ways in which her teaching experiences began to stir and galvanise other aspects of her personality:[44]

39 Butler, 'Proctor, Alethea Mary (Thea) (1879–1966)'.

40 Hetti Perkins, cited in Art Gallery of New South Wales, '"The Brown Pot (1940)": Margaret Preston'.

41 Gascoigne, interview by North, 13. In 1997, when Helen Topliss commented that 'Thea Proctor and Margaret Preston loved flower arrangement', Rosalie responded: 'Yes they did, but that was the women's world.' Gascoigne, interview by Topliss, 32.

42 Ibid.; Mollison and Heath, 'Rosalie Gascoigne', 7–8.

43 'Watercolours for Sale at Garden Party', *Canberra Times*, 25 March 1960, 2: 'Watercolours of Canberra, painted by local artist, Pamela MacFarlane will be on sale at the Pan 'Pacific and South-East Asia Women's Association garden party in the grounds of the Canadian High Commissioner's home to-morrow afternoon. Also on sale will be arrangements of dried flowers for winter decoration, made by Mrs. Gascoigne.' MacFarlane was married to ANU physiologist Walter Victor MacFarlane.

44 'Dried Arrangements', in Papers of Rosalie Gascoigne, box 3.

> I used to get invited to give demonstrations of dried flower arrangements … the Red Cross … never thought of paying … You did all this work, and you loaded the car up. 'Thank you, thank you, thank you.' … I did a lot of that. I was quite well known for dried arrangements, but native stuff, in Canberra.[45]

But flower arranging, while satisfying for a period, was not enough for Rosalie. She yearned for something all engrossing: 'I was all the time looking for something that was endless … something that you could empty everything you'd got into.'[46] It would be a while before she found what she yearned for; however, before the end of the decade her talent would be spotted and she would be launched on her stellar trajectory.

'Glory struck': The Australian Academy of Science

One day in 1959, Rosalie picked up the telephone to hear her Stromlo neighbour Jack Deeble, assistant secretary of the Australian Academy of Science, which was located on ANU grounds, on the line.[47] Deeble was preparing for a major conference in the academy's remarkable dome-shaped structure, one of Canberra's many new buildings (see Figure 7.10). He wanted Rosalie to make arrangements for the building during the conference.[48]

As the then research-only university grew, the Australian Fellows of the Royal Society of London had founded the Australian Academy of Science in 1954; they fundraised for a building and invited six architects to submit designs. The Fellows selected the most radical design, a copper-skinned reinforced concrete dome by modernist Melbourne architect Roy Burman Grounds. Now a Canberra icon known as the Shine Dome, when Governor-General Sir William Slim officially opened the space-age building in 1959, it was seen as making a statement about the importance of science to Australia.[49]

45 Hughes et al., 'Rosalie Gascoigne Artist', tape 3.
46 Ibid.
47 Gascoigne, interview by North, 12.
48 See Hamann, 'Grounds, Sir Roy Burman (1905–1981)'. The Australian Academy of Science building is a remarkable dome in shell concrete drawing on Finnish-American architect Eero Saarinen's neo-futurist sculptural design. Fondly known as the 'Shine Dome', it won the Royal Australian Institute of Architects' Canberra chapter's award and the Sulman award (1959), and, in 1984, was nominated for the international register of significant twentieth-century architecture.
49 Ibid.

In his book *Experiments in Modern Living: Scientists' Houses in Canberra 1950–1970*, the architect and writer Milton Cameron describes the nexus between rationality and creativity—between science, art and architecture—that Grounds expertly navigated when he worked on the Academy of Science building with scientists Otto Frankel, Mark Oliphant and John Eccles.[50] The three scientists had homes designed by modernist architects and Cameron tells how Grounds decided that scientists knew more about art than artists know about science. Just as Cameron describes the ways in which the scientists and their artist wives' houses were 'evidence of their passion for the modern world, of optimism, and of an underlying rationalism', so too was the Academy of Science building.[51] Australia's national capital represented a new beginning to the scientists and the new building contributed to the new world. It also contributed to a new beginning for Rosalie. It was for this unique building that Deeble proposed she provide regular dried flower decorations. This proposition boosted her confidence, opening up possibilities that ultimately led her further into the art world and nudged her into the public eye:

> Glory struck one day. Really glory struck. Because he [Jack Deeble] rang up, he said, 'Look we're having something at the Academy [of Science]. Would you do the decorations?' … I couldn't believe I'd been singled out … I did huge dried [arrangements with] … the Academy colours, all those greys and Roy Grounds colours.[52]

One of Australia's leading architects, Grounds was a proponent and practitioner of modernism. He was known for his radical handling of geometric form in his modernist design.[53] Grounds admired Rosalie's early arrangement organised by Deeble and suggested she be paid to do regular arrangements for the Academy of Science building.[54] Astounded to be recognised by such an illustrious figure, she exclaimed to North when telling him the story: 'The great Roy Grounds!'[55] This response gives an

50 Cameron, 'Where Science Meets Art', 192.

51 Ibid., 192–3.

52 Gascoigne, interview by North, 12.

53 Stephen, McNamara and Goad, *Modernism & Australia*. See also Hamann, 'Grounds, Sir Roy Burman (1905–1981)'. Grounds was knighted in 1969.

54 See Martin Gascoigne's annotations on Gascoigne, interview by North, 12, footnote 25: 'Academy documentation suggests she had an arrangement with the Academy from October 1960 to supply indoor plants and arrangements for major occasions (some of which she handed over to a commercial operator in October 1964). Rosalie still had works in the building in 1974.'

55 Ibid.

insight into her sense of identity as a 'nobody' who was suddenly recognised by a celebrated architect. Following Grounds's recognition, she began to move from outsider to insider in artistic circles.

Creating arrangements for the Academy of Science presented Rosalie with an opportunity to work on a larger scale than was previously possible. Until then, she had been confined and limited by her domestic space; however, the Shine Dome's uncluttered larger-scale foyer, stair halls and Fellows' Room, with their natural light, suddenly both challenged and freed her to create in a different way.[56]

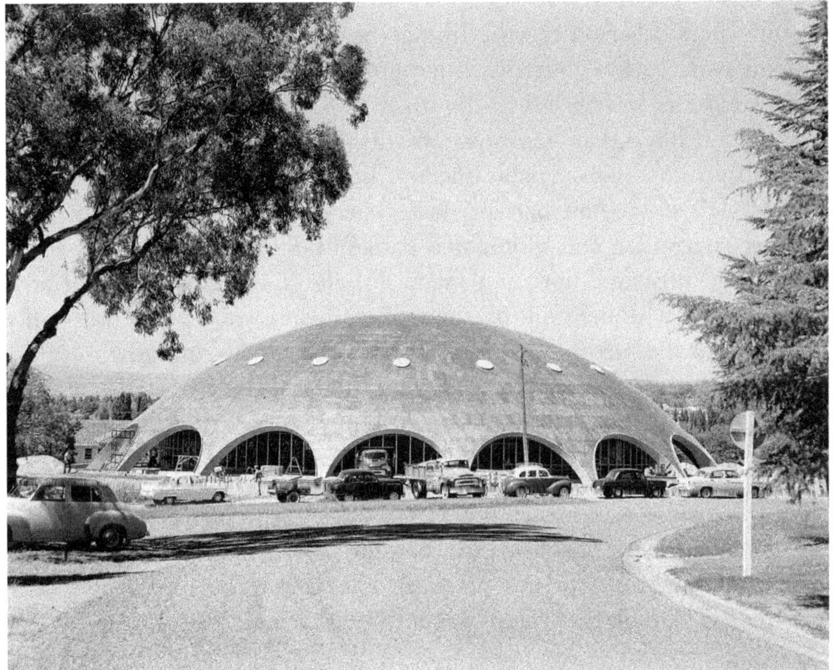

Figure 7.10: Australian Academy of Science, The Australian National University, Gordon Street and McCoy Circuit, Acton, ACT, 1959.

Notes: Designed by (Sir) Roy Grounds and completed in 1959, the building won the 1959 Sir John Sulman Award and the 1961 Canberra Medallion. It was placed on the National Heritage List in 2005. Rosalie said 'glory struck' when she was asked to create arrangements for the new building.

Source: NAA: 1200, L30871. Photograph: W. Pedersen.

56 Roberts and Australian Academy of Science, 'A Big, Bold, Simple Concept', 137.

Cutting through the isolation

By way of her self-narrative, Rosalie continued to depict herself as a lonely outsider who turned to nature for friendship in the absence of anything else on offer. Like the marigold she found pushing its way through the garden rubbish, she persistently sought a place for herself in her roles of wife and mother, gardener, flower arranger and observer that was marginal, singular, different. As this chapter has shown, flower arranging, and Constance Spry's aesthetic, played a greater part in the development of her artistic practice than has been previously recognised or credited, including by Rosalie herself.

Nature spurred her on to other things, as she sought ways to express her rapport with the hill, 'bitter with meagre stones'. She developed this trope years later. Her interview with North in 1982 made less of the difference and the loneliness than her interview with Hughes in 1998 by which time she had achieved considerable success. Increasingly, it seems, she wanted her listeners to see how bare her life was and how far she had come. She adapted, magnified and spotlighted parts of her story to fit her oft-stated belief that artists are born not made. Rosalie did with her life narrative what she did with her quilt on the mountain and with her later artworks: she laid out the pieces, selected some, rejected others, and assembled her selection in patterns that achieved what she needed—a story that assured her followers she was always an artist; one who had to suffer before she found herself. We all make sense of our lives in this way. Looking back over time, we attribute meaning to events and experiences of long ago.

By the end of the 1950s, Rosalie had begun to move from outsider towards insider through her artistic practice. The gesture of recognition from Grounds via Deeble had begun to cut through her sense of isolation.

8

1960–64: 'An expanding universe'

In 1960, Rosalie and her family moved off their mountain to one of Canberra's growing suburbs, Deakin. They were fortunate to do so in the face of chronic housing shortages. The 1960s were a period of huge change nationally and internationally, socially and artistically. Canberra forged ahead under Prime Minister Robert Menzies. The city was a virtual building site. Rosalie enjoyed the construction cranes. She roamed nearby Red Hill and farm paddocks bordering the new suburbs, collecting discarded farm iron. With Canberra's rapid growth, the environmental sensibility that was part of the capital's original design developed further, paving the way for the acceptance of her art and its response to the region's environment. Increasingly, Rosalie socialised with women who were generally as well educated as she, the wives of scientists and academics, and together they gardened and arranged flowers. During this time, her popularity as a teacher and flower arranger grew.

Rosalie's sense of herself as a woman and a mother also changed during this period. Her visibility grew and her confidence blossomed: she defined herself less by motherhood and compared herself less with other women (see Figure 8.1).

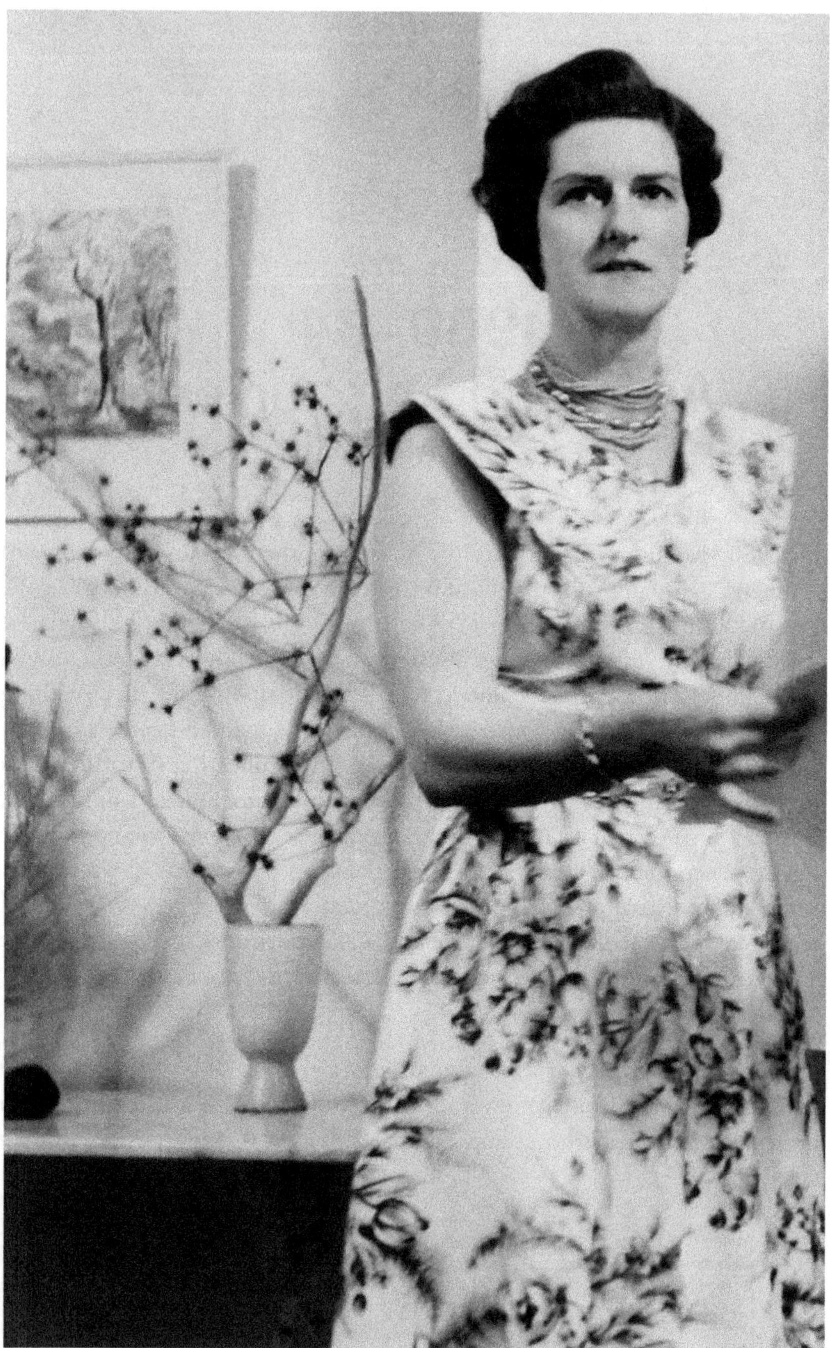

Figure 8.1: Rosalie c. 1961.

Source: Courtesy of the Gascoigne family.

'A national capital befitting Australia'

The Australian National University (ANU) owned the Gascoigne's new home in Dugan Street, Deakin. The family enjoyed the privilege of gaining access to such a property after the Department of the Interior transferred responsibility for the Mt Stromlo Observatory to the university in 1957, thereby making Ben an ANU academic. Within the capital's none-too-subtle suburban hierarchies, not only was academic standing an asset, but Deakin was a distinctly 'good' address. At the beginning of 1960, Martin was sixteen, Toss fourteen and Hester ten. They moved 'mostly because of the children, the after school cut off, you know, when they can't do things other children can do'.[1] The family would become much more integrated into the dynamics of a rapidly changing community at a time when their own lives were also in transformation.

Menzies was determined to build up the national capital 'in the eyes and minds of the Australian people', and, under his prime ministership, Canberra changed rapidly.[2] Having increased in population from around twelve thousand in the 1940s to fifty thousand in the 1950s, Canberra's population swelled to ninety-three thousand in 1966, reaching 140,000 by the end of 1969.[3] Public servants and members of the Australian Defence Force moved to Canberra in great numbers as offices relocated from Melbourne, causing housing shortages that meant a three-year wait for a house by 1961. Many families lived in government hostels that the National Capital Development Commission (NCDC) set up to complete the establishment of Canberra as the seat of government. Charged with shaping the environment in which people lived, worked and experienced Australia's national capital, the NCDC struggled to keep up with housing demand.[4]

The Gascoignes were fortunate to have the opportunity to move from one house to another when the majority of people were forced to wait. Again, such privileges were a reflection of the hierarchies that mattered in Canberra's stratified community.

---

1 Hughes et al., 'Rosalie Gascoigne Artist', tape 4.
2 Menzies, *The Measure of the Years*, 144; Boden and Brown, 'Made in Canberra', 175.
3 Sparke, *Canberra 1954–1980*, 145, 224.
4 Ibid., 91; Museum of Australian Democracy at Old Parliament House, 'National Capital Development Commission Act 1957'.

In addition to housing for new Canberrans, offices were under construction to house relocated government departments. Infrastructure was built to cope with the expanding population, ranging from roads and schools to national institutions that would define the city. Projects through the early 1960s included the National Library of Australia, Lake Burley Griffin, Scrivener Dam, Russell offices, the Canberra Theatre Centre, and The Australian National University's Menzies and Chifley libraries. In his study of Canberra in 1954–80, Sparke describes how, in the seven years to 1965, 'Canberra changed from a semi-rustic town to an integrated, if still small and incomplete, national capital'.[5] According to the chief government architect, and then first commissioner of the NCDC, Sir John Overall: 'There were signs of action and movement everywhere.'[6]

The critics of the 1950s, such as architect Robin Boyd, who lamented the chaos into which the development of the capital had fallen, were countered by those such as historian Hugh Stretton who praised the 'quiet revolution' the city represented in modern planning.[7]

Rosalie's habit of looking at her surroundings was broader than the natural environment; she enjoyed some of the action including the 'beautiful' construction cranes that abounded on the Canberra skyline.[8] Her visual acuity developed further. The cranes were signs of change, expansion and promise. As Canberra expanded, so did Rosalie's universe.

Change surrounded Rosalie in the more immediate environment of Dugan Street, then a dusty building site, now a leafy established inner south suburb. Imagine Deakin as a hive of activity with the business of constructing homes, the beat of hammers, and the gritty churning of cement mixers and shouts of construction workers filling the air; in the hot summers and dry winters, dust and empty cement bags blow around the reforming landscape.

With the children at school all day, Rosalie found the new house restrictively small after the 'big bony house' on Stromlo.[9] In the physical and metaphorical confines of Canberra's expanding suburbia, she roamed not the 'natural' environment of Stromlo but a more transitional space of suburban transformation. She collected material for a new art form that

---

5 Sparke, *Canberra 1954–1980*, 103.

6 Ibid.

7 Brown, *A History of Canberra*, 123.

8 Rosalie told Hughes: 'I used to look at the cranes around Canberra. Beautiful cranes'. See Hughes et al., 'Rosalie Gascoigne Artist', tape 4.

9 Ibid.

reflected the modernism embraced in the domestic and public spaces of the capital. Milton Cameron ascribes the move to build modernism into Canberra to the influx of scientists who sought forms and materials that represented particular physical attributes of the modern world.[10] Certainly, Rosalie and Ben and the majority of people in their social circles at the time were part of Canberra's growing scientific world.

Rosalie had branched out into making flower arrangements on a bigger scale to suit the capacious internal spaces in the Academy of Science building; however, Dugan Street's 'more polite' spaces restricted her experiments at home (see Figure 8.2). She said: 'when I wanted to do something, there was nowhere to do it in the house … there was nowhere to settle in the house'.[11]

Rosalie's sense of restricted physical space mirrored restrictions she felt in her life, and they now assumed new dimensions. She told Topliss she had wanted 'an expanding universe … to see more and to feel more and to be aware of more'.[12] In the early years of the 1960s, she was still very much a housewife and mother. However, women were beginning to question their restricted roles in society. The momentum building to the arrival of second-wave feminism manifested in the form of the women's liberation movement, in which women marched, lobbied and protested against the limited definition of a woman's role.

Although she chafed against housework, there is no evidence that Rosalie questioned women's roles. Having had her working, chief breadwinner mother as a role model she had no doubt what women could do. Yet that was not a role she was keen to embrace herself. The dynamics of her own family were beginning to create greater spaces in which she could begin to explore wider dimensions of her own identity. Rosalie sought more than domesticity. Just as she searched discarded iron for the right piece for a container for her flowers, her narrative tells how she continued to seek roles beyond housewife or mother:

> you peel yourself like an onion to make visible what you really are. And I didn't know what I was. I just knew I was out of step and always looking.[13]

10 Cameron, 'Where Science Meets Art', 189–93.

11 Hughes et al., 'Rosalie Gascoigne Artist', tape 4.

12 Gascoigne, interview by Topliss, 33.

13 Hughes et al., 'Rosalie Gascoigne Artist', tape 8.

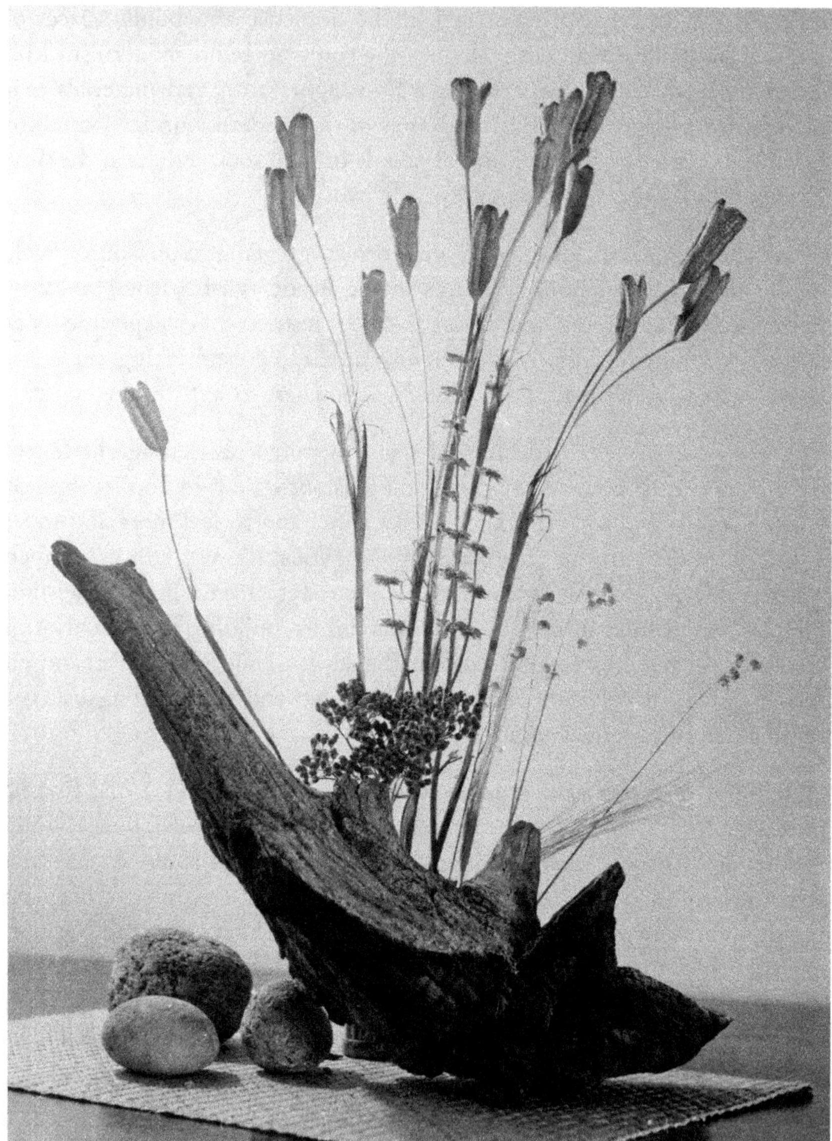

Figure 8.2. Rosalie's arrangement with driftwood and grasses at the Spring Flower Show in 1960.

Source: Courtesy of the Gascoigne family.

Rosalie was 'always looking' for who she was and she was 'always looking' at nature—from the Michaelmas daisies and shadows on the wall of her childhood in Auckland, to the Monaro landscape, and now the transitional spaces of Canberra's suburbia.

With time to herself while the children were at school, Rosalie collected quantities of the farm iron that pleased her eye. Around 1964 she started using this iron to contain her flower arrangements and was soon making small sculptures. In 1965, she moved on to making larger sculptures.[14] With alacrity she colonised her suburban garden with iron, laying it out on the grass with paths in between so she could choose pieces for particular purposes. Her apparent lack of concern for what the neighbours thought illustrates that she was now less dependent on approval and provides insights into her single-minded character and focus on artistic pursuits. In earlier times she was concerned with people's opinions about the way she hung her washing or the rusty petrol can and other discards she took into her house for decoration. No such concern is evident at Dugan Street.

Dugan Street's lack of space continued to rankle and the Gascoignes began to dream of building a home designed for their specific needs. At the same time, Canberra's horizons expanded. The city's new influences were to play significant roles in her rise to artistic acclaim.

Environmental sensibility

With Canberra's rapid expansion and influx of highly educated residents, a distinct sensibility began to emerge that was a product of the local landscape, of current social concerns and, not least, an ethic of conservation that intersected with the bush capital's own identity. Canberra was born with and of an environmental sensibility. The late nineteenth and early twentieth century Garden City (UK) and City Beautiful (US) urban planning movements, which aimed to counter overcrowding and industrial pollution in cities by providing plentiful green spaces, inspired Walter Burley Griffin and Marion Mahoney Griffin's Canberra design for Australia's new national capital. However compromised in its implementation, the architects' sensitivities to Canberra's landscape continued to influence the city's development. Equally, in response to a culture of rampant development

14 These metal pieces that Rosalie made from the 1960s to the early 1970s can be viewed in Gascoigne, *Rosalie Gascoigne: A Catalogue Raisonné*, 147–55.

at any cost after World War II, environmental awareness and sensibilities blossomed throughout the developed world and had advocates in the national capital. Two publications signifying this were Harvard economics professor John Kenneth Galbraith's *The Affluent Society* (1958) questioning such unbridled growth, and Rachel Carson's classic *Silent Spring* (1962), linking synthetic pesticides to environmental problems.[15] Carson's work addressed pressing environmental concerns and so engaged international public imagination that it sold half a million copies in hardback and stayed on bestseller lists for over thirty weeks.[16]

In Australia, Donald Horne's *Lucky Country* (1964), an indictment of 'Australia's laid-back, self-satisfied society and its mediocre leaders', spoke to local concerns about Australia's escalating postwar expansion.[17] The national capital's rapid growth, with the population doubling every seven years, stimulated its own environmental concerns. Environmental awareness grew among the well-educated populace in the bush capital, a city that, according to historian Keith Hancock, possessed the richest treasury of native plants close to its centre of any capital city in the world.[18] This growing environmental awareness and sensibility saw the Australian Conservation Foundation established in Canberra in 1964.[19] In 1969, the Canberra branch of the National Council of Women established an environment sub-committee.[20] Around the country, individuals raised public awareness of environments at risk.[21]

Rosalie's flower arrangements, in which she assembled materials found in the landscape, reflected the natural environment. The sometimes jarring, eroding, tarnishing relics of human land use meshed with this growing environmental sensibility. She caught the resilience as well as the transience of a local place in her works made with grasses, thistles and seed heads: 'spiky pods from the river bank, gum leaves dried the colour of parchment

15 Galbraith, *The Affluent Society*; Carson, *Silent Spring*.

16 Williams, *Green Power*, 13.

17 Horne, *The Lucky Country*.

18 Hancock, *The Battle of Black Mountain*, 1–3. Hancock also commented on the numerous birds, members of the kangaroo family, small mammals, reptiles, frogs and insects close to the city that were at risk from hasty development.

19 Williams, *Green Power*, 13.

20 Brown, *A History of Canberra*, 185.

21 Horne, *The Lucky Country*; Williams, *Green Power*, 196; Wildlife Preservation Society of Queensland, 'Monograph 1'. Poet Judith Wright, who settled near Canberra and became part of its literary circles, and who Rosalie was to meet later, took up the cudgel for environmental activism when she helped found the Wildlife Preservation Society of Queensland in 1962 with scientist and author, David Fleay, painter and author, Kathleen MacArthur, and publisher Brian Clouston.

… black banksia branches with their heavy black cones'.[22] She had moved from the brighter colours advocated by Constance Spry to the Monaro's greys, browns, blacks, golds and creams. This sensibility, combined with the central place of landscape art in Australia, were significant factors in the development of Rosalie's art and its successful reception by the art world and the general population.

Although she was sought after for her flower arranging skills and demonstrations, Rosalie told Vici MacDonald that she never recognised this as a special talent because she was not 'used to being good'.[23] It is difficult to imagine how, in the face of such demand, she might not have recognised her talent.

In addition to her contract with the Academy of Science since 1959, Rosalie arranged flowers for The Australian National University's University House until the 1970s.[24] She made formal arrangements for the Pan Pacific and South East Asia Women's Association conference in 1961, where the international president Mrs Balbao of the Philippines urged women 'to unite and make peace and to keep it permanent'.[25] The event's themes demonstrate the milieu in which Rosalie lived and the intersecting groups of women of which she was part. Opportunities for women's expression were framed by a growing awareness of the restrictions on women's lives. First Assistant Secretary of the Department of External Affairs David Osborne Hay told the conference that the proportion of women to men in higher education in many countries, including Australia, was far too small: while half the students in Australian secondary schools were girls, only 20 per cent of university students were women.[26]

Rosalie's stature as a flower arranger grew. In March 1963 she created the floral display for the opening by Prime Minister Menzies of David Jones' Canberra store at the new Monaro Mall in Civic.[27] Between 1960 and 1965, she demonstrated or taught flower arranging for fundraisers for organisations including the Red Cross, the YWCA, the National Council of

22 'Dried Arrangements', in Papers of Rosalie Gascoigne, box 3.

23 MacDonald and Gascoigne, *Rosalie Gascoigne*, 21.

24 Harriet Barry, interview by author, Canberra, 27 January 2011; Jan Brown, interview by author, Canberra, 23 September 2011.

25 'What People Are Doing: Behind the Scenes at the Pan-Pacific and South-East Asia Women's Association Conference', *Canberra Times*, 17 January 1961, 25; 'Unity Hope for Peace, Women Told', *Canberra Times*, 10 January 1961, 1.

26 'Not Enough Women in Higher Education', *Canberra Times*, 12 January 1961, 3.

27 MacDonald and Gascoigne, *Rosalie Gascoigne*, 102.

Women of the ACT and the Canberra Hospital Nurses' Home.[28] Her talent and teaching skills engaged and inspired her students, while also providing social activity and making money for local organisations.

Her artist's eye is evident in one of the few available primary sources from this period—a script she wrote around 1960 for her talks on dried arrangements. The typed carbon copy affirms her eye for detail, form, texture and colour as she describes the types of materials she used and recommends where and how to keep them:

> Some years I gather ordinary roadside grasses in the spring and tie them in bundles and hang them under the house … Grasses hung in the dark will keep their delicate colour … Grass gathered in the late spring won't drop its seed when dry … Other grass I pick when it has burnt brown and blond and orange in the summer sun.[29]

And so she continued in her poetic language, describing tall thistles with bold, starry shaped heads that go silver grey; small thistles with yellow flowers and short, thin stems like a candelabra; spiky pods from the riverbank; and gum leaves dried the colour of parchment.[30] Rosalie had learned about grasses from looking at them during her lonely years on Stromlo. She passed her sharpened eye over entries in the horticultural shows to see how others organised their flowers into prize-winning pieces. It is likely she read newspaper articles on flower arranging and some of the burgeoning number of books and pamphlets published on the art during the 1950s and 1960s.[31]

In her talk, a work of art in itself, colour, shape and form are her language:

> Colours vary from bronze and brown and tan to indefinite dark shades with a purplish bloom on them … a thin branch of bleached willow wood, found by the river, adds an interesting white curve through … dark material.

28 'Official Opening by Mr Menzies Tomorrow', *Canberra Times*, 5 March 1963, 1; 'What People Are Doing: Demonstration of Flower Display', *Canberra Times*, 11 October 1962, 5: 'Mrs Gascoigne illustrated decorations for varied functions including first birthdays, weddings and a harvest festival. One sophisticated arrangement was made of plastic artificial flowers, dried leaves and seedpods sprayed in gold. Mrs Gascoigne showed a more versatile decoration of a few very large an expensive blooms in a spectacular arrangement.' 'Flower Arrangement', *Canberra Times*, 10 August 1962, 5; 'Flower Lesson for Nurses', *Canberra Times*, 19 May 1964, 11.

29 Gascoigne, 'Dried Arrangements'.

30 Ibid.

31 Blaxland, *Collected Flower Pieces*; Blaxland, *Flower Pieces: On the Arrangement of Flowers*; O'Brien, *Designed Flower Arrangement*.

She describes graceful drooping lines and advises her audience to start by adding grasses to a simple vase and to keep adding until you 'get your eye in'.[32] In contrast to her later, retrospective self-deprecation, her words exude confidence. This is a subject she is comfortable with. It involves her friend nature and is an activity she does for herself.

Rosalie had got her own 'eye in' and believed it was simply a matter of time and practice before others did the same. Her teacher training showed in her specific directions and concrete language. Poems of line and colour emerged from her instructions: 'weary tattered stuff, pale green grasses dried in the dark, or burnt brown and pale gold by the sun, but never greyed by frost and winter rain'. Playfully, she warned her listeners to take care of their arrangement: 'keep it where the cat can't get it!'[33]

Yet demonstrations could also provoke her ire. In early 1961 she wrote to Ben, who was then at the Goddard Space Flight Centre at NASA Headquarters in Washington DC, about having to cart 'stuff up and down long flight of slate steps inside house from garage to kitchen' for a recent demonstration.[34] The abrasiveness attributed to Rosalie by others is evident in the negative comments she made about some of the women attending the class. Frustration and discontent with elements of the demonstration and with the secretary's proposal simmer through her words:

> Secretary afterwards said that all the ladies were dying to get out in the paddocks and look for stuff. I should come and lead them and we could take a picnic lunch. Likely! But I am going to charge a fee for next demonstration, if any. Too much work carrying things.[35]

She finished: 'And anyway I feel I've made my mark now.'[36]

Reflecting on her interactions with Stromlo refugees in her interview with Hughes, Rosalie described the 'terrible fate … [of] doing good works with your life'.[37] Although she clearly enjoyed flower arranging, her demonstrations were largely 'good works'—fundraising events for community organisations or groups. While she had been happy initially to

32 Gascoigne, 'Dried Arrangements'.

33 Ibid.

34 Rosalie Gascoigne to Ben Gascoigne at NASA, Washington DC, August 1961, Papers of Ben Gascoigne, box 3.

35 Ibid.

36 Ibid.

37 Hughes et al., 'Rosalie Gascoigne Artist', tape 3.

support worthy causes, Rosalie did not want her life taken up with meeting the needs of others. Her sights were set on other things. She wanted an expanding universe, telling Hughes in 1998: 'I think it's a basic human fear to be boxed in.'[38]

Rosalie gained more confidence during this period. Her popularity for demonstrating flower arranging and her continued success in Canberra Horticultural Society shows—her arrangement *Forest Fire*, showing ikebana's influence in composition, won the Champion Award in 1962—boosted her self-confidence and visibility (see Figure 8.3). Her words to Hughes in 1998 convey her sensitivity about recognition: 'all women need … to know they're on the map. Otherwise they just disappear, you see. And I think women do need that. That they're somebody and they—they're important.'[39]

Rosalie neither allowed herself to be boxed in nor to disappear. She used her agency to expand her universe by growing flowers, collecting material from the Canberra countryside, drying some of it and arranging the materials artistically. In this way, she made herself visible. Flower arranging was a popular pastime for middle-class women, but she excelled at it in a way that ensured she was seen and recognised for her talent. Through her blossoming confidence, Rosalie began to assert her agency and claim a new role. She was determined to express her creativity.

Her letter to Ben provides a rare glimpse into other aspects of Rosalie's daily life—brief details about family, friends and social occasions. She had taken Toss to his football game and dashed off the letter in a spare half hour before the match. She flew through her news, seldom constructing complete sentences, usually abbreviating names and weekdays, and was sparing with pronouns and verbs. Her life was as full as the letter. Sunday afternoon drinks at the home of fellow New Zealanders Alice and Mick Borrie, the latter a leading ANU academic, had been 'Pleasant and quiet'.[40] Galloping through the events of the week just past, she regaled Ben with stories of her social engagements and Hester's social life. Martin, at eighteen, was already interested in art and Rosalie recorded his attendance at silversmith Darani Lewers's exhibition in Sydney, where he saw their friend, artist Carl Plate, in 'a very loud check suit'.

---

38 Ibid., tape 8.

39 Ibid.

40 The Borries were W. D. 'Mick' and Alice Borrie, New Zealanders who moved to Australia in 1942. Mick Borrie worked at ANU from 1947, where he was eventually appointed professor of demography.

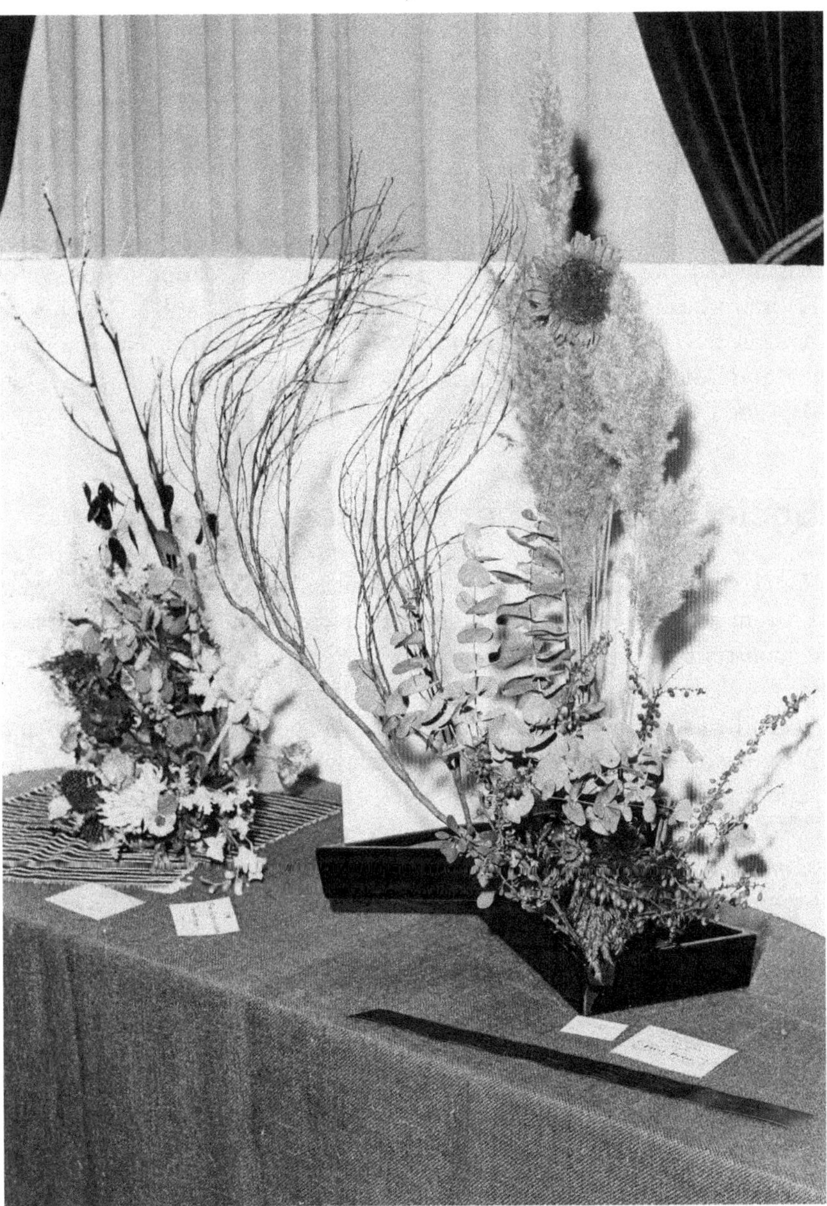

Figure 8.3: Rosalie's arrangement *Forest Fire* was the champion decorative exhibit at the Canberra Horticultural Show held at the Albert Hall in March 1964.

Note: It featured in the *Canberra Times*, 16 March 1964, 10: 'The champion decorative exhibit of the Canberra Horticultural Show, called Forest Fire, was entered by Mrs S.C. Gascoigne of Deakin.'

Source: Courtesy of the Gascoigne family.

Without pause for breath or paragraph breaks, she wrote of an income tax rebate—'and we could use all of it'.[41] She detailed bills paid and debts cleared, and remarked about how pleased Marion was to see Ben in New Zealand, presumably en route to the US. Marion, wrote Rosalie, was glad to see that Daintry's husband Mac (Campbell Percy McMeekan, university professor, agricultural scientist and for some years a senior agriculturalist with the World Bank in New York), was impressed with Ben's achievements. Rosalie did not prevaricate in her description of Marion's opinion of Daintry's husband: 'She always thinks Mac so egotistical.'[42] A series of cameos, the letter resembles her later grid-pattern artworks. The aerogram is a continuous running line of text broken only by full stops, starting 'Dear Ben' and ending 'Lots of love Rosalie'.

Social circles: 'It got so incestuous'

Rosalie's acute observations of Canberra people in her letter to Ben were far from gentle. The names of women at coffee mornings and dried flower demonstrations were those of wives of ANU professors and Canberra scientists, but this did not necessarily mean they were congenial or sympathetic company. Social circles in Canberra were still small and Rosalie would have come across the same women time and again in the various groups with which she engaged. Nicholas Brown, in his *A History of Canberra*, quotes Hope Hewitt's observation in 1961 that, as well as more trees and children per head, Canberra boasted more societies.[43] Apart from formal societies, special interest groups flourished in the city where many were newcomers who lacked extended family, social networks and old friends. Societies and classes provided a means of meeting people and connecting with others of like interests. Rosalie was a member of the Horticultural Society of Canberra and, in 1962, helped to found the First Canberra Garden Club. She belonged to the University House Ladies' Drawing Room (see Figure 8.4) at ANU and a group who loosely referred to themselves 'the Academy of Science ladies'.

41 Rosalie Gascoigne to Ben Gascoigne at NASA, Washington DC, August 1961, Papers of Ben Gascoigne, box 3 (original emphasis).
42 Ibid.
43 Brown, *A History of Canberra*, 152.

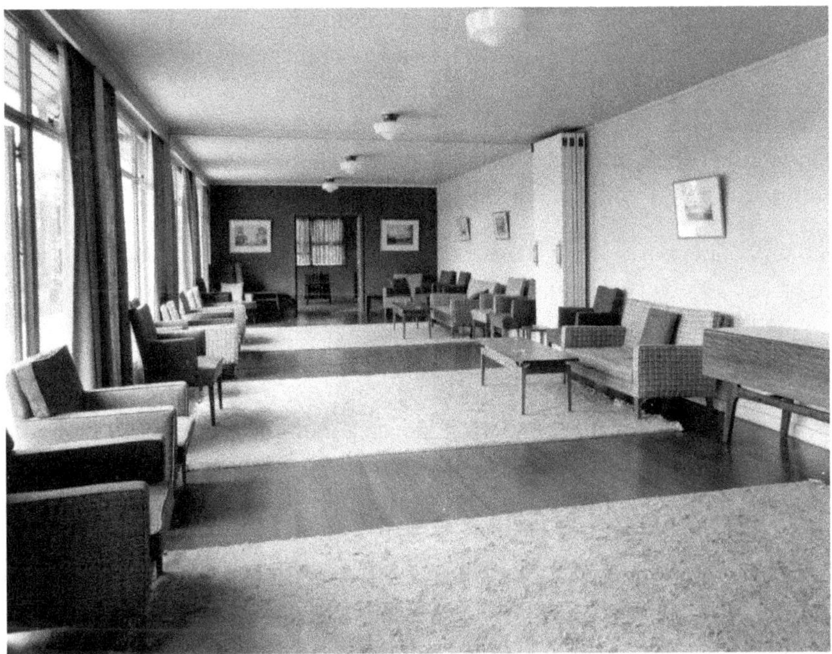

Figure 8.4: The Ladies' Drawing Room, University House, ANU, c. 1955, with furniture designed by Fred Ward.

Source: Courtesy of The Australian National University Archives, ANUA295-21.

She had been part of the Ladies' Drawing Room at ANU since its inception in 1956 and was co-convenor with Monica Freeman in 1959.[44] Freeman, who later enjoyed a successful artistic career and also made her name as an ethnographer, was married to New Zealand–born ANU anthropologist Derek Freeman.[45] Rosalie's friend, sculptor Jan Brown, said of the Ladies' Drawing Room: 'You couldn't get out of it but it got so incestuous—very small group.'[46] It was also a privileged group, having been established for the few female academics at the time and for wives of ANU academics. It aimed to create opportunities for like-minded women to meet and enjoy intellectual stimulation in the small city still lacking in social or cultural

44 Waterhouse, *University House*; Moran, 'University House Ladies Drawing Room'.

45 Fox, 'Emeritus Professor Derek Freeman'.

46 Jan Brown, interview by author, Canberra, 23 September 2011. Like Rosalie, Brown was tertiary-educated, having trained at the National Art School in Sydney and London's Chelsea Polytechnic with celebrated British modernist sculptors Henry Moore and Bernard Meadows. She also taught ceramic sculpture part-time at the precursor of ANU School of Art—the Canberra Technical College—from 1956. See Agostino and The Australian National University School of Art, *A History*. Jan Brown and Rosalie remained friends until Rosalie's death.

facilities despite its rapid growth.[47] The group was small and competitive; Brown remembered that she and Rosalie would wash the dishes to avoid gossip about whose husbands had achieved promotion and who had not.[48] Their avoidance of such gossip suggests that they had their own interests and senses of self, and did not need to engage in one-upmanship about their husbands' roles.

The 'Academy of Science ladies' comprised wives of academy members who met once or twice a year. Dawn Waterhouse, wife of the Commonwealth Scientific and Industrial Research Organisation (CSIRO) entomologist Dr Douglas Waterhouse, persuaded Rosalie to host a group lunch at Deakin at which Rosalie treated the women to a tour of her farm iron laid out in the backyard.[49] Another time Waterhouse remembered the group planning a morning tea for which she suggested they serve hot buttered cheese scones. Rosalie disagreed because they were 'too fattening', so an alternative was agreed upon. According to Waterhouse: 'There was no question about the scones. Rosalie had spoken so we couldn't have them!'[50] Such directness suggests that Rosalie experienced increasing confidence and self-assurance at this time. The elements of that shift in her identity are important to note: that she received affirmation and recognition through Horticultural Society activities and wins; that she was in demand for flower demonstrations and displays; that she felt fewer pressures to conform as an archetypal housewife following her move from Stromlo, where she had felt intense scrutiny, to suburban Canberra, where she enjoyed more privacy; and that she had more time, energy and personal space for her own activities with the children growing and Ben often away.

Few of the women she mixed with passed muster with Rosalie, so it stands out when one got her seal of approval. In her 1961 letter to Ben, she related that: 'Terry Milton Moore has gaiety—one of my favourite qualities after some of these uninspired and factual morning coffees I go to. We will see more of her I feel.'[51] Theresa 'Terry' Moore (née Ryan) arrived in Canberra in 1937 and married ecologist and scientist Raymond Milton Moore. Whether the Gascoignes did see more of Moore is unclear, but the qualities Rosalie admired in her reveal what she was searching for.

47 Moran, 'University House Ladies Drawing Room'.
48 Brown, interview by author.
49 Dawn Waterhouse, interview by author, Canberra, 24 July 2014.
50 Ibid.
51 Rosalie Gascoigne to Ben Gascoigne at NASA, Washington DC, 1961.

Rosalie's art practice: Gardening, flowers, ikebana

Two things happened in 1962 that were to contribute further to Rosalie's art making practice, one leading to another. In July 1962, she and a group of Canberra women founded the First Canberra Garden Club Inc. Born of Canberra's garden city status and tradition, a love of gardening and the need for a women's group that could meet during the day when children were at school and husbands at work, the club fostered friendship through gardening. In July 1962, Barbara Day, Grace Gurnet-Smith, Phyllis Jacobs, Molly Shoobridge, Mary Griffith, Jean Hurrell, Dot Hardy and Rosalie met at Hardy's home, where they formed a provisional committee to establish a garden club affiliated with the Garden Club of Australia.

The Horticultural Society of Canberra (HSC) had been going since 1927 and most of the women, including Rosalie, competed in its shows at the Albert Hall.[52] Men largely ran the HSC and they met in the evenings. Married, middle-class women did not generally work outside the home and provisions for childcare still lay in the future, so, in a city where most inhabitants had moved from elsewhere, the club gave women who were keen gardeners an opportunity to develop friendships while exchanging information about gardening. Canberra's hot, dry summers, frosty winters and generally poorly drained clay soil presented particular challenges. The club also provided a forum for swapping cuttings, bulbs and plants.[53] Despite the emphasis on friendship, the formality and conservatism of the time and place meant that the women addressed each other as Mrs, Miss or Lady in personal exchanges and meeting minutes. Their names were recorded with their husband's initials, as in 'Mrs S.C. Gascoigne'.[54]

Rosalie's time in the First Canberra Garden Club was short-lived. The family spent six months living in England in 1963 and, on her return to Canberra, she did not re-engage with the club. By that time she was immersed in Sogetsu Ikebana, a modern version of the complex and often minimalist Japanese art of flower arranging that dates back to the fifteenth century. The Sogetsu

52 First Canberra Garden Club Inc., 'The First Canberra Garden Club Inc'.
53 Mary Riek, interview by author, Ainslie, 26 November 2012.
54 Ibid.

school, founded in 1927, considers ikebana 'a three dimensional art form' or installation.[55] Its role in the next iteration of Rosalie's development is worth close attention.

Ikebana

In 1962, one of the early members of the First Canberra Garden Club, Dawn Waterhouse, invited Rosalie to join a class in Sogetsu Ikebana.[56] Waterhouse's mother-in-law Janet Waterhouse (née Kellie), wife of the camellia expert and University of Sydney professor of German and modern languages and literature Gowrie Waterhouse, had taken up ikebana in the 1920s, learning it from Eva Botan Sadler, the Anglo-Japanese wife of Arthur Sadler, professor of Oriental studies at the University of Sydney.[57] In 1959, Janet Waterhouse became the founding president of the Sydney chapter of *Ikebana* International. Through her love for the practice, she inspired her daughter-in-law Dawn to organise a class in Canberra.[58] Janet turned to renowned Australian ikebana master Norman Sparnon, who had studied in Japan for fourteen years under Sofu Teshigahara, the founder of the Sogetsu school. On returning to Australia in 1960, Sparnon based himself in Sydney and offered classes around the country.[59] As Sparnon would teach only classes with a minimum of twenty people, Dawn Waterhouse encouraged women in her social circles to join the class. Rosalie was one of those she persuaded.[60]

The women in the group represented the educated and privileged nature of Canberra society, spotlighting the circles in which Rosalie moved. Most of the women had held interesting jobs prior to their marriages, a number were tertiary educated, and virtually all were married to senior scientists, public servants and/or academics. Dawn Waterhouse had met her husband when she worked as a research assistant at CSIRO. Mary Riek had moved from Tasmania to Canberra to train as a librarian with the public service in

55 Shimbo, 'Ikebana to Contemporary Art', 50.

56 Mary Riek, interview by author.

57 O'Neil, 'Waterhouse, Eben Gowrie (1881–1977)'; Day, Whitten and Sands, 'Douglas Frew Waterhouse 1916–2000'.

58 Dawn Waterhouse, interview by author.

59 Roberts, 'Discovering Tradition'. Norman Sparnon was a member of the international board of directors of the Sogetsu school in Tokyo; in Australia, he had the titles of grand master of the Ikenobo school and representative of the Sogetsu and Ohara schools.

60 Dawn Waterhouse, interview by author.

Canberra where she met her husband, CSIRO entomologist and winemaker Dr Edgar Riek. Phyllis Nicholson was a botanist and school teacher who married another CSIRO entomologist, Dr A. J. Nicholson. Dorothy de Salis was married to Dr Eric James Fane De Salis, director of the Canberra Health Laboratory and from an old Monaro pastoral family. Jean Hurrell's husband George was the headmaster of Griffith Primary School. Rosalie mixed with the educated and affluent. Flower arranging and ikebana were provinces for those with a certain kind of aesthetic as well as spare time and financial resources. Waterhouse told me: 'We had time [for ikebana]. Nearly everyone had a cleaning lady.'[61]

Rosalie quickly took to ikebana. She told Hughes it provided her with the first inkling she could do anything:

> It was the first time I realised I was good at anything … I could always write a bit, you know, and that sort of thing. But nothing solidified. And with this, I learnt Ikebana for seven years I think. And it helped me with my art. It helped me with form.[62]

She said Constance Spry was all about colour, whereas ikebana was about form and it led her to start 'looking sculpturally at things'.[63]

The affirmation of success further inspired Rosalie, who looked forward to the monthly classes held in the Wesley Methodist Church hall in Forrest. She recalled: 'At his first lesson, Norman Sparnon said that the best way to translate the word Ikebana is "awareness of nature". I'd got that already. I was *acutely* aware of nature'.[64] She said: 'From practising Ikebana I got the vision of how to use the things I liked.'[65] Ikebana's tradition of mass and size appealed to Rosalie. Its influence is visible in her later work in the profusion of identical materials, especially in her carved-up and rearranged reflective road signs and assemblages of deconstructed wooden soft drink crates. Rosalie's involvement in ikebana and its impact on her artistic practice will be discussed further in the following chapter where it fits chronologically.

61 Ibid.

62 Hughes et al., 'Rosalie Gascoigne Artist', tape 1.

63 Ibid.

64 MacDonald and Gascoigne, *Rosalie Gascoigne*, 21 (original emphasis).

65 Mary Eagle, cited in O'Brien, Savage and City Gallery Wellington, *Rosalie Gascoigne: Plain Air*, 38.

Henry Moore's *Standing Figure: Knife Edge* and Rosalie's own small sculptures

Rosalie left the Antipodes for the first time in 1963. She and Hester spent six months in England on Ben's sabbatical at the Royal Greenwich Observatory, then next door to Herstmonceux Castle in East Sussex. The shipping company with whom the family travelled from Australia to Greece mislaid Ben's scientific papers, so he had a shaky start. Hester studied by correspondence with lessons sent from Australia. Toss travelled with the family, but, at seventeen years of age, chose to spend his time in London rather than the small East Sussex village, of Hailsham, the village neighbouring Herstmonceux, where the family lived in the home of astrophysicist Bernard Pagel and his wife Annabel and their children while they were elsewhere on sabbatical. The cottage was called 'Red Dwarf' (a type of star) a fitting name for one whose work involved the stars.[66] Martin, then a student at ANU, remained in Canberra where he lived in Bruce Hall, the The Australian National University's first student hall of residence, opened in 1961 and the first co-ed university hall of residence in Australia.[67] In further trans-Tasman connections, Bruce Hall's warden (for twenty-five years) was New Zealand Rhodes Scholar William (Bill) Packard.[68]

At this stage Rosalie, supported by Ben, actively sought exposure to art. From Sussex the Gascoignes took advantage of the easy train ride to London where they visited exhibitions and saw contemporary American art and work by Francis Bacon.[69] Henry Moore's *Standing Figure: Knife Edge* (1961) excited Rosalie when she and Ben saw it at the fourth *Sculpture in the Open Air* in London's Battersea Park.[70] The work, 2.845 metres high and cast in bronze, reminded her of a monumental ikebana construction.[71] Other work in the open-air exhibition included works by American artists John Chamberlain and Jason Seley, both of whom used car parts.

66 Hester Gascoigne, emails to author, 19 March 2023, 27 September 2023.
67 The Australian National University, 'Acton Campus—Site Inventory'; Cheng, 'Historic Bruce Hall'.
68 Kent, 'Packard, William Percival (Bill) (1925–2009)'.
69 O'Brien, Savage and City Gallery Wellington, *Rosalie Gascoigne: Plain Air*, 83.
70 Martin Gascoigne, email to author, 9 December 2014.
71 MacDonald and Gascoigne, *Rosalie Gascoigne*, 21.

Back in Canberra, the sculptures Rosalie had seen inspired her to look at shape 'and the only shape around here which was durable was the iron in the paddocks, so I used it'.[72] The iron, she told North, 'breathes the Australian landscape'.[73]

From 1964, Rosalie began using rusty iron to make small sculptures of people and creatures described by MacDonald as being 'in sharp contrast to the abstract linearity of Ikebana'.[74] Significantly, these works began to register some of the pressures of contemporary social change, as if clarity on the issue of form allowed greater attention to that of purpose. MacDonald described one of Rosalie's early pieces, *Conscription*, as:

> A mass of flat-headed spikes from Captains Flat railway station crammed into a small pierced metal slab, depicting a hurrying crowd of people. One spike had its head 'turned back'—a reluctant Vietnam conscript looking over his shoulder.[75]

Rosalie's son Toss had his birthdate drawn in the national service ballot but was declared unfit for military service because of a broken ankle he had suffered playing football some months earlier.[76] Rosalie was far from alone in being a mother brought to political awareness by the immediacy of issues such as conscription. But still, characteristically, and not convincingly, she disowned too direct a political connection. While lamenting 'all those poor blighters who had to go', she described *Conscription* as a reference to current events rather than a political statement: 'I never made a statement of any sort at all.'[77]

Few of Rosalie's early small sculptures survive because she packed them together without fixatives so they eventually fell apart. Ben later took a course in welding to help create more permanent works, but Rosalie (eventually) felt his involvement threatened her creative autonomy:

> I felt he was getting into my world that belonged just to me, where what I said went. And it was the first time in my life that what I said went.[78]

72 Ibid., 20.
73 Gascoigne, interview by North, 16.
74 MacDonald and Gascoigne, *Rosalie Gascoigne*, 20.
75 Ibid.
76 Toss Gascoigne, email to author, 14 January 2015.
77 MacDonald and Gascoigne, *Rosalie Gascoigne*, 20.
78 Ibid.

By the time Ben graduated from his welding course in 1973, Rosalie had gone 'right off' iron sculptures.[79] Rare surviving works include *Sir Bagby* (1974) in the Art Gallery of New South Wales, and *Adam and Eve* in the family collection.

Moving on

The first four years of the 1960s were significant for Rosalie. This was due, in part, to Canberra's rapid growth; to her increasing visibility and success in flower arranging and demonstrating; to her introduction to, and immediate success at, ikebana; to the artistic influence of her exposure to Henry Moore's sculptures in England; and to her branching out into making small iron sculptures. The years were in-between ones as she began to feel unfulfilled in her roles as a flower arranger and demonstrator. At the same time, she achieved recognition for her skills, lifting her confidence and encouraging her to pursue more opportunities for creative expression. She was fortunate that Canberra was expanding in ways that began to make it possible for her own universe to do the same. Having made her mark with flowers and dried arrangements, she was ready to move on and a number of factors conspired to make this possible. Ikebana taught her form and composition, and her stint in England gave her access to a wider range of art. The *Sculpture in the Open Air* exhibition at Battersea Park sparked her imagination. Women were reflecting on their place in society and beginning to challenge the restraints placed on them. Although she was not actively involved in formal women's movements, Rosalie's networks included women who were aware of their rights and who were discussing issues about representation and interests. These factors, combined with the increased time available to her as her children grew, paved the way for her developing art practice.

79 Ibid. Ben's pass is recorded in 'Technical College Results', *Canberra Times*, 11 January 1973, 17.

PART III

1969–99

PEARCE

‘I needed this art’

9

1965–70: 'Lift-off'[1]

A photograph of Rosalie in the *Canberra Times* in November 1969 shows a quintessentially affluent-looking woman wearing a neat, vertical-striped shirtwaist dress, shortish bouffant hair and cat-eye spectacles. She is pictured holding her ikebana instructor Norman Sparnon's latest book, *A Guide to Japanese Floral Arrangement*. An ikebana arrangement sits in a Sparnon bowl behind her. She is quoted as saying of the book: 'It removes all the mystique of the east and puts Ikebana squarely on the Australian scene.'[2]

Rosalie's visibility grew from this point. She emerged from the shadow of her husband and domesticity. And it was from this time that people often commented unbidden on her appearance, providing us with a strong sense of her physical presence. There are risks in describing a successful woman's appearance—of reducing her to her hair style, body type or choice of clothing. But, for Rosalie, such descriptions enable her to materialise in our line of vision, and into the public eye, an unusual occurrence for a woman of her age when women usually begin to disappear as their hair greys and their fertility diminishes. As an older, menopausal woman, Rosalie stood in strong contrast to other artists achieving acclaim. For instance, Sydney painter Brett Whiteley was young, male and lived a life of excesses often seen to be a successful artist's due. Rosalie's appearance was noted because

1 In O'Brien, Savage and City Gallery Wellington, *Rosalie Gascoigne: Plain Air,* Daniel Thomas described Rosalie's physical presence and her work as 'airborne' and wrote: 'two of her masterpieces jolt all Canberran observers with a gut feeling of physical lift-off'. I have used 'lift-off' here in the sense that her artistic practice 'lifted off' during the period covered by this chapter.

2 Lax, 'Ikebana: A Flight to Creativity … and a Popular Art', *Canberra Times*, 18 July 1969, 12.

of her difference. She was steady and no-nonsense. She had begun living for her art and nothing was going to get in the way. This is how people saw her—as straightforward, direct and having no pretensions. She was seen as honest and, together with her direct gaze, this made her stand out.

Compared to her family of origin, Rosalie was tall. At 170 centimetres, she stood taller than her parents and siblings: 'I was bigger. I was the biggest one in the family, which is strange. Both my mother and father were short.'[3] Her brother Douglas was 162 centimetres.[4] That she carried her height with elegance became increasingly apparent as her public profile grew. In television features, she moves slowly and deliberately across the landscape, graceful in every way.

The new friends who began to enter her life from the late 1960s onwards frequently mentioned her physical appearance, almost as if it was part of the impact she made: an impressive, mature woman exerting sudden influence over the then predominantly masculine world of Australian art. Meeting her in the 1970s and getting to know her in the early 1980s when he was senior curator of Australian Art at the then Australian National Gallery (ANG), Daniel Thomas described her as 'tall and slim and graceful, and especially when older, had physical presence'.[5] James Mollison, foundation director of the ANG from 1982, told me Rosalie 'was always very attractively dressed. She had good clothes sense—it had nothing to do with fashion. Understated handcrafted elegance—good in texture, size of pattern.'[6]

Some comments about Rosalie's attire might have reflected assumptions about bohemian artists who expressed their difference through dress, which was definitely not Rosalie's style. If anything, her care over her appearance was likely a legacy of her genteel Auckland upbringing. Her daughter-in-law, art historian Mary Eagle commented that, even though 'she felt she was the odd one out in society … throughout her life she adhered, without deviation to the conventions of her Auckland upbringing'.[7] All of these elements added to the incongruity but also the appropriateness of the figure she began to cut in an art world keen for a new synthesis.

3 Hughes et al., 'Rosalie Gascoigne Artist', tape 1. Rosalie's height is recorded in her passports, which are in Papers of Rosalie Gascoigne, box 4.

4 Douglas Hamilton Walker, army no. 46701, service record supplied by Headquarters New Zealand Defence Force Te Ope Kātua O Aotearoa.

5 Thomas, 'Rhythm & Lift-Off', 15.

6 James Mollison, interviewed by author, Melbourne, 2 November 2011.

7 Eagle, 'Rosalie Gascoigne's Lyrical Derailments', 203.

Friend and fellow artist Marie Hagerty who knew Rosalie from the 1990s said:

> she didn't seem like an old woman. She dressed with great style … she was agile mentally; and physically, too … the phone would ring and she'd skate the rug across the floor on the way to answer it.[8]

Another friend and fellow artist, Jan Brown told me:

> You'd never have picked her as an artist as people are these days—wearing funny clothes, funny haircuts and behaving in an outrageous manner. I've … seldom met a serious artist who does that … Henry Moore was … like a country bank manager—wore a tweed coat with leather things on his elbow, knitted tie, always clean.[9]

Eminent Aotearoa New Zealand photographer Marti Friedlander commented on Rosalie's elegance, having met her in Auckland in 1999:

> I was taken aback by the stylishness. You would never have guessed from Rosalie that she was this amazing artist. [She was a] … beautifully stylishly dressed woman … totally different to how I imagined an artist would be. Groomed, utterly groomed … to me that was quite amazing because I would have thought that being this artisan artist she might have let go … isn't that an interesting aspect of her? That in a way you always hold on to the integral part of who you really are because you can never let it go—it's so important—you might want to change a bit for fashion, but I think that's part of Rosalie that she could never change for fashion because she was herself.[10]

Rosalie was comfortable in her own skin at this time of her life. Her confidence manifested itself in the way she carried and presented herself. Descriptions of her appearance highlight her increasing visibility as she became well-known in Canberra for her flower arranging and ikebana. Her personal visibility coexists with that of women generally through the manifestation of women's movements that questioned women's roles and limitations on their lives.

8 Marie Hagerty, quoted in Thomas, 'Rhythm & Lift-Off', 15. Hagerty and her partner Peter Vandermark also mentioned Rosalie's easy agility and habit of skating on the rug in our interview on 24 January 2011.

9 Jan Brown, interview by author, 2011.

10 Marti Friedlander, interview by author, Auckland, 19 October 2010.

Ikebana from the mid- to late-1960s

During the mid- to late-1960s Rosalie's art practice continued to include ikebana and sculptures made from rusty farm iron. She told Ian North in 1982 that ikebana was good for her because it gave her discipline and enabled her to give shape to some of the amorphous areas of her practice.[11] Significantly, she told Hughes: 'it gave me the whole free open world. I could do what I liked.'[12] When Hughes asked her what she got out of ikebana, she responded:

> I got a lot, I did get a lot ... it made possible things that I didn't particularly know were possible. And that you could make art. Ikebana doesn't need a flower in it ... it can be like sculpture.[13]

Having gained confidence from her success at ikebana, Rosalie was beginning to see herself and her creativity in a different light—one full of possibility.

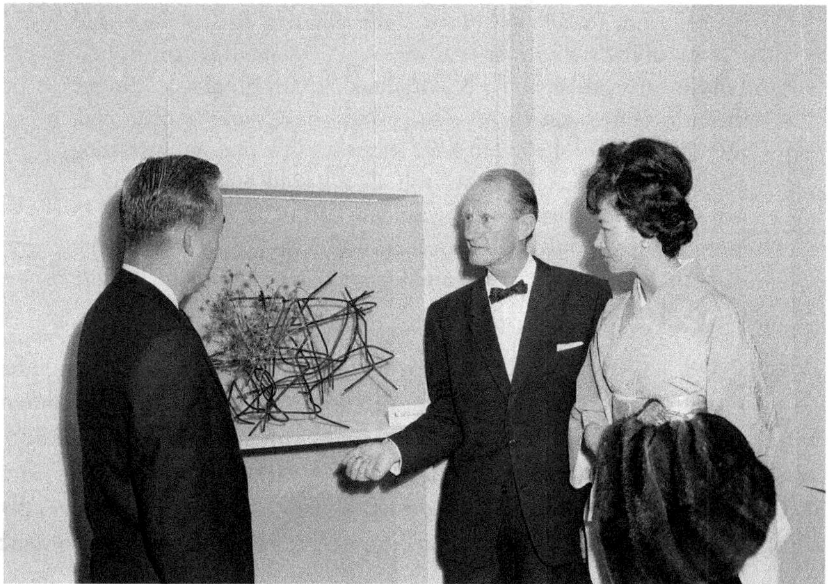

Figure 9.1: 'He emasculated it!'—Norman Sparnon (centre) in front of Rosalie's tangled iron with blue devil, with the consul general for Japan, Mr Nissi Sato, and Mrs Sato at Farmers Blaxland Gallery, Sydney, in 1965.
Source: NAA: 1501, A5765/2.

11 Gascoigne, interview by North, 12.
12 Hughes et al., 'Rosalie Gascoigne Artist', tape 3.
13 Ibid.

In 1965 the practice so engaged Rosalie that she trained as an ikebana teacher, gaining a teaching diploma from Tokyo's Sogetsu School.[14] In June of that year, Farmers Blaxland Gallery in Sydney displayed an innovative piece of her work in which she arranged the noxious weed blue devil with a rusty tangle of iron from reinforced concrete (see Figure 9.1). However, Rosalie's pleasure in having her work displayed dissipated when she discovered Sparnon had coated the rusty iron with black paint. To Vici MacDonald in 1998 she cried, 'he emasculated it!'[15]

Rosalie's ikebana career peaked in September 1967 when the Japanese master Sofu Teshigahara, founder of the Sogetsu Ikebana school, visited Canberra with an extensive entourage, including sixteen kimono-clad assistants. Rosalie was in awe of Teshigahara who was 'reputedly the highest paid artist in Japan', the 'Picasso of flower arranging'.[16] The visit brought recognition for her when Sydney-based Sparnon asked her to collect material for Teshigahara that reflected the Canberra countryside. Having spent weeks collecting plant material that she stuffed into the Academy of Science basement in preparation for the visit, Rosalie told how she trembled as she followed 'the great man' down the stairs to the basement where he was to view the material. She was overwhelmed and relieved when he turned around and said to her, 'you have a great eye'.[17]

> Talk about the accolade! … it was great praise … He went back to Japan and apparently he said … It's got wonderful material in Australia but the best in Canberra … Everybody else was doing the lush and the orchid and the camellia … I gave him the brown look.[18]

Rosalie's reputation as an excellent Sogetsu ikebana practitioner flourished in the years following Teshigahara's accolade. Designer Arthur Robinson commissioned her to create displays for the opening of the National Library of Australia in 1968, and the Japanese Embassy commissioned her to make

14 'Reception to Honour Indian MP', *Canberra Times*, 23 November 1965, 13, reported that Rosalie and another Stromlo astronomer's wife, Mrs B. Westerlund, received teachers' diplomas from the Sogetsu School of Ikebana in Tokyo. During 1968 and 1969, Rosalie advertised her classes in the *Canberra Times*, for example: 'Classes in Japanese flower arrangement, Wednesday mornings and afternoons. Beginners and advanced students. Enquiries Mrs Gascoigne 811285.' See *Canberra Times*, Tuesday 1 October 1968, 21. Ikebana classes were advertised in the *Canberra Times*, Saturday 1 February 1969, 118.

15 MacDonald and Gascoigne, *Rosalie Gascoigne*, 18.

16 Roberts and Australian Academy of Science, 'A Big, Bold, Simple Concept', 139.

17 Gascoigne, interview by North, 15.

18 Ibid.

a display for the opening of their new chancery in 1970.[19] In addition to building her confidence, Rosalie's experience with Teshigahara left a lasting legacy for her art. In the catalogue *Rosalie Gascoigne: Plain Air*, Daniel Thomas notes that Rosalie attended Teshigahara's performances in Sydney (at the Art Gallery of New South Wales) and in Canberra where he 'danced around with broom-sized brushes making a huge, wildly gestural black calligraphy painting … [and] transformed a supply of tree branches into an over-human-height, artfully-angled mound, an Ikebana woodpile'.[20] Rosalie recalled these events in a later letter to Martin: 'I remember Sofu doing his vast dragon calligraphy and think that I could well do a visible WHISPER out of feathers.'[21] As Thomas points out, she did so with *Feathered Fence* in 1979:

> One would like to think that watching Sofu's performance helped confirm her direction not only towards big things hoisted up in the air, which is the essence of Sogetsu Ikebana, but also towards works that transparently reveal their simple processes of making.[22]

The following year, 1968, Rosalie's confession to her 'total involvement in the art of Japanese flower arrangement' sparked *Canberra Times* reporter Doreen Hungerford's tribute:

> Even if all your fingers are thumbs and you have the artistic soul of a concrete mixer—and I speak for myself, naturally—you can't help responding to the enthusiasm of Rosalie Gascoigne when she talks about the art of Ikebana.[23]

Having achieved recognition through her ikebana practice and found an aesthetic that resonated with her acute awareness of nature, Rosalie wholeheartedly embraced the exotic art form. But that same year something happened that was to become a factor in her move away from ikebana.

---

19 Hughes et al., 'Rosalie Gascoigne Artist', tape 3. A letter from the Japanese Embassy thanking Rosalie for the 'magnificent arrangement of dry and fresh materials' she made to decorate the reception room at the Lakeside International Hotel when the Crown Prince and Crown Princess of Japan visited is among her papers at the National Library of Australia. Kiezo Kimura, Embassy of Japan, to Mrs S. C. Gascoigne, 8 May 1973, Papers of Rosalie Gascoigne, box 16.

20 Thomas, 'Rhythm & Lift-Off', 15.

21 Rosalie to Martin in Hong Kong, cited in Thomas, 'Rhythm & Lift-Off', 15.

22 Thomas, 'Rhythm & Lift-Off', 15.

23 Doreen Hungerford, 'Ikebana Is Evoking Lots of Enthusiasm', *Canberra Times*, 13 November 1968, 20.

A number of aspects of ikebana had begun to irk Rosalie, not least was her increasingly problematic relationship with Sparnon whose plagiarism of one of her creations for his book initiated the deterioration of their working relationship.

Tiring of the expensive ikebana vases, Rosalie had begun to use discarded farm iron as bases for her displays 'because it had the shape in it … some marvellous shapes'.[24] Sparnon used one of Rosalie's containers made 'with two somethings and a bit of wire' for a camellia arrangement and included it in his book *The Magic of Camellias*.[25] It was Rosalie's first published assemblage, and Sparnon described it as if it were his own creation.[26] Rosalie was furious.[27] She angrily attributed Sparnon's autocratic behaviour to ikebana's culture of the supremacy of the master and the relative insignificance of the student: 'You feed everything into the Master and you remain nothing.'[28] As her confidence in her own ability grew, her ardour for ikebana dwindled.

Despite her fury, in a *Canberra Times* article in 1969, the reporter described Rosalie as 'an ardent admirer of Norman Sparnon' and quoted her as saying: 'He [Sparnon] brings a pure strain of Ikebana to Australia.'[29] In a telling comment on the social transitions underway and the evolving possibilities in her own life, Rosalie lauded ikebana as another means of a 'flight to creativity' for housewives, alongside pottery.[30] More significantly, in relation to her move away from ikebana, she made these positive statements just one year after the publication of *The Magic of Camellias* with her plagiarised iron pot, and around the time of the publication of another book by Sparnon entitled *A Guide to Japanese Floral Arrangement*.[31] The contrast between Rosalie's words about ikebana in 1969 and her 1998 comments about the place of ikebana in her artistic practice illustrate the process of reflection and interpretation she had engaged in during the years in between. The confidence she acquired as a result of achieving artistic acclaim validated her anger at Sparnon's plagiarism in 1968 and she felt able to express it publicly,

24 Hughes et al., 'Rosalie Gascoigne Artist', tape 4.

25 Ibid., tape 3; Sparnon, *The Magic of Camellias*.

26 MacDonald and Gascoigne, *Rosalie Gascoigne*, 102.

27 Hughes et al., 'Rosalie Gascoigne Artist', tape 3.

28 Gascoigne, interview by North, 15.

29 Carole Lax, 'Ikebana: A Flight to Creativity … and a Popular Art', *Canberra Times*, 18 July 1969, 12.

30 Martin Gascoigne told me: 'Rosalie did pottery classes for a few weeks in the 1950s at the tech—she made an ice-cream tray and a pot. Pottery was the thing in Canberra and there were women potters.' Martin Gascoigne, interview by author, 2014.

31 Sparnon, *A Guide to Japanese Floral Arrangement*.

whereas in 1968 she was more restrained in her response. She still needed the discipline of ikebana, which, as she said in the interview, 'involves the subtlest forms of self-expression often in the most dramatic form'.[32] Nevertheless, tensions with Sparnon grew. Rosalie's anger at Sparnon for his use of her work without due credit snakes through her ikebana narrative.

Kelly Gellatly suggests that Rosalie's relationship with Sparnon 'became an increasingly complex bundle of mutual respect and creative competitiveness'.[33] At the same time, a number of other factors combined to contribute to this problematic mix, including Rosalie's growing impatience with ikebana's impermanence, disillusionment with ikebana's 'hierarchical approach and deference to "all things Japanese"' and her wish to engage more directly with the local countryside than ikebana permitted.[34]

By the end of the period covered in this chapter, Rosalie was tiring of ikebana's impermanence:

> Well ... I started making things that would last. I got a bit sick of the fact that Ikebana things if they lasted for four days this was absolutely marvellous, you see, and that was like eternity.[35]

Added to her frustration at ikebana's ephemeral nature and her precarious relationship with Sparnon, Rosalie also began to feel impatient with the fact that ikebana derived from a culture that was not Australian and that this was reflected in structures as well as aesthetics. She likened ikebana's hierarchical structure to the Roman Catholic Church, calling it a 'big pyramid, the Japanese ikebana pyramid' with 'mere practitioners' elevating the very few people at the top.[36] To Hughes in 1998 she said the ikebana schools were very rich 'because you pay for every certificate you get ... Didn't seem right, or Australian to me.'[37] By now she identified as Australian and wanted her work to reflect this and the Australian landscape.

In terms of aesthetics, Sparnon's insistence that she must 'learn to understand the Japanese' irritated her:[38]

32 Lax, 'Ikebana: A Flight to Creativity.'
33 Gellatly, 'Rosalie Gascoigne', 11.
34 Hughes et al., 'Rosalie Gascoigne Artist', tape 3.
35 Ibid.
36 Ibid.
37 Ibid.
38 MacDonald and Gascoigne, *Rosalie Gascoigne*, 19.

> There were more things that I wanted to explore about the Australian countryside than I could say with Ikebana. It also troubled me that it was a foreign art. I thought that was too limiting. My work was becoming very Australian.[39]

Rosalie 'wanted a bigger world than the one Ikebana offered' in the rural Australian context.[40] Although she was ready to move on, she acknowledged ikebana's gift to her. In a message for a Tokyo audience in 1983, Rosalie described the place of ikebana in her practice:

> The primary emphasis on form and line and the secondary emphasis on colour sharpened my eye and heightened my enjoyment in the things I saw in the hills and paddocks around Canberra.[41]

She had found a means of making art that gave meaning to her feelings for the Monaro countryside and a form by which to represent them. Ikebana, she said, 'confirmed in me many of the feelings I already had for nature and it provided some necessary discipline in expressing those feelings'.[42] 'Ikebana taught me to use the unusable.'[43]

Despite her frustrations with ikebana, Rosalie continued with classes and, during 1968 and 1969, advertised herself as a teacher. Decades after her death, debate continues over the magnitude of the significance of ikebana to her art. Art commentators recognised the influence of ikebana on Rosalie's art making. Melbourne curator Kelly Gellatly suggested that the study of ikebana gave 'purpose' to Rosalie's already fervent 'hunting and gathering'.[44] The 'almost classic formality' of her works with their 'staunchness and discipline as well as a scrupulous eye' recognised by New Zealand's Wellington City Gallery director in 2004, Paula Savage, was probably a legacy of ikebana's discipline.[45]

---

39 Jacobs, 'Rosalie Gascoigne', 110–13.

40 Gascoigne, 'Message to the Japanese', Papers of Rosalie Gascoigne, box 3.

41 Ibid.; Holland, 'Innovation, Art Practice and Japan', 29: '*Continuum '83* toured twenty-seven Australian artists to fifteen commercial galleries and studios across Tokyo, including seven video artists to the SCAN Gallery. This was an exceptional art experience for Tokyo's local audience and for the Australian artists who visited during the exhibition period, which included Rosalie Gascoigne, Mike Parr and Lyndal Jones. Paula Dawson, Ken Unsworth and John Letherbridge [displayed] media works at galleries in the Ginza where there was a concentration of exhibitions.'

42 Gascoigne, 'Message to the Japanese'.

43 Edwards, *Rosalie Gascoigne: Material as Landscape*, 12.

44 Gellatly, 'Rosalie Gascoigne', 11.

45 Savage, 'Introduction', 12.

However, one person seeking to use Rosalie for art historical cultural purposes pulls in another direction. Melbourne ikebana artist and academic Shoso Shimbo claims that ikebana was crucial for her art.[46] He takes exception to Mary Eagle's contention that ikebana was a 'gateway' to Rosalie's art, asserting that it was much more than this.[47] He regards her work as 'a case study of cultural transformation across borders' and argues that 'the visual and sustained metaphor Gascoigne recognised in Ikebana places her assemblages at an extreme end of contemporary Ikebana'.[48]

There is no doubt that Rosalie's engagement with ikebana was significant for her artistic development. Rosalie acknowledged this herself; however, she was irritated when some commentators accorded Sparnon and ikebana more influence in her career than she considered either deserved. She told North in 1982:

> I don't like the sense that it invented me because I was going great guns before. I have this little thing against Norman Sparnon whom I think used me a lot.[49]

Fifteen years later, she was feeling much the same when she expressed similar frustrations to MacDonald:

> I always fight the belief that Norman Sparnon invented me. He didn't, I was already there. I got the point of the Japanese thing, and then I went through it and it wasn't for me. Ikebana disciplined me in a way I wouldn't have been otherwise. It taught me I was good at something. But it left great big pieces of the Australian ethos out.[50]

In the meantime, Rosalie had become more aware of other forms of artistic expression and was learning about modern painting and sculpture. Around this time, her son Martin began collecting contemporary art and introduced her to work by promising young Australian artists. As Martin entered adulthood and independence, the close relationships Rosalie had nurtured in her children blossomed in Martin through his sensitivity to her creativity and a particular aesthetic they shared, both of which he, in turn, nurtured and affirmed in her.

---

46 Shimbo, 'Ikebana to Contemporary Art', 57.
47 See Eagle, 'Rosalie Gascoigne's Lyrical Derailments', 205.
48 Shimbo, 'Ikebana to Contemporary Art', 49, 57.
49 Gascoigne, interview by North , 16.
50 MacDonald and Gascoigne, *Rosalie Gascoigne*, 19.

The arrival of dealer galleries

Along with these transformations in Rosalie's personal practice, the arrival of dealer galleries in Canberra in the 1960s brought two new dimensions to the recognition her work would achieve. The galleries ushered in a wider range of art than had been previously available through the Artists Society of Canberra exhibitions at the Canberra Art Workshop, Riverside, from 1948, the Riverside Gallery in Barton from 1953 and Les Arts in Kingston from 1957.[51] During the 1950s and particularly in the 1960s, reports in the *Canberra Times* attest to frequent exhibitions in the earliest commercial galleries, including the Canberra Theatre Centre Gallery on Ainslie Avenue in Civic (founded in 1959); Anna Simons Gallery in her Campbell home (early 1960s), which then became Canberra's branch of Sydney's Macquarie Galleries in Manuka in 1969, reverting to Anna Simons in 1972; and Gallery A, which operated out of the Town House Motel in Rudd Street, Civic, from 1964 to 1966. Dutch-born potter Riek LeGrand opened Studio Nundah in her O'Connor home in 1963 'to foster city art and provide a meeting place for artists'.[52] It continued to operate until around 1972.[53]

In addition to making more art available for the Canberra public to experience firsthand, public galleries around Australia increasingly purchased from the dealer galleries, changing the previous practice of purchasing from art society exhibitions. In *Suburbs of the Sacred* (1988), Humphrey McQueen describes how the era of amateurism ended in 1961 when state galleries stopped buying from art society exhibitions.[54] Sales and purchases were increasingly mediated via dealers to exert their own taste and make their own market. The dealers made their money by taking a proportion of the sale price; accordingly, they sought to foster artists who might sell. The base of power shifted as 'trustees no longer came to the painters: dealers waited upon the curators. Artists moved away from group shows towards one-person exhibitions with dealers who were becoming more professional.'[55]

51 See *Canberra Times* during the 1950s for advertisements and articles about Artists' Society of Canberra exhibitions at Canberra Art Workshop, the Riverside Gallery and Les Arts.

52 'New Gallery', *Canberra Times*, 21 March 1963, 12. Art critic and art historian, Sasha Grishin wrote about galleries in Canberra but only covered the period from the mid-1970s, by which time the major changes in the art world had already occurred vis-à-vis dealer galleries, and Rosalie was already establishing and aligning herself with Macquarie Galleries and Anna Simons.

53 'The Story of Studio Nundah: Oral History Interview with Michael Legrand'.

54 McQueen, *Suburbs of the Sacred*, 153.

55 Ibid.

Just as Rosalie began to find acceptance as a creator, the structure of the professional art world began changing. The increasing number of dealer galleries provided more venues for artists to exhibit in solo and group exhibitions. The new dealer galleries not only exposed Rosalie to more art, but also symbolised changes in the Australian art industry that were to benefit her within the next decade. The galleries provided opportunities to exhibit her art and enabled it to be seen by the critics and buyers who would facilitate her rise to fame.

Rosalie and Ben had attended Artists Society of Canberra shows in the 1950s and by the mid-1960s Rosalie was making the most of opportunities provided by the new dealer galleries. In 1965, she was excited to attend an exhibition of Pro Hart's work at Studio Nundah:

> When people first had shows in Canberra, there was one artist, one gallery, way over on the north side, and we used to put on our best arty clothes and go over, and it was marvellous. And you used to have advertisements in the paper like 'And the artist will be there' … the artist! Well that was touching glory for me. And I remember the time … when Pro Hart came to town. Pro Hart! And everybody rushed over, and he was supposed to be quite a voice in those days. Canberra was very backward.[56]

The rise of the dealer gallery, the replacement of group shows with solo artist exhibitions and the new practice of public galleries purchasing from these shows would prove timely for Rosalie's art career, along with other, later factors including Canberra's developing national gallery structures. Martin Gascoigne, who was to become a significant influence in Rosalie's artistic development in the late 1960s and 1970s, attended dealer gallery exhibitions.[57]

Martin Gascoigne

Martin told me he grew up with a sense of art as a family value, saying it went back to his father's friendship with Sydney artist and gallery/bookshop owner Carl Plate, which, in his recollection, is meshed with an expanding awareness of contemporary art:

56 Hughes et al., 'Rosalie Gascoigne Artist', tape 7. Donald Brook, 'New Nundah Gallery', *Canberra Times*, 16 December 1965, 27, reports the opening of the gallery on 15 December 1965.

57 'We went to the commercial galleries that were set up': Martin Gascoigne, interview by author, 2014.

> Carl … would visit. I can remember going to [Plate's] Notanda Gallery Bookshop in the 1950s [and] selecting postcards and things and seeing Carl. They would visit us. We stayed at their house on the Woronora River south of Sydney for a couple of weeks one summer in the fifties … [Ben and Rosalie] used to go to the Canberra Art Society shows a bit in the 1950s and bought a painting by one of the local schoolteachers. And they had a couple of prints including the Braque—a real Braque … and when Dad went to the States in 1956 … for six months, he came back with some reproductions from New York … a John Marin water colour, can't remember what else. In 1963 she [Rosalie] brought a classic Modigliani print back from London.[58]

In addition to the exposure to art through Ben's friendship with Plate, Rosalie's visuality was part of family life. She had taught all three of her children to always look with a discerning eye.

Martin's own interest in art developed steadily, alongside his mother's. As a new university graduate in his first job, he began buying original artworks in 1965, including a lithograph by Roy Lichtenstein (*Shipboard Girl*, 1965) and Dick Watkins's *Charming Study*. Martin kept an eye on new publications of art books and bought Douglas Duncan's *Picasso's Picasso* for Rosalie in 1961 as a combined Christmas and birthday present. Like his parents, he was a frequent visitor to 'the commercial galleries that were set up'.[59]

At Lesta O'Brien's Australia Sculpture Centre in Red Hill, Martin met a young man who had arrived in the city in November 1968 to work for the Commonwealth Arts Advisory Board (CAAB).[60] James Mollison (see Figure 9.2), formerly director of the Ballarat Fine Art Gallery, had just purchased a Hilda Rix Nicholas painting for the CAAB. The two young men struck up a conversation about the colour of the subject's eyes. As Martin recalled:

> That's where I met him [Mollison] the first time. So we'd see each other, run into each other. I was with him and some other people he knew going out to see Christo's wrapped coast.[61]

58 Ibid.

59 Ibid.

60 Lesta O'Brien was also a New Zealander and had attended Epsom Girls' Grammar School at the same time as Rosalie. An undated letter in Rosalie's archive from Rosalie to O'Brien suggests they were having a feud of sorts and demonstrates Rosalie's forthrightness: 'I do what I think right, or what pleases me, not what you think right, or what pleases you.' See Papers of Rosalie Gascoigne, box 24.

61 Ibid. Christo's *Wrapped Coast* was an artistic installation in which a two-and-a-half-kilometres long, twenty-six metres high area of Little Bay in Sydney was wrapped with ninety thousand square metres of synthetic erosion-control fabric for ten weeks.

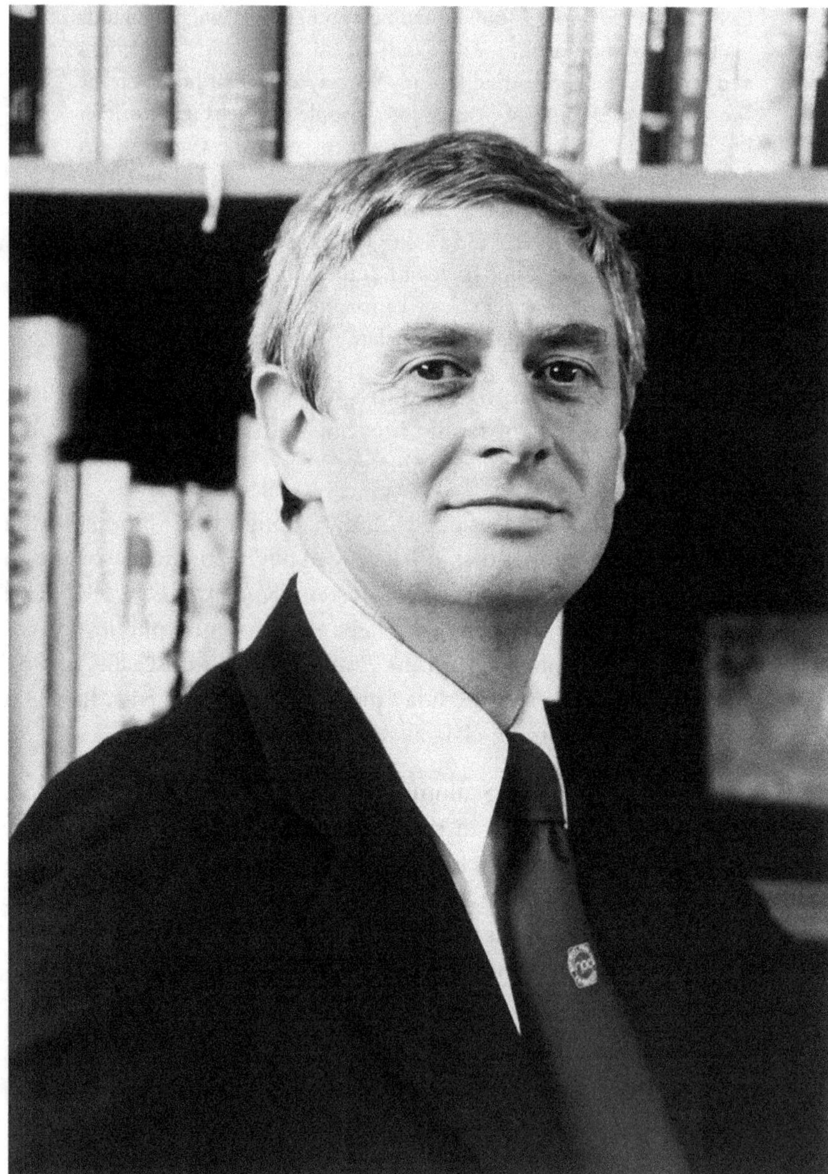

Figure 9.2: James Mollison, c. 1977.

Note: Having been appointed by the Commonwealth Arts Advisory Board to build the national art collection and later as acting then foundation director of the Australian National Gallery (later the National Gallery of Australia), Mollison played a significant, even crucial, part in Rosalie's development as an artist.

Source: Photograph and courtesy: Matt Kelso.

Mollison's arrival in Canberra heralded the beginning of a focus on the development of the Commonwealth Art Collection and the eventual development of the national gallery to be based in Canberra. Mollison described to me how his friendship with Rosalie began with Martin's invitation: 'Why don't you come and have Sunday dinner with us? My mum always has a Sunday meal.'[62] Mollison recalled that, for the next ten to fifteen years:

> Sunday dinner every night I had in town was with Professor Ben Gascoigne who became a particular friend, Rosalie and Martin. Mostly the same meal, leg of lamb [and] a marvellous dish of tomatoes, onions with breadcrumbs on top.[63]

So began an important friendship between Rosalie and Mollison, one of the key people in the Australian art world that decade. He was to speak to her about her developing art practice, instruct her in art history and introduce her to the Australian art community.

The art world in which Mollison was a central player was in a process of flux. Tastes were changing. Painting's primacy waned and other art forms like pop art, minimalism and assemblage gained acceptance. Structures changed, with the commercialisation of art through the rise of the dealer galleries and the developing bureaucracy of curators, administrators and critics around the planned for new national art gallery. Both taste and bureaucracy were to play significant parts in Rosalie's rise to fame and pave the way for her reception.

62 James Mollison, interview by author, 2011.

63 Ibid.

Australian National Gallery and James Mollison

A national art gallery had always been part of the vision for Canberra, but the economic hardships and austere years of two world wars and the Great Depression delayed plans. It was not until 1965 that the ANG, which was to be a major influence in Rosalie's life, began to take shape when Prime Minister Sir Robert Menzies set in train its establishment as part of his vision to build a national capital befitting Australia.[64] It was 1982 before the building was complete and officially opened.[65]

The initial vision was for a collection of 'portraits of "representative men" of the new nation—Governors-General, leading politicians, pioneers'.[66] In 1938, this brief broadened to include 'suitable landscape paintings by Australian artists from time to time' on the recommendation of the then chair of the CAAB, which had been established in 1912.[67] By the early 1950s, the CAAB began to acquire art for the 'Lending Collection', which made works available on loan to Australian diplomatic posts overseas and official establishments in Australia.[68] By the 1960s, this policy was seen by the CAAB as a way of encouraging young Australian painters; by the late 1960s, it had broadened further on the basis of James Mollison's assessment of the collection and the 1966 Lindsay Report's recommendation for an acquisition policy 'that extended the scope of collecting beyond Australia's shores to its geographical region and to the wider world'.[69]

64 Helen Hyland, bibliographic services librarian, National Gallery of Australia, email to author, 16 July 2014: 'The Gallery name was changed from Australian National Gallery to National Gallery of Australia on 24 October 1992. This coincided with the 10th anniversary of the opening of the Gallery. The name change is documented in the annual report for 1992–1993 and is also mentioned more informally in the NGA members' magazine, National Gallery news.' In this book I use the name that was appropriate chronologically: ANG until 1992 and then National Gallery of Australia (NGA).

65 Sparke, *Canberra 1954–1980*, 309; Green, ed., *Building the Collection*, 1.

66 Green, ed., *Building the Collection*, 1.

67 Ibid., 3.

68 Ibid., 5.

69 Ibid., 14. In 1965, Prime Minister Robert Menzies established the National Art Gallery Committee of Inquiry chaired by Sir Daryl Lindsay. The committee presented its report to Prime Minister Harold Holt in 1966.

Mollison's assessment included a recommendation for acquiring truly contemporary Australian works, modernist works and examples of colour-field, non-figurative painting from the National Gallery of Victoria's groundbreaking *The Field* exhibition in 1968.[70] The collection lacked work from Western Australia, South Australia and Queensland, so Mollison set about filling those gaps. He emphasised his awareness that his personal taste should not be a factor when choosing works for the collection and said of CAAB chair Sir William Dargie: 'he was very aware that you should never allow anything personal to intervene in what you are doing for a Gallery'.[71] Dargie, said Mollison, is the unsung hero of Australia's national gallery:

> He is often spoken of as being a conservative; in fact he had a very clear head for what a National Gallery might in due course contain, and that it had to pay keen attention to current art practice.[72]

With Dargie behind him during the expansive 1970s, when Australian confidence was strong and ambitions high, Mollison felt the sky was the limit.

Mollison was in his late thirties, having been born in 1931; Rosalie was in her late fifties. Like Rosalie, Mollison had trained as a teacher. He had taught art at Reservoir High School and Melbourne High School.[73] In 1960, after time in Europe, he was appointed education officer at the National Gallery of Victoria (NGV) from where he took up a role as director of Gallery A, Toorak, in 1964. In 1967, he was appointed director of Australia's oldest and largest regional gallery, the Ballarat Fine Art Gallery.

Mollison was passionate about art, and he was driven. At the age of sixteen, he had asked NGV director Daryl Lindsay for a job, and there he met critic and pioneering modernist painter Arnold Shore (1897–1963), who was a guide-lecturer. Shore's studio was the first Mollison visited. From there he established close relationships with key Australian artists including William 'Jock' Frater (1890–1974), Eric Thake (1904–1982) and Danila Vassilieff (1897–1958).[74] Mollison immersed himself in the art world; he learned about art from the artists themselves and quickly became a highly respected member of the Victorian arts community. At one stage he had wanted to be an artist, writing home from London in 1957 that he planned to get himself

70 Ibid., 15.

71 Mollison and Gray, 'James Mollison in Conversation with Anne Gray', 25.

72 Ibid.

73 Douglas Aiton, 'The Big Art Spender', *Age*, 16 October 1974.

74 Mollison, interview by author, 2011.

a studio so he could work more regularly. But, he conceded, he 'found other people's work infinitely more interesting. Anything I did was so clinical that there didn't seem to be any place for it.'[75]

In 1967, when CAAB experienced difficulty in finding someone to build a national collection in preparation for the ANG, they turned to Mollison. He had proven himself to be someone who knew the business of art, museums and exhibitions. The board invited him to Canberra to discuss the new position. Lindsay, whom Mollison had known then for two decades, was chair of the CAAB. Mollison, happy at Ballarat, declined the position; when asked what it would take for him to accept the job, the thirty-six-year-old nominated double his Ballarat salary, weekly flights around Australia to establish the content of every Australian collection, three months each year on overseas art buying trips, and a car and driver at all times while working wherever he was in the world.[76] Such was the esteem in which Mollison was held that CAAB acceded to all his requests. Mollison, confident, young, trendy and elegant with his long hair and flared trousers, was appointed to the role in October 1968 and moved to Canberra.

His rise had been rapid and his task was colossal. The CAAB commissioned Mollison to catalogue the national collection, arrange exhibitions of Australian art to tour overseas and advise on acquisitions. This role gave Mollison considerable standing in the art community. The trust in him demonstrated by CAAB, which included Sir Daryl Lindsay, and renowned painters Sir William Dargie (1912–2003) and Sir Russell Drysdale (1912–1981), rendered Mollison one of the most powerful people in Australia's art world. It is not surprising that Rosalie held him in awe.

Like Rosalie, Mollison was a deeply private person. During his time as director of the ANG, he was known for his refusal to divulge personal information in interviews. In 1974, he told an *Age* journalist: 'It's not important who I am … who is the director of the Louvre? No one knows. It doesn't matter.'[77] So private was he that for some time during the 1970s, he refused to allow photographs of himself to be taken. Mollison's focus was on art and making a great gallery for Australia. Gordon Darling, chair of the ANG Council from 1982 to 1986, said of Mollison that 'he lived and breathed the Gallery; his whole life was devoted to putting together a

75 Mollison and Gray, 'James Mollison in Conversation with Anne Gray', 28.

76 Ibid., 24.

77 Aiton, 'The Big Art Spender'.

wonderful collection'.[78] Committed, private and at times acerbic, Mollison and Rosalie shared similar character traits. Mollison told me that Rosalie welcomed him 'and a couple of other youngsters on the very small [ANG] staff'.[79] Over the next decade, Rosalie supported Mollison, and Mollison advised Rosalie in a way that positioned her well for success in the art world.

Mollison could be harsh on Rosalie, as will be demonstrated in the following chapter. Yet Rosalie said she got into the habit of leaving her work around when Mollison visited, finding affirmation in his engagement with it, even when he was critical. She felt it an accolade when he patronisingly told her: 'You really are very good with your bits of twig.'[80] Other times, she said, 'he wouldn't look at them and I used to find him stealing looks and not saying anything'.[81] To me, Mollison described some of the small metal sculptures Rosalie made during the decade from 1964 to 1974 as 'pretty horrible things'.[82] He said he deliberately tried to stop her from making work he considered 'empty-headed': he disliked her figures made out of farm iron because some of her other work was 'extraordinarily creative'. Already very impressed by Robert Klippel's metal sculptures that included found objects, Rosalie's sculptures did not measure up for Mollison.[83] The comparison with Klippel's work was tough. Klippel had made art since his early twenties, having studied at the East Sydney Technical College and the Slade School of Fine Art in London, and was later proclaimed 'Australia's greatest sculptor'.[84] Without Mollison's guidance at this point in her artistic career, Rosalie might have got stuck in her small metal sculpture stage. He was key in encouraging her to push herself further artistically so that she eventually found her métier.

Moving on again — to a room of her own

Rosalie felt increasingly cramped and restricted at Dugan Street. As she branched out into making larger works and collecting bigger and more materials from rubbish dumps, roadsides and paddocks, she needed more space than the little university house had to offer. She and Ben had been

78 Butler and Darling, 'A Twenty-Year Relationship', 137.
79 Mollison, interview by author, 2011.
80 Hughes et al., 'Rosalie Gascoigne Artist', tape 4.
81 Gascoigne, interview by Topliss, 3.
82 Mollison, interview by author, 2011.
83 Ibid.
84 Scarlett, 'Robert Klippel'.

casting their eyes around Canberra real estate, eventually deciding that 'you can't have what you want unless you build it yourself'[85] In July 1967, the Gascoignes purchased a lease for a block of land at Anstey Street, Pearce, for $2,200. It was a block on the rising ridge of a new suburb in Canberra's first 'new town', Woden, again with the bush behind it.[86] By then, new purchasers had to vie for land with speculators and big developers. The *Canberra Times,* however, recorded that on Tuesday 20 June 1967, S. C. B. and R. N. K. Gascoigne purchased section 26 of block 19 in Pearce in an unrestricted sale.[87] Once again, Rosalie was to live by a hill. The elevated site on Mt Taylor's north-east slope provided views across the Woden Valley to Black Mountain.

With their land secured, the Gascoignes set about looking for an architect. Rosalie knocked on the doors of houses she liked and asked residents for the name of the designing architect. Eventually it was a visit to the home of the founding general editor of the *Australian Dictionary of Biography*, Douglas Pike and his wife Louisa Pike, in the Canberra suburb of Campbell that decided Rosalie and Ben.[88] They were drawn to the light and airy nature of architect Theo Bischoff's Pike house, which had been designed for maximum sun in cold Canberra winters and copious natural light. Shortly after purchasing the land, the Gascoignes began discussions with Bischoff about the new house. They knew what they did not want from their experiences of Residence 19 on Stromlo and Dugan Street in Deakin.[89] Rosalie's sense of relative freedom in making installations for the spacious Academy of Science building made her appreciate the freedom to create in larger spaces. Residence 19 had made her aware of the importance of the private enclosed domestic space—intimate space where she could study the materials she brought in from paddocks and hillsides. It was in such spaces that she discerned how she would use her materials. The process of

85 Hughes et al., 'Rosalie Gascoigne Artist', tape 4.

86 The Reserve Bank of Australia's inflation calculator calculates that $2,200 in 1967 equates to $33,135.57 in 2023. Note that, at this stage, all land 'sold' in the ACT was leasehold; however, ongoing controversy over the high cost of land rent and the fact that it was not financially viable led to it being dropped in 1971 and a rating system established in its place. See Sparke, *Canberra 1954–1980*, 197–201. Rosalie said: 'the land was going cheaper out in Pearce. You know, we had a slump. So we, of course, being not terribly saving people, thought, ah, this is our chance. We can just afford a block of land out there.' Hughes et al., 'Rosalie Gascoigne Artist', tape 4.

87 'Buyers at Tuesday's Auction', *Canberra Times*, 22 June 1967, 12.

88 Cameron, 'Where Science Meets Art', 142–3.

89 All comments about searching for an architect from ibid.

discernment took time: 'It was very gradual. I had to bring things into my house to look at.'[90] Milton Cameron described the domestic spaces where Rosalie studied her finds as:

> 'intensely private' places, inner sanctums where she attempted to create order out of chaos … she would rearrange objects until she reached a point where they recalled 'the feeling of an actual moment in the landscape'.[91]

Cameron explained how Ben's and Rosalie's different approaches informed their notions of what they wanted in their new house. He described Ben's approach as 'rational and scientific' and Rosalie's as 'instinctive and intuitive: a combination of gut instinct and practicality'.[92] Rosalie's instructions, in poetic aphorisms, were informed by her experience of working in the Academy of Science's large spaces. But while their approaches differed, Ben and Rosalie agreed on core design elements. The aspect was important for both light and view; they wanted the house to be a natural extension of the site and they wanted it to facilitate the display of art—Rosalie's own art, which at that stage was still primarily ikebana, and their growing collection of other artists' work.[93] Rosalie's request to Bischoff for space echoed her literal and metaphorical fear of being boxed in: 'don't shut us in … I need space … lots of air: high ceilings and wide windows to allow the elements in and frame views of the distant hills'.[94] She hoped that the custom-designed house with room for the work she longed to make would free her to be who she was. The dining space, which was to double as Rosalie's ikebana studio, was to be a long simple room, with white-painted brick walls and abundant natural light, with a large table and strong shelves for supporting vases and containers.[95] It was to provide her with the kind of space she needed to create both herself and art. In July 1968 Rosalie and Ben signed a contract for the construction of the Anstey Street house and work was underway by Christmas. They moved in the following year (see Figures 9.3–9.5).

90 Edwards, *Rosalie Gascoigne: Material as Landscape*, 8.
91 Cameron, 'Where Science Meets Art', 141; Edwards, *Rosalie Gascoigne: Material as Landscape*, 8.
92 Cameron, 'Where Science Meets Art', 144.
93 Ibid.
94 MacDonald and Gascoigne, *Rosalie Gascoigne*, 22.
95 Cameron, 'Where Science Meets Art', 145.

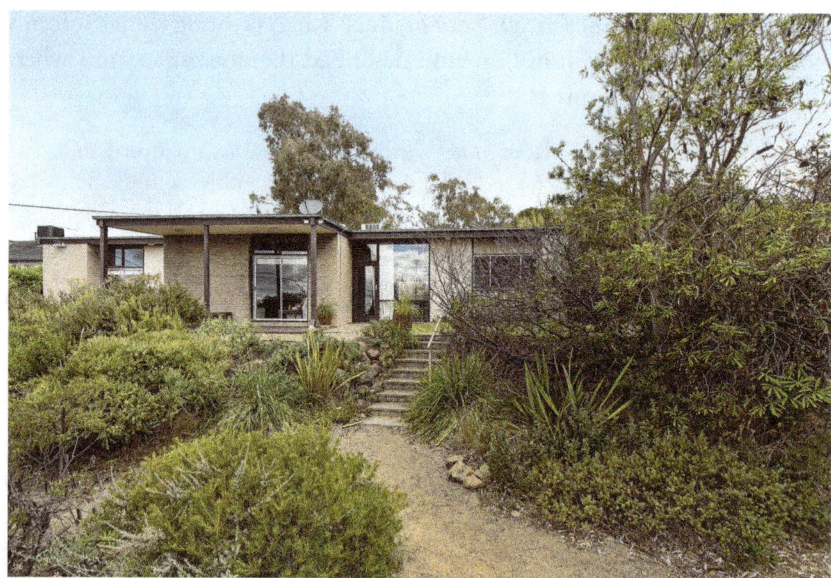

Figure 9.3: 3 Anstey Street, Pearce, the mid-century modern Gascoigne home designed by architect Theo Bischoff.

Source: Photograph and courtesy: Kasey Funnell Photography, Queanbeyan, NSW.

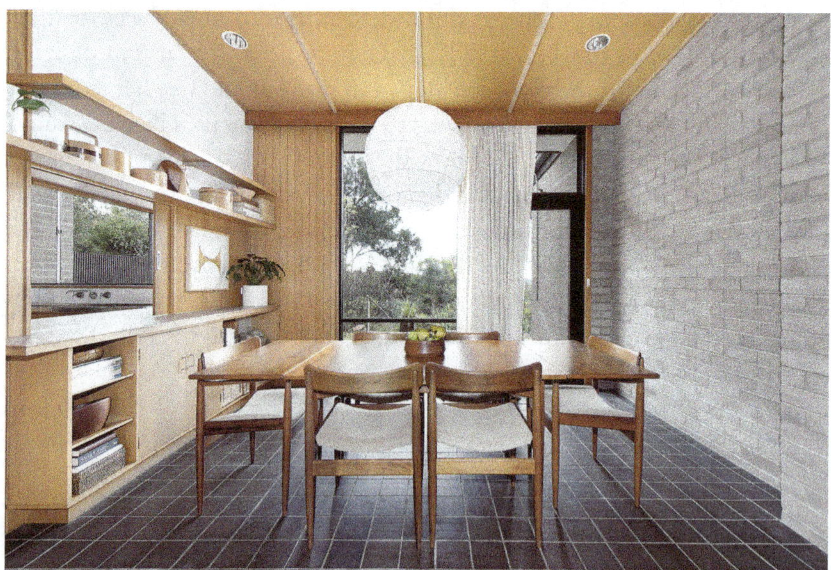

Figure 9.4: The dining room at 3 Anstey Street, Pearce.

Note: It was to double as Rosalie's ikebana studio, with white-painted brick walls, abundant natural light, a large table and strong shelves for supporting vases and containers.

Source: Photograph and courtesy: Kasey Funnell Photography, Queanbeyan, NSW.

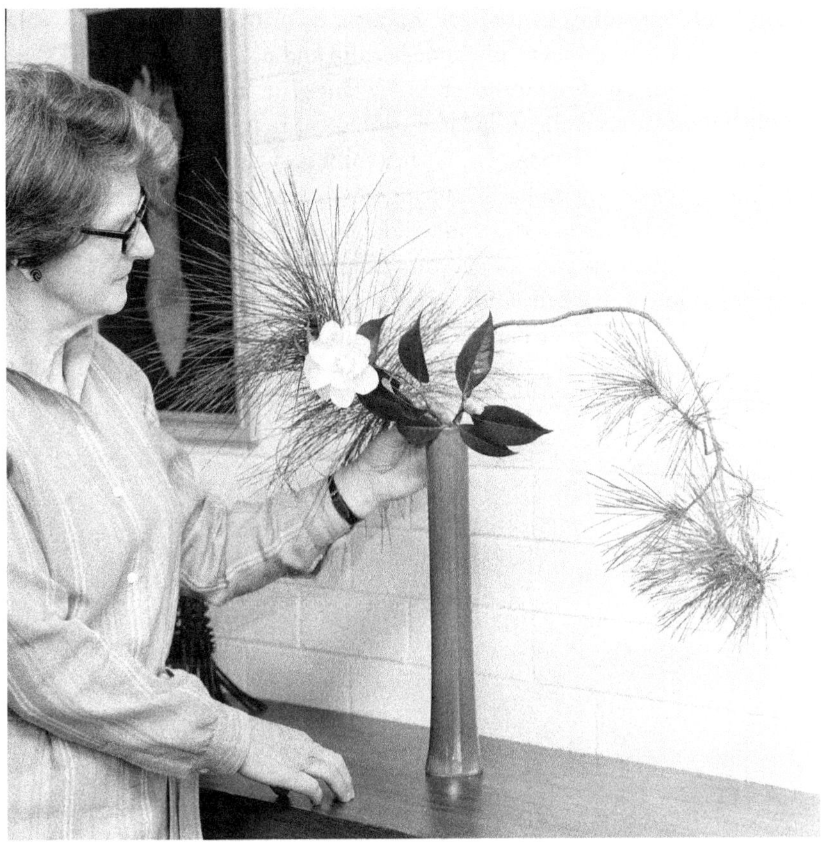

Figure 9.5: Rosalie with one of her ikebana arrangements, Anstey Street, Pearce, 1969.

Source: NAA: 1501, A9510.

Lift-off

The five years from 1965 to 1970 marked a transition period in Rosalie's practice. She launched from flower arranging and ikebana into making art that was her felt response to the local environment. Until now, many of the chief protagonists in her life had been women; however, the main ones she spoke about in her self-narrative of this period were men—Sparnon, Mollison, Martin and, of course, Ben, whose job provided the financial security that enabled Rosalie to explore and extend her creative practices.

A range of coinciding factors collaborated to provide lift-off for Rosalie as she moved into the next phase of her life and art. These included skills she learned, social developments and changes in the art world. Flower arranging encouraged the individual expression that became a hallmark of her artistic practice. Ikebana taught her form and composition. Canberra's developing environmental sensibility resonated with her art and provided fertile ground for her practice and for the reception of her work. Changing art tastes and the unseating of painting from its primacy opened the way for the recognition and appreciation of her assemblage art. In addition, Martin introduced her to contemporary art, Mollison arrived in her life and the new house at Pearce provided her with the space and light necessary for her art making. Her narrative covering these years moved from deficit to positive change.

10

Early 1970s: 'I'm an artist!'

One summer day in the early 1970s Rosalie flew outside the Anstey Street home to Ben who was painting the garden fence while he listened to a New Zealand – Australia cricket match on the radio. Her excited voice broke into the radio commentary: 'Ben, Ben, I know what I am—I'm an artist!'[1] The story is contested by Mollison who told me he finds it 'impossible to believe … she might have said it jokingly but there was no epiphany'.[2] Mollison said the story did not fit with what he knew of Rosalie as a grounded person, albeit with a poetic sensibility. In the face of contested stories, oral historians Alessandro Portelli and Luisa Passerini tell us it is not the absolute truth of the event that is important but its meaning: here the meaning could be that, during this period in her life, Rosalie began to fully identify as an artist.[3]

During the early 1970s, Rosalie's artistic confidence consolidated as she moved further into the art world assisted by the development of her friendship with James Mollison, and a new friendship with artist Michael Taylor. She said of Taylor: 'he was … the first practising artist with whom I had real conversations'.[4] Taylor made her feel like an artist.[5] He and Rosalie shared a distinct environmental sensibility that grew in Rosalie's evolving art practice as an aesthetic response to the scenic natural environment of the Canberra region. Rosalie shared this sensibility with other new friends

1 Hester and Ben Gascoigne, interview by author, 2010. The story could possibly be placed in January 1974 when Australia and New Zealand played the second test at the Sydney Cricket Ground.

2 James Mollison, interview by author, 2011.

3 Portelli, *The Death of Luigi Trastulli*; Passerini, 'A Passion for Memory', 72.

4 Hughes et al., 'Rosalie Gascoigne Artist', tape 7.

5 Ibid., tape 4.

she made during this period, including poets Rosemary Dobson and David Campbell, who formed part of a loose artistic and poetic/literary circle reflecting a regional sensibility. Rosalie came to see herself as a regional artist. She described herself as such in a talk she gave to the Canberra School of Art in 1985.[6] She told Steven Heath and James Mollison in 1997: 'My country is the eastern seaboard, Lake George and the Highlands.'[7] To MacDonald, she described artists as being 'like the bards of old, they sing a song of their district'.[8]

Rosalie's introduction to Dobson and Campbell and their circles of people who shared her sensibility paralleled her inclusion in the visual arts culture that grew around dealer galleries and planning and staffing of the planned-for Australian National Gallery. She made friends among artists, curators, dealers and critics. Her entry into these circles, together with a number of other factors, coloured the 1970s golden years for Rosalie. The new house at Pearce, the increasing independence of her children and Ben's intense involvement in the Anglo-Australian Telescope, which meant he regularly spent long periods away, provided her with the physical and emotional space that enabled her to further develop her art and clarify her identity.

At the beginning of the 1970s, ikebana remained one of Rosalie's prime creative activities; however, by February 1972 she had written to Norman Sparnon: 'I feel I must withdraw from classes for a while and do my own thing.'[9] She never returned. Her attention had shifted to the local landscape. Rosalie wanted to make art that reflected the Monaro region. She continued making sculptural works from the discarded farm machinery components she found in former mining sites and paddocks, and began to work with other materials such as cattle bones and weathered wood. In 1972, this consolidating, extending sensibility was recognised nationally for the first time when Faye Bottrell and Stacey Wesley included Rosalie in their book, *The Artist Craftsman in Australia, Aspects of Sensibility*.[10]

Letters she wrote to Martin from 1971 to 1974 provide a frame for this period. Replete with energy, drive and her excitement at the thrill of making art and discovering kindred spirits who accepted her, the letters spotlight the space and time for reflection Rosalie now enjoyed. They illuminate the

6 Rosalie Gascoigne, 'Regional Art', talk to the Canberra School of Art, 21 August 1985, Papers of Rosalie Gascoigne, box 21.

7 Mollison and Heath, 'Rosalie Gascoigne', 7.

8 MacDonald and Gascoigne, *Rosalie Gascoigne*, 37.

9 Rosalie to Martin, 8 February 1972, cited in Eagle, *From the Studio of Rosalie Gascoigne*, 35.

10 Bottrell and Stacey, *The Artist Craftsman in Australia*.

sympathy she had developed with Martin as a mentor and confidante about her art. Several times she expressed the wish that he were present to advise on her work. Her descriptions of art making, invitations to exhibit, and relationships with artists, arts administrators, curators and commercial gallery owners, convey an expansive lightness that reflected the Canberra region's big skies and great blonde paddocks that inspired her. All these processes opened her world, but she also became a figure with a particular role and significance within them.

Rosalie and Ben

Rosalie found her expanding world created new tensions in her marriage. When Martin described his parents' relationship at Rosalie's service of thanksgiving in November 1999, he used an image from their Auckland University College years:

> At the end of a dance one night, they had the job of turning out the lights. In the half light Rosalie played a game of hide and seek in the long curtains surrounding the room.[11]

'That image', said Martin, 'could stand for their life together … Ben … found Rosalie a perennial challenge'.[12] Rosalie did not talk publicly about the intimate details of her marriage, but she did talk about how busy Ben had always been with his work and what she perceived as his dismay at her success. Ben's absorption in his work, as Martin's image suggests, was perhaps matched by the elusiveness her own journey brought to their marriage.

Ben had often been required to spend long periods away from home, particularly during the late 1960s and early 1970s when he was involved in the Anglo-Australian Telescope (AAT). The AAT had been established in response to representations from the Australian Academy of Science and the Royal Society of London to the Australian and British governments in the 1960s. Ben was involved in site selection from the beginning, making several trips to Siding Spring on the edge of the Warrumbungle National Park near Coonabarabran in western New South Wales. The Australian National University (ANU) had operated an observatory there since 1965.[13] Once the decision to proceed had been made, Ben was one of two Australian

11 Martin Gascoigne, 'Rosalie—M.B.G. Eulogy', 1999, Papers of Ben Gascoigne, box 3.

12 Ibid.

13 Bhathal, Sutherland and Butcher, *Mt Stromlo Observatory*, 119–24.

representatives appointed to the AAT's technical committee.[14] His trips to the construction site, six hundred kilometres north-west of Canberra, took him away from home for ten days at a time, returning for a brief two days before setting off again. When he was at home, Rosalie felt he was not present because his mind was on the telescope:

> I'd think, thank goodness for some company. But he didn't see you. It was like the man who climbed Everest—you saw this dream in his eyes. That's when I got into art in a big way. I thought, I've got to have something to fill the vacuum. So I made things all over the house.[15]

In Ben's absence, Rosalie acted out new dimensions of her independence. She became proficient with saws and drills. Ben would return to find the Anstey Street house full of Rosalie's work. Milton Cameron told a story of the occasion Rosalie showed Ben a saw cut she had accidentally made on the dining table and Ben said: 'Well, we're not going to fill that, not for anybody—this was made by Rosalie Gascoigne!'[16]

Such enthusiasm might have come readily enough, but both Hester and Martin acknowledged their father's ambivalence towards Rosalie's artistic career. Her father, Hester suggests, supported her mother:

> in his own time and his own way and with some reluctance on some occasions. I think a large part of Dad would have liked a regular wife who had dinner parties and neat houses and tidy hair and frocks and he didn't like the mess. And he liked parties. He liked the success but I think the actual hard grind of making art was something quite else ... part of him would have liked interesting dinner parties, bridge parties ... and people to stay—lots of house guests, which she couldn't stand at the end because it threw out her working days.[17]

Martin also acknowledged his father's occasional ambivalence, writing that Ben enjoyed his new role as artist's assistant and homemaker but with some reservations: 'I think he liked all the attention that came with it, though as Mum's engagement deepened he sometimes felt left behind.'[18] The trajectories of their working lives were, in middle age, beginning to diverge: he was overseeing the construction of a new facility for future researchers; she was making her own work.

14 Australian Astronomical Observatory, 'The Anglo-Australian Telescope'.
15 MacDonald and Gascoigne, *Rosalie Gascoigne*, 25.
16 Cameron, 'Where Science Meets Art', 131.
17 Hester Gascoigne, interview by author, 20 February 2011.
18 Strickland, *Affairs of the Heart*, 38.

Ben's dedication to his wife's developing career was plain to see when, in 1972, during her metal sculpture phase, he made time in his busy schedule to attend welding classes at Canberra Technical College to assist Rosalie in making her rusty iron constructions 'as steady as a rock'.[19]

But she soon tired of the sculptures, writing to Toss in November 1973:

> Junk sculptures, nothing! That's really not what I'm at any more and whatever it is I *am* doing, it takes all my time. Any vestige of a nice homemaker type in me is fast vanishing. Vanished even.[20]

By the time Ben had completed the welding course, Rosalie had moved on to bone and wooden works. He could not keep up.

Rosalie apparently had difficulty publicly acknowledging Ben's support. As to whether she did so privately, I cannot say. It may have served Rosalie's narrative to convey an impression of Ben's lack of understanding about her passion for art and this may have been the truth. But regardless, he did provide practical support and it was the financial stability of his work that made her single-mindedness possible. Ben, who heard the story second-hand from a woman who was present, quotes Rosalie's response to a question put to her at the end of a talk to art school students:

> a student asked 'what is the most important thing you need if you are setting out to be an artist?', and Rosalie replied, 'A partner with enough money to keep you for the rest of your life.'[21]

'At least', said Ben, 'I satisfied that criterion'.[22] For her part, Rosalie identified a discontinuity in the roles that defined her life. She acknowledged that she could not have been an artist if she had had to keep a family: 'I couldn't have done it. I couldn't have been single-minded enough … you've got to have a lot of solitude … And you can't be … selfless.'[23] She was only able to give undivided attention to art once she was freed from some of the demands of family life when her children had become independent.

19 Ben to Martin, 26 March 1972, cited in Eagle, *From the Studio of Rosalie Gascoigne*, 35.

20 Fink, 'The Life of Things', 150.

21 Gascoigne, 'The Artist-in-Residence', 15.

22 Ibid.

23 Hughes et al., 'Rosalie Gascoigne Artist', tape 7. Note that the former director of the National Gallery of Australia, Betty Churcher (1931–2015), said the same of painting: she was unsure she could be both a good mother and a good painter so focused on mothering her four sons. See Francis, 'Churcher, 1931–2015'.

One remark of Ben's stirred an enduring fury for Rosalie:

> And Ben, I remember saying to me, 'I've never seen obsession like it.' This is when I first started and I was doing it all over the house. And he'd been obsessed, lawfully, legally, legitimately, with his mathematics, his science, all his life, you see. And he didn't … understand my passion for it.[24]

Rosalie's comment expresses her frustration at Ben's perspective on her artistic passion. Her sense of imbalance was not peculiar to the Gascoigne's marriage. Then, as now, couples navigated the divergent expectations of, and opportunities for, men and women of comparable education. Rosalie's friends who also had husbands in academia compared notes. The women felt their husbands were happy if their wives had interests outside the home, as long as the interests did not impinge on family life:

> as other university wives have said, men like you to have an interest, but as long as you put it away when they come home, you see. And that's very true. A lot of academic men were like that. And the women joined the art school and were part time artists. But they put it away, you see.[25]

Rosalie did not put her art away despite the fact that she clearly experienced the weight of social expectations of women. Her narrative tells how she felt that, in making art, she did not measure up to those expectations: 'it's all right if you bring up the children and you make the cake … and have people to dinner. Then you're being a real woman.'[26] Yet her original circles, which comprised largely the wives of academics and scientists, did include women who shared her artistic sensibility. Sculptor Jan Brown who taught at the precursor of the School of Art, New Zealand–born potter Margaret Frankel (wife of CSIRO geneticist and executive member Sir Otto Frankel), painters Elizabeth Davies and Pamela McFarlane, painter and sculptor Hilary Wrigley, and ceramicists Shirley Storey, Hiroe Swen, Mim Smyth, and Vicky Mimms were among her friends. All were successful artists in their own right. As measures of success came to her, Rosalie again sought to set herself apart from these women. Her narrative expressed in the quotation above is an older refrain that cultivates a sense of difference.

24 Hughes et al., 'Rosalie Gascoigne Artist', tape 7.

25 Ibid.

26 Ibid.

In 1970, Ben's work on the AAT took the couple overseas again: they visited Japan, Denmark, Sweden, England, France, Portugal and Thailand.[27] Rosalie's identification as an artist was assisted by the extent of contact she enjoyed with other, prominent artists during this trip. They visited Ben's old friend Carl Plate and his wife Jocelyn in Paris; painter Charles Blackman and his wife Barbara; abstract painter John Coburn and his wife Barbara; New Zealand–born, Australian-raised sculptor Matcham Skipper; and the Rumanian-born Leonard Hessing, who had studied with Fernand Léger in Paris in the 1950s while Rosalie was raising her children and growing and arranging flowers in Canberra.[28] It is not clear how the Gascoignes made all these connections at this rising stage in Rosalie's career and early in her acquaintance with James Mollison. It is possible they met the artists through Plate. Comments Rosalie made to Hughes about 'real artists' evoke her likely excitement at the meetings: 'real artists and … people who knew about art were magic to you [me], you know, unattainable. To be an artist of course was absolutely beyond one's dreams ever.'[29]

A treasure trove: Letters to Martin in Manila

From 1971 to 1974, Martin lived in Manila where he worked for the Asian Development Bank.[30] His time away had two effects on Rosalie. First, he left his art collection with his parents who displayed it at Anstey Street, exposing Rosalie on a daily basis to a greater range of original art than that to which she was accustomed. According to Eagle, one of Martin's artworks—Dick Watkins's *A Charming Study* (1963), described by Eagle as 'a splendid, ugly collage'—'teased' Rosalie, inspiring her to discard the disciplined outlet of flower arranging and go for 'the bigger game' of serious art.[31] If Eagle is right, perhaps the nature of the collage got under Rosalie's skin. The apparently slapdash application of brush strokes, cutout magazine photographs and torn newsprint stuck together in one space provided a stark contrast to ikebana's lean, balanced structures and offered her new possibilities for making art.

27 Gellatly et al., *Rosalie Gascoigne*, 124.
28 Ibid., 124.
29 Hughes et al., 'Rosalie Gascoigne Artist', tape 7.
30 Eagle, *From the Studio of Rosalie Gascoigne*, 29. Martin later worked in Hong Kong from March 1977 to March 1980.
31 Eagle, *Rosalie Gascoigne, 1985*, 1.

Second, Martin's absence resulted in a rich archive of letters from Rosalie, testaments to the support she gleaned from her eldest child and perhaps to the intensification his absence brought to her reflections on art and being an artist. An edited selection of these appear in Mary Eagle's *From the Studio of Rosalie Gascoigne*, the catalogue that accompanied the exhibition of the same name at The Australian National University's Drill Hall Gallery the year after Rosalie's death.[32] These letters provide the largest contemporary primary source direct from Rosalie herself of any period in her life. Martin and his wife Mary Eagle edited the collection. I had access only to the catalogue's edited versions. The archive emphasises her friendship with Mollison, one of the most powerful people in Australian art, and the support she received from him. It also illustrates Rosalie's growing relationships with other well-known art world figures. The picture painted by the letters is different from the Rosalie we encounter in the 1998 Hughes interview and other interviews. The letters portray her as a happy and fulfilled woman who delights in the artistic and literary worlds in which she is finding her place during this period. Her sometimes-acerbic voice, experienced in other sources, softens as she finds her milieu. The letters were for the family who knew her well, unlike the interviews, which, she would have understood, were to play an important role in the construction of her public identity.

A 'maverick' artist who understood aesthetics: National recognition

During the 1970s, Rosalie moved from making discarded farm iron sculptures to creating box constructions using a pile of old bee boxes she found in 1973, a move that took her further towards her own distinctive 'legitimate' style. Her first exhibition, at Macquarie Galleries in 1974, included small metal sculptures and box constructions. She embraced a distinctive artistic identity.

Rosalie's first national recognition came about through a random meeting with textile and design artist Fay Bottrell, who recalled that she had 'stumbled on' Rosalie through art circles in Canberra.[33] The two women hit it off and walked up a hill together to admire the vista. Bottrell recognised

32 Eagle, *From the Studio of Rosalie Gascoigne*.

33 Fay Bottrell, telephone conversation with author, 29 July 2014. Fay Bottrell, born in New South Wales in 1927, art teacher, textile artist and design artist, taught at the Mary White School of Art in Sydney with John Olsen and Robert Klippel.

Rosalie as a 'maverick' artist, while realising that 'she really did understand aesthetics'.[34] She decided to include Rosalie in her book about 'mavericks'—'people who were doing their own thing, were not famous at the time and who demonstrated a nonconformist sensibility in their work'.[35] At the end of 1971, Rosalie was 'bowled over' with her invitation to feature in *The Artist Craftsman in Australia* to be published the following year. Rosalie wrote to Martin: 'I am in a daze.'[36] Ben described to Martin author Fay Bottrell and photographer Wesley Stacey's visit, leaving no doubt as to Rosalie's excitement at this recognition:

> On Friday [the phone rang] at 7.30, this woman [Bottrell] is arriving at 8, and in one smooth continuous motion your mother springs out of bed, showers, dresses, breakfasts, washes up, tidies up and is there on the doorstep all composed at 8 a.m, just as well too. Well, this went like a house on fire; I haven't seen her so elated since Hester turned out to be a daughter and not a third son.[37]

Rosalie described her inspiration in a page of text in Bottrell's book: 'I am greatly moved by the Australian countryside, especially by the part I know well, within a fifty-mile radius of Canberra.'[38] She recounted that she liked 'foraging with an open mind and happening upon things' and was committed to showing 'how beautiful and visually exciting ordinary things can be'.[39] Gellatly rightly asserts that Rosalie's presence in Bottrell and Stacey's book marked the first official acknowledgement of her work.[40] Until this time, the only recognition Rosalie had received was in newspaper reports. Bottrell and Stacey's book represented recognition by respected artists within the Australian arts community. As such, it marked a major turning point in her career.

By now Rosalie was venturing further afield on her foraging trips. She wrote in Bottrell's book that she liked searching riverbanks, paddocks and dumps:

> especially if there is any old farm iron, a bit battered, with traces of faded paint. It seems to have tremendous vigor [*sic*] and something of the spirit of the country in it.[41]

---

34 Ibid.

35 Ibid.

36 Rosalie Gascoigne to Martin Gascoigne, 16 November 1971, cited in Eagle, *From the Studio of Rosalie Gascoigne*, 33–4.

37 Letter from Ben Gascoigne to Martin Gascoigne, 16 November 1971, cited in ibid., 34.

38 Bottrell and Stacey, *The Artist Craftsman in Australia*, 39.

39 Ibid.

40 Gellatly, 'Rosalie Gascoigne', 125.

41 Bottrell and Stacey, *The Artist Craftsman in Australia*, 39.

Rosalie roamed further onto the Monaro plain, into country rubbish tips in Bungendore, Gunning and Captain's Flat. She and Ben purchased a second car for Ben in 1972, freeing the Holden station wagon for Rosalie's exclusive use: the Canberra hinterland and rubbish tips were hers for the taking.[42]

During 1971 and 1972, Rosalie discovered animal remains on her sallies into the country. Tony Coleing's creative licence with his wire sculptures in Sydney freed her to experiment with threading cattle bones onto wire, creating large bone constructions in her backyard.[43] Sack in hand, Rosalie roamed paddocks on the edges of Canberra's new suburbs. She raced to salvage remains of sheep savaged by the domesticated dogs that had arrived with the new suburban dwellers. She needed to get there before the farmers buried their sheep. As her compulsion to make art grew, she allowed little to get in the way of her creativity, abandoning all niceties in her drive to get the materials for her art:

> It was rather invidious to say to a farmer, 'Do you mind if I pick up all your dead lambs?' Because he wasn't very pleased about them. I just gave away Canberra and all its pretensions.[44]

Rosalie scraped flesh off the bones because boiling or bleaching them would destroy the natural 'beautiful grey-white colour'.[45] She made several large-scale constructions of animal bones threaded on thick wire. *Last Stand*, nine tall columns of vertebrae 'threaded on new spinal cords of rusty wire' was shown at the Academy of Science's Shine Dome in place of her usual ikebana arrangements.[46] *Last Stand* triggered in-house humour among Canberra's scientists with the quip: 'It's about time somebody put a bit of backbone into this place!'[47]

42 After Rosalie's death in 1999, Miriam Eagle ended her condolence letter to the family: 'Oh Rosalie! Only a woman of your calibre could rummage at the tip with such dignity!' Miriam Eagle to 'Ben, Martin, Hesters and Mary', 27 October 2010, Papers of Rosalie Gascoigne, box 23.

43 MacDonald and Gascoigne, *Rosalie Gascoigne*, 23. She may have seen Tony Coleing's work at exhibitions at Gallery A or Frank Watters Gallery in 1970 and 1971. See also Gellatly, 'Rosalie Gascoigne', 40.

44 MacDonald and Gascoigne, *Rosalie Gascoigne*, 23.

45 Ibid.

46 Ibid.

47 Ibid.

Groups and connections

While still fashioning arrangements for the Academy of Science, Rosalie was beginning to move away from the social circle of scientists, academics and their wives of which she was a part through Ben's professional contacts. In the early 1970s, the arts community in Canberra comprised several groups: one around the Commonwealth Arts Advisory Board, including James Mollison; another around the Canberra School of Art with which Rosalie had little contact at this time apart from Jan Brown, her artist friend from her University House days; and a more general artistic and literary group of which she also became a part.

As Canberra continued to grow, new people arrived. The new National Library of Australia opened in August 1968, and Alec Bolton joined as director of publications in 1971. The Bolton family moved back to Australia from London where Alec had been editor for publishers Angus & Robertson.[48] Bolton's wife, poet Rosemary Dobson, became an important friend to Rosalie after the two met in 1972. With Rosalie's love of poetry and Dobson's brilliance at writing it, the two shared much in common, including the environmental sensibility that underpinned their respective arts. Contemplative and meditative, Dobson's poetry is rich with references to art, history, human relationships and the Australian landscape.[49] Through Dobson, Rosalie found herself in the orbit of other poets with kindred sensibilities: Canberrans David Campbell and Geoff Page; Judith Wright; poet and academic A. D. Hope; and, on her brief visit to Australia, British-born American poet Denise Levertov. Dobson, Campbell, Page and Levertov were inspired to write poetic responses to Rosalie's work.[50]

At a time when the concept of conservation was relatively new, Wright advocated responsibility towards the environment and greater awareness of the relationship between humans and their environment. A letter from her among Rosalie's papers at the National Library of Australia indicates

48 From Federation in 1901, the Commonwealth Parliamentary Library served both federal parliament and the nation. In 1927, when parliament relocated from Melbourne to Canberra, the library moved with it. In 1960, an act of parliament formally separated the National Library from the Parliamentary Library.

49 Francis, 'Dobson, Rosemary De Brissac (1920–2012)'.

50 MacDonald and Gascoigne, *Rosalie Gascoigne*, 23; Levertov, 'Two Artists'. 'Monaro', a poem in memory of Rosalie Gascoigne by Geoff Page, see Page, *Darker and Lighter*. Elaine Baker wrote *Mixed Media* about Rosalie's exhibition at the Art Gallery of New South Wales in 1997–98. New Zealand poet Jenny Bornholdt wrote *Jigsaw* inspired by Rosalie's work c. 2004; Tony Beyer wrote *Rosalie Gascoigne* c. 2004.

that they met in early 1975. Wright's letter from University House at ANU on 26 March 1975 shows that she had enjoyed the hospitality for which Rosalie was well known:

> Dear Rosalie, A belated thank you for that delightful lunch you gave me when Rosemary [Dobson] brought me out last month. I've been hoping to get in touch and ask you here for dinner before I left but time's been too quick for me. I hope for better luck sometime in the future. I did enjoy meeting you and seeing your work.[51]

How much Rosalie and Wright saw of each other after this meeting is not known. Dobson, though, became one of Rosalie's favourite companions for foraging expeditions. She left Rosalie free to make her own explorations and did not impede her.[52] In late 1972, Rosalie wrote to Martin about her growing friendship with Dobson and her delight in her as a foraging partner:

> Rosemary Dobson is ready and eager to come with me. I can see it would be the ideal outing for her—real escapism; ideal companion for me too—wouldn't get between me and nature.[53]

Her previous companion had not appealed: 'Last person I took kept holding up things and saying, "Look!" I had to gallop over the nearest hill whenever I stopped the car, to get out of earshot.'[54] The arrangement suited both women. They understood the demands of family and each other's need for creative solitude. Dobson valued Rosalie's friendship, as she described in a memoir for the exhibition *Rosalie Gascoigne: Plain Air* at City Gallery, Wellington, in 2004:

> Friendship with Rosalie was a treasured experience. There was always an element of chance in it. We both had our withdrawals due to work and family—but Rosalie would simply ring and say that it was going to be a lovely day and how about going out with her to enjoy it. From early on these were nearly always 'collecting days'. Rosalie would have in her mind some place that she wanted to investigate, and we would drive out of town into the Canberra landscape.[55]

---

51 Judith Wright McKinney, 26 March 1975, Papers of Rosalie Gascoigne, box 1. The 2010 edition of Wright's collection of poetry originally put together in 1990 when she gave up writing for activism, has a detail of Rosalie's work *Parrot Country* (1980–1983) on the front cover.

52 Rosalie Gascoigne to Martin Gascoigne, c. 16 November 1972, cited in Eagle, *From the Studio of Rosalie Gascoigne*, 39.

53 Rosalie to Martin, c. 16 November 1972, in ibid., 39.

54 Ibid.

55 Rosemary Dobson, 'Rosalie Gascoigne 1917–1999: A Memoir', Papers of Rosalie Gascoigne, box 1.

Rosalie's new and widening social networks suited her more than the groups in which she had awkwardly moved since arriving in Australia. According to her narrative, until this point she had never moved in circles in which she felt completely comfortable. Now she was affirmed in her own interests, environmental sensibility and artistic ability through overlapping circles of people who shared her views and passion for art. She was free to cast off presumed and unwanted shared identities, such as 'university wife'.

These new circles, in their role if not their identity, had parallels elsewhere in Australia and the United Kingdom. One precursor might be the Bloomsbury set in England, the members of which (including writer Virginia Woolf and her sister, artist Vanessa Bell) were connected by shared class and educational backgrounds. Welsh writer on culture and society Raymond Williams points out that the smallness of such groups hinders significant statistical analysis, and acknowledges that social and cultural groups are important because of what they can tell us about the wider societies of which they are a part.[56] Williams uses the Bloomsbury set or 'fraction' as an example in describing such cultural groups. All Cambridge graduates, the so-called Bloomsbury set also shared a consciously stated commitment to a new style of critical frankness.[57] I write 'so-called' because one of the chief protagonists in the 'set', Leonard Woolf, claimed the group was 'largely imaginary'—it was, he said, 'a group of friends'.[58] Given that many such groups begin as groups of friends, Williams proposes that we need to understand whether anything particular, in terms of shared interests and activities, brought them together and what this reflects about the wider society.

The Canberra group of which Rosalie became part was not as clearly defined as some other cultural groups based on the arts. The St Ives School of artists in the United Kingdom developed around an aesthetic of Cornwall's raw beauty in the provincial seaside town after potters Bernard Leach and Shoji Hamada and painter Ben Nicholson moved there in the 1920s. The growing artistic community enticed more artists and from the 1940s to the 1960s St Ives was the hub of modern and abstract developments in British art.[59] In Australia, near Melbourne, the Heide set included Sidney Nolan, Albert Tucker, Joy Hester, Mirka Mora, John Perceval and Charles Blackman. It grew around the patronage of Sunday and John Reed who

56 Williams, 'The Bloomsbury Fraction', 148–54.
57 Ibid., 148–9.
58 Ibid., 149.
59 Bird, *The St Ives Artists*.

invited artists to spend time at their self-conscious utopian community 'Heide' at Bulleen in Victoria, where life was lived with intense emotions that saw rifts and break-ups.[60] In the bohemian Merioola Group in Sydney's Woollahra, an ethic of community saw the artists live under one roof in a Victorian mansion.[61] Painter Clifton Pugh established an artists' commune, 'Dunmoochin', at Cottlesbridge, thirty kilometres from Melbourne in 1950.[62] The Boyd family of artists had their own family collective, 'Open Country', in the Melbourne suburb of Murrumbeena in 1913.[63]

All the groups mentioned above, apart from the latter, were founded on friendship; however, friendship is based on some commonality, which, for these groups, was art. The Canberra hinterland of the Monaro sparked poetry and a particular aesthetic in Rosalie and fellow members of the Canberra 'group'. The friends in this group gravitated towards each other in a small town full of national institutions, public servants, administrators and scientists. They reflected a particular sector of the new population moving into Canberra as the city expanded. The shared environmental and poetic aesthetic granted welcome relief to Rosalie. At last, she found herself among people with whom she felt at home. The affirmation of kindred spirits and the creativity in their interactions enabled her to further explore her own creative potential.

A fluid group, the Canberra set were all tertiary educated. Unlike the Bloomsbury group, however, they had not known each other at a particular university. Neither did they share a patron or patrons like the Heide group, nor be driven by a community ethic like Merioola. In contrast with the artists who adopted St Ives as their home, they had not moved to Canberra for its particular aesthetic. The Canberra group were a generally socially conservative group of artists and writers who did not display many of the bohemian traits often expected of creative people.[64] Living in stable, heterosexual marriages, in family units, in the salaried ranks of academics or senior public servants, the artwork of many was caught somewhere between leisure and professionalism, but rarely pursued as a sole occupation.

60 Grishin, *Australian Art*, 287–9.

61 France, 'Merioola and after'.

62 McCaughey, *Strange Country*, 233.

63 Ibid., 189.

64 I have been unable to find any references to their political leanings apart from anecdotal evidence that 'several were openly associated' with Gough Whitlam's 1972 'It's time' election campaign, and that White and Wright openly supported Whitlam. Nicholas Brown, email to author, 20 March 2015. Also see (under the subheading 'Widening art circles' in this chapter) Rosalie's cheeky comment about Bob Hawke at Frank Watters's dinner party in Sydney in 1972.

Two less conservative writers hovered on the fringes. Writer Patrick White, who was only open about his homosexuality in his 1981 autobiography, moved in and out of the circle on visits to Canberra through his friendship with Campbell. Poet and activist Judith Wright had moved to the region in 1975. Both Wright and White were environmental activists.

All had washed up in Canberra for their own or their partner's work as the national capital expanded. These well-educated, socially well-connected and financially stable artists and writers were able to ply their crafts relatively unhindered by economic need. Social and artistic circles overlapped in the group that characterised a section or, in Williams's terms, 'fraction' of Canberra society at that juncture in history.

Rosalie enjoyed this circle, and the overlapping one based around the bureaucracy that flourished around the developing national gallery, including curators James Gleeson, Ian North and Diana Woollard. Others, like Michael Taylor and Rominie Taylor, were involved in the private dealer galleries that emerged in Canberra from the late 1950s, burgeoning in the 1960s and 1970s. Donald Brook, art critic for the *Canberra Times* for several years, lived in Canberra from 1962 until 1968 when he took up an academic position in Sydney. Painter Gray Smith, who had been married to artist Joy Hester, lived in Canberra with his second wife and young family.[65] These people tended to be well connected nationally and internationally. Such connections brought Rosalie in contact with artists, writers, collectors, curators and poets from around Australia and the world, consolidating her self-confidence and artist identity, and cementing her place in a network of powerful people who would be significant to her success.

Mollison

During this period, Rosalie's friendship with Mollison continued to grow. Her letters to Martin reveal that Mollison was a frequent visitor to Anstey Street where they discussed other people's art and he watched what she made on a month-by-month basis.

65 Martin Gascoigne, annotations on transcript of Gascoigne, interview by North, 18, footnote 36.

The relationship between Mollison and Rosalie reads like one of acolyte and master, with Rosalie apparently in awe of 'Jim' as she called him. Looking back, Mollison described Rosalie as 'a likeable woman'.[66] His descriptions of her activities at the time he met her, while focusing on the visual, have a decidedly domestic flavour:

> her garden was marvellous, her flower arranging was truly creative, her patchwork was as good as such things can be, her touch about the house was excellent—even then things on the table would be arranged and she would have brought a few things in from the garden to look at—stones and dead leaves and things of that sort.[67]

Mollison's influence on Rosalie and the art world grew in the mid- to late-1970s. It will be discussed in the next chapter.

Rosalie's connections were widening in ways that would influence her career. At a party following Carl Plate's exhibition opening at Macquarie Galleries Canberra in July 1972, gallery owner Anna Simons told Rosalie she was: 'besotted by what I was doing and I must have a show and I must have it with HER'.[68]

Mollison had begun to consult Rosalie over purchases for the Australian National Gallery and had asked her to select some of Canberra ceramicist Hiroe Swen's work for the collection. Swen had offered her services to Mollison to select ceramics for the gallery collection, but Mollison told Rosalie, 'I have *you*!'[69] Rosalie was not only beginning to achieve recognition as an artist; Mollison recognised and valued her eye for art.

Michael Taylor: 'A real artist'

Rosalie found herself surrounded by what she described as the 'magic' of real artists. In 1972, she attended an exhibition in Canberra by Michael Taylor, a rising artist who taught at the art school. The flurry of private galleries that occurred in Australia's major cities after 1961 had arrived in Canberra.[70] One of these, Macquarie Galleries in Manuka, played an important role in Rosalie's rise. A regular visitor to Macquarie Galleries, she purchased one of

66 James Mollison, interview by author, 2011.

67 Ibid.

68 Rosalie to Martin, 24 July 1972, cited in Eagle, *From the Studio of Rosalie Gascoigne*, 37.

69 Letter from Rosalie to Martin, 24 July 1972, in ibid.

70 McQueen, *Suburbs of the Sacred*, 153–7.

Taylor's paintings having been advised by Mollison that Taylor was 'a very bright young man and the Boys [*sic*] were all coming up from Sydney for the show'.[71] Taylor's wife Rominie, a ceramicist who worked at Macquarie Galleries, introduced Rosalie to her husband, rightly thinking they would enjoy talking art.

Rosalie and Taylor became regular visitors to each other's homes (see Figure 10.1). They shared a passion for making art. Taylor and Rominie visited her at Anstey Street or she would drive the seventy-five kilometres along the Monaro Highway to their home at Bredbo. Rosalie acknowledged to North that her friendship with Taylor was formative for her, 'an absolute bonus':

> because there was a real artist [who] knew what your priorities were in life … And he needed someone at the time and he used to come in here and talk … sometimes twice a week, stay all afternoon … And this went on for quite some time and it was a very formative thing, because I felt I had identified myself [as an artist].[72]

To Hughes, Rosalie affirmed Taylor's importance:

> He was … the first practising artist with whom I had real conversations. We used to talk for hours and hours … it was a real treat for me to … have serious talks about what I was learning about art.[73]

Although Taylor's work was different from Rosalie's—he made large, lively abstract oil paintings while she made box constructions full of found objects—they both shared a distinct environmental sense that was to become increasingly evident in Rosalie's evolving art practice. Both she and Taylor were intrigued by landscape. Her belief in herself grew and her sense of identity was strengthening.

Taylor's friendship would prove invaluable. He encouraged her to exhibit in Canberra and was instrumental in her first public acclaim as an artist when he nominated her for the artist's choice exhibition in Sydney. This will be discussed in detail later in the chapter.

71 Rosalie to Martin, 17 September 1972, cited in Eagle, *From the Studio of Rosalie Gascoigne*, 37: 'The Boys turned out to be Daniel [Thomas] [art historian and curator] in magnificent … white panama hat, Frank Watters [owner of the private Watters Gallery in Sydney since 1964, a significant gallery for Australian contemporary art] and a woman who used to run Macquarie with Treania Smith [1901–1990 artist and Macquarie Galleries, Sydney owner].'

72 Gascoigne, interview by North, 19.

73 Hughes et al., 'Rosalie Gascoigne Artist', tape 7.

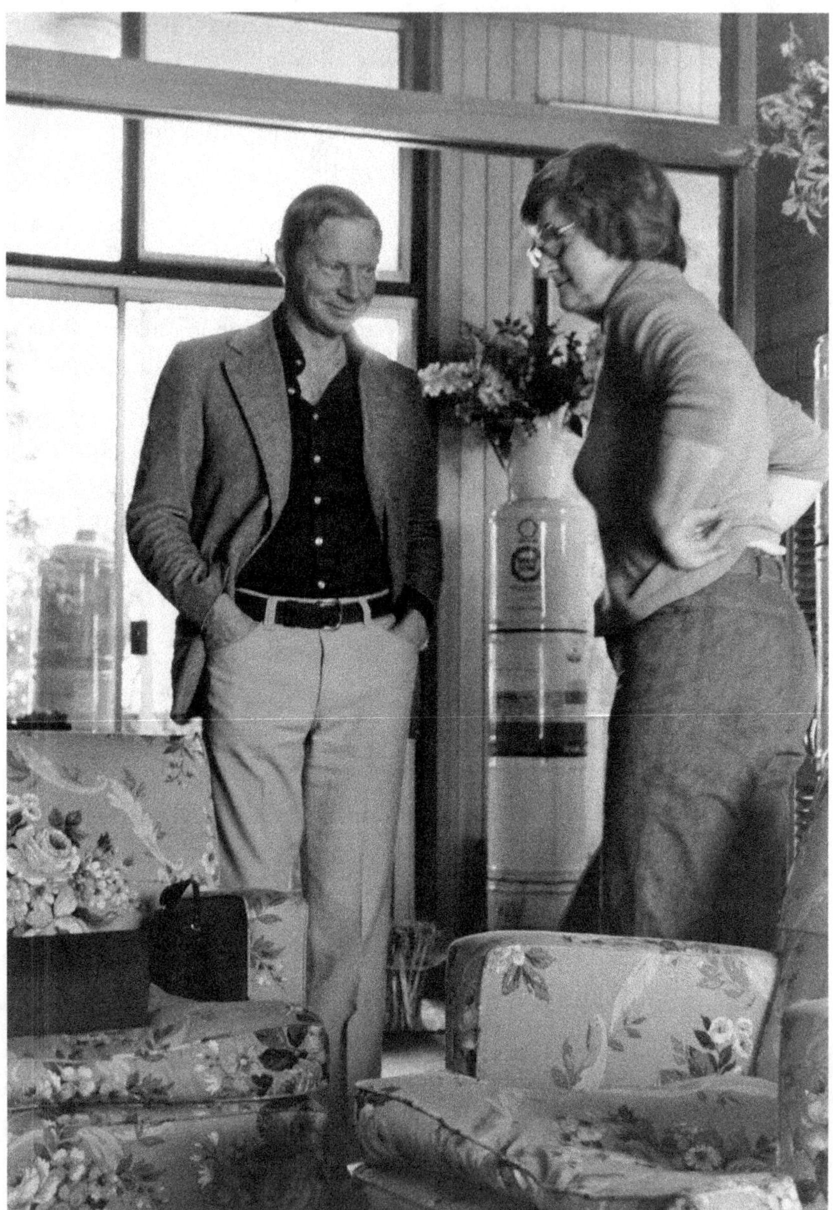

Figure 10.1: Rosalie with Michael Taylor at Anstey Street, Pearce, c. 1974.

Note: Their conversations 'fed a great hunger' in Rosalie: 'Michael was the first person who made me feel I could be a real artist'.[74]

Source: Photograph and courtesy: Matt Kelso.

74 MacDonald and Gascoigne, *Rosalie Gascoigne*, 25.

Widening art circles

Having got to know Taylor, Mollison and others, Rosalie realised that just as there was 'shop' talk in astronomy that she had listened to for years with her husband and his colleagues, there was also 'shop' talk for art.[75] This fed a hunger in her. The fact that successful artists engaged with her increased her sense of recognition and buoyed her confidence. In October 1972, Frank Watters, owner of the private Watters Gallery in Sydney since 1964—a significant gallery for Australian contemporary art—visited with Mollison. The same year she and Hester attended a dinner party given by Watters in Sydney where the powerful and eminent dined alongside each other. Rosalie listed the guests in a letter to Martin: 'Prof Richie, Fine Arts from Yale … John Lane, the elegant man's tailor from Double Bay who owns a National Trust house … Geoffrey Legge (who backs the Watters Gallery)' and assemblage artist John Armstrong and his wife. She continued:

> the wine was plied. Everyone shouted … 'What about Bob Hawke for PM?' I said to John Lane, a very strong Lib. Everyone shouted some more. It was all very jolly. I did enjoy it.[76]

Rosalie was in her element. She enjoyed the company and the art: 'Huge [painting by Richard] Larter along one wall. Several Armstrongs standing about … a lovely Max Watters on the mantel.'[77] Her circles widened to include the Brisbane, Sydney and Melbourne art scene. Canberra friendships provided her with entrée to these other cities.

By 1973 Rosalie was also broadening her knowledge of international art. She had taken up reading art periodicals, including *Artforum*, *Art International* and *Art in America*, opening her eyes to art in the wider world.[78] Hester had moved to Sydney; Rosalie visited regularly and together they enjoyed Sydney galleries.[79]

75 Hughes et al., 'Rosalie Gascoigne Artist', tape 7.

76 Rosalie to Martin, c. 16 November 1972, cited in Eagle, *From the Studio of Rosalie Gascoigne*, 39.

77 Ibid.

78 MacDonald and Gascoigne, *Rosalie Gascoigne*, 25.

79 Rosalie to Martin, 6 August 1972, cited in Eagle, *From the Studio of Rosalie Gascoigne*, 37; Gellatly et al., *Rosalie Gascoigne*, 124.

In a letter to Martin in 1973, Rosalie chronicled a turning point in her career. She found a hoard of discarded bee boxes between Gundaroo and Murrumbateman while out foraging with local painter Jean Conron.[80] Her use of the boxes led to later suggestions that her work was influenced by the box constructions of American Joseph Cornell and Australian John Armstrong.[81] Rosalie's reasoning, however, was entirely pragmatic. She wanted the boxes to stabilise her work:

> I was just making a pink circus at the time and every time anybody went past it went (rumble) and fell to the ground you see, or people knocked it and it got to be a terrible domestic curse. And I thought I must contain it, you know. And suddenly I thought, well, you know, I'll box it. So that will stop it falling over. And that's what got me into boxes.[82]

While denying that she knew of Cornell's work at this time, Rosalie did know Armstrong's work, having seen it at Watters Gallery in 1972 and later at the National Gallery's Fyshwick repository.[83] Armstrong worked with new materials. That did not appeal to Rosalie's aesthetic. She said she preferred the weathered look 'and the old unpretentious look'.[84] Although Armstrong's aesthetic was very different from Rosalie's, Martin suggested that some of Armstrong's work 'would find echoes' in her work.[85]

It was not until Christmas 1973, when Martin sent Rosalie *The Art of Assemblage* by William C. Seitz, published by the Museum of Modern Art in New York in 1961, that Rosalie became aware of Cornell's box assemblages of found objects. It arrived at just the right moment for Rosalie. She had found the bee boxes seven months earlier and had worked with them ever since. The book included illustrations of box works and she immediately felt at home among many of the featured artists whose work resonated with hers.[86]

---

80 Gascoigne, interview by North, 18, see annotation by Martin Gascoigne on transcript, footnote 40. Jean Condon was trained in London. See mention of her in 'An Artistic Line-up of Four', *Canberra Times*, 31 May 1967, 20.

81 Two *Canberra Times* reviewers in 1975 likened her work to Cornell's. See Chapter 4.

82 Gascoigne, interview by North, 19, see annotation by Martin Gascoigne on transcript, footnote 41: 'Rosalie first became aware of Joseph Cornell's works in boxes in late December 1973 when Martin sent her a copy of William Seitz's book on assemblage for Christmas. It included illustrations of Cornell's work amongst many others. William Seitz, *The Art of Assemblage*, The Museum of Modern art, New York 1961.'

83 Rosalie to Martin, c. 16 November 1972.

84 Hughes et al., 'Rosalie Gascoigne Artist', tape 4.

85 Martin Gascoigne, 'Rosalie's Artists', 41.

86 Rosalie to Martin, 30 December 1973, cited in Eagle, *From the Studio of Rosalie Gascoigne*, 39.

'Knowing the right people'

'It's a question in Canberra especially, of knowing the right people, I think', Rosalie told Hughes.[87] During this period Rosalie began to know Mollison and Taylor, but also Dobson, Bolton, Campbell and Hope. They were 'the right people' in terms of social and art connections but also, and just as importantly, they shared her aesthetic, lived for art and/or loved poetry. Their friendships and commonality alleviated her sense of feeling a misfit, affirmed her and encouraged her to push on with her vision. She began to see herself in a more positive light—no longer the odd one out who lived with the discomfort of feeling an outsider. This affirmation, together with Bottrell's inclusion of Rosalie in her book, Mollison's positive comments about her 'bits of stick' and his confidence in her eye for others' art, strengthened her belief in herself and propelled her on towards further success.

87 Hughes et al., 'Rosalie Gascoigne Artist', tape 4.

11

1974–79: 'Breathless times'

In 1974, Rosalie held her first solo exhibition, encouraged by Michael Taylor. Just four years later, in 1978, the National Gallery of Victoria mounted a survey of her work, an accolade usually reserved for mid- to late-career artists who had already achieved significant acclaim. Her fast-track career was propelled by James Mollison's mentoring, and Taylor's friendship and affirmation, which bolstered her passion and drive for art making. Mollison and Taylor set Rosalie on a trajectory that was to go into orbit, Mollison assuming the role of tutor to Rosalie in art history. And so she made art, she learned and she moved further into artistic circles. Her trajectory during this period would culminate in an invitation to represent Australia at the 1982 Venice Biennale.

James Mollison: Arbiter of national taste and creator of a national art collection

Appointed director of the Australian National Gallery (ANG, later renamed the National Gallery of Australia) in 1977, Mollison determined which art was to be seen by the Australian public. Crucially for Rosalie, he had a sense of the role she might play in satisfying the national taste he was nurturing.

Mollison's and Rosalie's stories could have been different. During the selection process for the appointment of the new national gallery director in 1969, Prime Minister John Gorton opposed the council's recommendation of Western Australian Laurie Thomas because Thomas had not built a gallery.[1] Gorton proposed the council appoint American Dr John Walker, director of the National Gallery in Washington DC. The council minutes of 6 July 1970 record that Gorton's recommendation was rejected 'because his [Walker's] experience in building galleries was limited and because his interest is in the academic side of art'.[2] The council suggested instead they appoint James J. Sweeney, director of New York's Solomon R. Guggenheim Museum, who had provided extensive consultative services to the ANG. Two years later, when no progress had been made and the ANG was still without a director, the council appointed Mollison as interim director. In February 1977, he was appointed director.[3] Had Gorton got his way, or had Thomas or Sweeney been appointed, Rosalie would have lacked a crucial patron, and Australian art would have had a very different figure to craft its national collection. The acceptance of her work and her rapid rise to fame relied on more than talent. It was highly dependent upon her social and cultural capital with members of the developing art bureaucracy in which Mollison played a central role.

As part of the expanding agenda of the ANG, Mollison's task was to advise on the Commonwealth's acquisitions of Australian art, catalogue the national collection and arrange exhibitions of Australian art to tour overseas.[4] Later his brief was expanded to include the purchase of overseas art. Under a Labor government after 1972, the ANG had more money to spend on acquisitions than any other gallery in the world. The national collection was building in earnest. By 1974, thanks to the beneficence of the Whitlam government towards the arts, Mollison had 'assembled a dazzling and representative collection of Australian art' that was still held in the temporary repository at Molonglo Mall in Fyshwick, Canberra's industrial district.[5] In addition to Australian art, Mollison bought major international works from a broad range of media, including contemporary works from New York and Europe under 'Art Current', a proposal he initiated to give the Australian public 'a first-hand experience of new art developments'.[6]

1 Green, ed., *Building the Collection*, 47. Green footnoted the fact that Sir Daryl Lindsay later noted that Thomas had been responsible for drawing up plans for a new gallery in Queensland but lack of finance meant it had not gone ahead. 'Letters to the Editor: The Reasons Why Sir Daryl Quit', *Canberra Times*, 1 March 1971, 2.

2 Green, ed., *Building the Collection*, 15–16.

3 Ibid., 15–21.

4 Sparke, *Canberra 1954–1980*, 310.

5 Anderson, 'Mollison's Creation', 23.

6 Ward, 'Art Current', 149–51.

This educative, almost didactic role was deeply entrenched in Mollison's approach. As well as exposing the public to cutting-edge art, he aimed to show Australians a variety of international art including African and Pre-Columbian American as well as Asian and Western art, together with 'a concentration of highest-quality international modernism and contemporary art and an extremely comprehensive collection of Australian art'.[7] Mary Eagle described Mollison as 'zestfully following an international mainstream of adventurous art'.[8] Curator, art critic and gallery director Daniel Thomas wrote that Mollison's choices were largely based on modernist aesthetics. Mollison, wrote Thomas, created a national gallery that was 'startlingly different from the overly British collections formed previously in Australia' and free of the parochialism of the state-based Australian art collections.[9] In 1990, Mollison's successor as gallery director, Betty Churcher, paid tribute to his crucial part in building the collection: 'he had single-handedly built a great and comprehensive collection from the ground up'.[10] This was the context in which Rosalie found her patron.

Mollison took Rosalie to the gallery's Fyshwick repository where art was stored in the years prior to the ANG's opening in 1982. For security reasons, few knew the location. Mollison showed Rosalie new works as they arrived. She said he gave her a personal course in art history.[11] She saw masterpieces by the likes of Man Ray, Duchamp, Brancusi and Tiepolo, and assemblages by Joseph Cornell and Robert Rauschenberg.[12] Kelly Gellatly described Mollison as a hard taskmaster, saying he interrogated people in a way that challenged them to form their own ideas and stand by them: 'That was part of Rosalie's training.'[13] Louise Pether, curator at the Auckland Art Gallery Toi o Tāmaki, told me in 2010 how fortunate Rosalie was to 'get picked up by James Mollison. You couldn't want for a more superhero supporter.'[14]

---

7 Thomas, 'Art Museums in Australia'.

8 Eagle, *From the Studio of Rosalie Gascoigne*, 47.

9 Thomas, 'Art Museums in Australia'. After gaining a degree from Oxford, Thomas returned to Australia where he was, by turn, professional assistant, curator and then senior curator, Australian Art, at the Art Gallery of News South Wales (1958–78); art critic at the *Sunday Telegraph* (1962–66, 1968–69), *Sydney Morning Herald* (1970–75) and *Bulletin* (1976–77); senior curator then head, Australian Art, at the National Gallery of Australia (1978–84); and director of the Art Gallery of South Australia (1984–90).

10 Churcher, 'The Years 1990 to 1997', 175.

11 MacDonald and Gascoigne, *Rosalie Gascoigne*, 25.

12 Ibid.

13 Kelly Gellatly, interview by author, 3 November 2011.

14 Louise Pether, interview by author, 2010.

Mollison challenged Rosalie to clarify her opinions on the art. He was known as a disciplined thinker and demanded the same of his 'pupils', including Rosalie, who described his expectations: 'If you really thought something, you had to be very sure you could argue it out. You'd hammer away and hammer away and sometimes James would say you were right.'[15] Thus, although Rosalie may not have 'read the book' as she often claimed, she was tutored in art and art history by one of Australia's most influential art historians, and saw the national gallery's splendid collection of Australian and international art close-up and hands-on in a way accessible to a select few.

Rosalie and her art benefited from her engagement with Mollison while he and his curatorial team relished Rosalie's creative, poetic approach. The relationship worked both ways—Mollison enjoyed Rosalie's visits to the repository:

> She was a very good visitor … literate and often interested in what things meant … from having taught poetry she had many tricks of reciting something quite appropriate to the work.[16]

In my interview with Mollison in 2011, he made light of his role in Rosalie's rise, attributing such suggestions to her 'mawkish letters' to Martin published in *From the Studio of Rosalie Gascoigne* (2000).[17] He said that she was just one of many artists with whom he engaged during his life and 'the only one in Canberra'.[18] However, without Mollison it seems unlikely Rosalie would have achieved the renown or developed her work in the way she did.

As well as challenging Rosalie's thinking about art, Mollison told me that he had questioned her practice of:

> using such impermanent material as torn blocks of newspapers nailed to a plank of timber put out into the sun for years until the sunlight stains them, the wind tears them they become very beautiful looking pages. The life of that will be fifty years. It couldn't be conserved so why doesn't she try to use more permanent materials?[19]

15 MacDonald and Gascoigne, *Rosalie Gascoigne*, 25.
16 James Mollison, interview by author, 2011.
17 Ibid.
18 Ibid.
19 Ibid.

Rosalie felt Mollison was hard on her: 'He was very cruel, he could be very cruel. And he discarded a lot of stuff, but after a while, he came to be convinced that I was something different.'[20] Mollison claimed it took Rosalie years to get over his 'bullying' of her, saying he bullied her 'because I couldn't be bothered being kind about it. If she's wrong she's just wrong. And if she goes wrong she's no longer an artist.'[21] He deliberately discouraged her from the small metal sculptures she made during the late 1960s and early 1970s because he considered them 'empty-headed'. He had seen what she was capable of with the 'extraordinarily creative' bone sculptures for the Academy of Science.[22] Rosalie's letters to Martin relate a compelling story of the importance of Mollison's advice for her growing practice. In 1997, she told journalist Janet Hawley that she 'didn't dare have the pretension to call what [she] was doing "art"' until she got to know Mollison.[23]

Where Martin affirmed and encouraged Rosalie, Mollison kept her on her mettle. Spare with his compliments, after watching her for a few years he told her: 'your work is lyrical'.[24] If he was parsimonious with praise, his actions spoke volumes when he purchased work from her first solo exhibition in 1974 for the Philip Morris Arts Grant Collection of work by bold and innovative artists.[25]

Despite his unkindnesses to Rosalie, she confirmed her trust in Mollison by following his advice. She travelled to New York on his recommendation, and bought Michael Taylor and Ken Whisson paintings when he recommended them. In 1974 he had told her Whisson was 'a man to buy'.[26] So buy she did, but beyond the purchase, there was an implicit resonance in style, approach and temperament. In Whisson's *And What Should I Do in Illyria?* Rosalie saw what she wanted to achieve in her own art—'the feel of things'. She loved 'the quality of air his paintings had'.[27] Whisson's expression of the natural environment resonated with her own. Mollison could mould Rosalie. She was happy to be shaped and guided by such eminence.

20 Hughes et al., 'Rosalie Gascoigne Artist', tape 4.

21 James Mollison, interview by author, 2011.

22 Ibid.

23 Janet Hawley, 'A Late Developer', *Sydney Morning Herald*, 15 November 1997, 42.

24 Eagle, *Rosalie Gascoigne, 1985*, 1.

25 Sponsored by a multinational cigarette company between 1973 and 1988, the collection, guided by Mollison, purchased an extensive body of works by emerging Australian artists for the gallery.

26 Hughes et al., 'Rosalie Gascoigne Artist', tape 7. Note, Rosalie paid $800 for the Whisson painting. Martin Gascoigne, email to author, 28 January 2015.

27 Eagle, *From the Studio of Rosalie Gascoigne*, 53.

Rosalie and Mollison served each other. Given that the Commonwealth Arts Advisory Board had given Mollison everything he wanted to entice him to accept the job in Canberra, it is unlikely he needed recognition from Rosalie. She did however offer him, a man living away from his family of origin, a connection with a family. Mollison said Rosalie mothered him and some of his young curators; he admired Ben enormously and had huge respect for his standing and knowledge in astronomy.[28] He enjoyed the Sunday evening meals at Anstey Street.

1974: *Assemblages* — first solo exhibition

Rosalie was fifty-seven at the time of her first solo exhibition, *Assemblages*. It showed from 15 to 26 June 1974 at Macquarie Galleries in Canberra. Michael Taylor had encouraged her: 'I was getting on, going merrily into my fifties, and still hadn't had a show, so he pushed it.'[29] Painter Keith Looby agreed with gallery manager Anna Simons that Rosalie's work could be shown, so she 'shovelled' it into the gallery.[30] Most of the fifty works exhibited were her earlier small iron sculptures, but she included ten of her box constructions, the works that now engrossed her. Most were on sale for $140 each. Rosalie was disappointed that only two of the boxes sold while the small iron works all sold. Perhaps wrestling with the lure of an easy market, she did not make iron sculptures again.

The exhibition launched her, but did not dampen her insecurity, which she revealed to *Canberra Times* reporter Jacqueline Lees when she said that she liked to add 'a bit of paint, of wallpaper' to a piece to show viewers that people were present in her art, despite not being visible:

> Of course, this is all very unacceptable to people who want you to be cosy and live up to the houseproud image that doesn't jar. People sometimes look upon me now as dangerous. They meet me in my denims and look at my work and wonder if I would be safe to have to lunch when they ask the ambassador's wife.[31]

---

28 James Mollison, interview by author, 2011: 'Ben was a man for whom I had huge admiration. And Rosalie was a likeable woman.'

29 MacDonald and Gascoigne, *Rosalie Gascoigne*, 25.

30 Hughes et al., 'Rosalie Gascoigne Artist', tape 4. Anna Simons ran one of the first commercial galleries from her home in the Canberra suburb of Campbell from the early 1960s then exhibited in the gallery space at the Canberra Theatre Centre playhouse for the Sydney-based Macquarie Galleries (directors Treania Smith and Lucy Swanton) before moving to Furneaux Street in Manuka. Simons retained the gallery as the Anna Simons Gallery when Macquarie Galleries withdrew from Canberra.

31 Jacqueline Lees, 'Gang Gang: Dried Flowers to Bones', *Canberra Times*, 20 June 1974, 3.

Rosalie's use of the word 'dangerous' reflects her sense of the convention she was challenging, perhaps as much in herself as beyond. Was she secretly proud to be considered dangerous? The image captured the ambivalent space she was beginning to occupy, and the purpose she was perhaps beginning to serve, in the shifting currents of Australian art: the sudden eruption of an unlikely artist on the tipping point of many conventions and stereotypes.

Of Rosalie and this first solo exhibition, Eagle wrote that 'she came into the art world, like Athena from the head of Zeus, full-grown and artistically fully-armed'.[32] Whether Rosalie was as fully formed as Eagle suggests is a moot point. That she continued to grow and develop her artistic practice suggests she was not quite fully formed. Whatever her own journey, she was finding broad acceptance.

In September 1974, Mollison purchased two works from the show at Macquarie Galleries: *Untitled No. 7* (1974) and *Untitled No. 25* (later known as *The Dredge)* (1974). Early the following year, he purchased two more: *Untitled* (1975) and *Woolshed* (1975).[33] Mollison's purchases of her work dazzled Rosalie. She told Hughes that she remembered 'lying on the carpet. I was so impressed with this fact that the things had been bought by such as Jim Mollison.'[34] To North in 1982 she expressed elation:

> You know, I mean, glory again, surprise, surprise. So then I felt I was real, so if anybody had a go at me I could say Philip Morris, you know … And you needed … a bit of identity.[35]

The four works were shown in the Philip Morris Arts Grant Second Annual exhibition in Melbourne and Sydney in March 1975.

Late in 1975, Rosalie showed her work again, this time alongside seven other recognised local artists, including her friend Jan Brown.[36] The exhibition, *Capital Art*, was an indication of the increasing depth and recognition of art made in the city. *Canberra Times* reviewers described one of Rosalie's works, *Moth Box* (then titled *Specimen Box*), as 'charming although influenced by

32 Eagle, *Rosalie Gascoigne, 1985*, 1.

33 Martin Gascoigne's annotations on Gascoigne, interview by North, 19, footnote 43. These four works can be seen in Gascoigne, *Rosalie Gascoigne: A Catalogue Raisonné*, 156–62.

34 Hughes et al., 'Rosalie Gascoigne Artist', tape 4.

35 Gascoigne, interview by North, 20.

36 Other artists who exhibited were Patricia Carr, Brian Cowley, Ante Dabro, Geoffrey de Groen, Keith Looby and Valerie Parr.

Joseph Cornell', and 'deeply indebted to Joseph Cornell'.[37] However, as mentioned in the previous chapter, Rosalie told North she did not know about Cornell at the time she started making box constructions: 'I … didn't know about Cornell anyway.'[38] She did not receive Seitz's book until Christmas 1973, but had found the bee boxes seven months earlier, in May, and quickly found they provided stability for her assemblages:[39]

> I arranged things happily in there, because I could fix them and they could stay, you see. But I was never into boxes the way say Cornell [was]. I didn't know about him … Didn't know about anything. And he was coming from a very different platform you see … Mine was stability problems and it was really making little Ikebanas in boxes.[40]

Made with a weathered bee box, *Specimen Box* reflected the gold, sun-bleached colours of the Monaro countryside Rosalie loved to explore. She donated the work to the *Artists for Labor* exhibition at the Anna Simons Gallery in November 1975 to raise funds for Gough Whitlam's re-election campaign.[41] This donation was a rare example of Rosalie's political inclination, possibly inspired by Labor's generosity to the visual arts, in particular the funding for the ANG collection. This was a singular indication of commitment beyond her work: politics was not the world in which she was finding a place.

Jim's Picnic: Hobnobbing with the international arts elite

In April 1975, Mollison invited Rosalie to an event that showed that she was truly an insider in Canberra's and Australia's art world. Rosalie was one of few Canberrans Mollison invited to a picnic at Tidbinbilla with Blanchette Ferry Hooker (Mrs John D. Rockefeller III) and the thirty-seven members of the International Council of the Museum of Modern Art (ICMMA). Other members of the ICMMA who attended the picnic included a European prince—Prince Franz von Bayern—and arts

37 'Edna Boling's Notes and Quotes', *Canberra Times*, 16 October 1975, 18; Geoffrey de Groen, 'Diverse Styles Exhibited', *Canberra Times*, 22 October 1975, 15.

38 Gascoigne, interview by North, 19, footnote 41. See annotation by Martin Gascoigne on transcript: 'Rosalie first became aware of Joseph Cornell's works in boxes in late December 1973 when Martin sent her a copy of William Seitz's book on assemblage for Christmas. It included illustrations of Cornell's work amongst many others.'

39 Seitz, *The Art of Assemblage*; Eagle, *From the Studio of Rosalie Gascoigne*, 42.

40 Hughes et al., 'Rosalie Gascoigne Artist', tape 3.

41 MacDonald and Gascoigne, *Rosalie Gascoigne*, 20.

administrators Porter McCray (US), Steingrim Laursen (Denmark) and Monroe Wheeler (US). The Australian members of the council included such rich, powerful and influential people as newspaper magnate and art patron James Fairfax, Gallery A owner Ann Lewis, writer and painter Lady Maie Casey and architect Penelope Seidler.[42] Visiting Australia for their biannual meeting and for the touring exhibition *Modern Masters: Manet to Matisse*, the councillors were feted by the Australian government with a banquet at Sydney's opera house, and meals at Kirribilli with the Whitlams and at the homes of some of the Australia's arts and cultural elite, including renowned Viennese-born architect Harry Seidler and his wife Penelope.[43]

In Canberra, Mollison showed them the national collection, the artworks leaning against filing cabinets and cinder block walls in the Fyshwick repository.[44] With other Canberrans—art historian and writer Felicity St John Moore and ANG donor Dimity Davy—Rosalie boarded a bus for the picnic at Tidbinbilla Nature Reserve with these influential people who were to be presented with the 'real' Australia. They delighted in it, 'encountering emus and kangaroos and … eagles' under a drizzly sky.[45] Rosalie made *Jim's Picnic* afterwards using wire mesh, Arnotts biscuit box parrot cutouts, dried grasses and glass jars (see the Gascoigne, *Rosalie Gascoigne: A Catalogue Raisonné*, 164), and later described the lunch in a talk to the Canberra School of Art: 'It was a marvellous impractical picnic with the clouds coming over, the kangaroos hopping up and down.'[46] Mollison clearly considered that her presence at the picnic would reflect well on the national gallery.

42 Fink, 'Jim's Picnic'.

43 Ibid.: 'During their ten-day tour, the Council was entertained in Sydney by a seven-course banquet at the Opera House, a dinner dance at Rosemont with Lady Lloyd-Jones, lunch with Mrs Whitlam at Kirribilli House and a dinner party (one of many) hosted by Penelope and Harry Seidler. The entourage travelled to Canberra (via lunch at James Fairfax's in Bowral) to view the national collection.'

44 Ibid.: 'In Shop 14 Molonglo Mall, *Blue poles* was stored in a specially built crate, covered in graffiti after its nation-wide tour, de Kooning's *Woman V* hung on a cinderblock wall, and Duchamp's *Bicycle wheel* was perched on top of a filing cabinet. There, in what must have felt like the middle of nowhere, the Council inspected works by Morris Louis, Malevich, Duchamp, Man Ray, Lichtenstein and Bacon laid out on the warehouse floor and stacked against walls.'

45 Ibid.

46 Ibid.

Stealing the show: *Artists Choice* at Sydney's Gallery A

A month after the picnic, in May 1975, Rosalie's star skyrocketed into orbit when her work stole the show in the *Artists Choice* exhibition at Gallery A in Sydney. Taylor had nominated her for the show, which was based on the idea that established artists chose promising young artists to exhibit. Taylor said to her: 'Look, I don't want to choose anybody at the art school. I want you to go in.'[47] Rosalie was flabbergasted: 'Heavens, you know! … That was Sydney, boy, Sydney!'[48] Sydney was a sophisticated metropolis compared to Canberra; it had a dynamic art scene and an audience for her work that was far greater than she could ever imagine in the national capital. She was also delighted because it felt less risky and exposing than first exhibiting in Sydney in a solo show.[49] Rosalie took Taylor's selection to Sydney. She described the scene at Gallery A:

> all these bright lads … leaping around … very large young men putting up things they'd been taught in Sydney schools. And you could tell who their teachers were mostly, because they did similar work. Big things … great big twelve-foot-long paintings.[50]

Overwhelmed, Rosalie quickly left the gallery: 'I put my little things down and crept out into Sydney.'[51] *Standing Piece*, *Collection*, *Leaning Piece* and *Lying Piece*, all made in 1974, were displayed under a window in the gallery, which Fink described as showing Rosalie's originality in greater relief because 'there was still a sense in the gallery of the house it had once been, a domestic scale that suited works made in a living room and on a dining table'.[52] Rosalie may have moved from the traditional female arts of flower arrangement but her work was still viewed partially in the gendered light of domesticity.

Rosalie crept out into the Sydney evening, seeking escape from the import and exposure of the exhibition, so missed seeing her works snapped up by keen buyers. Someone from the gallery phoned her that night to tell her she had stolen the show. Daniel Thomas's review in the *Sydney Morning Herald* reflected the success of her work:

47 Hughes et al., 'Rosalie Gascoigne Artist', tape 4.

48 Gascoigne, interview by North, 20.

49 'Much less fraught and painful than going in with a one-man show in Sydney': Rosalie to Toss Gascoigne, February 1975, cited in Fink, 'The Life of Things', 150.

50 Ibid., 152.

51 Hughes et al., 'Rosalie Gascoigne Artist', tape 4.

52 Fink, 'The Life of Things', 150.

> She turns out to be not a young post-graduate student but a mother of grown-up children, recently self-taught. She assembles disparate objects, like a neat horizontal stack of dried stalks in a piece of convex metal, with a marvellously sure and fully sculptural taste in setting up contrasts of texture, colour, direction and weight.[53]

Rosalie was fifty-nine. Four days after the exhibition opening, Gallery A invited her to hold a solo exhibition. She was over the moon: 'I was so high I tell you!'[54] The show, in 1976, was a huge success. It earned critical acclaim and several public collections acquired exhibited works. Fink expressed the exhibition's vitality: 'Rosalie did not so much install the exhibition as colonise the gallery. It was ebullient, theatrical, a carnival of art.'[55] The show celebrated discards. Sideshow throwaways discovered at the Bungendore tip included kewpie dolls 'like ladies sitting at the opera or a crowd at the football' who greeted the viewer with incurious eyes set in their battered heads, their 'arms ripped off like Aunty Jack'.[56] James Gleeson bought four works for the ANG: *The Colonel's Lady*, *Blackbird Box*, *Tiepolo Parrots* and *Triptych*. Daniel Thomas bought *Crop* and *Enamel Ware* for the Art Gallery of New South Wales. Five state galleries acquired work: 'It was very, very heady', said Rosalie, 'it just went from unreality to unreality. The world opened up; I found I was legitimate. And then there was no holding me.'[57] In a letter to Toss, Ben described Rosalie's elation: 'She is floating on this cloud, most of the time, except when she thinks she ought to cook a meal or iron a shirt.'[58] Even at this time, the early days of her stellar rise, Rosalie felt the pressures of domesticity's demands, but as she herself recognised, and as was confirmed by a number of art critics, she was launched.[59]

Momentously, in April 1977, Robert Lindsay invited Rosalie to hold a survey show in a new series of contemporary art shows planned by the National Gallery of Victoria (NGV). Such survey exhibitions were usually

---

53 Daniel Thomas, 'Interesting Artist's Choice', *Sydney Morning Herald*, 8 May 1975, cited in Fink, 'The Life of Things', 150.

54 Gascoigne, interview by North, 21.

55 Fink, 'The Life of Things', 156.

56 Rosalie Gascoigne quoted in MacDonald and Gascoigne, *Rosalie Gascoigne*, 20. The reference is to 'The Aunty Jack Show' that featured on Australian television from 1972 to 1973. In its theme song, Aunty Jack warns viewers that if they do not tune into the next show she will 'come around to your house and rip your bloody arms off'.

57 Ibid., 29.

58 Ben Gascoigne to Toss Gascoigne, 22 September 1974, in Gellatly, 'Rosalie Gascoigne', 14.

59 Gascoigne's own understated words were, 'I was sort of launched'. See Hawley, 'A Late Developer'. Gellatly et al., *Rosalie Gascoigne*, 125: 'This effectively launches her career'.

restricted to mid- or late-career artists who had achieved considerable acclaim. Mollison, usually wary and full of advice about the right times and places to exhibit, was 'very much in favour'.[60]

After the invitation from the NGV, the Arts Council invited her to exhibit at the Venice Biennale in 1982. Rosalie's excitement bubbled through her words when she recalled the thrill of those heady days to North:

> Me! Victoria! A show! Well. I died the death, but I pulled myself up again by my bootstraps and went in … And then very soon after that—this was breathless times—they said, 'You're going to Venice'![61]

In the meantime, her first Brisbane shows—at the Institute of Contemporary Art and a group show at Ray Hughes Gallery in 1977—illustrated the variety of work she made during this period. Hundreds of swan feathers woven through newspaper in *Pale Landscape* carpeted the floors of both galleries. Like a giant rug (3,965 x 7,320 mm), *Pale Landscape* sprawled in front of the viewer, daily news threaded with the means of flight, but grounded.[62] Rosalie made new friends in Brisbane, one of whom was Pam Bell, the *Australian* newspaper's recently appointed Brisbane art critic who liked Rosalie's works very much.[63] Rosalie partied with Ray and Jill Hughes and their artists' circle, and found a kindred spirit and admirer in conceptual artist Robert McPherson who sent her one of his line drawings. She told Martin she would go to McPherson's opening at Channy's in Sydney.[64]

Also in 1977, Rosalie was getting to know James Gleeson, surrealist painter, art critic, art historian and advisory curator for the national collection. His poetic appreciation of art resonated with Rosalie's.[65] He became a popular dinner party guest with both Rosalie and Ben who appreciated his 'really meaty conversation … full of scholarship'.[66] In Canberra she reported that acclaimed Australian novelist Patrick White was to have visited her with Rosemary Dobson and David Campbell and she had baked an apple cake for the occasion, but he 'got bogged down at National Gallery's Fyshwick

60 Ben Gascoigne to Martin Gascoigne, 4 July 1977, cited in Eagle, *From the Studio of Rosalie Gascoigne*, 49.

61 Hughes et al., 'Rosalie Gascoigne Artist', tape 4.

62 In 1983, Rosalie reconstructed *Pale Landscape* when visiting Wellington and gifted it to the National Gallery, later to become Te Papa. See Gascoigne, interview by North, 26.

63 Rosalie to Martin, 7 March 1977, cited in Eagle, *From the Studio of Rosalie Gascoigne*, 45.

64 Channy was Chandler Coventry who opened a gallery in Hargreave Street, Paddington, in 1970.

65 Hughes et al., 'Rosalie Gascoigne Artist', tape 5; O'Brien, Savage and City Gallery Wellington, *Rosalie Gascoigne: Plain Air*, 84.

66 Rosalie to Martin, 1 May 1977, cited in Eagle, *From the Studio of Rosalie Gascoigne*, 47.

repository looking at pictures with James Gleeson' and did not make it to Anstey Street. Dobson mentioned her name at the gallery and 'James G's face lit up'. He produced Rosalie's *Triptych* for White to see. White liked it: on leaving, he repeated Rosalie's name twice out loud and said: 'If I were an artist, I'd like to work like Rosalie Gascoigne.'[67] Rosalie wrote to Martin that White's comment made up 'for having to sit in my clean house with my freshly baked apple cake, waiting in vain'.[68]

Rosalie's circle continued to extend further into the art world. She made frequent mention in her letters to Martin of seeking Mollison's advice about particular works or invitations to exhibit, and of her visits to him at the Fyshwick repository and his visits to her at Anstey Street. English-born collage artist Mildred Kirk became a friend and companion on Rosalie's foraging trips.[69] Rosalie held and attended dinner parties with the inner circle of Australian art in Canberra and Sydney. In April 1977, she and Ben dined with art world notables Channy Coventry, Bridget Riley, Kerry Crowley, Gunter Christmann, Ray Hughes, Michael and Rominie Taylor, Robert Owen, Nola Yuill and Robert McPherson.[70] This event and Robert McPherson's widely spread comments around Sydney that Rosalie's *Pale Landscape* was the best thing that had ever happened for Brisbane brought home to Ben the significance of the attention Rosalie was receiving.[71] He wrote to Martin that he had begun to carefully and consistently photograph each and every one of Rosalie's finished works.

April 1978: *Survey 2: Rosalie Gascoigne* at the National Gallery of Victoria

April 1978 arrived and, with it, the opening of *Survey 2: Rosalie Gascoigne* at Melbourne's NGV.[72] Martin returned to Australia to support his mother during the installation and opening of the show, and Ben travelled to Melbourne in June to see it. The show was so popular that, unusually for exhibitions, the catalogue sold out, and the second printing also sold fast.[73]

---

67 All references to White's planned visit in Rosalie to Martin, April 1977 in ibid., 46.

68 Rosalie to Martin, April 1977, in ibid.

69 Rosalie to Martin, 11 October 1977. in ibid., 51: 'Tomorrow I am going out with Mildred … Will maybe to go Gundaroo and see if any more bee boxes.'

70 Eagle, *From the Studio of Rosalie Gascoigne*, 46–7.

71 Ibid., 49.

72 The show was open from 29 April to 4 June 1978.

73 Eagle, *From the Studio of Rosalie Gascoigne*, 46–7.

In a review in the *Sun*, artist, writer and educator Rod Carmichael described Rosalie as 'a magpie' with her collection of 'the detritus of society'. He alleged that 'not all her collage and assemblages work. When they fail, they are trite and sentimental.'[74] Perhaps it was this critic about whom Rosalie scribbled in blunt pencil on a scrunched-up sheet of paper now in her archive in the National Library of Australia:

> The critics in their trendy gear
> will tell us what it's all about
> but they didn't make the journey
> packing their few portables
> and moving away from comfort
> into the desert
> where nothing is there
> unless you put it there.[75]

As her scrawled poem suggests, the going was not all smooth. Despite the huge audiences, sell-out catalogue and the fact that director Robert Lindsay said that all the curators liked it, Mollison went to the exhibition but inexplicably refused to comment as did Rosalie's friends who knew him.[76]

Rosalie's practice took a new turn that year when she discovered piles of discarded crates at the Schweppes soft drink depot at Queanbeyan a small town across the Australian Capital Territory border in New South Wales.[77] The crates' coloured wooden slats were to provide her with material for the next twenty years and lead to some of her greatest works including *Monaro* (1989). In 1979, she showed her first work made of soft drink crates, *March Past* (1978), at Ray Hughes Gallery, Brisbane. Mollison gave *March Past* his stamp of approval when he purchased it for the Philip Morris Collection.[78]

Rosalie's reputation as an artist continued to grow. If the previous decades—dealing with the shock of difference on Stromlo, developing her eye there and in Deakin while growing and arranging flowers and creating ikebana—were formative, then Rosalie's isolation, shock and developed habit of intense looking blossomed and bore fruit in the 1970s. The consolidation of her own progress was matched by an art world and market keen for what she represented, both in her work and also, to some extent, her persona.

74 Rod Carmichael, 'Don't Scrap the "Junkies"', *Sun*, 10 May 1978.

75 Papers of Rosalie Gascoigne, box 1.

76 Eagle, *From the Studio of Rosalie Gascoigne*, 47.

77 Hughes et al., 'Rosalie Gascoigne Artist', tape 3.

78 The Philip Morris Arts Grant gifted it to the National Gallery of Australia in 1982.

Art historical context

The story of visual art in Australia from the 1950s conveniently coincides with Rosalie's maturing as an artist. The art historical context at the time of, and leading up to, her recognition as an artist is part of her story, not so much because it formed her (it did not; she came to the art world well formed as an artist), but because art tastes and structures changed during the 1960s and 1970s in ways that primed the art world to receive Rosalie and her art. Three major factors contributed to an environment in which her work would gain recognition: social change, changing art tastes and changing art structures.

Social change

Increasing affluence after World War II, the rise of feminism with the publication of Germaine Greer's groundbreaking *The Female Eunuch* (1970), and the growth of the environmental movement with the Australian Conservation Foundation's birth in 1964 and the Wilderness Society in 1976 were all signs of Australia's changing social tides. Patrick McCaughey notes that, in terms of art, the roots of the women's movement lay in the late 1960s 'with such disparate talents as Janet Dawson and Vivienne Binns' but came to fruition in the early 1970s.[79] While Rosalie was not part of this movement, she benefited from the increasing acceptance by art hierarchies of rising numbers of women artists. Changes in Australian society impacted the general public's access to, and interest in, art. Meanwhile, higher incomes meant more Australians enjoyed the leisure time to appreciate art and had the means to buy it.[80]

Three writers who have commented on Australian art from the 1950s to the 1980s diverge in their opinions about what accounts for the transformations of those decades. In *Strange Country: Why Australian Painting Matters* (2014), McCaughey asserted that 'Australian art boomed domestically in the late 1950s', stimulated by an increasing belief that Australia produced its own distinctive art.[81] However, Terry Smith, in his influential essay 'The Provincialism Problem' (1974), argued that art in Australia remained a projection of art worlds in other metropolitan centres such as New York

79 McCaughey, *Strange Country*, 299.
80 Eagle and Jones, *A Story of Australian Painting*, 220–1; Allen, *Art in Australia*, 189.
81 McCaughey, *Strange Country*, 203.

and was not distinctive.[82] Writing in 1997, Christopher Allen claimed that the situation had recently changed: Australian confidence in its art at home and overseas had been greater since 1980, as the focus was less on single centres and, therefore, people were 'more willing to accept Australia as one of a constellation of centres making up a contemporary cultural world'.[83] Rather than contradictory, these three analyses point to the major changes occurring in the art world and the contexts of Rosalie's reception.

The situation was not as black and white as implied by McCaughey, Smith and Allen, particularly Smith. Their perspectives can be reconciled by the reality that Australian art continued to be informed by, and influenced by, other metropolitan centres, albeit in distinctive ways in the Australian context. There is little doubt that trends in art centres like New York led to the rise and acceptance of alternative ways of making art, including the assemblage that became Rosalie's medium of expressing her feelings about the Canberra hinterland.

Art tastes

By the 1960s, overseas influences had diminished painting's supremacy and introduced new ways of making art: pop, minimalism and various forms of abstraction appeared, along with assemblage and avant-garde sculpture. In 1968, the NGV organised a comprehensive exhibition of Australian abstract colour field painting called *The Field*, which, according to Andrew Sayers, made it clear that 'there were many other ways in which artists could engage with the nature of the art object'.[84] In addition to abstract painting, assemblage, which Rosalie was to take up, was one of these new ways.[85] Robert Klippel began making assemblages while living in New York in the 1960s and continued on his return to Australia after 1963. John Armstrong started making his witty assemblages in the early 1970s.[86] We know from her letters to Martin that Rosalie knew the work of both men and, indeed, met them.[87] Richard Haese, however, claims that the Annandale Imitation Realists introduced assemblage to Australian art as early as 1962 in their

82 Smith, 'The Provincialism Problem'.

83 Allen, *Art in Australia*, 203.

84 Sayers, *Australian Art*, 198. 'The Field' included work by Peter Booth who was to exhibit with Gascoigne at the 1982 Venice Biennale.

85 Smith and Smith, *Australian Painting 1788–1990*, 443.

86 *Carry* (1972), *One Two Three Fur* (1972) and *Footstool* (1972) are in the NGA collection.

87 Letters, Rosalie to Martin, 1971–80, cited in Eagle, *From the Studio of Rosalie Gascoigne*, 32–61.

exhibition at Melbourne's Museum of Modern Art.[88] From whatever perspective, assemblage art found receptive practitioners in Australia: if it was the new trend, it also connected with ways of understanding a context of discontinuous, residual and displaced elements.

Taste inevitably involved style. According to McCaughey: 'The 1960s brought a sea change to contemporary art across the globe. Pop, minimalism and a variety of abstract styles pushed their way to the centre of the stage.'[89] He felt that decade was 'probably the last … in which painting and formalised sculpture held sway over all other media … installations, performance, language art, video and other post-minimal manifestations'.[90] Jill Trevelyan described the 1970s as 'the decade of post-object art, which focused on environments, installation and performance'.[91] The resulting challenge to the hierarchy of painting and sculpture opened the way for Rosalie's assemblages of found objects to achieve a level of recognition that would probably have been denied in previous decades.

While Rosalie resisted classification, she did say her art was made in response to the landscape, and it is generally recognised by curators, art historians and theoreticians as landscape art. Art historians understand the importance of landscape to the Australian imagination. McCaughey attributes to Rosalie one of the most original responses to the Australian landscape post-1970.[92] Sasha Grishin also acknowledges her importance: 'Rosalie Gascoigne is another artist who has challenged our perception of the Australian landscape.'[93] Deborah Edwards curated an exhibition of Rosalie's work in 1998, calling it *Material as Landscape* in acknowledgement of the artist's use of materials found in the countryside to express her feelings about what she called her 'country'—'the eastern seaboard, Lake George and the Highlands'.[94]

Rosalie declared: 'I am not making pictures, I make feelings.'[95] Her friend and Adelaide dealer Paul Greenaway wrote in her obituary in 1999: 'There was never a literal representation of nature but an interpretation of the

88 Haese, *Permanent Revolution*, 2; McCaughey, *Strange Country*, 203.
89 McCaughey, *Strange Country*, 217.
90 Ibid., 305.
91 Trevelyan, *Peter McLeavey*, 187; McCaughey, *Strange Country*, 217.
92 McCaughey, *Strange Country*, 335.
93 Grishin, *Australian Art*, 436.
94 Mollison and Heath, 'Rosalie Gascoigne', 7.
95 Rosalie Gascoigne, in conversation with Max Cullen, 12 July 1998.

feeling which that landscape evoked.'[96] The NGV online document 'Rosalie Gascoigne: Landscape—Place, Memory and Experience' comments that 'the art of Rosalie Gascoigne has a unique place in the rich landscape tradition in Australian art'.[97] Edwards described the works she included in *Material as Landscape* as hovering 'between their cultural associations, including the weight of the Australian landscape tradition, and their place as Modernist abstract assemblages'.[98] Rosalie's art belongs in the landscape tradition that, as Grishin claimed, 'has remained a central concern for Australian artists as a vehicle for the interrogation of our environment and of our physical and spiritual place in it'.[99]

Grishin observed how the changes in contemporary art affected landscape art. The tradition of Australian landscape art started to change following World War II 'with the influx of European modernism, and especially expressionism and Surrealism'.[100] In the wake of the stylistic diversity that, according to Terry Smith, characterised the 1950s and 1960s, painters such as Russell Drysdale, Arthur Boyd and James Gleeson moved away 'from the naturalistic images of pastoral wealth and rural Arcadia popularised by artists of earlier generations'.[101] But it was not until the late 1950s and the 1960s, during the time that Rosalie was flower arranging, making ikebana and iron sculptures, that the conventions of Australian landscape art underwent fundamental change.

Fred Williams, on his return to Australia in 1957 after five years in London, was so struck with the shock of recognition of the landscape he determined to paint it, transforming the landscape tradition.[102] Rosalie's shock of difference in response to the Monaro landscape and Williams's shock of recognition on returning to Australia provided similar impetuses for each artist: a shift in perspectives, of senses of distance, a sense of space as much as subject. Other artists who transformed the tradition were printmaker, painter and installation artist Bea Maddock and sculptor John Davis. While challenging Australian perceptions of the landscape, Rosalie's art fitted into an existing genre that had long held the Australian imagination, but that was also undergoing radical reassessment.

96 Greenaway, 'Rosalie Gascoigne AM'.
97 National Gallery of Victoria, 'Rosalie Gascoigne: Landscape'.
98 Edwards, *Rosalie Gascoigne: Material as Landscape*, 11.
99 Grishin, *Australian Art*, 443.
100 Ibid., 431.
101 Ibid.
102 Ibid.

Rosalie combined the long-held Australian tradition of landscape with avant-garde assemblage. She brought to it her restless hands, and capacity for seeing, together with gifts for composition and form finely honed by her ikebana practice and poetic thought. She told Mollison and Heath: 'it was not a restless hobby I was grasping. I needed art as an extension of what I honestly did like, air, hills, freedom, grass growing.'[103] For Rosalie, art involved catering to her own needs. She made the art for herself. So, while art history provided her with space at the right time in terms of structures and tastes, she was not entirely formed by the context.

Commercialisation of art

A crucial development for Rosalie's career was the increased commercialisation of art that led to an increase in dealer galleries, and the burgeoning of art bureaucracies around public art institutions that enjoyed unprecedented funding in the 1970s, in particular the preparation and planning for what is now the National Gallery of Australia.

The art market in Australia grew in response to the financial boom and the maturing art market. Commercial dealer galleries increased around Australia, beginning in the 1950s and mushrooming in the 1960s.[104] In response, private collectors proliferated and public galleries began to collect and exhibit contemporary art.[105] During the 1950s and 1960s, the *Canberra Times* recorded the openings and activities of commercial galleries in the city, as outlined in Chapter 9.[106] Artists began moving away from group shows towards one-person exhibitions with dealers who were becoming more professional, more attuned to a market among a broader stratum of a more affluent society.[107] These changes provided the opportunity for Rosalie to show her work in her first solo exhibition at Macquarie Galleries in Canberra in 1974, making it visible to gallery curators and administrators from early in her exhibiting career.

At the same time, a boom was occurring in state and federal government-funded art institutions around which a bureaucracy—grant administrators, gallery directors, curators, magazine editors, critics, publicists, teachers,

103 Mollison and Heath, 'Rosalie Gascoigne', 7–8.
104 Allen, *Art in Australia*, 189.
105 McCaughey, *Strange Country*, 203; Allen, *Art in Australia*, 189.
106 McQueen, *Suburbs of the Sacred*, 153.
107 Ibid.

art historians and art theorists—proliferated.[108] In Canberra, on Rosalie's doorstep, plans for the national gallery saw the collection of a range of art styles from around the world, including up-to-the-minute contemporary art. Academic specialisation was increasing by the 1970s with the growth of art schools: the Canberra School of Art was founded from the Canberra Technical College Art Department.[109] Art had become an industry.

Rosalie: 'An artist whose relation to history is highly ambiguous'

While some art of the time influenced Rosalie's work, any attempt to classify her art or try to fit her into a particular art historical slot would deny her uniqueness. Christopher Allen describes Rosalie as an 'artist whose relation to history is highly ambiguous'.[110] He suggests that, like some other artists in the 1970s such as Mike Parr and Peter Booth, she was less influenced by current postmodern trends than many other artists.[111] Ian North described her work to me as innovative and in the spirit of the experimental 1970s, a period described by Allen as a time when art looked 'like a disparate group of artistic movements in search of a theory'.[112] Rosalie did not search for a theory, she eschewed it. Her former studio assistant, sculptor Peter Vandermark, recalled that she was not distracted by art world politics or fashions:

> she really stuck to her thing that she worked with the landscape around Canberra—the Monaro … she wasn't distracted by post-modernism … she knew what was happening in the art world but … she knew that this was her place, this was where she worked and she didn't really try and go out there and get recognised by doing work for a particular issue or a curator … she was the landscape, installation sculptor.[113]

Honesty was of paramount importance to Rosalie and, by honesty, she meant art that came directly from within the artist's 'own nature—NEVER the other fellow's art'.[114] She said artists 'must have the desert …

108 Allen, *Art in Australia*, 189.

109 Agostino and The Australian National University School of Art, *A History*, xi. The School of Art was amalgamated into ANU in 1992.

110 Allen, *Art in Australia*, 209.

111 Ibid., 203.

112 Ian North, interview by author, Adelaide, 13 December 2012; Allen, *Art in Australia*, 191.

113 Marie Hagerty and Peter Vandermark, interview by author, 2011.

114 Rosalie Gascoigne, 'Opening Address, 1993 Sydney *Perspecta*', Papers of Rosalie Gascoigne.

Not everybody else telling you [what to make].'[115] A letter she wrote to Martin in 1974 about Seitz's *Art of Assemblage* and a library book about Marcel Duchamp illustrates her struggle:

> I have taken on influences. Rewarding but in the end clouding my own vision … false, false … this a.m. returned to my true loves and think I have pulled it off.[116]

Rosalie displayed high expectations of herself in her attempts to avoid any influence.

For Rosalie, art was to be looked at. The 'big secondary industry of words' was a distraction, although she did acknowledge the interdependence of artists and the 'secondary industry' of galleries and exhibitions.[117] She told Stephen Feneley: 'I really don't like … "artspeak", people who put the words before the art. Art is a seeing thing … And "artspeak" clouds the issue.'[118] To theorise her into an art community, as if she had been formed by that community, when she clearly shunned theory and embraced the notion of art coming directly from the artist, would be to impose something alien on her. It would deny the innovative nature of her art and the impulse that drove her to make it. At the same time, a critical biographical study must address context and formation.

'Poised for a smart leap forward'

At the beginning of 1978, the *Canberra Times* reported that three of Rosalie's mixed media assemblages were on show at the Canberra Theatre Centre along with other recent ANG acquisitions.[119] After her second exhibition at the Ray Hughes Gallery, she prepared for the *Third Sydney Biennale: European Dialogue* curated by Nick Waterlow who became a friend and important supporter of her art. In March 1979, Ben wrote to Martin that Rosalie seemed 'all poised for a smart leap forward'.[120] During April–May 1979, *Feathered Fence* was shown in the Sydney Biennale alongside the work of important European artists including Gerhard Richter, Joseph Beuys, Hanne Darboven, Mario Merz, A. R. Penck, Valie Export, Daniel Buren

115 Hughes et al., 'Rosalie Gascoigne Artist', tape 6.

116 Letter to Martin, 9 January 1974, cited in Eagle, *From the Studio of Rosalie Gascoigne*, 43.

117 Gascoigne, 'Opening Address, 1993 Sydney *Perspecta*'.

118 Feneley and Gascoigne, 'Express Highlights'.

119 'Recent Acquisitions on Show', *Canberra Times*, 4 January 1978, 17.

120 Ben to Martin, March 1979, cited in Eagle, *From the Studio of Rosalie Gascoigne*, 58.

and Armand Arman, as well as performance art from Marina Abramovic and Ulay, Jürgen Klauke, Ulrike Rosenbach and others. The Biennale website states that Rosalie's *Feathered Fence* epitomised for the visiting Europeans the psyche of the Australian landscape.[121] Rosalie felt confirmed in her work as an artist by the Biennale, and was buoyed by the responses to her work, but she was not excited by the exhibition overall.[122]

So confident and confirmed was she feeling that, in November 1979, she complained to Mollison that she found the Sydney and Melbourne art scenes boring. He snarled: 'Get to the States—see what the big boys are doing'. He told her she was doing things too easily and needed to 'stand in the British museum' and think which of her work would she put up beside the Elgin marbles.[123] Not one to duck a challenge, Rosalie took up the idea. She did not go the British Museum but, the following year, she made an art pilgrimage to New York.

Glory years

At the close of 1979, Rosalie was sixty-two years old. If there was one period in which the stars aligned for her artistic rise, this had been it. The developing friendship with Mollison meant she had the eyes and ears of one of the most powerful tastemakers and administrators in Australian art. With Taylor, she experienced her first real sense of engagement with an artist and was affirmed by his recognition. His nomination of her in Gallery A's *Artists' Choice* led to such acclaim that invitations to exhibit flowed from important galleries like Brisbane's Institute of Contemporary Art and the Ray Hughes Gallery. Glory struck again when she was invited to do a survey show at the NGV, and to represent Australia in 1982 at the Venice Biennale. Her rise during these years was astronomical, especially for a woman in the second half of her life who had no formal art training. Her talent, drive, application and ambition, combined with the networks she wove during this period, all contributed to her becoming a familiar name in Australian art. But these events were all part of the bigger story of her life in that everything that went before led to this point—and there was more to come.

121 Biennale of Sydney, 'About Us'.

122 Rosalie to Martin, 30 April 1979, cited in Eagle, *From the Studio of Rosalie Gascoigne*, 58.

123 Rosalie to Martin, 16 November 1979, in ibid., 59. Ben was present; he described Mollison's challenge as 'very trenchant'. See Ben Gascoigne to Martin, 12 December 1979, in ibid.

12

The 1980s: 'An artist is like someone in the desert'

Rosalie began the 1980s with a visit to New York that affirmed her feelings about the truth and honesty of her art. She was sixty-three. Much has already been written of her career during this period. Art historians and theorists have interpreted her work, chronicled aspects of her life narrative, and composed catalogues and essays about her exhibitions.[1] Curators hung her art in galleries throughout Australia and in New Zealand, Japan and Sweden. Critics reviewed her work in newspapers, art journals and magazines. Family, friends and admirers wrote about her. She gave two talks at the Canberra School of Art, was visited in her studio by representatives from New York's Guggenheim Museum and a group of 'distinguished scholars, artists, art collectors and museum docents' from the Princeton University Art Museum.[2] Rosalie had made it as an artist and achieved recognition, not just in Australia but also internationally. Avoiding duplication of this material, this chapter provides fresh perspectives through an overview of her rise to fame in the context of her networks, and analyses her perpetual sense of being misunderstood—of being an outsider and alone.

1 For example, see MacDonald and Gascoigne, *Rosalie Gascoigne*; Edwards, *Rosalie Gascoigne: Material as Landscape*; Gellatly et al., *Rosalie Gascoigne*; O'Brien, Savage and City Gallery Wellington, *Rosalie Gascoigne: Plain Air*; North, 'Rosalie Gascoigne: Signs of Light'; North, Cattapan and University of South Australia Art Museum, *Expanse: Aboriginalities*; Fink, 'That Sidling Sight'; Eagle, 'Rosalie Gascoigne's Lyrical Derailments'.

2 Elizabeth Lawson, Guggenheim Museum, to Rosalie Gascoigne, 18 December 1984 and 29 March 1985, and Margaret B. Consedine, Princeton University Art Museum, to Rosalie Gascoigne, 10 October 1985, Papers of Rosalie Gascoigne, box 21, folder 1972–1985.

Perhaps she was so at ease with discomfort that she was unable to let it go? She may have felt increasingly isolated from family and friends as she became more committed to art making and needed to withdraw in the way she described to Hughes: 'an *artist is like someone in the … metaphorical desert* and there's nothing there unless you put it there yourself'.[3] She expanded on this theme later in the interview:

> [making art is] like being drowned. And there's … one piece of driftwood you can hang on to—honesty … otherwise you destroy yourself … every artist needs solitude. You must have the desert.[4]

This chapter also focuses on particular key events—her 'art pilgrimage' to New York in 1980, her time at the Venice Biennale and her return to New Zealand in 1983 for the first time since 1957—events that, in turn, show both her acclaim and her lingering sense of alienation.

Rosalie's sense of alienation is best expressed in her interview with Ian North in February 1982. Trusting North as a friend and fellow artist, and feeling recognised by him, Rosalie emphasised the 'sense of utter isolation' in her art, and her fight against what she 'knew other people wouldn't like'.[5] She told North that Brisbane art dealer Ray Hughes 'got her wrong', that he did not appreciate the seriousness of her work when he and some writers and critics misconstrued it as nostalgic.[6] Her rejection of this interpretation may have revealed a nerve she was determined to protect.

Recognition: James Gleeson and the Australian National Gallery

In February 1980, James Gleeson, then acknowledged as Australia's greatest surrealist painter and renowned for his substantial intellect, included Rosalie among the ninety-eight artists he interviewed for the Australian National Gallery's catalogue.[7] This inclusion was significant for an early career artist like Rosalie. The fact that the gallery had acquired five of her works and

3 Hughes et al., 'Rosalie Gascoigne Artist', tape 3 (emphasis added).

4 Ibid., tape 6.

5 Gascoigne, interview by North, 17.

6 Ibid., 22.

7 The James Gleeson Oral History Collection can be accessed via the of the National Gallery of Australia's website, see nga.gov.au/media/dd/documents/gascoigne.pdf. Former director of the Art Gallery of New South Wales, Edmund Capon, described Gleeson as 'an amazingly gifted scholar, critic and painter'. See Capon, 'Art Review'.

included her in Gleeson's oral history collection indicates her standing. The interview with Gleeson was her first major interview and the focus was on her art in the Australian National Gallery (ANG), not her life.

Rosalie generally felt uncomfortable in interviews and regarded with scepticism 'the big secondary industry of words' that accumulated around art.[8] The fact that Gleeson was a friend probably put her at ease and, as Mollison told me when talking about Rosalie: 'You're not an artist because you don't want anybody to know anything about you.'[9] If Rosalie sought recognition, he argued, she needed to accept having a public face. Two issues emerged from Gleeson's interview. First, four attempts were required to satisfactorily complete it; of the earlier attempts, Rosalie recorded in a letter to Martin on 5 February: 'Felt I talked a great deal too much about me and my art', a comment suggesting either a lack of confidence or, possibly at this point in her career, a question of wanting to manage her image.[10] Second, she wrote to Martin that she was in a 'doing mood' and hoped she could get in a talking mood: to relax into the 'artspeak' that seemed to preoccupy people 'who put the words before the art'.[11] However, Rosalie trusted Gleeson and, on 8 February, she managed to achieve the appropriate mood to successfully complete the interview.

In the interview she provided information about the works the ANG had purchased from her solo show at Gallery A in 1976—*Triptych* (1976), *Blackbird Box* (1976), *Tiepolo Parrots* (1976) and *The Colonel's Lady* (1976)—and the gallery's more recent purchase, *Country Air* (1978).[12] Rosalie talked about her process for making art. She told Gleeson that she aimed for a classical look, with dignity and beauty regardless of the materials used. She said she selected materials purely on aesthetic grounds, with no interest in their emotional or nostalgic value or history. She had no preconceived notions about what she would do with the materials she collected; rather, she took what dropped in front of her: 'I just like ordinary stuff … ordinary stuff is so good.' She likened new and old materials to people: 'brand new people … are not quite so interesting … people who are a bit battered are much … more interesting'.[13]

8 Gascoigne, 'Opening Address, 1993 Sydney *Perspecta*'.
9 James Mollison, interview by author, 2011.
10 Rosalie to Martin, 5 February 1980, cited in Eagle, *From the Studio of Rosalie Gascoigne*, 60.
11 Rosalie Gascoigne, interview by Stephen Feneley, 4 December 1997.
12 See these artworks in Gascoigne, *Rosalie Gascoigne: A Catalogue Raisonné*, 167, 168, 174, 175.
13 Gascoigne, interview by Gleeson.

Rosalie took the 'ordinary stuff'—the battered, weathered materials—and transformed them. Her practice had evolved considerably in just a few years. At the same time, an audience had developed for her work, appreciating her use of everyday materials and expression of feeling for the landscape. Gleeson's interview, then, is primarily a marker of her considerably increased status and her recognition by the Australian art establishment as a significant artist. It highlights the aesthetic approach of her artistic process and differentiates her work from that of other artists working with found objects such as Robert Klippel and the German Dadaist, Kurt Schwitters. Gleeson demonstrated his grasp of Rosalie's work by eliciting a strong artist statement in terms as concrete as her work.

In March 1980, in further evidence of her rising reputation and success, Rosalie exhibited *Paper Square* (1980) in *Drawn and Quartered—Australian Contemporary Paperworks* at the Adelaide Festival Exhibition in the Art Gallery of South Australia.[14] The same month, Gleeson affirmed her for successfully achieving recognition with a piece of art where renowned painter Albert Tucker had failed. Rosalie had shown Gleeson her work *Parrot Country*, made with weathered coloured slats of soft drink crates with jagged edges. She recounted Gleeson's response in a letter to Martin: '"Ah", said James G[leeson] happily, "The parrot is the country." "It screeches", I said … and he said "Albert Tucker TRIED to do that".'[15] One commentator on an exhibition of Tucker's parrots in 2013 likened them to a Hitchcock nightmare.[16] Gleeson appreciated the aesthetic of Rosalie's parrots, bright raucous birds who were not aggressive like Tucker's. He also found in them a truth, an objectivity, lacking in Tucker's motifs. Gleeson's response clearly delighted Rosalie. That an eminent curator like him favourably compared her with someone of Tucker's eminence was a real boost for her.

14 There appears to be another work called *Paper Square* or *Harvest* that she made in 1982.

15 Rosalie to Martin, 14 February 1980, cited in Eagle, *From the Studio of Rosalie Gascoigne*, 61. Tucker (1914–1999), a modernist painter who was a member of the Heide Circle in Melbourne, had been exhibiting since the 1940s and had achieved considerable renown at the time of this exchange. He had made a series of paintings featuring parrots in the 1950s and 1960s after a parrot he had nursed back to health bit him. He usually depicted them as aggressive creatures tearing into people's flesh.

16 Book, 'Albert Tucker'.

New York: A strengthened sense of her own truth

Rosalie took up Mollison's challenge and travelled to New York to look at art. She wrote to Martin on 7 January 1980 that Diana Woollard, a curator at the ANG, had told her 'Jim wants to be in New York with me'.[17] Mollison was travelling on one of his legendary buying trips with an open chequebook and was in New York for some of the three weeks Rosalie was there.[18]

She set off in May 1980 on her pilgrimage. She did the trip in style, staying at the historic luxury Algonquin Hotel near Times Square on Gleeson's recommendation.[19] She saw Mollison just once on the trip. While he had encouraged her to go, he virtually ignored her at their one meeting.[20] This bolstered, even served, her image of a 'solo pilgrimage'. Using words that evoked grit and mettle in the face of hardship, she told MacDonald she 'toughed out' hectic Manhattan alone.[21] Although Rosalie characterised her trip as lonely, she did not want people getting in the way of her plans. She told MacDonald: 'I wanted to see the art by myself. I didn't want other people to waste time.'[22] She recounted the troublesome aspects of her trip—it rained incessantly and 'her friends failed to meet her, she was beset by lunatics.'[23] Rosalie described herself as 'very brave in those days'.[24] Yet, the other side of the story is the privilege of her financial situation, which made the trip possible, and the patronage she received from Mollison, who perhaps had in mind to leave her to herself once there, as another dimension of his tough love.

Undeterred by these difficulties, Rosalie crammed her days with gallery visits, but was not impressed by much of what she saw, finding it 'very false'.[25] She considered Walter De Maria's *The Earth Room*, a second-floor apartment in Manhattan where the floors were completely covered in twenty-two inches of earth, 'the product of a decadent society'; she thought

17 Rosalie to Martin, 7 January 1980, cited in Eagle, *From the Studio of Rosalie Gascoigne*, 60.
18 Rosalie to Martin, 14 February 1980, in ibid.
19 Rosalie to Martin, 14 February 1980, in ibid.
20 Martin Gascoigne, interview by author, 2014.
21 MacDonald and Gascoigne, *Rosalie Gascoigne*, 32.
22 Ibid.
23 Ibid.
24 Ibid.
25 Ibid.

the earth 'should be out in the sun with a pigeon sitting on it'.[26] She was equally unimpressed by De Maria's *The Broken Kilometer*—'a mile of brass pipe encased in an upstairs room'.[27] With her chosen aesthetic of weathered, battered things, big skies and lots of air, she did not have much that was positive to say about busy, densely populated New York City, with its high-rise buildings crowding sky and air, except that 'the vibe in the street was something you just had to experience'.[28]

Loneliness, again, comes readily into her account of this time: 'You know loneliness when you've been to New York by yourself.'[29] However, she did make connections that reflected her standing and her networks. She watched Volker Schlöndorff's recently released screen version of Günter Grass's epic novel *The Tin Drum* with the eminent Australian art historian and academic Patrick McCaughey and his father, academic and theologian Davis McCaughey.[30]

The core impact of Rosalie's New York trip was a strengthened sense of her own truth. Honesty was central to her notion of art: 'I think art is definitely about truth … mostly the bottom line in this life is money … But an artist has got to be honest.'[31] She understood honesty in art to mean the art must be made as an end in itself, not for commercial reasons or to fill an exhibition.[32] This, perhaps, was a position that New York clarified for her.

She said that art was a search for honesty on one's own terms: 'The journey to self-recognition took me decades' and she was not about to be sidetracked by what the 'big boys' were doing.[33] The New York visit boosted her confidence in her own work. She told Hughes that it made her realise 'there's other art and it's truer to me [than New York's "false" art]'.[34] When Hughes responded with the question: 'So it gave you a lot more confidence in your

26 Ibid.

27 Ibid.

28 Ibid.

29 Ibid.

30 Martin Gascoigne, email to author, 5 October 2011. McCaughey was appointed Monash University's first professor of fine arts in 1962 and director of the National Gallery of Victoria in 1981. He moved to the US in 1990 where he held positions such as Chair of Australian Studies at Harvard University and director of the Yale Center for British Art. As a measure of his esteem, in 2012, the University of Melbourne awarded him an honorary doctor of laws for his contribution to art history and to Australian cultural life.

31 Hughes et al., 'Rosalie Gascoigne Artist', tape 6.

32 Ibid.

33 MacDonald and Gascoigne, *Rosalie Gascoigne*, 9: 'People think art's like you strike it lucky and you're famous tomorrow, but it isn't like that, it's a search for honesty on your own terms. The journey to self-recognition took me decades.'

34 Hughes et al., 'Rosalie Gascoigne Artist', tape 6.

own work?' Rosalie replied: 'Well yes, you stick to your guns.'[35] Mollison's challenge was, in fact a gift: Rosalie gained more certainty and confidence that her work was true.

'I feel a lot more than he [Ben] does'[36]

The same year that Rosalie made her New York art pilgrimage, Ben retired from The Australian National University as emeritus professor of astronomy (see Figure 12.1). In a reversal of the roles the couple had played for thirty-seven years, Ben took over management of the house and became Rosalie's assistant and archivist, freeing her for her work. Still, she continued to feel that Ben neither understood her need to make art nor the solitude she required. She felt he was dismayed at her passion for art, 'he was rather surprised that this meant so much to me … I'd changed so much from what I was when I was a girl in New Zealand … Not pleased he wasn't.'[37]

It is conceivable Ben felt conflicted—happy to see Rosalie developing her own passion and achieving significant success and recognition in the art world, while at the same time longing for more engagement with her after he retired, and wondering where the young woman he married had gone. Ben may have felt Rosalie was slipping away as her passion drew her further into art. She had spent years searching for something to fill a void in her life, for something constant that meant she was not dependent on anyone.[38] She had found it in art, but there was a cost: 'the more you do something, the further you get from the understanding of everybody else who doesn't do it'.[39] The journey, she said, gets lonelier and more isolated, 'because your art is a whole world … people have got to put up with it, because that's what you're going to be and that's what you are'.[40] Rosalie apparently felt that people tolerated her and her art, rather than embraced it. It is not clear whether this position was a reflection of her lived experience, or how much it reflected the sense of herself that she projected onto others. Her insecurities are evident in her habit of assuming what people thought of her and imagining the worst:

35 Ibid.
36 Ibid., tape 8.
37 MacDonald and Gascoigne, *Rosalie Gascoigne*, 9.
38 Hughes et al., 'Rosalie Gascoigne Artist', tape 8.
39 Ibid.
40 Ibid.

> the first things you do … it's like home decoration. They think … 'that's okay … I can stomach that'. And then you get further … and people think … 'I don't like that. I like what she used to do.'[41]

Her use of the word 'think' to describe people's actions, rather than 'said' or 'say' implies that it was imagined rather than something people actually said to her: her indirectness renders it impossible to be sure. What is certain is that her self-doubt was deeply entrenched.

Rosalie felt that Ben did not understand her art. She expressed the differences between them with a stoicism that belied the frustration behind her words. She described him as 'a paper man, and a clean hands man … an intellectual man'.[42] In contrast, she said of herself: 'I feel a lot. I think I feel a lot more than he does.'[43] At the same time, she acknowledged the difficulty in ever fully knowing another person. By this point in their relationship, her frustration with Ben was evident, yet, in contrast to her parents, and in spite of Ben's ignorance of, or complicity in, 'the long littleness' of women's lives, she was determined to stay in the relationship.[44]

She said her art making put a strain on her marriage, and also that Ben did not realise what it was like to live in a man's shadow. He had his career, his recognition, his renown and his colleagues; he also had a wife who managed the home and had taken primary responsibility for the children. Ben was of a generation for which such a gendered role definition was the norm. His family of origin had functioned along these conventional social lines. Rosalie's family had not; she knew other possibilities existed, and she also carried the scars of compensating for that difference. Regardless of whether it was an assumption on her part that Ben did not understand her or her art, or the result of discussions they shared, Rosalie and Ben remained married until her death. When an interviewer commented on their fifty years of marriage, Rosalie's response suggested she lived with compromise, which of course is part of any relationship:

> You live the way you can … if there's … an eruption of difference … you work that out … But you know what you've got to be, and they know what they've got to be.[45]

41 Ibid.
42 Ibid.
43 Ibid.
44 Ibid. Rosalie referred to 'the long littleness of female life' in her interview with Hughes. The line 'long littleness of life' is from a poem, 'Youth', by Frances Croft Cornford (née Darwin) in *Poems*, 15.
45 Hughes et al., 'Rosalie Gascoigne Artist', tape 8.

Alongside Rosalie's expressed frustrations in her marriage, a vignette from Miriam Eagle, a member of the extended family, paints another picture. In her condolence letter to the family after Rosalie's death, Eagle, who knew Rosalie in her final two decades, described her memories:

> It is at home on a Sunday that I see Rosalie with her most intimate creations around her—family, and her artworks retained. I think of her calmness, her sharpness, her slim figure in pants, cricketers forever bowling, bowls of stones, and serving home cooked lunches she has prepared with Ben (in his apron). You could feel the love between Ben and Rosalie, and the house was always light and sunny.[46]

As Rosalie told Hughes, she lived the way she could and she worked out differences in the relationship, which was inevitably fluid and contingent according to time and events. Bright times sat alongside gloomier moments during their six decades of courting and marriage, inevitable when two people live together, each finding their way in an ever-changing world and when one, a woman, struggles with the limiting gendered expectations of their time.

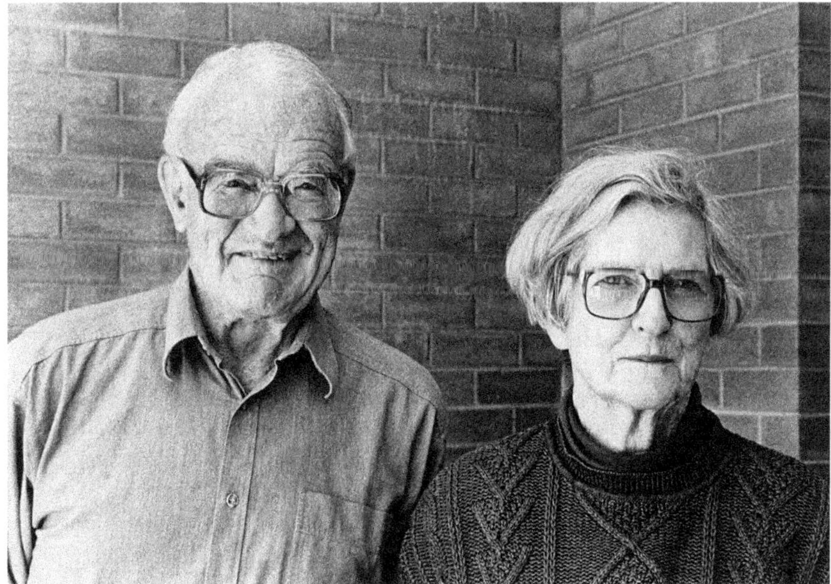

Figure 12.1: Rosalie and Ben, Anstey Street, 1997.

Source: Courtesy of William Yang and the Gascoigne family. Photograph: William Yang.

46 Miriam Eagle to 'Ben, Martin, Hesters and Mary', 27 October 2010, Papers of Rosalie Gascoigne, box 23. Note the 'cricketers forever bowling' probably refers to Rosalie's artwork that she made from cutout newspaper photos of cricketers arranged in a box. See Hughes et al., 'Rosalie Gascoigne Artist', tape 6.

'I don't like other people involved [in my art making]'[47]

As Rosalie's universe expanded, Ben considered that she became territorial about her art. In 2009, he told Cameron that Rosalie could be 'very jealous' about other people being involved in her work.[48] Ben was reflecting on Rosalie's view that he 'got credit for some of the things she did. Oh she didn't like this.'[49] Rosalie herself told Vici MacDonald that she did not like other people to be involved in her art making.[50]

In a 2007 interview with Milton Cameron for the latter's doctoral thesis about scientists' houses in Canberra in 1950–70, Ben described an episode in which he interpreted Rosalie's actions as territorial. After reading about the incident and her father's interpretation of it in my doctoral thesis, Hester gave me a different reading. Both Hester and Ben recalled the incident in the same way but interpreted it differently.

The incident took place in the 1980s when their granddaughter, sitting on the floor near Rosalie, picked up some of Rosalie's odd scraps and stuck them on a board. Ben described the occasion thus:

> A few odd bits of yellow, and there was the sun up there … And she [the granddaughter] said 'oh look'. Rosalie [was] not pleased! I was really surprised by this. I thought, being challenged by your own granddaughter—doesn't happen to many people! I was rather pleased with it [the child's creation] … But she [Rosalie] was always like that.[51]

On the other hand, Hester told me:

> I think 'jealous' is the wrong word. And this is all rather overblown. Mum was protective of her work. I assume most artists are. As she said to Vici, she did not like other people involved in her art making. To the extent people were, it was out of necessity—she had helpers to do heavy lifting and to fix elements so works were sound. Her art was her passion, as astronomy had been for dad. Making art was deadly serious; she wanted and needed people to respect that. I find

47 MacDonald and Gascoigne, *Rosalie Gascoigne*, 33.
48 Cameron, 'Experiments in Modern Living', 353.
49 Ibid.
50 MacDonald and Gascoigne, *Rosalie Gascoigne*, 33.
51 Cameron, 'Experiments in Modern Living'.

> it hard to believe she was 'challenged' by a grandchild. I recall her being on a roll with her work at the time, so studio as play room would have been a mixed blessing.[52]

Aotearoa New Zealand academic Caroline Daley discovered in an oral history study that men and women in the same families often gave her radically different versions of the same childhood events, and different understandings of events and situations. Initially she wondered if one was wrong or misremembering, but when it recurred on multiple occasions over many families, she came to the conclusion that people in the same family can experience and interpret events differently. Daley was mainly concerned with gender, and found not only that men's and women's experiences are different, but also that 'their memories have been shaped by prevailing ideas of gender-appropriate behaviour and values'.[53] 'In the shared family environment then', Daley states, 'men and women often present very different pasts'.[54] They also often present very different interpretations because spaces and experience are gendered.

It could be that Ben, as a long successful, internationally recognised and respected astronomer, could not understand Rosalie's response because he had never had to struggle with invisibility and lack of respect. Rosalie, on the other hand, had travelled the long road to her own recognition of herself as an artist. She had achieved recognition in the art world, but it was still relatively early days in a long history of feeling she did not fit and finding recognition. Thus, while her husband immediately praised their little grandchild's work with pieces of Rosalie's art, Hester, as a woman, could empathise with her mother, understand the issues and see beyond the surface.

Ben suggested this was a pattern of behaviour for Rosalie—'she was always like that'. It may be that what Ben saw as competitiveness towards their young granddaughter was really a legacy of growing up with an alcoholic parent. Psychologist Janet Geringer Woititz asserts that adult children of alcoholics take themselves very seriously because life with an alcoholic parent is 'a serious, angry business' with little room for fun.[55] Rosalie's stories of her childhood support this assertion. She talked about the dourness and abrasiveness in her family. She described herself as 'silly' in comparison

52 Hester Gascoigne, pers. comm., 2 April 2023.

53 Daley, 'He Would Know'.

54 Ibid.

55 Woititz, *Adult Children of Alcoholics*, 38–9.

with her siblings, identifying with her father's 'unacceptable' Irishness in contrast to what she called the others' 'Scotchness'.[56] While she may have felt 'silly', there is little evidence of silliness in her life. Although she was known by some for her streaks of humour and playfulness, Rosalie adhered to the middle-class conventions of her upbringing; she was a serious person who expressed her differentness through creativity. The shadow of her father's alcoholism may have lain behind the challenge she felt her when her granddaughter played at something central to her own being. Despite Rosalie's love for her granddaughter, she would not be trivialised.[57]

Even watching the television soap opera *Days of Our Lives* constituted a serious ritual. Rosalie was candid about the fact that she knocked off work at midday to watch the American program, telling Vici MacDonald: 'I know, it's escapism.'[58] But she also emphasised the visual stimulation television could provide:

> I think the television is very useful for exercising your art eye … the line of a head and shoulder … television is very x-ray. You exercise your eye all the time.[59]

She and Junette Greenaway, mother of her Adelaide dealer Paul Greenaway, talked regularly by telephone about the program and kept each other up-to-date if either one missed an episode. Junette gave up watching after Rosalie's death.[60]

Some of the frustration Rosalie expressed about Ben may be attributable to the recognition he received through contributing to her success by cataloguing her work, managing the household after his retirement and building her studio. How often is the wife of a successful man so generously and publicly acknowledged for her contribution in the way Ben was with regard to Rosalie's career? Although she dismissed any notion of feminism for herself, what she experienced was a gender bias towards the male. Where she had been invisible during Ben's career and was seldom if ever publicly acknowledged as having enabled him in his professional success, Ben was and still is frequently credited with a significant role in her success. For example, Professor Bob Crompton, in his interview with Ben for the Australian Academy of Science in 2000, emphasised Ben's part: 'He has also devoted

56 Hughes et al., 'Rosalie Gascoigne Artist', tape 1.
57 Cameron, 'Experiments in Modern Living', 353.
58 MacDonald and Gascoigne, *Rosalie Gascoigne*, 33.
59 Ibid., 32.
60 Paul Greenaway, interview by author, Adelaide, 10 July 2012.

much of his time to assisting his late wife, the distinguished artist Rosalie Gascoigne, including cataloguing her extensive works of art.'[61] Ben himself stressed his practical involvement in his chapter, 'The Artist-in-Residence', in *From the Studio of Rosalie Gascoigne*.[62] Admittedly there is little doubt that that his role was important for her career: Rosalie acknowledged this herself in terms of his income providing the means for her to be an artist. But there was no equivalent acknowledgement of her part in his career.[63]

Blossoming career: Australia, Japan, New Zealand, Italy, Sweden

Despite Rosalie's continuing sense of alienation and isolation, as well as her frustration with Ben, her career blossomed. Recognition continued when she was selected as one of 158 artists to exhibit in *Australian Perspecta 1981*, the first major survey of contemporary Australian art since 1973. Rosalie's piece, *March Past* (1979)—twenty panels of weathered painted wood arranged vertically—was informed by her recent experience of an Anzac Day March in Melbourne. There she was 'struck also by the aural texture of the city with its "trams full of clinking medals"'. *March Past* was shown with work by prominent artists such as Frank Watters, Ken Whisson, Dick Watkins, Denise Green, Mandy Martin, Clifford Possum Tjapaltjarri, Ken Unsworth, Imants Tillers, Micky Allan and Mike Brown.[64] Rosalie was the oldest by two decades and more. Most of her fellow exhibitors were her children's generation and were art school trained. Yet her work owned a place among 'the most recent, and often challenging, forms of art evolving in Australia today'.[65]

61 Crompton, 'Professor Ben Gascoigne'.

62 Gascoigne, 'The Artist-in-Residence', 9–15.

63 Hughes et al., 'Rosalie Gascoigne Artist', tape 8. When asked by a student at the Canberra Art School 'what is the most important thing you need if you are setting out to be an artist?', Rosalie replied: 'A partner with enough money to keep you for the rest of your life.'

64 'Trams full of clinking medals' described in Art Gallery of New South Wales, ed., *Australian Perspecta 1981*, 11.

65 Ibid., 3.

In 1982, Rosalie became the first woman to represent Australia at the Venice Biennale. Visual Arts Board (VAB) member Nick Waterlow, who was especially keen on Rosalie's work, nominated her and board members agreed that the combination of an outstanding artist like Rosalie and painter Peter Booth would make an impact in Venice.[66]

On arriving in Venice, Rosalie and VAB Venice Biennale Commissioner Katrina Rumley were shocked to discover that the pavilion set aside for the Australian exhibition had been given to Italian artists. It was six weeks before an alternative exhibition space was ready.[67] Rosalie was disconcerted and unhappy. She told Hughes: 'It's your big opportunity, and you're kicking your heels … you're seeing other people's art, and you haven't got your art up … Oh, it was terrible.'[68] She and Rumley stayed in a hotel 'near the gardens' and over lunches and dinners the two talked about art, artists and art making.[69] While Rumley negotiated with Venetian authorities over the construction of a new space, Rosalie sometimes sat on the wall by the building site, studying the artefacts workers uncovered as they prepared the site.[70] The old coins, pipe bowls and ancient china shards fascinated her, as one would expect of an artist who made her work from found objects.

Rosalie did not particularly enjoy Venice. The ornamented and decaying visuals were too fancy for her taste: 'Everything man-made and so decorated. Look at what we have [in Australia]: space, skies.'[71]

Progress was slow and tensions were high. But there were light moments. In addition to Rumley, a number of influential members of the Australian art world were in Venice to assist, including one of Rosalie's favourite painters Ken Whisson, who had travelled from his home in Perugia; her friend, gallery owner Ray Hughes from Brisbane; Venice-based Australian literary academic Bernard Hickey; Sydney College of Fine Arts head and former VAB member Ken Reinhart; VAB chair, Ann Lewis; the VAB's Tasmanian representative Geoff Parr; and Bernard Shirley from the Australian Embassy in Rome. Rosalie enjoyed many evenings with the Australian contingent at

66 Katrina Rumley, email to author, 10 July 2014.

67 Australia was not alone. The same happened to China, India, East Germany and Chile. See Visual Arts Board of the Australia Council, 'News from the Visual Arts Board, October 1982', Papers of Rosalie Gascoigne.

68 Hughes et al., 'Rosalie Gascoigne Artist', tape 4.

69 Rumley, email to author, 10 July 2014.

70 Hughes et al., 'Rosalie Gascoigne Artist', tape 4.

71 Mollison and Heath, 'Rosalie Gascoigne', 7.

Harry's Bar, long favoured by the rich and famous, near the Grand Canal and St Mark's Square.[72] One night they shared the bar with Liza Minnelli, Joel Grey and other stars.

Frustrated with waiting for the exhibition space to be made available, Rosalie and Rumley travelled to the *Documenta* exhibition curated by Rudi Fuchs in Kassel, Germany. There Rosalie saw works by acclaimed international artists Joseph Beuys, On Kawara, Robert Mapplethorpe, Cy Twombly, Cindy Sherman and Gerhard Richter; the Australian artist Imants Tillers; and the New Zealand–born artist Boyd Webb—some of whom she would exhibit alongside at the 1988, 1990 and 2000 Sydney Biennales. Rosalie recalled her pleasure at attending *Documenta* and her readiness to pack up and leave Venice if an exhibition space were not provided:

> it was wonderful that they [the Venice Biennale and *Documenta*] coincided, and if the Italians hadn't built that hut and filled up those holes in the ceiling and what not we were going to leave, you see. And this was strong stuff, but it was my independent opinion … I felt the dignity of the nation was at stake.[73]

But, as she said, they 'battled through, got there'.[74] Although the building was still incomplete the day before the opening, Rumley installed the exhibition in roofless spaces in time for the press reception and opening.[75] The VAB reported that, during the three opening days, over 160 international critics and journalists saw the exhibition and registered their names in the visitors' book with favourable comments. London's *Times* and *Guardian* published positive reviews.[76]

Rosalie showed ten works in Venice, including *Pink Window* (1975), a window frame primed with flaking pink paint with a rusty corrugated iron curtain floating across the top right-hand corner.[77] When asked, years later, why she

72 Rumley, email to author, 10 July 2014.

73 Hughes et al., 'Rosalie Gascoigne Artist', tape 4.

74 Ibid.

75 Visual Arts Board of the Australia Council, 'News from the Visual Arts Board, October 1982', 9, 10.

76 Ibid.

77 Other works exhibited were: *Country Air* (1978, corrugated galvanised iron and weathered wood); *Feathered Fence* (1979, swans' feathers, wood and fence wire); *Parrots* (1980, weathered wood and paper); *Side Show Parrots* (1981, weathered wood and paper); *The Bird House* (1981, weathered wood and paper); *City Birds* (1981, weathered wood and paper); *Scrub Country* (1981, weathered wood [soft-drink crates] and aluminium strip backing); *Crop 2* (1978, salsify heads, wire netting and galvanised iron sheet); *Harvest* (1982, newspaper and nails on pineboard). See Hughes et al., 'Rosalie Gascoigne Artist', tape 4. All these works can be seen in Gascoigne, *Rosalie Gascoigne: A Catalogue Raisonné*: *Pink Window*, 165–6; *Feathered Fence*, 185–6; *Parrots*, 193; *Side Show Parrots*, 200–1; *The Bird House*, 196; *City Birds*, 197; *Scrub Country*, 206; *Harvest*, 204.

had called the work *Pink Window*, she responded with her refreshingly direct, no-nonsense approach to art: 'Well, it's a window and it's pink.'[78] She went on to say that she had made it with Australian outback women in mind:

> left alone in her house, looking out … to see if something was happening. Nothing. Absolutely nothing was happening … there's a nothingness in the Australian landscape … And the sort of hope that that might be a car or galloping hooves or something … nothing happened on Stromlo a lot, you know. And people did sort of yearn for other places, familiar times, friends.[79]

The art she took to Venice reflected her early sense of isolation on Mt Stromlo. Even at a moment of great acclaim, she referred back to a time when she felt isolated and alone, when she sought nature as a friend and found comfort in visuals.

News of her unique art had reached her country of origin across the Tasman. The National Art Gallery in Wellington, headed by Luit Bieringa (1942–2022), mounted a survey show—*Rosalie Gascoigne: Sculpture 1975–1982.* Part of a Sculpture Australia Project organised by New Zealand's National Art Gallery with assistance from the VAB and the Australia–New Zealand Foundation, the project was seen as part of the growing trans-Tasman exchange of artists and their work.[80] Two other Australian sculptors exhibited separately as part of the project: Ken Unsworth (6 September – 20 October 1983) and Adrian Hall (28 October – 11 December 1983).

Rosalie's show was held at the then National Art Gallery and Dominion Museum in Mt Cook close to Wellington's city centre, an imposing building considered one of the finest examples of Stripped Classical architecture in Aotearoa New Zealand.[81] The exhibition ran from 15 December 1983 – 12 February 1984, before being toured to Auckland City Gallery (10 March – 11 April 1984), Manawatu Gallery, Palmerston North (28 April – 24 June 1984) and the Govett-Brewster Gallery in New Plymouth (5–30 September 1984).[82]

78 Hughes et al., 'Rosalie Gascoigne Artist', tape 6.

79 Ibid., tape 4.

80 Sculpture Australia/Rosalie Gascoigne, exhibition files, 1983–84, Museum of New Zealand, Te Papa Tongarewa, MU000006/017/0008.

81 Heritage New Zealand Pouhere Taonga, 'The National Art Gallery and Dominion Museum'.

82 Sculpture Australia/Rosalie Gascoigne, exhibition files, MU000006/017/0008. The works exhibited were: *Pink Window* (1975), *Tiepolo Parrots* (1976), *The Colonel's Lady* (1976), *Early Morning* (1976), *Grass Rack* (1977), *Pale Landscape* (1977), *Parrot Country* (mark II) (1980), *Step through* (1980), *Sharp Bros Horizontal* (1981), *Piece to Walk around* (1981) and *Blossom* (1982). See these artworks in Gascoigne, *Rosalie Gascoigne: A Catalogue Raisonné*.

Rosalie had not been in New Zealand since 1957 and curator Louise Pether (previously Upston) told me it took some persuasion to win her agreement to exhibit and travel there. It was only when Pether told her that the gallery was showing Colin McCahon at the same time that Rosalie agreed.[83]

Colin McCahon (1919–1987) was credited with pioneering modernism in New Zealand art along with fellow painters Rita Angus and Toss Woollaston. He was known for his large dark paintings overlaid with biblical text, words from Christian liturgy and poetry; and for landscapes in which he sometimes placed figures from biblical stories and Christian symbols. As Anne Kirker wrote in the *Sense of Place* catalogue to accompany the joint exhibition of McCahon's and Rosalie's work in Sydney in 1999, each had an 'unswerving commitment to a particular landscape': Rosalie to the Monaro, McCahon to New Zealand.[84] McCahon's stated aim was 'to throw people into an involvement with the "raw land, and also with raw painting"'.[85] He intended that his work would invite the viewer to engage directly with existential issues. Like Rosalie, he believed in an unmediated relationship between artwork and viewer.

In 1997, Rosalie told Hughes: 'I would cross the seas to go anywhere with Colin McCahon' because 'I really think he's the greatest Antipodean—he gives you the country that they would never know in the northern hemisphere.'[86] So she flew to Wellington in January 1983. Pether met her at the airport and drove her into the city in her Mini. She recalled that Rosalie shielded her eyes as they drove around the city's bays, Rosalie saying:

> This is why I didn't want to come back—the landscape is so strong here. I don't want to let this landscape impinge on the work I'm making, which is all about the Monaro, the scale of Australia.[87]

Yet, despite Rosalie's implying that her aesthetic had become fully Australian, she remained deeply moved and inspired by McCahon's stark New Zealand landscapes that were flat in plane and modernist in style. Her need to blinker her eyes from Wellington's hills, as Pether drove her from the Miramar Peninsula around the city's inner harbour bays, suggests that she may have continued to feel the pull of her childhood landscape. Pether said there was

83 Louise Pether, interview by author, 2010.

84 Kirker, Wedde and McDonald, *Rosalie Gascoigne—Colin McCahon*, 14.

85 North and Catalano, *Australia, Venice Biennale 1982*. Colin McCahon, quoted in Auckland City Art Gallery, *Colin McCahon: A Survey Exhibition*, 89.

86 Hughes et al., 'Rosalie Gascoigne Artist', tape 6.

87 Louise Pether, interview by author, 2010.

no discussion of her earlier life in New Zealand: Rosalie was clear that she was working with the gallery as Rosalie Gascoigne the artist. She feared 'being dragged into places and memories she had put behind her'.[88]

Her art was well received in New Zealand. Wellington critic and poet Ian Wedde listed Rosalie's work in 'Where Was the Best Art This Summer?', an article in *New Zealand Art News*, describing it as 'at once desolate and lyrical, a celebration and an elegy'.[89] Rosalie herself was also well received. Curator Louise Upston (later Pether) wrote to Margaret Rich, director of the Ballarat Fine Art Gallery on 24 January 1984: 'Rosalie herself was also a delight and has quite charmed everyone here. We're proud to have a small and distant claim to her!'[90]

During her time in Wellington, Rosalie took the opportunity to visit the Peter McLeavey Gallery in the city. Through an anonymous, graffitied doorway and up a flight of wooden stairs from quirky, bohemian Cuba Street, the gallery had been the launching pad for modernist art in New Zealand, and McLeavey modernism's champion.[91] On his green velvet chaise longue—the same one Rosalie and he sat on in 1983—McLeavey told me of Rosalie's visit to purchase a McCahon painting (see Figure 12.2).[92] He remembered her 'driven, ambitious, kindly, nurturing intelligence, [and] as someone who was well informed on contemporary art and the history of art'. In his lyrical fashion, he sensed that:

> She came to New Zealand … trying to make contact with her New Zealand past … through the vehicle of McCahon … I sense she was trying to reclaim a memory of a time and place that was gone, that she knew in her heart of hearts she could never ever ever be part of. It was like she was trying to capture a cultural memory that had eluded her and she came into these rooms … looking for something that would key her back into it … my overriding impression was someone looking for something, like trying to find a love that had eluded her.[93]

88 Ibid.
89 Wedde, 'Where Was the Best Art This Summer?'.
90 Sculpture Australia/Rosalie Gascoigne, exhibition files, MU000006/017/0004.
91 Trevelyan, *Peter McLeavey*.
92 Peter McLeavey, interview by author, 15 April 2010.
93 Ibid.

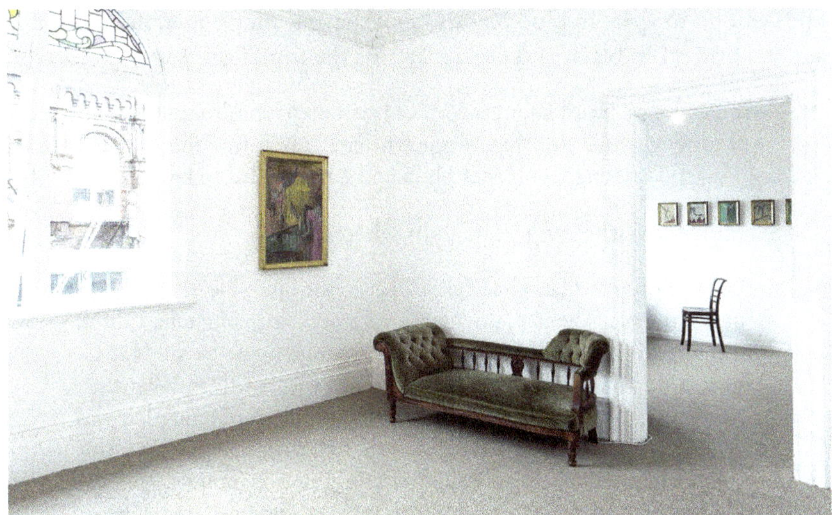

Figure 12.2: The green velvet chaise longue on which Rosalie chatted with Peter McLeavey in 1983.

Source: Courtesy of Shaun Waugh, the McLeavey Gallery, Cuba Street, Wellington and the estate of Bill Hammond whose paintings feature in the background from the 'Permanent Maroon' exhibition' at the McLeavey Gallery, 27 November – 24 December 2013. Reproduced with permission from Jane McBride from the Bill Hammond Estate. Photograph: Shaun Waugh, Te Whanganui-ā-Tara Wellington, Aotearoa New Zealand.

If McLeavey was right and Rosalie sought a connection to her past, it is unlikely she would have admitted it, firm in her expressed opinion that New Zealand was a backwater, a 'little Britain' where nothing interesting happened.[94] McLeavey said she was interested in McCahon and what had made him as an artist. She quickly chose a McCahon painting from the *Gate* series and took it back to Canberra.

Back in Canberra, Rosalie wrote to Louise Upston:

> I really enjoyed the NZ trip and have been singing the praises of the NAG to everyone in general and the ANG in particular. I have never felt so relaxed about setting up a show, thanks to your professionalism and sensitivity.

94 Ibid.

She went on to write in blue-black ink on the pale blue paper, her name and address printed in black and centred across the top of the page:

> You will have heard about my McCahon purchase. Although it's not an early religious painting or one with green hills (my first choice), it is a good strong Colin McCahon and I am thrilled to have it.[95]

She explained that she rang McCahon when she:

> finally got to Auckland but I didn't get to see him. 'Not a very good time of the year', he said, unarguably. But we had a long talk. I think I probably did a bit of over-kill in my genuine praise of the N.A.G. show. Told him how marvellous I found the Northland Panels.[96] 'Not really a very good painting', he said. This comment I felt was no measure of the viewer's response. I found the painting radiant and moving, human & accessible and whatever he found to quibble at in the execution of the work it in no way impinges on the spirit of the painting.[97]

Rosalie may have remembered the colours, shape and spirit of the Tai Tokerau Northland landscape from her time spent teaching at Whangārei Girls' High School in 1938; that may have been part of her response to McCahon's painting. Regardless, her admiration for McCahon's work was undimmed by his criticism of it. Rosalie told Upston that she was 'wrestling with a five-hundred-word piece for *Art and Australia* for "Artist's Choice"'. She had to write about any Australasian painting in the ANG and had chosen McCahon's *Victory over Death*.[98] 'Both Daniel Taylor and Ian North support the choice as they feel Colin has not yet been given the attention he deserves in Australia.'[99] In her article, Rosalie referred to the honesty of McCahon's work, emphasising the importance to her of truth and honesty in art:

> Recently I was lucky enough to catch a retrospective show of Colin McCahon's work at the National Art Gallery in Wellington. The power of its honesty was almost overwhelming. Here is an artist who draws his art from within himself. He speaks of who he is, where he lives and what life has made and is making of him.[100]

95 Rosalie Gascoigne to Louise Upston, National Art Gallery, Wellington, 10 January 1984, Sculpture Australia/Rosalie Gascoigne, exhibition files, MU000006/017/0004.

96 See Phillips, 'Arts and the Nation'.

97 Gascoigne to Upston, 10 January 1984.

98 Rosalie Gascoigne, 'Colin McCahon', 490.

99 Gascoigne to Upston, 10 January 1984.

100 Gascoigne, 'Colin McCahon'.

***

Rosalie did not stop at New Zealand that year. Five of her works were featured in *Continuum '83* at Gallery Yamaguchi, Tokyo, the first exhibition of Australian contemporary art in Japan.[101] In the same year, Ben used some of the proceeds of his retirement 'special golden handshake' to build a studio for Rosalie.[102] At this time, Rosalie was still working in the dining room Bischoff had designed with her ikebana in mind. Her work overflowed to the hallway and the room next door. Ben said they needed to 'get to the dining room' so he told Rosalie: 'We're going to build that [the studio], whatever you think.'[103] Ben was proud of the contribution the large studio (around five by eighteen metres) made to Rosalie's art making practice and career: 'this was heaven for Rosalie. And every artist who visited the place would look around and [say] "Oh, you're lucky to have all of this space!"' (see Figure 12.3).[104]

Rosalie finally had the 'room of one's own' advocated for women by Virginia Woolf as necessary in order to be able to write (or create art) at a time when societal limitations made this difficult unless a woman's 'parents were exceptionally rich or very noble'.[105] The extra space enabled Rosalie to spread her vast collection of materials out, making it easier for her to see how pieces worked in relation to each other; it freed her to make larger works.

With the increased workspace, and after the highlights of Venice, Wellington and Tokyo, Rosalie's work became a familiar part of exhibitions in public galleries around Australia. *Set Up*, *The Colonel's Lady* and *Graven Image* were included in *Australian Sculpture Now: The Second Australian Sculpture Triennial* at the Art Gallery of New South Wales in 1984. In addition to public galleries in Australian capital cities, during the 1980s and 1990s her work was shown in small galleries and regional public galleries including Wollongong, Canberra Museum and Gallery, Museum of Modern Art Heide, Monash University Gallery, Australian National University Drill

101 Eagle, *Rosalie Gascoigne, 1985*, 4. Works shown were: *Spring* (1982), *Wattle Strike* (1983), *Herb Garden* (1982), *Blue Bands* (1981) and *Scrub Country* (1982).

102 Cameron, 'Experiments in Modern Living', 344–5. 'I retired in eighty—I got a golden handshake. In what was a special golden handshake … So we said "ah, we're going to build a proper studio"'.

103 Ibid., 345.

104 Ibid.

105 Woolf, *A Room of One's Own*, 52.

Hall Gallery and the Perth Institute of Contemporary Art.[106] In September 1985, the Tasmanian School of Art in Hobart mounted a solo exhibition—*Rosalie Gascoigne, 1985*—at which her now renowned yellow and black retro-reflective road sign works were first displayed.

In 1988, American critic Dan Cameron described Rosalie as 'one of the … true discoveries' at the Australian Biennale at the Art Gallery of New South Wales and later at the National Gallery of Victoria.[107] Critical of the overall exhibition, Cameron singled out Rosalie and McCahon's work for positive comment:

> Certain moments are quite compelling, as for example a pair of walls on which the late Colin McCahon's intensely quiet paintings face a group of three recent wood reliefs by Rosalie Gascoigne.[108]

So impressed was Cameron that he invited Rosalie to participate in his *What Is Contemporary Art?* exhibition in Malmö, Sweden, the following year along with prominent international artists including Jeff Koons, Rebecca Horn, On Kawara and Mike Kelley. With honesty and directness central ethics in her art practice, Rosalie would have been delighted by Cameron's recognition that her work belonged with that of other artists he chose because they made art he considered 'as legible as possible as if to refute art's obscurantist reputation'.[109] Cameron also acknowledged Rosalie's place in Australian art, proclaiming as unique her 'evocation of a sense of place that is both nowhere and everywhere at once, an edgelessness that is a recurring motif in Australian art'.[110] He explained the relationship between the landscape and her work: 'the intimate presence of the land itself is part of the texture of the work'.[111]

106 Her dealer galleries in Melbourne, Sydney and Adelaide held successful shows. Pinacotheca in Melbourne showed solo exhibitions in 1984, 1986, 1991 and 1993. In November 1989, Roslyn Oxley9 Gallery held Rosalie's first solo exhibition in Sydney since 1976 at which *Monaro* made its first public appearance. She showed here again in 1992, 1993, 1994, 1995, 1998 and 1999.
107 Cameron, 'Showdown at the Southern Cross', 12.
108 Ibid. Cameron described Rosalie's work as 'projecting humour, pathos and poetry'.
109 Cameron, 'Introduction', 9.
110 Ibid., 17.
111 Ibid., 18.

Seventy-two and rising, but misunderstood

At the end of the 1980s Rosalie was seventy-two years old. The growth of her reputation and demand for her work increased her awareness of the necessity of solitude in an artist's life and convinced her that her art set her further apart from the people in her life who were not artists. As a result, even though she had discovered a passion for art, identified as an artist and achieved considerable acclaim, she continued to feel a misunderstood outsider.

Rosalie's notion of truth, as much as the process of making art, set her apart—in art and in life. Perhaps because she maintained a determined silence on much in her childhood, she valued truth and honesty in other aspects of her life. She frequently referred to the necessity for honesty and her search for truth, always directly in relation to her art. To Aotearoa New Zealand painter Ewen McDonald in 1990s, she described art as 'almost like a religion, it's a search for truth of a sort'.[112] To Topliss she said: 'you've got to guard your own patch and keep yourself as honest as you can. You're the only person who's got to like it.'[113] So art represented honesty and truth to Rosalie, and she was fortunate to make art during a time of social change when such honesty was well received and recognised by the likes of Dan Cameron. Edmund Capon's preface to the *Material as Landscape* catalogue articulates how ready the art world was to receive her: 'Most powerfully of all, these works demonstrate the honesty of a distinctive and individual response and that indefinably quality of affinity with that source of inspiration, the landscape.'[114]

Rosalie had achieved recognition, not only for her illuminating talent, but also for the honesty she prized. She stepped into the next decade, her eyes, as ever, wide open, her feet firmly on the ground, and her star high in the sky.

112 McDonald, 'There Are Only Lovers'.

113 Gascoigne, interview by Topliss, 33.

114 Edwards, *Rosalie Gascoigne: Material as Landscape*, preface by Edmund Capon, 5.

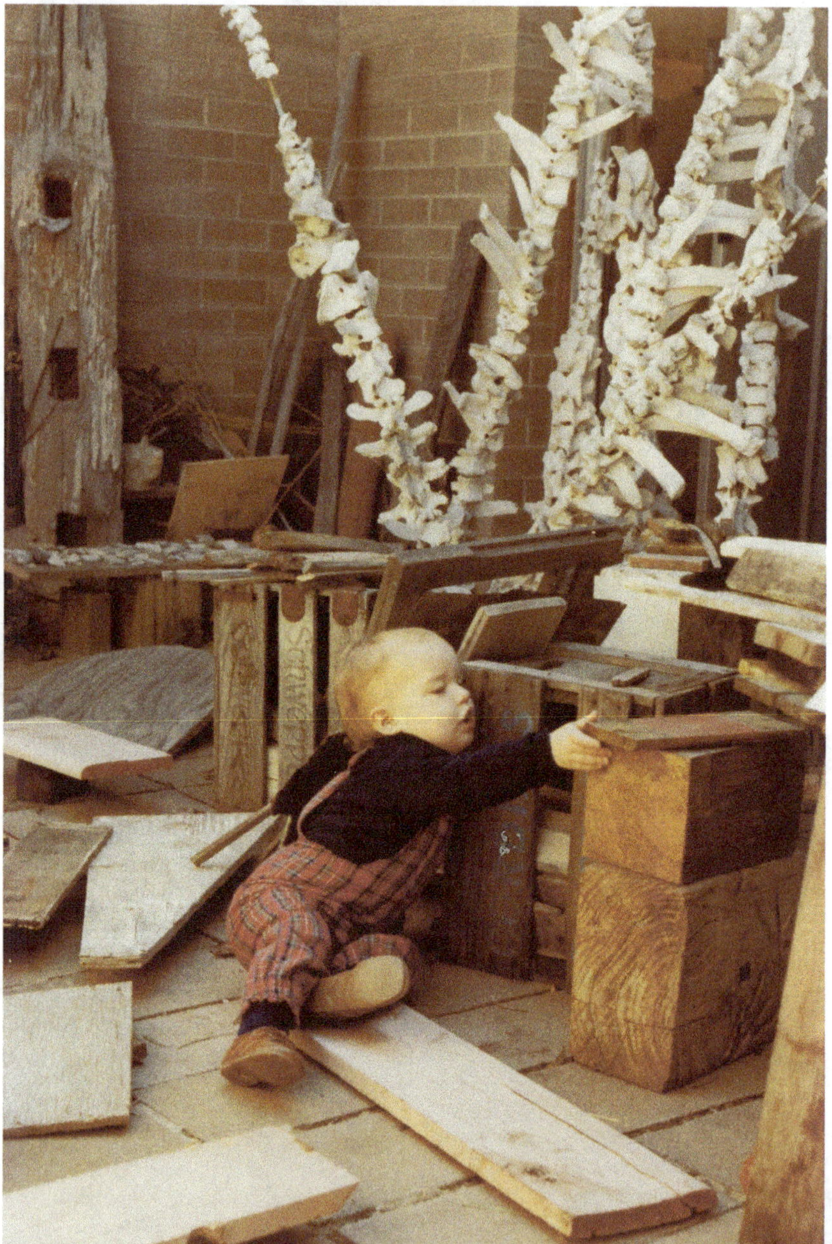

Figure 12.3: Rosalie's grandson, Charles Gascoigne, with her materials in the courtyard at Anstey Street, 1983.

Note: In addition to the studio space, Rosalie enjoyed the adjoining courtyard space for work and storage.

Source: Courtesy of the Gascoigne family.

13

The 1990s: 'Only artists understand other artists'

Rosalie's sense of being an outsider textured her life and was central to her self-narrative. Even when she had the freedom to make art full-time and her work attracted serious attention, she felt no more settled with her lot: 'If you're that sort of animal, you never feel at ease with absolutely anything.'[1] She believed that art is 'a private inward thing, and you get out what's already inside you'.[2] She also believed that 'only artists understand other artists'.[3] She continued to feel unsettled and isolated from the people around her who were not artists, in particular Ben.

While her confidence and assuredness grew, brief correspondence with American novelist Josephine Humphreys (b. 1945) and American sculptor Anne Truitt (1921–2004) reflected her continuing struggle with feeling a misfit. In her 1982 interview with Ian North, this feeling was not pronounced, perhaps because she was then riding the crest of the wave of her early success. By 1997, however, she described to Topliss how 'artists huddle together … because they … don't have to explain themselves'.[4] In 1998, when Hughes interviewed her, she seemed particularly disturbed that Ben did not understand her, although she wrapped this concern in a more general sense of distance.

1 Hughes et al., 'Rosalie Gascoigne Artist', tape 8.
2 Ibid.
3 Anne Truitt to Rosalie Gascoigne, 26 November 1986, Papers of Rosalie Gascoigne, box 1.
4 Gascoigne, interview by Topliss, 34.

In contrast with previous decades, when the chief protagonists with regard to her artistic career were male, the artists with whom she communicated about this new aspect of her identity were often women, possibly because, although she disliked being labelled a 'woman artist' and eschewed feminism, she found her experience had more in common with women who, like her, had known the truth of 'being a sort of *shadow behind* the *man* all the time'.[5] Mollison said that Rosalie did not discuss her artist identity with him—he was her patron and provocateur rather than colleague. The painter Marie Hagerty, who became Rosalie's friend in the 1990s, said Rosalie 'saw herself as an artist and she talked about it all of the time in terms of what sort of animal you are, almost like talking to herself'.[6]

This chapter traverses Rosalie's final years, from 1990 to her death in 1999. It provides only an overview of her continued success because this is recorded in detail in Martin Gascoigne, *Rosalie Gascoigne: A Catalogue Raisonné*, and in catalogues, particularly those edited by Gellatly, Edwards, O'Brien and Eagle.[7] This chapter examines instead the last stages of her lifelong sense of feeling out of step. Her struggle is a core part of her self-narrative—the narrative about herself that she constructed; yet, until now, it has been accepted uncritically. Its examination is integral to the objectives of this biography: to enlarge our understanding of Rosalie Gascoigne through reflecting on the identity she constructed for herself and the contexts in which she gained recognition as an outstanding artist of her generation.

Montpellier (1990) to New York (1993)

In 1990, as well as going to Montpellier, France, in *L'Été australien à Montpellier: 100 chefs d'oeuvre de la peinture australienne* (Australian summer in Montpellier: 100 masterpieces of Australian painting), Rosalie's work was again paired with McCahon's, this time for *Sense of Place*, Aotearoa New Zealand's sesquicentenary exhibition in Sydney. The exhibition, examining both artists' responses to the landscapes in which they lived, was initially shown at Sydney's Ivan Dougherty Gallery, where it was so popular the gallery's usual attendance doubled, before moving to Melbourne's Ian Potter

5 Hughes et al., 'Rosalie Gascoigne Artist', tape 8 (emphasis added).

6 Ibid.; Marie Hagerty and Peter Vandermark, interview by author, 2011.

7 Gellatly et al., *Rosalie Gascoigne*; Edwards, *Rosalie Gascoigne: Material as Landscape*; O'Brien, Savage and City Gallery Wellington, *Rosalie Gascoigne: Plain Air*.

Gallery.[8] McCahon's stark, expressive painted landscapes were juxtaposed again with Rosalie's lyrical assemblages of discarded objects. The Australian art-loving public, so long immersed in landscape art, flocked to this exhibition, but not all were impressed. Poet and art critic Gary Catalano wrote in the *Age* of his scepticism about the quality of McCahon's work, feeling it was 'inseparable from a kind of narrowness [of provincial New Zealand] that … limits its appeal'.[9] He dismissed Rosalie's work with a swipe against her popularity: 'She does many things I know I should admire … but … I always find that her work leaves me cold.' He went on: 'In Gascoigne … we have an artist whose sensitivity of eye is not matched by any great ability as a maker.'[10] Despite her assertions that she made art for herself alone, 'not for what the viewer sees', responses from the 'uncaring world' bruised her self-image and left her feeling that only an artist could understand another artist.[11]

At the Queensland Art Gallery in March–May 1991, at the age of seventy-four and just seventeen years after first exhibiting her work, Rosalie was included in *Diverse Visions: Twelve Australian Mid to Late Career Artists* along with other respected artists, Charles Blackman, Mike Brown, Ray Cooke, Inge King, Robert Klippel, Les Kossatz, Alun Leach-Jones, John Perceval, Gareth Sansom, Gordon Shepherdson and John Wolseley.[12] In 1992, her *First Fruits*, torn linoleum on plywood, went to New York's Metropolitan Museum of Art after it was purchased from Roslyn Oxley9 Gallery's *Rosalie Gascoigne* exhibition, which ran from 15 April to 2 May.[13] This was the first work of hers acquired by a public gallery outside Australia and Aotearoa New Zealand.

Catalano's criticism might have been pushed aside in such a sequence of successes, or Rosalie might have brooded: did the fact that she was becoming a celebrity in the art world offer any consolation in the search for identity, that elusive thing that had always troubled her?

8 Louise Pether, interview by author, 2010.

9 Gary Catalano, 'Fractured View in Mccahon's Antipodean Art', *Age*, 29 August 1990, 14.

10 Ibid.

11 See Rosalie Gascoigne to Josephine Humphreys, 26 July 1993, Papers of Rosalie Gascoigne, box 1.

12 Hogan and Queensland Art Gallery, *Diverse Visions*.

13 Martin Gascoigne, email to author, 5 October 2011: 'The Metropolitan [Metropolitan Museum of Modern Art (MOMA), New York] bought the work. One of their senior people was in Sydney and saw the show [*Rosalie Gascoigne* at Roslyn Oxley9 Gallery, Sydney, 1992].' On its website, MOMA lists the work as a donation, and did not respond to my requests for information about how it came to be in the collection.

Artist identity

It is reasonable to expect that after her inclusion in major shows, Rosalie might have ridden the crest of the acclaim wave; after all, she had 'made it' in a relatively short time in a way that would arouse the envy of many an artist. A few letters between Rosalie and American novelist Josephine Humphreys tucked into Rosalie's archive at the National Library of Australia suggest otherwise (see Figure 13.1). The archive contains only three of the four letters—Humphreys's two letters to Rosalie and Rosalie's draft of her second letter to Humphreys.[14] The brief correspondence sheds rare light on Rosalie's self-understanding and provides insight into her ongoing sensitivities as an outsider. To Humphreys, Rosalie revealed more than she had anywhere else in the public sphere about her feelings on being an artist, the process of making art and her continuing sense of alienation.

In March 1993 Humphreys was visiting Australia to speak at the Canberra Word Festival 'and various other things'.[15] Sitting in her room in the Adelaide Intercontinental Hotel, Humphreys found her attention hooked by a television interview in which Rosalie spoke about her art practice.[16] Humphreys was 'struck by everything' Rosalie said—'its truth, and its relevance to writing as much as to art'—and so, she told Rosalie:

> I grabbed a pen and tried to jot down all I could, while nodding and smiling. I felt I was listening to a better, clearer explanation of what I have been trying to say about the writing of novels during my tour through Australia—especially the parts about how the artist can surprise herself … how we work to satisfy ourselves alone … how one is 'happy' when something's coming up, like the moment just before you net the butterfly, and 'it's rather downhill from there'.[17]

---

14 Humphreys thought she might have had Rosalie's letters 'somewhere' but was not able to locate them; neither letter is among her papers in the Duke University collection where most of Humphreys's papers are held.

15 Josephine Humphreys to Rosalie Gascoigne, 14 March 1993, Papers of Rosalie Gascoigne, box 1. Humphreys told me she visited Australia as part of a United States Information Service program that sent US writers to other countries. She was asked to go to Poland or Australia and chose the latter: 'Once in Australia, I did the Canberra festival and then a series of university and city programs. In Sydney it was a dark little bar where poets drank and read … then colleges in Perth, Melbourne, Adelaide—and one other city I can't remember. Sometimes I gave a talk, other times I met with faculty and classes.' Josephine Humphreys, email to author, 20 September 2012.

16 The interview was in connection with Rosalie's work then showing in the *Joan and Peter Clemenger Triennial Exhibition of Contemporary Australian Art* at the National Gallery of Victoria from 23 February to 16 May 1993. Works shown were *Lake* (1991), *Cow Pasture* (1992), *Fools Gold* (1992) and *Clouds 3* (1992).

17 Josephine Humphreys to Rosalie, 10 March 1993, Papers of Rosalie Gascoigne, box 1.

In her second letter, Humphreys responded with delight to Rosalie's reply, of which, unfortunately, there is no extant copy. She had visited the National Gallery of Victoria and seen Rosalie's work, which she found mysterious, exciting and inspiring, so much so that:

> the guards had to pull me away at closing time. I came home so full of your words and your images that I can't help talking about you everywhere I go. In Tennessee last week I had to give a speech about writing fiction but I mostly talked about the things you said in the television interview.[18]

Humphreys's words touched a deep need in Rosalie, a sensitivity and uncertainty about herself as an artist despite the acclaim lavished on her. Her response suggested that the novelist's comments palliated Rosalie's lack of confidence and diminished sense of self:

> There are some days when one's only hope is the postman and last week on one such day he did his *deus ex machina* act and brought me your letter … I was delighted to hear that my name was being bandied around in Tennessee by such as you and I felt a real person again.[19]

Rosalie's statement about feeling 'a real person again' is powerful testimony that, prior to receiving Humphreys's letter, she was not feeling validated or recognised and, equally, that she still craved attention to her 'name'. Rosalie and Humphreys met each other's basic human need for recognition, seeing each other as artists, a mutual recognition that included affirmation and validation. In this sense, recognition is about being seen and acknowledged for who you are. Writers and philosophers, including Abraham Maslow, Georg Hegel, Axel Honneth and Charles Taylor, have emphasised the need for recognition for decades.[20]

18 Humphreys to Rosalie, 14 April 1993, Papers of Rosalie Gascoigne, box 1.

19 Rosalie Gascoigne to Humphreys, 26 July 1993, Papers of Rosalie Gascoigne, box 1.

20 During the eighteenth and nineteenth centuries, Hegel asserted that recognition from others is essential to the development of a sense of self; in the 1940s and 1950s US psychologist Abraham Maslow posited a hierarchy of needs, which includes 'recognition' as one of the esteem needs. Maslow emphasised the importance of esteem needs for psychological health when he wrote: 'Satisfaction of the self-esteem needs leads to feelings of self-confidence, worth, strength, capability and adequacy of being useful and necessary in the world.' German philosopher Axel Honneth asserts that recognition is vitally important for humans, basing his claim on Hegel's stated necessity of recognition for humans 'to flourish as persons, both psychologically and socially'. In 1992, Canadian philosopher Charles Taylor promulgated 'due recognition' 'as a vital human need'. See Maslow, 'A Theory of Human Motivation'; Ikäheimo, 'A Vital Human Need'.

Canadian academic Alison Bain claims that recognition for visual artists is complicated by the fact that art is seldom seen as 'real work'.[21] As Neuhouser asserts: 'to desire recognition is to desire to have a certain standing in relation to the standing of some group of relevant others'.[22] In other words, recognition has more power when it comes from someone whose standing is relevant to that of the person seeking recognition. For recognition to work, the 'recogniser' must be someone who the 'recognised' admires and who has status in a field pertinent to that of the one seeking or hoping for recognition. Humphreys was an acclaimed novelist whose work Rosalie knew and admired. They agreed that visual artists and writers 'work within the same kind of nonverbal, intuitive scheme'.[23] They shared an identity as artists.

At the time the women wrote to each other, Rosalie lived in Canberra and Humphreys in Charleston, South Carolina. They exchanged four letters between March and July 1993 but never met in person. The women bypassed context and contingency, age and nationality; they ignored domesticity and feminism and went to the heart of the matter for them. Art was their common language and they wrote to each other of its identifying hallmarks.

Art was not all they had in common: both women had been teachers, were mothers and came to art later in life. Humphreys published her first book at the age of thirty-nine and Rosalie first exhibited when she was fifty-seven.[24] At the time of their correspondence, both women had successful professional husbands.[25] Humphreys loved nature and Gascoigne described nature as her friend. Rosalie made most of her art about the Monaro region; the locus of Humphreys's novels was her hometown, Charleston.

---

21 Bain, 'Constructing an Artistic Identity', 25.

22 Neuhouser, *Rousseau's Theodicy of Self-Love*, 32–3.

23 Gascoigne to Humphreys, 1993, Papers of Rosalie Gascoigne, box 1.

24 Humphreys was honoured with the 1984 Hemingway Foundation/PEN Award for *Dreams of Sleep* (1985), a Guggenheim Fellowship for Fiction (1986), the Lyndhurst Prize (1986–88) and the American Academy of Arts and Letters Award in Literature (1995). Her novel *Rich in Love* (1987) was made into a film starring Albert Finney and Jill Clayburgh in 1993, the year she visited Australia and corresponded with Rosalie.

25 Humphreys's husband Tom Hutcheson was, at the time the women corresponded, a lawyer in Charleston, South Carolina. He is now retired.

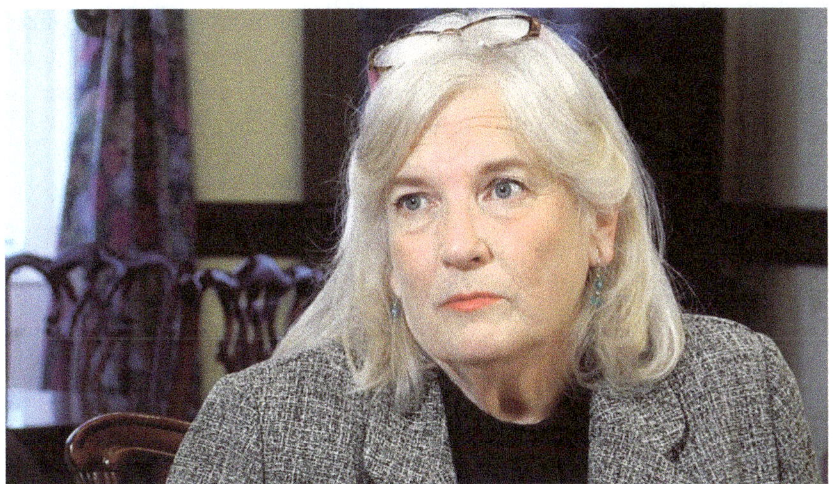

Figure 13.1: US writer Josephine Humphreys, c. 2013.

Note: 'I came home so full of your words and Sources that I can't help talking about you everywhere I go.' Humphreys to Rosalie, 1993.

Source: Courtesy of Josephine Humphreys and Phil Noble, from a video still produced by Phil Noble, Envision, South Carolina, US, and reproduced with their permission.

Despite this wealth of commonality, the surviving letters suggest that Humphreys and Rosalie wrote to each other only about the process of art making and the life of an artist. In Humphreys's letters she quotes from Rosalie's interviews and expresses her connection with Rosalie's comments by repeating them. She collages Rosalie's words onto the page just as Rosalie assembled weathered discards into the art Humphreys found 'to be mysterious and exciting and inspiring'.[26]

Humphreys agreed with Rosalie's comments:

> I [know my work is good when I] like the way it looks … [my art is] all for me; it's not for what the viewer sees. It reads back to me with something … And then I put it out upon the uncaring world.[27]

Rosalie's responses illustrated her all-encompassing sense of herself as an artist with little room for anything else. The passion and depth with which she wrote to Humphreys are compelling. Her words leave scant room for doubt. She quoted American painter Jasper Johns who said 'a picture is what a painter puts what he's got into'.[28] What 'one has' comes as the result

26 Humphreys to Rosalie, 14 April 1993, Papers of Rosalie Gascoigne, box 1.

27 Rosalie, quoted in ibid., Papers of Rosalie Gascoigne, box 1.

28 Rosalie Gascoigne to Josephine Humphreys, 26 July 1993, Papers of Rosalie Gascoigne, box 1.

of a lifetime—as Rosalie put it—'compulsively computerising experiences, attitudes and other people's endeavours and they hear voices and watch faces'.[29] These things, she wrote, become part of the artist and writer; the fruits of their lifetime of looking and listening go into their art:

> The truth as you see it is what you want, and that takes care of your personality, your conditioning and everything else. So all you need is solitude, honesty and hard hard unremitting work … I believe in passion too … I believe real creativity is possible only when one lets go of all support systems. I talk a lot about the need of the creative person to embrace the desert. It's between you and the empty space. Put something in it—your choice. With sweat, honesty and all of yourself. How one falls short! Better is possible! Always the beckoning finger![30]

Rosalie's correspondence with Humphreys illustrates that a sense of connection was close to her heart, and, perhaps, that it always existed in bitter tension with her feelings of isolation. She had written to American artist Anne Truitt about that need in 1981, having met her in June 1980 when Truitt visited Canberra as a guest of the Visual Arts Board. Rosalie took Truitt home where she served her a meal that Truitt described as 'perfectly delicious cauliflower cheese … crisp and creamy.'[31] Several years later they wrote to each other about the life of an artist, Truitt agreeing with Rosalie that: 'Only artists understand the life of artists.'[32]

In the 1990s, Rosalie also corresponded with poet and *Australian* art critic Pam Bell, who she met in 1974 at the opening of the *Genesis* exhibition at The Australian National University. A letter dated November 1992 suggests they had discussed poets and artists. Bell wrote to Rosalie about a quotation from poet Joseph Brodsky:

> A poet is a combination of an instrument and a human being in one person, with the former gradually taking over the latter. The sensation of this takeover is responsible for timbre; the realisation of it, for destiny.[33]

29 Ibid.
30 Ibid.
31 Anne Truitt to Rosalie Gascoigne, 26 November 1986.
32 Ibid.
33 Pam Bell to Rosalie, 9 November 1992, Papers of Rosalie Gascoigne, box 1.

It could be adduced from Bell's letter that the two women had been discussing the quotation and Bell had just found it in full. Bell continued: 'Poet … artist … What's the difference between them? Timbre being vibration being light or sound and both … Anyway that's my present to you this morning.'[34]

That an artist's life is not easy was something Rosalie wrote to fellow artists about, and probably discussed in person. She put it plainly to Hughes in 1998:

> Bette Davis [the actress] once said … 'Old age isn't for sissies.' Well, I'll tell you … art isn't for sissies, either … It's hard yakka … hard grind … a very isolated, isolating sort of way to live … you give up a lot for art.[35]

On the one hand, she asserted that she had felt an outsider because she was born an artist but did not discover that aspect of herself until later; on the other hand, she often spoke about the isolation of being an artist—that basic self-perception did not go away. Thus, she not only always felt an outsider but also she believed that an artist had to be an outsider; in this way, she established a mutually reinforcing pattern for herself.

The year after her correspondence with Humphreys, Rosalie received recognition from the wider Australian community when she was appointed a Member of the Order of Australia (AM) in the 1994 Queen's Birthday honours list, 'in recognition of service to the arts, particularly as a sculptor'.[36]

Despite his much longer career as an astronomer, it would be two years before Ben was appointed an Officer of the Order of Australia (AO). One level higher than Rosalie's AM, Ben's AO recognised his 'service to observational astronomy, specialising in the life history of stars, particularly in the Magellanic Clouds and for his contribution to astronomical optics and to the Anglo-Australian Telescope'.[37] Rosalie's rise had been quick, in the context of historical and social changes. Her art, with its directness and environmental aesthetic, resonated with both the art-appreciating public and the Australian government's newly developing cultural diplomacy, which will be discussed shortly.

34 Ibid.

35 Hughes et al., 'Rosalie Gascoigne Artist', tape 7.

36 See honours.pmc.gov.au/honours/awards/870155.

37 Ben received a further honour in the form of a Centenary Medal on 1 January 2001 'for service to Australian society and science in astronomy'.

1994–99: From the Antipodes to Asia, Germany and England

Rosalie's artistic star continued to rise in 1994 when the Art Gallery of New South Wales awarded her the John McCaughey Prize for *Clouds I* (1992). In Darwin, she exhibited in a group show celebrating corrugated iron—*100% Tracy*. In Aotearoa New Zealand, her works *Big Yellow* (1988) and *Skewbald* (1993) were included in *Aussemblage* at the Auckland City Art Gallery Toi o Tāmaki and Wellington City Gallery.[38] From February to March 1995, *Parrot Lady* (1974), *A Rose Is a Rose* (1986–88) and *Past Glories* (1988) were hung at the Perth Institute of Contemporary Arts as part of *In the Company of Women: 100 Years of Australian Women's Art from the Cruthers Collection.*[39]

Her work achieved further international exposure in 1995 when Germany's Goethe Institute invited her to provide an 'art kite' for the international event *Pictures for the Sky* in Sydney. Her *Highway to Heaven* hung alongside kites by artists of considerable international prominence like Robert Rauschenberg, Aman, Gerhard Richter and Antoni Tapies. In August of that year, she received further kudos when her enamelware piece *Set Up* (1984) won the Grand Prize Award at the *Chegu Pre-Biennale*, South Korea. Her work travelled to the United Kingdom for the first time when *Overland* (1996), *Afternoon* (1996), *All Summer Long* (1996) and *Highway Code* (1985) were part of *In Place (Out of Time): Contemporary Art in Australia* at Oxford's Museum of Modern Art in 1997.[40]

The same year her art was included in the Asialink exhibition *Other Stories: Five Australian Artists* that toured to the Bangladesh Biennale in Dhaka, Kathmandu, Hanoi, Colombo, Karachi, Lahore and Islamabad. This exhibition, created in response to the interest in narrative in South Asia, presented the work of five major Australian artists—Fiona Hall, Mike Parr, Rosslynd Piggott and Hossein Valamanesh—who told stories with their art. That her art was seen as 'narrative' is surprising: Rosalie herself saw her work as emotion recollected in tranquillity, paraphrasing Wordsworth. It was not

38 *Big Yellow* (1988), a large retro-reflective road sign work was purchased by the Chartwell Collection in 1988; the collection is held in the Auckland Art Gallery Toi o Tāmaki. *Skewbald* (1993), a work made with Masonite and old enamelware, was purchased by Auckland Art Gallery Toi o Tāmaki in 1994.

39 Miller, Cruthers Family and Perth Institute of Contemporary Arts, *In the Company of Women*. These artworks can be seen in Gascoigne, *Rosalie Gascoigne: A Catalogue Raisonné*.

40 Elliott et al., *In Place (Out of Time)*.

about story or picture, but 'about feeling, about how you feel. Not about how it looks, it's about how you feel about it.'[41] However, others saw her work as telling a story about what Australia was, or how it wanted to be seen.

In that role, and in these many overseas exhibits, Rosalie's work also gained popularity in the context of a new phase of cultural diplomacy that was becoming important for how Australia presented itself overseas in the aftermath of Cold War polarities and the search for cultural, educational and service-related international ties—or 'soft power' connections. American diplomat Cynthia P. Schneider defines cultural diplomacy as 'the exchange of ideas, information, art and other aspects of culture among nations and their peoples to foster mutual understanding'.[42] It recognised that culture can be a powerful instrument 'to pursue national interest in an un-intrusive, intelligent, convincing and cost-effective manner'.[43] Australia used the visual arts to build relationships that rose above old tensions, stereotypes and rivalries. Rosalie's career benefited from its 'fit' with such practices, her public persona serving to diversify older images of what Australia was. In the 1970s, she found a place in the expanding market of dealer galleries; in the 1980s, her work was shown alongside international artists at the Venice Biennale and also gained recognition in Aotearoa New Zealand, which would include her art for its own cultural diplomacy; in the 1990s, her work would become a different kind of commodity in cultural programs.

The Art Gallery of New South Wales mounted a major survey of her landscape-inspired work from November to January 1997 in *Rosalie Gascoigne: Material as Landscape* curated by Deborah Edwards.[44] This exhibition toured to the National Gallery of Australia, Canberra, in May 1998.

In November 1998, she was interviewed for the *Australian Biography* series made by SBS television 'profiling some of the most extraordinary Australians of our time'.[45] The program was shown on television on 1 August 1999.[46] Hester told me that her mother felt she said 'lots of stuff she didn't want to say' during the interview:

41 Hughes et al., 'Rosalie Gascoigne Artist', tape 4.
42 Schneider, 'Culture Communicates', 147; Byrne, 'Public Diplomacy in an Australian Context', 193.
43 Byrne, 'Public Diplomacy in an Australian Context', 192.
44 Edwards, *Rosalie Gascoigne: Material as Landscape*.
45 Hughes et al., 'Rosalie Gascoigne Artist'.
46 Cefn Ridout, Film Australia, to Rosalie Gascoigne, 5 July 1999, Papers of Rosalie Gascoigne, box 23.

> partly because they interviewed for so long and she probably forgot there was a camera … she really didn't like that program … it probably took her into places she didn't want to go.[47]

The same year, British writer Vici MacDonald published her monograph *Rosalie Gascoigne*, a richly illustrated overview of Rosalie's life including her path to becoming an artist, her aesthetic and her art making process. At the time of writing, this and the *Australian Biography* interview remain the only full biographical works about Rosalie that predate this book.

Aotearoa New Zealand also used Rosalie's work for cultural diplomacy. In 1999, René Block, director of the Museum Fridericianum in Kassel, Germany, selected eleven pieces of Rosalie's work for inclusion in *Toi Toi Toi: Three Generations of Artists from New Zealand*. The exhibition showed in Kassel (23 January – 5 March 1999), where Rosalie had attended the *Documenta* exhibition in 1982 while in Venice for the Biennale, and then Auckland (21 May – 8 August 1999). Along with Rosalie, Block selected significant Aotearoa New Zealand artists Len Lye, Billy Apple, Bill Culbert, Jacqueline Fraser, Lillian Budd, Ralph Hotere, Colin McCahon, Lisa Reihana, Peter Robinson, Mike Stevenson, Yuk King Tan, Ronnie Van Hout and Boyd Webb. Block chose these artists because of the 'degree to which they are rapidly gathering international exposures as they continue to make a distinctive mark in New Zealand'.[48] Rosalie, Lye, Culbert and Webb had made names for themselves in Australia, the United States and Europe, while others, like McCahon, worked and exhibited primarily in Aotearoa New Zealand. Curators Block and Chris Saines from the Auckland Art Gallery Toi o Tāmaki described *Toi Toi Toi* as: 'In part a proposition and in part a declaration. It seizes a moment in contemporary New Zealand art and weaves it through some key strands of its modern condition.'[49]

Rosalie was impressed to have been chosen by Block, who had curated Sydney's eighth Biennale in 1990, and delighted once more to be shown alongside McCahon. But she was less enchanted about being described as a New Zealander, because she had never made art in Aotearoa New Zealand.[50] She said: 'place of birth … doesn't deal with the places that formed you. And it was certainly circumstances in Australia that formed me, and the

47 Hester Gascoigne, interview by author, 20 February 2011.
48 Block et al., *Toi Toi Toi*, see foreword by René Block and Chris Saines.
49 Ibid.
50 Hughes et al., 'Rosalie Gascoigne Artist', tape 6.

taking on another country.'[51] The curators' foreword, however, states plainly that some of the artists lived and worked overseas but were included because of the visibility of their practice in Aotearoa New Zealand, and Rosalie is described as 'more visibly an Australian.'[52] Yet her art, by this time, was also highly visible in Aotearoa New Zealand and much appreciated there. Rosalie forged her relationship with nature during her early years in Aotearoa New Zealand, so her art expressed a sensibility that resonated with New Zealanders, but, perhaps more importantly, conferred a sense of wider impact. The success of her 2004 exhibition at City Gallery Wellington was reflected in high attendance numbers and positive reviews, and significant Aotearoa New Zealand public galleries subsequently purchased her work.[53]

The same year as *Toi Toi Toi*, Rosalie's work was included in *Drive* at the Govett-Brewster Gallery in New Plymouth, Aotearoa New Zealand. Despite this acclaim from across the Tasman and the international exposure, Rosalie told her Sydney dealer Roslyn Oxley: 'I'd rather be an Australian … I was never an artist in New Zealand.'[54] Oxley aptly replied: 'you might be both, darling'. Here, Rosalie was talking about her formation as an artist; however, reflecting the cultural role that her work was then performing on both sides of the Tasman, Oxley was talking about her standing as an artist.

Auckland Art Gallery Toi o Tāmaki curator Ron Brownson said that there were strategic reasons for including Rosalie with Aotearoa New Zealand artists. Of her, he said: 'we love her achievement because she was amongst the best of us'.[55] Australia had not included her in any group shows in Germany, but Aotearoa New Zealand curators saw the opportunity to do so, thereby boosting her reputation in another country. Aotearoa New Zealand kudos led her on to greater things in Germany and placed her in a coterie of great Aotearoa New Zealand artists.

51 Ibid.

52 René Block et al., *Toi Toi Toi*, 8.

53 For example, for reviews, see Lucy Chapman, 'Rosalie Gascoigne: "Australia's Most Famous NZ Artist"', *Salient*, 15 March 2004; William McAloon, 'Roadrunner: Rosalie Gascoigne, City Gallery, Wellington (to May 16)', *New Zealand Listener*, 17–23 April 2004. Rosalie's work is held in a number of public galleries and collections including the Museum of New Zealand / Te Papa Tongarewa; Auckland Art Gallery / Toi o Tāmaki; the Chartwell Trust; City Gallery, Wellington; the Govett-Brewster Gallery, New Plymouth; and the University of Auckland. It is also held in a number of private collections.

54 Hughes et al., 'Rosalie Gascoigne Artist', tape 6.

55 Ron Brownson, interview by author, 18 October 2010. Brownson died in February 2023.

1999: *Earth*, Auckland, Adelaide and death

In late July 1999, Rosalie's daughter Hester accompanied her to Auckland for the *Toi Toi Toi* and *Home and Away* exhibitions. Rosalie's large retro-reflective work *Big Yellow* (1988) was on show in *Home and Away* and a number of works were in *Toi Toi Toi*.[56] Her lecture and floor talk at the gallery attracted good crowds. The artist and her work were loved in her birth city by the art world and the public: venues were 'jam-packed'. Pether recalled: 'It was like a fan club of people. It was extraordinary—the enthusiasm and the ripple in the room—because she is so generous in her thinking.'[57] Brownson recounted how Rosalie showed no nerves prior to 'flooring' the audience with the provocation that art has no sex, no age and no gender. He described the talk as a 'one-person symposium where she articulated the raison d'être of her work as an artist'.[58] Marti Friedlander, one of Aotearoa New Zealand's greatest photographers and an expatriate artist herself, said Rosalie riveted listeners with her brilliant, witty presentation.[59]

Brownson had arranged for Friedlander to take Rosalie's photograph at the gallery, thinking the two would hit it off.[60] They did, but the meeting was not without minor tension. Rosalie, notoriously, did not like having her photograph taken. Friedlander, knowing what she wanted in terms of light and position, was exacting when she directed Rosalie at the photo shoot by the fountain outside the gallery, so exacting that Rosalie accused Friedlander of being a bully (see Figure 13.2).[61] Friedlander described how a moment of tension turned to shared humour:

> she [Rosalie] could give as good as she could get; she was a strong woman … I wanted to get good photos of her and what I loved about her was although she said 'you're a bit bossy' I said 'well so are you—look at the way you push your materials around' and she loved it.[62]

---

56 The following works by Rosalie were shown in *Toi Toi Toi*: *Beaten Track* (1992), *Scrub Country* (1981), *Grasslands II* (1998), *Love Apples* (1992), *Party Piece* (1988), *Solitude* (1997), *Please Drive Slowly* (1996), *Highway Code* (1985), *Loopholes* (1996), *Lasseter's Reef* (1997), *White Garden* (1995) and *Cockatoos* (1991).

57 Louise Pether, interview by author, Auckland, 2010.

58 Ron Brownson, interview by author, Auckland, 2010.

59 Marti Friedlander, interview by author, Auckland, 2010. Friedlander died in November 2016.

60 Brownson, interview by author, 2010.

61 Friedlander, interview by author, 2010. Friedlander also wrote to Hester Gascoigne about this. See Marti Friedlander to Hester Gascoigne, 10 February 2000: 'She was a reluctant subject and called me a bully when I persisted in photographing her against her works in the new gallery, I retorted that she bullied her materials and she laughed at that', in Papers of Rosalie Gascoigne, box 23.

62 Ibid.

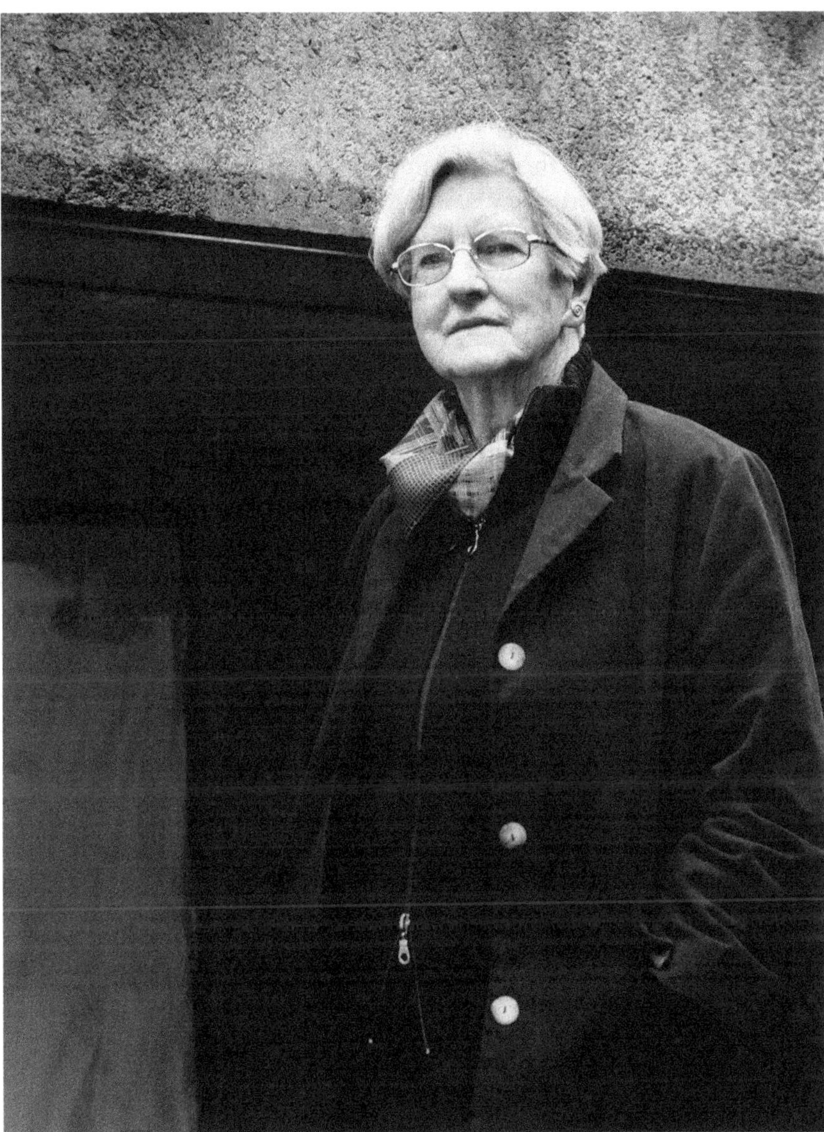

Figure 13.2: Rosalie Gascoigne at Toi o Tāmaki Auckland Art Gallery, July 1999.

Source: Courtesy of the Marti Friedlander Estate.[63] Photograph: Marti Friedlander.

63 As far as we know, Marti's photographs were the last ones taken of Rosalie.

Back in Australia, Rosalie's next stop was Adelaide and the Greenaway Art Gallery. Since meeting him at the *First Australian Sculpture Triennial* at La Trobe University, Melbourne, in 1981, Rosalie had developed a friendship with gallery owner Paul Greenaway and, in 1996, he presented her first South Australian solo exhibition. From time to time she visited him in Adelaide where she also enjoyed spending time with her friend Ian North. Greenaway and Rosalie would often drive into the countryside in his 1966 Datsun. Greenaway told me they left one day just as the sun was rising:

> we headed up to the hills … through thunderstorms and freezing cold sleet and then the sun came out in big rainbows … we drove … through Second Valley [coastal town on Fleurieu Peninsula] and … beautiful bald hills and rocky outcrops … to the waterside and the coastline.[64]

Around one bend the landscape reminded Rosalie of Aotearoa New Zealand. That day they enjoyed lunch at the 'Star of Greece' restaurant on the coast at Port Willunga where they watched a thunderstorm dramatically sweep across the sea, rapidly followed by bright sunshine.[65] Rosalie's visual literacy was deeply engrained and Greenaway shared her artistic sensibility. Unlike other road trips where she preferred silence and would not even countenance music, she talked non-stop to Greenaway, revelling in the natural environment and spotting everywhere connections with art:[66]

> Over every hill, around every bend there was something that reminded her of another artist or another person or another emotion … she would say 'ahhhhh, feel the breath!' or 'see the McCahon hills' or 'see that Sugimoto sea' [Japanese photographer, Hiroshi Sugimoto b. 1948]. Or wouldn't Michael Taylor love this![67]

---

64 Paul Greenaway, interview by author, Adelaide, 2012.

65 Ibid.

66 Peter Vandermark told me that Rosalie preferred silence when he drove her: 'when we used to do our tip runs and we'd quite often cover quite a few kilometres out to Collector and through to Captain's Flat and do this big loop but in silence—which she just loved … I eventually became the driver so she could just sit and look … no music … the silence in the car—it was never tense—just no music, me driving and Rosalie looking at the landscape—it was only when we arrived at the tip that she'd jump out of the car and start getting really excited.' Hagerty and Vandermark, interview by author, 2011.

67 Greenaway, interview by author, 2012.

At Rosalie's request, she and Greenaway spent a full day together plotting a strategy for her international career. They agreed she would exhibit at *ARCO*, the International Contemporary Art Fair in Spain and, accordingly, Greenaway took out full-page advertisements in international art journals.[68] He was to prepare a proposal for a museum exhibition in the United Kingdom, and they discussed the United Nations show acknowledging senior living artists. Rosalie was eighty-two years old and her career continued to flourish; her passion for making art prevailed.

The plans were not to be. Death crept up on Rosalie. Shortly after her planning day with Greenaway, she was diagnosed with the cancer that was to kill her. On the eve of her exhibition at the Roslyn Oxley9 Gallery in Sydney she was admitted to Canberra's John James Memorial Hospital, near Dugan Street in Deakin, where she had lived in the 1960s. Rosalie's daughter Hester arranged small items from her studio so that she could see them from her bed—remnants of retro-reflective road signs, tiny animal bones she had collected from Monaro paddocks in better times, a pattern of box-fragments.[69] This installation of found objects from Rosalie's life gifted her with visual reminders of how far she had travelled and the heights she had achieved. The fragments symbolised the variety in her life; they showed how the pieces of a life, like the pieces of her artworks, can be artfully arranged and shaped by context, contingency and fluidity.

Her friend from the University House Ladies' Drawing Room days, fellow artist Jan Brown AO, visited Rosalie in hospital the week before she died. Rosalie was intent that Brown should see one of her most recent works, the *Earth* (1999) panels. She considered they were the best things she had made. Brown remembers feeling concerned because Rosalie was weak and fragile yet had stretched herself across the armchair: 'I was going spare. I said "you're going to fall out of the bloody thing".'[70] Rosalie's body may have been fragile but her spirit was strong. Brown found her that day as any other day: 'arguing—always arguing—about art and things related'.[71]

68 Ibid.
69 O'Brien, 'Plain Air / Plain Song', 46; Hester Gascoigne, pers. comm., 19 June 2023.
70 Jan Brown, interview by author, 2011.
71 Ibid.

Just one year earlier, in her familiar pragmatic way, Rosalie had told Hughes she did not fear death because she saw little point given death's inevitability. But she also acknowledged, perhaps hopefully, the possibility that death might be more than final darkness:

> It's inevitable … [so] why bother [fearing death] … you don't know the whole story … Nobody knows anything for sure … so what about confronting the inevitable and going along with it … it's going to happen whatever you do.[72]

The inevitable happened. Rosalie died on 23 October 1999, aged eighty-two. But before she did, she smiled up at Ben from her hospital bed one day when they were alone, and whispered: 'Ben, I'm sorry I can't be with you for the rest of the journey.'[73] For Ben, her smile and look were as important as the words. He had been a constant in her life for ten years of friendship and courting followed by fifty-seven years of marriage. Letters between Ben and writer Hannah Fink convey that all was not rosy between Rosalie and Ben in her later years when she was sometimes difficult and often uncommunicative.[74] Perhaps she was making up for lost time, cramming as much art making as she could into her life in the face of the inevitable march of time and approach of death. Perhaps it was only when she faced imminent death that she was able to openly acknowledge Ben's importance to her.

The pattern of communication in her family of origin had been abrasive, as described in the early chapters of this book, and she and her siblings had not affirmed one another. It seems that just as Eagle had said that Rosalie adhered, without deviation, to the conventions of her Auckland upbringing, perhaps she had equally clung to aspects of the style of communication and relationship she had grown up with. The inevitability of death freed her.

Rosalie was cremated after a private funeral service at Norwood Crematorium, Canberra, on 26 October. A friend and fellow artist Marie Hagerty painted the casket. On Friday 5 November, her family, friends, colleagues and admirers celebrated her life at a service of thanksgiving in St Paul's Church, Manuka, the nearest thing in Canberra to an Anglican cathedral. Like her letters to Martin in the 1970s, the order of service reads

72 Hughes et al., 'Rosalie Gascoigne Artist', tape 8.

73 Ben Gascoigne to Hannah Fink, 7 May 2000, Papers of Ben Gascoigne, box 5.

74 Ibid.: 'As you mentioned, Rosalie was sometimes difficult in her later years, and often incommunicative.'

like a who's who of Australian art.[75] Apart from family, the speakers were from the art world—Michael Desmond, formerly of the National Gallery of Australia (NGA), then with the Powerhouse Museum and later with the National Portrait Gallery, and Edmund Capon, then director of the Art Gallery of NSW, gave eulogies. Daniel Thomas, then director emeritus of the Art Gallery of South Australia, read some of her favourite quotations. Ron Radford, then director of the Art Gallery of South Australia and chair of the Visual Arts/Crafts Fund of the Australia Council, later director of the NGA, talked about travelling with Rosalie. Old friends from Aotearoa New Zealand, ikebana, First Canberra Garden Club and the Horticultural Society did not speak, although many paid their respects from the pews. The service of thanksgiving for her life reflected the trajectory Rosalie's life had taken in her last three decades.

On their day together a few months earlier, Greenaway and Rosalie discussed *Earth*, a work that she had recently completed from discarded formwork plywood she had found on the Questacon building site in Canberra in 1984.[76] She had referred to the work—ten large panels of varying brown-ochre-russet-red-black colours sawn and arranged in grid patterns—as being 'from the earth'. Prophetically, she had said to Greenaway: 'it looks like death. Where do I go from here?'[77]

Rosalie was dead but not gone. A line from the 1937 Ira and George Gershwin jazz song 'They Can't Take That Away from Me' that played at her thanksgiving service aptly notes: 'the song has ended but as the songwriter wrote the melody lingers on'.

Rosalie lives through the legacy of her work that enabled Australians to see their country with fresh eyes. Death could not take that away from the art-loving public. The trail of her star continues to dazzle. In the weeks and months after her death, numerous obituaries appeared, not only in publications the length and breadth of Australia and Aotearoa New Zealand

75 'Service of Thanksgiving for the Life of Rosalie Gascoigne'.

76 In 1987, Rosalie wrote a letter to her son Toss describing her delight at finding materials on the Questacon building site in Canberra in 1987: 'My dining room floor is covered with builders' form board in various shades of brown, dull purple, and tan, I made a killing at a new building site opposite National Library. Stepped daintily down to the manager's office in my Carla Zampatti linen and my social shoes and asked if I might have any spare bits … I returned next day in my old pants and took a LOT … Plenty to go on with anyway! I wonder that no other artist is using it. I keep scrubbing concrete off it and laying it all over the floor until such time as it tells me what it wants to become.' Tony Wright, 'Rosalie's Old Trash National Treasure Now', *Age*, 19 March 2008, www.theage.com.au/news/arts/rosalies-old-trash-national-treasure-now/2008/03/18/1205602384225.html.

77 See Greenaway, interview by author, 2012.

but also in the United Kingdom and the United States.[78] Her work has since appeared in major exhibitions, including solo shows *From the Studio of Rosalie Gascoigne* at The Australian National University's Drill Hall Gallery in 2000; *Rosalie Gascoigne—Plain Air* at Wellington's City Gallery, Aotearoa New Zealand, in 2004; and *Rosalie Gascoigne* at the National Gallery of Victoria in 2008–09. Her work also appeared in group shows as significant as the *Australia* exhibition at the Royal Academy in London in 2013. The vast and magnificent *Monaro*, constructed from yellow and black painted wood Schweppes soft drink crates, was shipped across the world and hung in the Royal Academy where it gave viewers an experience of the Monaro's sweeping vistas and rippling blonde grass. She featured in the NGA's *Know My Name* exhibition celebrating Australian women artists in 2021 and 2022. Also in 2021–22, the Ian Potter Centre of the National Gallery of Victoria mounted an exhibition *Found and Gathered: Rosalie Gascoigne | Lorraine Connelly-Northey* that displayed the 'shared materiality at the heart of the practices of both artists, both of whom used found and discarded objects to create beautiful and surprising works of art'.[79]

Of course, her husband, children, daughters-in-law and grandchildren felt the greater loss by far. Ben struggled to come to terms with Rosalie's death. He was left surrounded by her art, leftover bits and pieces and 'the garden by which she set such store just outside the window'. He described his feelings to his friend Robbie from his university days in Auckland:

> if she could have chosen her time this might well have been it—at the height of her powers, her last show (which she never saw) possibly her best ever, and she just back from a most successful visit to Auckland, where she seemed at last to have come to terms with her long estrangement from New Zealand.[80]

Ben received scores of condolence letters stamped with postmarks from around the world—notes, letters and cards from old Auckland friends, from Stromlo and every phase of their lives. In a testament to the respect Rosalie commanded in the art world, letters of sympathy also poured in from artists and from those who, in Rosalie's words, 'move in after the fait accompli

78 In addition to obituaries in all the major Australian and New Zealand newspapers, obituaries were published overseas, including: Rebecca Hossack, 'Obituary: Rosalie Gascoigne', *Independent*, 2 November 1999, www.independent.co.uk/arts-entertainment/obituary-rosalie-gascoigne-1121898.html; 'Obituaries', *Art in America* 88, no. 1 (January 2000), 142.

79 National Gallery of Victoria, *Found and Gathered*.

80 Ben Gascoigne to Robbie (school and university friend, author Neil Robinson, who Ben described as his oldest and closest friend), Papers of Ben Gascoigne, box 3.

… the assessors, the labellers, the evaluators', the curators, art historians, writers, arts administrators.[81] These were the people who recognised her greatness and made her. Now they, with her family and friends, mourned her. She had commented to Topliss in 1995 about the layers and layers of defence people have, likely thinking of herself and yet again deflecting. She said she liked reading the 'warts and all' lives of artists because she found it interesting to know what made them tick, but she also said: 'After you are dead who cares anyway?'[82]

81 'Service of Thanksgiving for the Life of Rosalie Gascoigne.'
82 Greenaway, interview by author, 2012.

Conclusion

> She had a perpetual sense … of being out, far out to sea and alone.
>
> —Virginia Woolf, *Mrs Dalloway*

In 1993, when Rosalie gave the opening address at the Sydney *Perspecta* exhibition, she told the gathering that art is a visual medium and viewers:

> can only communicate with artists by standing in the presence of the work. They after all have gone the journey to arrive at this place … you [the viewer] have to meet the work first on their terms.[1]

'Afterwards', she continued, 'the big secondary industry of words takes over'. She spoke of critics and how 'the mighty art speak machine will roll into action and sometimes confuse the issue'. I do not think this was anti-intellectualism for its own sake, or a protective measure against harsh critics. During the years that I have researched Rosalie, she has convinced me that she made art because she needed to. Like a moth needs light and a sailor needs the sea, Rosalie needed an outlet for the layers of feelings that built up over the years of her life. Making art helped her to make sense of her isolation and confirmed it—even created it during her years of eminence. Her instinctive eye for beauty in the unexpected was born of the confusion, anxiety and emotional abandonment she felt in her childhood, then again on Stromlo and in Canberra's suburban circles. She turned isolation into creative space; she evoked wonder with her art and found truths there that eluded her elsewhere.

In focusing on Rosalie's self-narrative, this biography explores the purposes that narrative served in making sense of experiences that were deeply personal while also being emblematic of aspects of a generational context. Themes of grief, shame, dislocation, education and independence, of fraying certainties of class and new expectations of domesticity and self-realisation,

1 Gascoigne, 'Opening Address, 1993 Sydney *Perspecta*'.

and the particular path of a woman through those transitions, have been at the core of my interpretation. So have been the opportunities that came to her for expression, and the role she came to fulfil as an artist in a career that mapped significant transformations in the art world—that 'mighty art speak machine'—from which she sought distance. The tensions between her own narrative and these wider contexts energised my enquiry, not because the accuracy of one had to be traded against the other, but because the balance between the representative and the individual continually emphasised the truth of both.

She told guests at the *Perspecta* opening: 'People will write theses'. She was right. At the time I completed my PhD thesis, three others had been written, all in creative arts or curatorial faculties. In 1994, Campbell Banbury wrote a postgraduate diploma thesis in art curatorial studies at the University of Melbourne entitled 'Rosalie Gascoigne Reassembled: Ikebana and the Grid'.[2] Lolita Hamilton's 2010 master of creative arts thesis at the University of Wollongong, 'Physicality and Process: Representing an Evolving Practice through the Embodied Experience', examined the embodied experience of self and practice through the art making processes of Rosalie Gascoigne and Aida Tomescu.[3] And, in 2012, Peta Murray wrote a master's thesis in the Queensland University of Technology Creative Arts Faculty, 'Things That Fall Over: Women's Playwriting, Poetics and the (Anti) Musical', which explored the nexus between women, ageing and creative practice via an investigation into the oeuvre of two Australian artists, Rosalie Gascoigne and Elizabeth Jolley.[4]

None of these works critically examined Rosalie's life: they largely observed her injunction to attend mainly to 'the work'. However, the distinction between life and work, as Rosalie's narrative underscores, is far from neat. My book contributes to this body of work about Rosalie by illuminating her life and motivations, seeking to enlarge both our sense of her as a person, and the context in which she achieved fame.

The three strands woven through this study expand the currently limited understanding of Rosalie's life and artistic success. My study of her self-narrative illuminates aspects of her life and personality, while placing her in the historical context of Canberra during the 1960s and 1970s, illustrating how changes during that period created the context for the successful

2 Banbury, 'Rosalie Gascoigne Reassembled'.
3 Hamilton, 'Physicality and Process'.
4 Murray, 'Things That Fall Over'.

reception of her work. In addition to that social context (and without venturing too far into the distinct concerns of art history), I have also traced the development of her work in relation to changing art tastes in Australia.

Life narrative

Rosalie constructed and told a life narrative once she achieved artistic acclaim because people were interested in hearing the story of a woman who 'found herself' with such public success in the latter part of her life. Her story inspires many; it engages listeners with a tale of almost mythic proportions. She told how she spent decades struggling with her identity, weaving into her narrative stories of how she was caught between her siblings during childhood and lived in the shadow of shame—a family shame, the weight of which she assumed at a young age. Like Mrs Dalloway in Virginia Woolf's novel of the same name, she had a 'perpetual sense … of being out, far out to sea and alone'. Rosalie told and retold her story in interviews, the narrative culminating in her discovery of her self-identity and public reception as an artist.

This self-narrative has been uncritically received, both before and after her death. Repeated in art catalogues, articles and book chapters, it has served powerful purposes. This biography, however, illustrates that Rosalie's story is more complex. She emphasised certain aspects of her life in order to create a picture of herself as an artist who took decades to realise it and suffered from feeling isolated and out of step in the meantime. I am not suggesting this was a deliberate act of creating a fiction. Rather, I propose that, in constructing this version of her story, Rosalie sought to make sense of some of her past experiences. Contemporary sources provide evidence that events around her family during childhood could well have caused her to take on the shame she spoke of. This shame and events leading to it may have been behind her sense of being out of step. The artistic identity she discovered later in life, and the accompanying success, gave meaning to her earlier suffering. As Butler wrote:

> The further the subject is in time from the event, the greater is the tendency to reflect upon it rather than remember what was actually thought at the moment, and to present experience in a variety of romanticised modes.[5]

---

5 Butler, *Kitty's War*, 166.

In 1998, when interviewed by Hughes, Rosalie was eighty years on from her birth and fifty-four years removed from her arrival on Mount Stromlo. In Butler's terms, therefore, she was more likely to be reflecting on those years and presenting herself romantically as an outsider who had always felt that way until she discovered her artist identity. Then, she said: 'I found my own sort of heaven.'[6] Those closest to her—including her husband—expressed surprise at her accounts of a difficult childhood and her later escape. To some extent, that in itself reflects the secrecy that prevailed in her life until found, fragmented, weathered and boxed objects offered some form of respite. It also accords with Charles Fernyhough's assertion that early memories often function as creation myths.[7] Just as Rosalie made some of her art works by carving up discarded road signs or soft drink crates and rearranging the pieces on a grid pattern, she took elements of her life story and rearranged them, giving greater emphasis to the elements that worked as creation myths, reinforcing her claim to having been born an artist.

Historical intersections

Timing is everything. Rosalie's artistic path fortuitously coincided with historical changes in Australia during the 1950s to the 1970s, in particular, the growth of Canberra, a developing environmental sensibility, and changes in art bureaucracy and art tastes. These changes prepared the ground for the acceptance and acclamation of her work. During her time in the Australian Capital Territory, Canberra changed from a small rural town to an approximate national capital, bringing about significant changes that ultimately benefited Rosalie's career. The expansion brought large numbers of highly educated academics, scientists and administrators to the city, among them a number of people who were to become significant to her through a shared environmental and artistic sensibility and then acceptance and recognition of her as 'one of them'. Canberra suburbs—sites (as Hugh Stretton was to put it in 1970) of a 'quiet revolution' in the balancing of private and public lives in Australia—provided a context in which Rosalie experimented in expression, moving from flower arranging and the discipline of ikebana to her own aesthetic.[8] 'Mrs S. C. Gascoigne's' evolution through motherhood to 'Rosalie Gascoigne', a middle-aged

6 Hughes et al., 'Rosalie Gascoigne Artist', tape 4.

7 Egan, 'Review of Nicola King', 922; King, *Memory, Narrative, Identity*; Fernyhough, *Pieces of Light*.

8 Stretton's 'quiet revolution', see Brown, *A History of Canberra*, 123.

woman artist whose conservative appearance beguiled people intrigued by her art, was its own 'quiet revolution'—not hers alone, but one that again mapped a generational shift and specific historical context.

At the same time, and in the same context, moves towards the establishment of a national gallery in Canberra brought Rosalie into contact with an invaluable adviser in James Mollison, and new currents in Australian art practice that shaped and affirmed her journey.

A bureaucracy of curators, administrators and critics dealer galleries arrived, with their own ways of shaping an art market and promoting artists. The burgeoning acceptance of modern art in Australia paved the way for Rosalie's abstractions of the local environment, fusing the long-held primacy of landscape in Australia with the new sensibilities. Her hands-on physical processes and adoption of the conceptual over the pictorial marked her approach as modernist and enabled Rosalie to present a new vision of the Canberra hinterland. In a time of new nationalism, Australia used cultural diplomacy to project to the rest of the world a mix of high icons, popular images and the impact of its peoples on an old, weathered but clever country.

In 1997, Rosalie told James Mollison and Steven Heath: 'You are a fool if you want praise and fame and more fool if you think you have arrived.'[9] Rosalie needed praise and she achieved fame. In terms of her success and acclamation, she arrived. But, as her life and rise to fame show, Rosalie was no fool. As with this biography and me, she did not do it alone. This study has shown she had a remarkable eye and exceptional resilience. Rosalie was driven by powerful motivations and need. She was blessed with the right conditions of education and affluence that allowed her the freedom to create. She knew the right people and was in the right place at the right time. But it was a long road. Let us give her the final word:

'I have been given support to overcome self-doubts, to pull myself up. Now my art supports me. I only just believe it now.'[10]

9 Mollison and Heath, 'Rosalie Gascoigne', 8.
10 Ibid.

Epilogue

Writing a life is a massive enterprise. No account can cover every aspect of a life.

I am full of admiration for Rosalie Gascoigne. I hope my admiration shows in this book. I lived with her in my head for five years during my PhD candidacy and for a further six months preparing this manuscript for publication. During these times I developed a huge respect for her. I wanted to do my very best for her in this telling of her life.

Writing a person's life is also a sensitive exercise. Not everyone will be happy with my words about Rosalie. I have always been aware that Rosalie was a mother and a grandmother and a friend to people still living. I believe that my account manages to be both honest and respectful.

In revising my thesis for publication, I was advised to explore the challenges faced by creative women such as Rosalie, both during her time and earlier. Fitting this into the biographical narrative of my thesis, which was a completed piece of work with its own coherence, did not work well, either in the introduction or within the narrative. It distracted from Rosalie's story of self-discovery. To retain that original focus, which acknowledges the importance of context and contingency in all our life stories, I have placed it here at the end—in an epilogue. My intention is that, after enjoying the biography, readers can consider my latest conception of Rosalie's story, which explores the issues that affected her in the context of other work by women artists.

Women who made art and did not like being called 'women artists'

Rosalie disliked being described as a 'woman artist', telling Robin Hughes in 1997: 'I have no truck with it … Art has neither age nor sex.'[1] She was not alone. Australian Margaret Preston and American Georgia O'Keeffe also objected to the term and to being included in women-only exhibitions. In a review of the National Gallery of Australia's *Know My Name: Australian Women Artists 1900 to Now* (2021–22), Canberra art critic Sasha Grishin relates a famous anecdote in feminist art history about two famous American women artists: 'Elaine de Kooning and Joan Mitchell. At a party they were asked, "What do you women artists think?" Mitchell responded, "Elaine, let's get the hell out of here".'[2]

Australian modernist photographer Olive Cotton, who lived during the same era as Rosalie, equally disliked being described as a 'woman photographer', saying 'I'd rather be thought of as an artist.'[3] Austrian-born Australian photographer Margaret Michaelis preferred to be considered 'a photographer' rather than as a 'woman photographer' or a feminist.[4]

While it is understandable that a woman might prefer to be known as an artist without reference to race, sex or gender, feminist sociologist Kathleen Barry rightly states that 'the biographical subject is always a gendered subject'.[5] Political scientist Marian Simms wrote in 1978 that:

> One of the key issues facing students of women's history and politics is the nature of the relationship between sex, class and status in understanding the position of women in contemporary society.[6]

While contemplating this issue, I read the novel *Bad Art Mother* by Australian writer and musician Edwina Preston, which centres on the fictional character Veda Gray, a poet struggling for recognition in the 1950s–60s Melbourne,

1 Hughes et al., 'Rosalie Gascoigne Artist', tape 7. Rosalie had possibly read that Victorian artist, suffragist and feminist Louise Jopling-Rowe was described this way in Greer, *The Obstacle Race*, 320. See Jopling, *Twenty Years of My Life*, 307; de Montfort, 'Louise Jopling'.

2 Sasha Grishin, 'Know My Name: Australian Women Artists 1900 to Now at the National Gallery of Australia Is a Dazzling Visual Experience', *Canberra Times*, 14 November 2020, www.canberratimes.com.au/story/7009539/half-the-sky-and-equal-wall-space/.

3 Ennis, *Olive Cotton*, 415.

4 Ibid., 415.

5 Barry, 'Biography and the Search for Women's Subjectivity', 563.

6 Simms, 'Writing the History of Australian Women'.

a time just before second-wave feminism surfaced in Australia. This period, during which Rosalie was beginning to develop her oeuvre in Canberra, was, as Christos Tsiolkas described, 'a transformative moment in culture when everything [was] about to change'.[7] *Bad Art Mother* describes the challenges Gray faced in her creative life, challenges that other women creatives faced. Rosalie benefited from the changes set in motion at this time in Australia.

Feminism making waves in Australia

The years after Rosalie settled in Australia were watershed years for Australian women. She arrived in January 1943. In August of that year, women were elected to the federal government for the first time: Enid Lyons to the House of Representatives, and Dorothy Tangney to the Senate. It would take another twenty-three years (1966) for women in the Australian public service to win the right to remain employed after marriage.

In 1973, Prime Minister Gough Whitlam created the role of adviser on women's affairs, appointing Elizabeth Reid, who later commented that the revolution that was women's liberation in Australia in the 1970s exposed the fact that Australia was 'a bloke's world'.[8] Australian women became increasingly aware of the limitations placed on them, particularly around birth control, access to employment and male-dominated occupations, childcare, equal pay, and the impact of sexist and discriminatory language in texts and advertising.

Feminist historical scholarship in Australia in the 1970s revealed stories of women's experiences of family, sexual and other forms of violence.[9] Into the twentieth century, the belief persisted that husbands had the right to 'chastise' their wives, including through physical violence, while at the same time, there was general acknowledgement that wife-beating was a widespread problem. Legislation was in place to prevent physical and sexual violence; however, the expectation that men be physically and mentally tough, and that women, as the 'gentler sex', be neither, held sway.[10] Then, as now, as Piper and Stevenson assert, positive action to confront gendered violence was less forthcoming than expressions of concern about it.[11] As women

7 Preston, *Bad Art Mother*, see Christos Tsiolkas's comment on back cover.
8 Reid made this comment in a 2005 ABC *Stateline* interview.
9 Piper and Stevenson, 'The Long History'.
10 Ibid.
11 Ibid.

became more aware of the scale of domestic violence and sexual harassment, the impact on individual's lives and the silence around it, feminists called for action.

Throughout Australia, groups of women, including Anne Summers, author of the feminist history *Damned Whores and God's Police: The Colonization of Women in Australia* (1975), realised they would have to shape their own future through direct action: protests to gain media attention as well as lobbying to win funding for newly established women's refuges and health services commenced.[12] It would be another decade before 'domestic violence' was named as such.

The change had begun. Rosalie may not have actively participated in the feminist movement, but she benefited from the changing perceptions of women that grew out of it.

The cults of domesticity and motherhood in New Zealand and Australia

In 1975, the year of Rosalie's triumph at Gallery A, Anne Summers published *Damned Whores and God's Police: The Colonization of Women in Australia*. A bestseller on publication, the book is now acknowledged as a 'feminist blockbuster' and has remained almost continuously in print. Summers argued that 'colonization created a patriarchal gender order that reduced 19th-century women to one of two narrow roles: virtuous wives and mothers, dubbed "God's police", and the transgressive "damned whores"'.[13] She asserted that the social forces that determined women's lives in early colonial Australia continued to shape Australian women's lives in the 1970s. Such forces were like those that had dominated Rosalie's early years in New Zealand. The cult of domesticity and the propaganda surrounding it, likely factors in Rosalie's belief that she must have children, were integral parts of her formative years.[14] As with the Australian women of her generation, her education was designed to entice her into an ideal domestic role. Historians

12 Francis, 'Women Who Caucus'.

13 Arrow, 'Damned Whores and God's Police'. Arrow's comments on Summers's book should be noted here: 'It neglected class differences between women. It sidelined the experiences of Indigenous women with its metaphor of "colonisation"'; however, this is not the place for such discussion.

14 Hughes et al., 'Rosalie Gascoigne Artist', tape 1.

such as Barbara Brookes in Aotearoa New Zealand and Patricia Grimshaw in Australia have written extensively about these influences, some of which are addressed in earlier chapters.

Domesticity and motherhood comprised a significant part of Rosalie's life as a young wife and mother. In 1999, she told Robin Hughes in the *Australian Biography* interview series: 'I had to have children, I knew I had to have children … I just needed them … It was unthinkable for me not to have children.'[15] Yet, she also spoke of 'the long littleness of female life' during the same interview. A professional woman with a university degree, which was unusual in her era, Rosalie chose marriage over a career—a traditional marriage with Ben as the provider and her as the homemaker. She took Ben's name. As far as we know, she eschewed feminism, although she identified with women who felt 'sort of the shadow behind the man' and resented it.[16]

During Rosalie's childhood, there was an intense focus on mothers' responsibility for the health and welfare of children and men. The poor physical condition of World War I recruits was blamed on mothers' poor domestic skills. The death of 8,600 New Zealanders in the 1918 influenza epidemic was attributed to poor hygiene in the home. Health officials began to formulate policy to improve domestic hygiene. The combined forces of the government, the prohibition movement, the Society for the Protection of the Health of Women and Children and evangelical Protestantism placed the burden of responsibility for raising healthy children and making the home a place where husbands would want to return at the end of each day, thus keeping them out of pubs and away from the demon drink, on women.

At the heart of disquiet about motherhood and children in both Australia and New Zealand was concern for the kind of society each country wanted to build. In New Zealand, the official hope was for a 'white man's country … as completely British as possible'.[17] Australia nurtured similar hopes. In New Zealand, a falling Pākehā birth rate, especially after the high death toll of World War I and the influenza epidemic, raised serious concerns. Meanwhile, the Māori birth rate increased rapidly.[18] The declining birth

15 Ibid.

16 Ibid., tape 8.

17 Brookes, *A History of New Zealand Women*, 201.

18 The Māori birth rate grew rapidly, increasing by 34.8 per cent by 1930. This outstripped Pākehā rate by 68 per cent. The non-Māori population grew by only 10.6 per cent in the same era. See Brookes, *A History of New Zealand Women*, 191–5. There were various reasons for this including the increased availability of birth control.

rate among Pākehā was blamed on greater access to information about birth control by campaigners Marie Stopes in Britain and Ettie Rout in New Zealand. In Australia, the white colonial birthrate declined from the 1890s, triggering fears for the preservation of the white Australia race and leading government to place restrictions not only on the advertisement and sale of contraceptives but also on the availability of information about how to control fertility.[19]

As a result of such anxieties, motherhood in both countries developed into a vocation. Summers asserts that the motive behind compulsory education was to ensure that girls were educated sufficiently to fulfil their roles as mothers of the nation.[20] It was not considered feasible to combine this special vocation with any other work or career.

Rosalie's mother Marion Metcalfe had provided a role model for combining motherhood and a profession, albeit with the assistance of her mother and sister. The fact that Rosalie felt she had missed out on adult attention as a result, together with the prevailing thinking about women and motherhood in New Zealand throughout her childhood and early adulthood, is likely to have forestalled any thought Rosalie may have had about combining the two.

***

Inevitably, other women artists were also influenced by their times, although in different ways. In 1970, Germaine Greer's groundbreaking feminist work *The Female Eunuch* 'urged women to think beyond the stereotype patriarchal society had created for them, which limited their capacity to act'.[21] In 1972, Rosalie made a sculpture out of rusted scrap metal, nails, mesh, pipes and copper ballcock that she called *Germaine Greer*.[22] In a letter to her son Martin, she described it as 'a large woman waving her fists and railing against her obvious pregnancy (after all it was a very large ballcock)'.[23] The sculpture, much appreciated by artist Carl Plate and later given to him by Rosalie, indicates her low opinion of Greer.

---

19 Grimshaw, 'Gendered Settlements', 193–4.

20 Summers, *Damned Whores and God's Police*, 336.

21 Nelson, 'The Female Eunuch at 50'.

22 See an image of *Germaine Greer* in Gascoigne, *Rosalie Gascoigne: A Catalogue Raisonné*.

23 Rosalie to Martin, 11 January 1972, in Gascoigne, *Rosalie Gascoigne: A Catalogue Raisonné*.

Representation of women in public art collections

The patriarchal structures of society to which Germaine Greer referred in *The Female Eunuch* were reflected in the art world in terms of the perception of women as artists and public galleries' acquisition policies. For women who made art up to and including the time Rosalie began her art practice, two major factors were at play: general societal attitudes to and expectations of women, and the culture of the art world that tended to privilege male artists, particularly painters and sculptors. Expectations of motherhood and domesticity for women, and the undervaluing and under-representation of female artists' work in public art collections in museums and galleries, impeded women's artistic careers. The two factors are directly related to the structures of a patriarchal society, but it helps to identify them separately and the part they played in the lives of women who made art.

Another of Greer's books, published in 1979, *The Obstacle Race: The Fortunes of Women Painters and Their Work*, analysed the obstacles facing women painters from the time of the first female monasteries until the nineteenth century.[24] Greer explored the psychological, economic and aesthetic reasons for what American feminist Erica Jong termed 'the virtually unchallenged patriarchalism of all our artistic establishments'.[25] The obstacles Greer outlined included the lack of artistic training available to women until the nineteenth century, which meant that the only way a woman could train was through a male family member who was an artist. With the greater availability of art education, this is no longer an issue; however, my research shows that recognised Australian women artists in the late nineteenth and early twentieth centuries tended to come from cultured families (which often included male artists) that had sufficient resources to provide their daughters with an education, including the study of art. While Rosalie had not yet recognised the artist in her when she arrived in Australia, and it would take three decades before she did, her family of origin had enabled her to receive a good education, including a university degree in which she studied the English romantic poets who later inspired and informed some of her art.

24 Greer, *The Obstacle Race*.

25 Ibid., see Erica Jong's comment on back cover of 2021 edition.

Among Australian women artists up to the mid-twentieth century, I have yet to find a single one who did not come from a cultured or well-off family that enabled her to paint and, in many cases, travel to Europe to study. Nora Heysen (1911–2003), Margaret Preston (1875–1963), Grace Cossington Smith (1892–1984), Grace Crowley (1890–1979) and Stella Bowen (1893–1947) are just some of the women artists active during Rosalie's lifetime who enjoyed these privileges. Along with Rosalie, all were included in the National Gallery of Australia's *Know My Name: Australian Women Artists 1900 to Now* exhibition (2021–22) that was billed as:

> A celebration, a commitment and a call to action, *Know My Name* is a gender equity initiative of the National Gallery of Australia. *Know My Name* celebrates the work of all women artists with an aim to enhance understanding of their contribution to Australia's cultural life.[26]

***

Now recognised as one of Australia's great portrait painters, Nora Heysen, daughter of landscape painter Hans Heysen, was one of many women who experienced humiliation as an artist; Greer described humiliation as an obstacle for women making art. Not only did Heysen experience humiliation but also she was forgotten for four decades:

> it took 62 years before a painting by Nora Heysen was hung in the country's National Portrait Gallery. Yet for the first three decades of her life, she was something of a star. Showing prodigious talent from an early age, in 1938 she was the first woman to win the country's pre-eminent art prize, the Archibald, and, in 1943, as Australia's first female Official War Artist she created 170 paintings and drawings. However, after the war, her fame faded, and she was sorely neglected by the Australian art community until the late 1980s.[27]

Heysen, who studied painting in Adelaide, Sydney and Europe, explained how she was crushed by her experience in London where renowned painter, art historian and former director of London's National Gallery Charles Holmes laughed at her work. He later wrote her a letter of apology, but the damage was done. Other powerful men in the art establishment also

26 National Gallery of Australia, 'Know My Name'.

27 Jennifer Higgie, 'Archibald Winner Nora Heysen Was Crushed by Men Who Laughed at Her Art', *Sydney Morning Herald*, 1 April 2021, www.smh.com.au/culture/art-and-design/archibald-winner-nora-heysen-was-crushed-by-men-who-laughed-at-her-art-20210316-p57b4b.html.

criticised her work harshly. In Australia, painter Max Meldrum, grumpy that Heysen had won the Archibald Prize in 1938 and he had not, published an ungracious, patronising response to her win in Brisbane's Sunday Mail. Beneath the headline 'Domestic Ties Downfall of Women Art Careerists', he wrote: 'If I were a woman I would prefer raising a healthy family to a career in art. They are more attached to the physical things in life.'[28]

Heysen's win made her other enemies. Newspapers were inundated with letters from irate readers, some of whom alleged that the Heysen family and friends had influenced the judges.[29] Nora Heysen later said:

> That was a surprise to me; I wasn't aware of this [kind of attitude] as it wasn't in my home ... Among artists I wasn't conscious that women were being treated differently. Art's art to me, whoever does it, men or women or what.[30]

Emily Kam Kngwarreye (c. 1910–1996) started making batik in her remote Northern Territory community of Utopia around 1977. Ten years later she moved to paint on canvas, for which she quickly received institutional recognition in Australia, followed by international acclaim. Jeannette Hoorn suggests that Kngwarreye 'has achieved greater recognition than perhaps any other Australian artist', male or female, yet she suffered 'sexist and racist attacks on her sexuality and working practice even in catalogues which sought to honour her'.[31] Hoorn writes:

> One [male art historian and critic] famously referred to the brilliant Australian artist as 'profligate' and another [male art historian] attempted to disallow her status as one of the world's iconic artists suggesting that because she had passed the menopause, she now worked in a state of 'suspended femininity' and therefore was neither 'a great female artist' or 'a new modernist hero'![32]

'These are just two examples', writes Hoorn, 'of the many attempts that have been made by men who seek to minimise female greatness'.[33]

28 'Domestic Ties Downfall of Women Art Careerists', *Brisbane Mail*, 23 January 1939, cited in Speck, 'Nora Heysen', 190–1.

29 'Archibald Prize: Enquiry Urged', *Argus*, 11 March 1939; 'Knockabout', *Daily News*, 13 March 1939; 'Letter to the Editor', *Sydney Morning Herald*, 14 March 1939, cited in Speck, 'Nora Heysen'.

30 Higgie, 'Archibald winner Nora Heysen Was Crushed by Men Who Laughed at Her Art.'

31 Hoorn, 'Know My Name', 130.

32 Ibid.; Smith, 'Kngwarreye Woman Abstract Painter', 25; Benjamin, 'A New Modernist Hero', 52.

33 Hoorn, 'Know My Name', 130.

Under the heading 'Love', Greer discusses women artists who subjugated themselves to male artists, reflecting the relative social roles of men and women. The chapter is full of names from the history of art, including Australian artist Stella Bowen, who travelled to England in 1914 where she was 'completely crushed' by a professor who interviewed her for the Slade.[34] In 1918, Bowen fell in love with British novelist Ford Madox Ford. She devoted herself to him for the next eight years, including giving birth to their daughter Julie in 1920. Ford's infidelities, and the impact they had on Bowen who was left on her own to raise their daughter, are well known. But, even before their marriage breakdown, Bowen has described how her relationship with Ford 'hopelessly interfered with' her painting:

> for I was learning the technique of quite a different role: that of consort to another and more important artist, so that although Ford was always urging me to paint, I simply had not got any creative vitality to spare after I had played my part towards him and Julie and struggled through the day's chores.[35]

Olive Cotton (1911–2003) was one of Australia's pioneering modernist photographers. Like most of the other women artists I have mentioned so far, she had a privileged upbringing in an affluent, cultured family. The gift of a Kodak Box Brownie camera at age eleven inspired her to take up photography. After graduating with a bachelor of arts from the University of Sydney, she joined her childhood friend Max Dupain in 1934 in his studio as an assistant to him and his male employees Geoffrey Powell and Damien Parer. She managed to achieve what her biographer Helen Ennis described as 'an impressive and unusual degree of visibility' given her gender and 'comparatively low professional standing' as a studio assistant when her work was selected for two key shows in Australia and two of her images, *Winter Willows* and *Shasta Daisies*, appeared in the London Salon of Photography in 1938.[36]

The same year, the *Sydney Morning Herald*'s mid-week 'Women's Supplement' featured Cotton in an article entitled 'The Lady behind the Lens: Young Sydney Artist Discusses a Hobby for Women', which trivialised her work.[37] Nonetheless, the article enabled Cotton to provide some useful insights into her thoughts on photography.

34 Greer, *Obstacle Race*, 319.

35 Ibid., 53.

36 Ennis, *Olive Cotton*, 174.

37 Ibid.; 'The Lady behind the Lens', *Sydney Morning Herald*, 29 March 1938, 13.

When she and Dupain married in 1939, Cotton ceased working at the studio, possibly out of social convention; however, she later ran the studio while Dupain worked as a camoufleur during World War II. Within a few years, Cotton decided to leave the marriage: 'There … wasn't enough regard, consideration or affection … and she suffered multiple humiliations and betrayals, large and small, which she decided not to bear any longer.'[38] She disappeared from the art scene when she married Ross McInerney and moved to central western New South Wales where she gave birth to two children. The family lived simply, without electricity or running water, both essential for processing and printing photographs.[39] She taught at Cowra High School from 1959 to 1963, before leaving teaching to establish a commercial photography business in Cowra where she produced group and individual portraits and wedding and passport photographs. It was not until the 1980s that feminism and increasing interest in the history of photography drew her early work back into the art world's eye. An Australia Council grant encouraged her to reprint early negatives and a retrospective in Sydney attracted critical acclaim. She became a national name and was redefined as a key pioneer of modern photography, finally shaking off her connection with Max Dupain.[40]

By the time Rosalie was seriously making art, her children were grown and she had the freedom to create. In terms of criticism, James Mollison was direct with her if he disapproved of something she had made or the direction in which her art was moving. Rosalie said of Mollison: 'He was very cruel, he could be very cruel.'[41] Mollison himself said it took Rosalie years to get over his 'bullying' of her; as noted in Chapter 11, he said he 'couldn't be bothered being kind about it. If she's wrong she's just wrong. And if she goes wrong she's no longer an artist.'[42] There were other criticisms, too, which caused Rosalie some distress. For example, she was unhappy when Brisbane art dealer Ray Hughes and others misconstrued her work as nostalgic.[43] While Rosalie received more acclaim than criticism, the latter still hurt.

38 Ennis, *Olive Cotton*; Helen Ennis, 'Photographers Olive Cotton and Max Dupain Were 'Inseparable'—Until Married Life Came into Focus', *Sydney Morning Herald*, 19 October 2019, www.smh.com.au/culture/art-and-design/photographers-olive-cotton-and-max-dupain-were-inseparable-until-married-life-came-into-focus-20191015-p530uo.html.

39 Ennis, *Olive Cotton*.

40 Ahmed, 'Olive Cotton 1911–2003'.

41 Hughes et al., 'Rosalie Gascoigne Artist', tape 4.

42 James Mollison, interview by author, 2011.

43 Gascoigne, interview by North, 22.

An obstacle Greer highlighted that does not appear to have affected Rosalie was 'dimension'. According to Greer, the socialisation of girls and women to not draw attention to themselves and the resulting lack of confidence meant that they often made art on a small scale, which was considered inferior to the 'large heroic paintings by men'.[44] This was not Rosalie's experience. While she did begin with 'domestic' art, this reflected her life at the time. Inspired by the sight of a marigold pushing through weeds and rubbish on Mt Stromlo, she began growing flowers. She discovered a talent for flower arranging, subsequently branching out into Sogetsu Ikebana. While some of her initial works were small, the big works she also made suggest she was never confined by lack of confidence. A very early work, *Fountain* (c. 1966–68), made of rusted metal, was about one-and-a-half-metres tall.[45] *Last Stand* (1972), comprising nine towers of weathered sheep and cattle bones threaded on rusted iron steel rods, is three-metres tall.[46] In her earlier ikebana practice, she was drawn to making 'big things hoisted up in the air'.[47] Later, she made great canvases of road signs sawn into pieces and rearranged in grid patterns, the signs swapped for slabs of beer with roadworkers in the Canberra hinterland.

The constraints outlined by Greer in *Obstacle Race* varied at different times and places; however, as outlined above, a common thread of domesticity and childrearing, along with gendered attitudes and public gallery acquisition policies, created obstacles for women artists of Rosalie's era.

Some words on women artists and institutional amnesia about their work

The year 1975 was International Women's Year. Rosalie held her first exhibition that year and Janine Burke organised *Australian Women Artists: 1840–1940*. A touring exhibition, *Australian Women Artists*, the first exhibition to be devoted to art solely by women, had its first showing at the University of Melbourne's Ewing and George Paton Galleries. An earlier exhibition, the *First Australian Exhibition of Women's Work*, held in Melbourne in 1907, had dealt with a wider range of women's work—fine

44 Greer, *Obstacle Race*, 104–14.
45 Gascoigne, *Rosalie Gascoigne: A Catalogue Raisonné*, 147.
46 Ibid., 150.
47 Thomas, 'Rhythm & Lift-Off', 15.

arts, applied arts, photography, horticulture, literature, music and elocution, physical culture, needlework, cookery, laundry, teaching and nursing.[48] In mounting *Australian Women Artists*, Burke explained:

> I wanted to find painting of the highest calibre. I wasn't interested in special pleading for women artists and I never have been. I was looking for excellent work—not *excellent women's work*—but damned good paintings. I found them.[49]

Numerous subsequent exhibitions of women's art have been held. For example: *The Women's Show*, curated by the Women's Art Movement collective in Adelaide (1977; unselected—open to all); the Sydney Women's Art Festival (1983); *Aboriginal Women's Art Exhibition* (1991) at the Art Gallery of New South Wales (AGNSW); and *Review: Works by Women* (2021), which included three hundred works by more than eighty artists from AGNSW's Australian collection.[50] Another exhibition that deserves mention is *Contemporary Australia: Women* curated by Julie Ewington at the Gallery of Modern Art and Queensland Art Gallery in 2012, which featured the work of fifty-six female artists. This exhibition highlighted the ways in which Australian women's art practices have been essential to key developments in art, both nationally and internationally, over the previous forty years.[51]

A flurry of feminist activity and writing in the 1970s raised the issue of women's representation in the art world. Since 2008, the *Countess Report*, a collaboration between Elvis Richardson, Amy Prcevich and Miranda Samuels, has been gathering data on gender representation (non-binary, female, male) in Australian art, supported by the Sheila Foundation, a national philanthropic foundation with a mission to overturn decades of gender bias by writing Australian women artists back into our art history and ensuring equality for today's women artists.

Almost fifty years after Janine Burke's *Australian Women Artists*, the National Gallery of Australia in Canberra launched *Know My Name: Australian Women Artists 1900 to Now* (November 2020 – June 2022), a 'gender equity initiative' that was the largest exhibition of art solely by women launched in Australia, with 350 artworks by 170 artists.[52] The National Gallery of

48 Museums Victoria, 'First Australian Exhibition of Women's Work'.
49 Burke, 'Sex, Destiny and Amnesia', 15.
50 Marsh, 'Know My Name'.
51 Ewington, *Contemporary Australia: Women*.
52 Mendelssohn, 'Beauty and Audacity'.

Australia (NGA) claimed that the exhibition 'celebrate[s] the work of all women artists with an aim to enhance understanding of their contribution to Australia's cultural life'.[53]

The need for this exhibition suggests that, despite half a century of visibility, nothing much has changed, leading some commentators to ask why this is the case. Art writer Anne Brennan points out that:

> There is a good argument to say that large omnibus exhibitions such as this have outlived their usefulness as a strategy for making the work of women artists visible. If their purpose is to remind institutions of the rich contribution of women artists to the cultural life of the nation, why hasn't that task already been achieved by similar exhibitions that have preceded it?[54]

Jeanette Hoorn, referring to *Know My Name* and the 1975 exhibition, asked:

> Here the works of a great many artists who had disappeared from view were enthusiastically welcomed by spectators and reviewers alike. Will we again, in fifty years' time, see another exhibition desperately seeking recognition for Australian women artists?[55]

Professor Anne Marsh went further, calling it 'almost criminal that our national collection needs to be attended to in the 21st century'.[56] Because of the thin pickings of art made by women in the NGA collection, *Know My Name* borrowed much work from other collections and commissioned work especially for the exhibition. Only 25 per cent of art in the NGA's Australian collection and 33 per cent in the Aboriginal and Torres Strait Islander collection is made by women. And yet, as Jeannette Hoorn writes in the *Australian and New Zealand Journal of Art*:

> There is no doubt that the art of Australian women is equal in quality to the nation's male artists and that during several periods in our history has undoubtedly surpassed it.[57]

One period Hoorn refers to is the first thirty years of the twentieth century when, she says, 'Australian women were the leaders in the introduction of modernism, especially bringing post-impressionist practice to our [Australian]

53 National Gallery of Australia , 'About Know My Name'.
54 Brennan, 'Group Exhibition'.
55 Hoorn, 'Know My Name'.
56 Marsh, 'Know My Name'
57 Hoorn, 'Know My Name', 128.

shores.'[58] She refers to artists such as Margaret Preston, Hilda Rix Nicholas and Ethel Carrick. The last two 'were in the vanguard of [the] first wave of female modernists working in Europe before 1914, which also includes Iso Rae, Agnes Goodsir, Marie Tuck, Evelyn Chapman and Bessie Gibson.'[59] There is also Grace Cossington Smith, who Daniel Thomas suggests painted 'the first fully Post-Impressionist painting in Australia', *The Sock Knitter*.[60]

The next wave, larger than the first, includes Janet Cumbrae Stewart, Grace Crowley, Dorrit Black and Anne Dangar.[61] There are too many to name and do justice to. And with the increasing availability of art education, numbers have blossomed further.

In 'Sex, Destiny and Amnesia: The Fate of Women Artists', Janine Burke describes how, every time there is an exhibition or book of women's art or artists, she is asked the same questions over and over: 'why [do] these questions need to be asked again and again'? Echoing Hoorn's question above, Burke wonders why women artists need to be constantly rediscovered.[62] Regarding her book on Joy Hester, she wrote:

> I have found, particularly through my own writings on Joy Hester … that it is not enough to write one book, hold one exhibition and let it rest there. The price of recovery is, apparently, [to] again sink into obscurity. I would estimate it is *twice as difficult* to maintain the reputation of a woman artist as that of a man.[63]

Conclusion

Time will tell regarding Rosalie's art legacy. She did not have difficulty getting recognised. She was in the right place at the right time. Her family of origin meant she enjoyed the benefits of a good education. Her marriage to Ben Gascoigne gave her the time and means to develop her visual acuity and to explore the means of expression that led her to her art—gardening, flower arranging, Sogetsu Ikebana. She had no need to earn a living. Her social connections gave her access to James Mollison, the foundation director of the NGA, and to his team of curators. This is not to deny her talent, but talent

58 Ibid.
59 Ibid.
60 Thomas, 'Smith, Grace Cossington (1892–1984)'.
61 Hoorn, 'Know My Name', 128.
62 Burke, 'Sex, Destiny and Amnesia'.
63 Ibid.

alone is insufficient for recognition. As Anne Marsh acknowledges, 'it is … extremely difficult to maintain a long-term art practice without some form of institutional support or recognition'.[64] Rosalie achieved institutional support and recognition early in her artistic career. Within just a few years of her first solo exhibition, at Macquarie Galleries in Canberra, major public art institutions had begun purchasing her work for their collections. In 1978, just three years after her first exhibition, the National Gallery of Victoria held a major survey of her work; in 1982 she was the first woman chosen to represent Australia at the Venice Biennale; in 1983 the then National Art Gallery of New Zealand, in partnership with Sculpture Australia, held a touring exhibition *Rosalie Gascoigne: Sculpture 1975–1982*. And so it continued for her, with inclusion in exhibitions in Asia and Europe. In 2019 ANU Press published *Rosalie Gascoigne: A Catalogue Raisonné* compiled by her son Martin Gascoigne. Her work was included in the NGA's *Know My Name: Australian Women Artists 1900 to Now* and, in 2021–22, it appeared alongside that of Indigenous artist Lorraine Connelly-Northey at the National Gallery of Victoria's Ian Potter Gallery in Melbourne.

Although we can discern sociological patterns in constraints and responses, all these women artists' stories differ. Earlier women artists' stories differ from Rosalie Gascoigne in significant ways. Importantly, Rosalie did not come to recognise herself as an artist until later in life. Further, she began making art during a time when the public and art institutions were beginning to be more accepting of women in general.

That Rosalie does not fit into any neat art boxes, that she did not see herself as an artist when she arrived in Australia in 1943, that self-recognition as an artist was a long time coming—these are significant factors in her story. Likewise, that she lived in Canberra when the national collection and the NGA were being built; that she knew James Mollison personally; that he saw her promise and mentored her (although he denied that to me); that she enjoyed the luxury of not needing to earn a living; that attitudes to women were changing and with them public policies, thanks to feminism and the feminist women who advocated for change. Talent and circumstance—connections, right time, right place—came together for Rosalie. Her stars were in alignment to get her 'own sort of heaven'.

64 Marsh, 'Know My Name'.

Bibliography

Oral history

Rosalie Gascoigne's interviews

Feneley, Stephen and Rosalie Gascoigne. 'Express Highlights—Rosalie Gascoigne. Interview with Stephen Feneley, 4 December 1997'. Australian Broadcasting Corporation. www.abc.net.au/arts/express/stories/rose.htm (site discontinued). Transcript in author's possession.

Gascoigne, Rosalie. In conversation with Max Cullen. *Sunday*. Nine Network, 12 July 1998.

Gascoigne, Rosalie. Interview by Stephen Feneley for *Arts Express*, ABC TV, 4 December 1997. Transcript in Papers of Rosalie Gascoigne, 1930–2011. National Library of Australia.

Gascoigne, Rosalie. Interview by Helen Topliss, 26 February 1995. Transcript. National Library of Australia.

Gascoigne, Rosalie. Interview by Ian North, 9 February 1982. Transcript. National Gallery of Australia Research Library.

Gascoigne, Rosalie. Interview by James Gleeson, 8 February 1980. Transcript. National Gallery of Australia. nga.gov.au/media/dd/documents/gascoigne.pdf.

Hughes, Robin, Rosalie Gascoigne, Film Australia and SBS Television. 'Rosalie Gascoigne Artist'. Interview for *Australian Biography*, November 1999. www.australianbiography.gov.au/subjects/gascoigne/interview1.html (site discontinued). See www.collection.nfsa.gov.au/title/420947.

Survey 2, Rosalie Gascoigne: National Gallery of Victoria, 29 April 1978 to 4 June 1978. Melbourne: National Gallery of Victoria, 1978. Videocassette, 17 min. Includes interview with Rosalie Gascoigne by Robert Lindsay.

Author's interviews

Barry, Harriet. Interview by author. Canberra, 27 January 2011.

Brown, Jan. Interview by author. Canberra, 23 September 2011.

Brownson, Ron. Interview by author. Auckland, 18 October 2010.

Friedlander, Marti. Interview by author. Auckland, 19 October 2010.

Gascoigne, Ben and Hester. Interview by author. Canberra, 20 March 2010.

Gascoigne, Hester. Interview by author. Canberra, 20 February 2011.

Gascoigne, Martin. Interview by author. Canberra, 9 December 2014.

Gellatly, Kelly. Interview by author. Melbourne, 3 November 2011.

Greenaway, Paul. Interview by author. Adelaide, 10 July 2012.

Hagerty, Marie and Peter Vandermark. Interview by author. Canberra, 24 January 2011.

McLeavey, Peter. Interview by author. Wellington, 15 April 2010.

Mollison, James. Interview by author. Melbourne, 2 November 2011.

North, Ian. Interview by author. Adelaide, 13 December 2012.

Pether, Louise. Interview by author. Auckland, 19 October 2010.

Riek, Mary. Interview by author. Canberra, 26 November 2012.

Waterhouse, Dawn. Interview by author. Canberra, 24 July 2014.

Archival records

Auckland Council. 'Lot 84, MacMurray Road'. Property Records, 1915–23.

Auckland Council. 'Lot 92, Robert Hall Avenue'. Property Records, 1915–23.

Dobson, Rosemary. 'Rosalie Gascoigne 1917–1999: A Memoir'. In Papers of Rosalie Gascoigne 1930–2011. National Library of Australia.

Fröhlich, Ernest Frederick. 'Diary of Ernst Fröhlich, 1940–1941'. National Library of Australia.

Marriage of Marion Hamilton Metcalfe and Stanley King Walker, St Mary's, Parnell. Auckland Anglican Archives, Register 1027.

Metcalfe, George Hamilton—WW1 13056—Army. R107880509, 18805. Archives New Zealand Te Rua Mahara o te Kāwanatanga, Wellington. ndhadeliver.natlib.govt.nz/delivery/DeliveryManagerServlet?dps_pid=IE11884759.

New Zealand Department of Internal Affairs, Births, Deaths and Marriages. 'Death Registration, Auckland District, No. 955, Quarter Ending 31 September 1931, Ellen Mary Metcalfe'.

New Zealand Department of Internal Affairs, Births, Deaths and Marriages. 'Death Registration Printout Number 3528/1977, Douglas Hamilton Walker'.

New Zealand Electoral Roll, 1914, Parnell Roll, 172. See ancestry.com.

Numerical List of Reservists—Alphabetical Index. Archives New Zealand Te Rua Mahara o te Kāwanatanga, Wellington.

Official Assignee. 'Walker, Stanley King. Auckland Insolvency File'. Supreme Court of New Zealand, Northern District, R12170174, 1922–23. Archives New Zealand Te Rua Matura o te Kāwanatanga, Auckland.

Papers of Ben Gascoigne 1938–2007. National Library of Australia.

Papers of Clabon Walter Allan, 1922–1953. National Library of Australia.

Papers of Rosalie Gascoigne, 1930–2011. National Library of Australia.

Probate for METCALFE, Ellen Mary. BBAE 1570 153 570/1931. Archives New Zealand Te Rua Matura o te Kāwanatanga, Auckland.

Sculpture Australia/Rosalie Gascoigne. Exhibition files, 1983–84. MU000006/017/0008. Museum of New Zealand Te Papa Tongarewa, Wellington.

'Service of Thanksgiving for the Life of Rosalie Gascoigne, Friday 5 November 1999, St Paul's Anglican Church, Manuka ACT'. Order of service in author's possession.

Walker, Douglas Hamilton. Army no. 46701. Service record supplied by Headquarters New Zealand Defence Force Te Ope Kātua O Aotearoa, Personnel Archives, Private Bag 905, Upper Hutt 5140, New Zealand.

Newspapers and periodicals

Age (Melbourne)
Ashburton Guardian (NZ)
Auckland Star (NZ)
Auckland Weekly News (NZ)
Canberra Times
Chicago Tribune (US)
Christchurch Press (NZ)
Colonist (NZ)
Evening Post (NZ)
King Country Chronicle (NZ)
Kiwi (Auckland University College, NZ)
Nelson Evening Mail (NZ)
New Zealand Graphic and Ladies Journal
New Zealand Herald
New Zealand Listener
New Zealand Observer
New Zealand Truth
North Otago Times (NZ)
Northern Advocate (NZ)
Poverty Bay Herald (NZ)
Salient (NZ)
Sun (Melbourne)
Taranaki Daily News (NZ)
Te Korero (EGGS magazine, NZ)
Te Puke Times (NZ)
Telegraph (London)
Thames Star (NZ)
Waikato Times (NZ)
Wairarapa Daily Times (NZ)
Wanganui Chronicle (NZ)

All other sources

Agostino, Michael and The Australian National University School of Art. *The Australian National University School of Art: A History of the First 65 Years.* Canberra: The Australian National University School of Art, 2009. doi.org/10.22459/ANUSA.2010.

Ahmed, Hannah. 'Olive Cotton 1911–2003'. Hundred Heroines. hundredheroines.org/historical-heroines/olive-cotton/.

Albers, Robert H. 'Shame: A Dynamic in the Etiology of Violence'. *Dialog* 36, no. 4 (1997): 254–65.

Albers, Robert H. *Shame: A Faith Perspective.* New York: Routledge, Taylor & Francis Group, 1995.

Allen, Christopher. *Art in Australia: From Colonization to Postmodernism.* London: Thames and Hudson, 1997.

Anderson, Patricia. 'Mollison's Creation'. *Australian Book Review*, no. 256 (November 2003): 23.

Arrow, Michelle. 'Damned Whores and God's Police Is Still Relevant to Australia 40 Years On—More's the Pity'. *Conservation*, 21 September 2015. theconversation.com/damned-whores-and-gods-police-is-still-relevant-to-australia-40-years-on-mores-the-pity-47753.

Art Gallery of New South Wales, ed. *Australian Perspecta 1981: A Biennial Survey of Contemporary Australian Art.* Sydney: Art Gallery of New South Wales, 1981. Exhibition catalogue.

Art Gallery of New South Wales. *Colin McCahon: A Survey Exhibition.* Auckland: Auckland City Art Gallery, 1972.

Auckland Botanic Gardens. 'Meryta sinclairii'. www.aucklandbotanicgardens.co.nz/plants-for-auckland/plants/meryta-sinclairii/.

Auckland Council. 'Ōhinerau / Mt Hobson Path'. www.aucklandcouncil.govt.nz/parks-recreation/get-outdoors/aklpaths/Pages/path-detail.aspx?ItemId=394.

Australian Astronomical Observatory. 'The Anglo-Australian Telescope'. Australian Government Department of Industry and Science. www.aao.gov.au/about-us/anglo-australian-telescope (site discontinued).

The Australian National University. 'A Home on the Hill'. saa.anu.edu.au/observatories/mount-stromlo-observatory/heritage-trail-and-director-s-residence.

The Australian National University. 'Acton Campus—Site Inventory'. content.anu.edu.au/files/campus-map-poi/124.-innovations-building-final.pdf.

Australian War Memorial. 'Rationing of Food and Clothing during the Second World War'. www.awm.gov.au/articles/encyclopedia/homefront/rationing.

Bain, Alison. 'Constructing an Artistic Identity'. *Work, Employment and Society* 19, no. 1 (2005): 25–46. doi.org/10.1177/0950017005051280.

Bainbridge, Scott. 'The Death of Elsie Walker'. In *Shot in the Dark: Unsolved New Zealand Murders from the 1920s and 30s*, 193–272. Crows Nest: Allen & Unwin, 2010.

Banbury, Campbell Grant. 'Rosalie Gascoigne Reassembled: Ikebana and the Grid'. PGDip thesis, University of Melbourne, 1994.

Bancroft, Angus, Sarah Wilson, Sarah Cunningham-Burley, Kathryn Backett-Milburn and Hugh Masters. *Parental Drug and Alcohol Misuse: Resilience and Transition among Young People*. York: Joseph Rowntree Foundation, 2004.

Barry, Kathleen. 'Biography and the Search for Women's Subjectivity'. *Women's Studies International Forum* 12, no. 6 (1989): 561–77. doi.org/10.1016/0277-5395(89)90001-0.

Beeby, C. E. *The Biography of an Idea: Beeby on Education*. Wellington: New Zealand Council for Educational Research, 1992.

Belich, James. *Paradise Reforged: A History of the New Zealanders from the 1880s to the Year 2000*. Auckland: Penguin Press, 2001.

Benjamin, Roger. 'A New Modernist Hero'. In *Emily Kame Kngwarreye: Alkahere: Paintings from Utopia*, edited by M. Neale, 52. South Yarra: Macmillan, 1998.

Bhathal, Ragbir, Ralph Sutherland and Harvey Butcher. *Mt Stromlo Observatory: From Bush Observatory to the Nobel Prize*. Canberra: CSIRO Publishing, 2013. doi.org/10.1071/9781486300761.

Biennale of Sydney. 'About Us'. www.biennaleofsydney.art/about-us/#overview.

Bird, Michael. *The St Ives Artists: A Biography of Place and Time*. Aldershot: Lund Humphries, 2008.

Blaxland, Helen. *Collected Flower Pieces*. Sydney: Ure Smith, 1948.

Blaxland, Helen. *Flower Pieces: On the Arrangement of Flowers*. Sydney: Ure Smith, 1949.

Blaxland, Helen and Elaine Haxton. *Flower Pieces*. Sydney: Ure Smith, 1946.

Block, René, Gregory Burke, Museum Fridericianum and Auckland Art Gallery. *Toi Toi Toi: Three Generations of Artists from New Zealand.* Kassel and Auckland: Museum Fridericianum and Auckland Art Gallery Toi o Tāmaki, 1999. Exhibition catalogue.

Boden, Susan and Nicholas Brown. 'Made in Canberra'. In *Canberra Red: Stories from the Bush Capital,* edited by David Headon and Andrew MacKenzie, 171–92. Crows Nest: Allen & Unwin, 2013.

Book, Natalie. 'Albert Tucker: Explorers and Intruders'. *Time Out.* www.au.timeout.com/melbourne/art/events/7967/albert-tucker-explorers-and-intruders (site discontinued).

Bottrell, Fay and Stacey Wesley. *The Artist Craftsman in Australia, Aspects of Sensibility.* 2nd ed. Crow's Nest: Jack Pollard, 1972.

Boyarin, Jonathan, ed. *Remapping Memory: The Politics of Timespace.* Minnesota: University of Minnesota Press, 1994.

Brennan, Anne. 'Group Exhibition "Know My Name: Australian Women Artists 1900 to Now"'. The Review Board, 17 August 2021. thereviewboard.com.au/review/group-exhibition-know-my-name-australian-women-artists-1900-to-now/.

Brookes, Barbara. *A History of New Zealand Women.* Wellington: Bridget Williams Books, 2016. doi.org/10.7810/9780908321452.

Brown, Hayley Marina. 'Loosening the Marriage Bond: Divorce in New Zealand, c.1890s–c.1950s'. PhD thesis, Victoria University of Wellington, 2011.

Brown, Nicholas. *A History of Canberra.* Cambridge: Cambridge University Press, 2014.

'"The Brown Pot (1940)": Margaret Preston'. www.artgallery.nsw.gov.au/collection/works/7223/.

Burke, Janine. 'Sex, Destiny and Amnesia: The Fate of Women Artists'. *Art Monthly Australia,* no. 126 (December 1999–February 2000): 15.

Butchers, Arthur Gordon. *Education in New Zealand.* Dunedin: Coulls Somerville Wilkie, 1930.

Butler, Janet. *Kitty's War: The Remarkable Wartime Experiences of Kit McNaughton.* St Lucia: University of Queensland Press, 2013.

Butler, Roger. 'Proctor, Alethea Mary (Thea) (1879–1966)'. *Australian Dictionary of Biography.* National Centre of Biography, The Australian National University. Published first in hardcopy 1988. adb.anu.edu.au/biography/proctor-alethea-mary-thea-8122/text14187.

Butler, Roger and Gordon Darling. 'A Twenty-Year Relationship: L. Gordon Darling in Conversation with Roger Butler, Senior Curator of Australian Prints and Drawings'. In *Building the Collection*, edited by Pauline Green, 128–47. Canberra: National Gallery of Australia, 2003.

Butlin, S. J. and C. B. Schedvin. *War Economy, 1942–1945*. Canberra: Australian War Memorial, 1977.

Byrne, Caitlin. 'Public Diplomacy in an Australian Context: A Policy-Based Framework to Enhance Understanding and Practice'. PhD thesis, Bond University, 2009.

Caine, Barbara. *Biography and History*. Basingstoke: Palgrave Macmillan, 2010.

Cameron, Dan. 'Introduction'. In *What Is Contemporary Art?*, edited by Peter Edstrom, Helene Mohlin and Anna Palmqvist. Malmö: Roosmuseum, 1989.

Cameron, Dan. 'Showdown at the Southern Cross: Notes on the 1988 Australian Biennale'. *Artlink* 8, no. 3 (September 1988): 10–14.

Cameron, Milton. 'Where Science Meets Art: Bischoff and the Gascoigne House'. In *Experiments in Modern Living: Scientists' Houses in Canberra 1950–1970*, 131–60. Canberra: ANU E Press, 2012. doi.org/10.22459/EML.05.2012.

Cameron, Milton Provan. 'Experiments in Modern Living: Scientists and the National Capital Private House 1925–1970'. PhD thesis, University of New South Wales, 2009.

Capon, Edward. 'Art Review'. artreview.com.au/contents/570568117-james-gleeson-1915-2008 (site discontinued).

Carmichael, Gordon, ed. *Trans-Tasman Migration: Trends, Causes and Consequences*. Canberra: Australian Government Publishing Service, 1993.

Carson, Rachel. *Silent Spring*. Boston: Houghton Mifflin, 1962.

Cheng, Linda. 'Historic Bruce Hall Loses Fight against Demolition'. *Architecture, AU*, 7 April 2017. architectureau.com/articles/historic-bruce-hall-at-anu-loses-fight-against-demolition/.

Churcher, Betty. 'The Years 1990 to 1997'. In *Building the Collection*, edited by Pauline Green, 164–75. Canberra: National Gallery of Australia, 2003.

Clark, Deborah. 'Standing on the Mountain: The Landscape Impulse in Rosalie Gascoigne's Art'. In *Rosalie Gascoigne*, edited by Kelly Gellatly, 28–33. Melbourne: Council of Trustees of the National Gallery of Victoria, 2008.

Clarke, Patricia. *Eileen Giblin: A Feminist between the Wars*. Clayton: Monash University Publishing, 2013.

Cohen, Deborah. *Family Secrets: Shame and Privacy in Modern Britain*. USA: Oxford University Press, 2013.

Commonwealth Rationing Commission. *Departmental History of Rationing of Clothing and Food, 1942–1950*. Melbourne: Commonwealth Rationing Commission, 1950.

Coxhead, Elizabeth. *Constance Spry: A Biography*. London: Luscombe, 1975.

Croft Cornford, Frances. *Poems*. Hampstead: Priory Press, 1910.

Crompton, Bob. 'Professor Ben Gascoigne, Astronomer'. Interview. Australian Academy of Science. www.science.org.au/learning/general-audience/history/interviews-australian-scientists/professor-ben-gascoigne-1915-2010.

Daley, Caroline. '"He Would Know, but I Just Have a Feeling": Gender and Oral History'. *Women's History Review* 7, no. 3 (1998): 343–59. doi.org/10.1080/09612029800200173.

Dalley, Bronwyn. 'The Cultural Remains of Elsie Walker'. In *Fragments: New Zealand Social and Cultural History*, edited by Bronwyn Dalley and Bronwyn Labrum, 140–62. Auckland: Auckland University Press, 2000.

Day, Maxwell F. C., Maxwell J. Whitten and Don Sands. 'Douglas Frew Waterhouse 1916–2000'. *Historical Records of Australian Science* 13, no. 4 (2001): 495–519. doi.org/10.1071/HR0011340495.

de Montfort, Patricia. 'Louise Jopling: A Biographical and Cultural Study of the Modern Woman Artist in Victorian Britain', *Journal of Victorian Culture* 23, no. 1 (January 2018): 137–9. doi.org/10.1093/jvcult/vcx008.

Donald, Richard. *Painting Out the Past: The Life and Art of Patricia France*. Dunedin: Longacre Press, 2008.

Downer, Helen and the New Zealand Free Kindergarten Union. *Seventy-Five Years of Free Kindergarten in New Zealand*. Dunedin: New Zealand Free Kindergarten Union, 1964.

Eagle, Mary. *Rosalie Gascoigne, 1985. 6–28 September 1985*. University of Tasmania Fine Arts Gallery. Hobart: University of Tasmania, 1985.

Eagle, Mary. 'Rosalie Gascoigne's Lyrical Derailments'. In *Brought to Light II: Contemporary Australian Art 1996–2006 from the Queensland Art Gallery Collection*, edited by Lynne Seear and Julie Ewington, 198–205. Brisbane: Queensland Art Gallery Publishing, 2007.

Eagle, Mary. *From the Studio of Rosalie Gascoigne, 5 September – 8 October 2000.* Canberra: The Australian National University, Drill Hall Gallery, 2000.

Eagle, Mary and John Jones. *A Story of Australian Painting.* Sydney: Macmillan, 1994.

Edstrom, Peter, Helene Mohllin and Anna Palmqvist, eds. *What Is Contemporary Art?* Malmö: Roosmuseum, 1989.

Edwards, Deborah. *Rosalie Gascoigne: Material as Landscape.* Sydney: Trustees of the Art Gallery of New South Wales, 1997. Book to accompany the Art Gallery of NSW exhibition *Rosalie Gascoigne: Material as Landscape*, 14 November 1997 – 11 January 1998.

Egan, Susannah. 'Review of Nicola King: *Memory, Narrative and Identity*'. *Biography* 24, no. 4 (2001): 922–4. doi.org/10.1353/bio.2001.0083.

Elliott, David, Howard Morphy, Rebecca Coates and Museum of Modern Art (Oxford). *In Place (Out of Time): Contemporary Art in Australia.* Oxford: Museum of Modern Art, 1997.

Ennis, Helen. *Olive Cotton: A Life in Photography.* Sydney: Harper Collins, 2019.

Erikson, Erik. *Childhood and Society.* 2nd ed. New York: W.W. Norton & Co., 1963.

Ewington, Julie. *Contemporary Australia: Women.* South Brisbane: Queensland Art Gallery, 2012.

Fernyhough, Charles. *Pieces of Light: The New Science of Memory.* London: Profile Books, 2013.

Fink, Hannah. 'Jim's Picnic'. Bonhams. www.bonhams.com/auctions/21362/lot/25/.

Fink, Hannah. 'The Life of Things: Rosalie Gascoigne at Gallery A Sydney'. In *Gallery A Sydney 1964–1983*, 147–63. Campbelltown: Campbelltown Arts Centre and Newcastle Region Art Gallery, 2009.

Fink, Hannah. 'Rosalie Gascoigne (1917–1999): Sunflowers 1991'. Bonhams. www.bonhams.com/auctions/21362/lot/51/.

Fink, Hannah. 'That Sidling Sight: Wondering about the Art of Rosalie Gascoigne'. *Art and Australia* 35, no. 2 (1997): 200–8.

First Canberra Garden Club Inc. 'The First Canberra Garden Club Inc: Our History from 1962 to 2012'. Canberra, 2012.

Flusser, Vilém. 'The Challenge of the Migrant'. Translated by Kenneth Kronenberg. In *The Freedom of the Migrant: Objections to Nationalism*, edited by Anke K. Finger, 13. Urbana: University of Illinois Press, 2003.

Flusser, Vilém. 'Exile and Creativity'. Translated by Kenneth Kronenberg. In *The Freedom of the Migrant: Objections to Nationalism*, edited by Anke K. Finger, 81–7. Urbana: University of Illinois Press, 2003.

Flusser, Vilém. *The Freedom of the Migrant: Objections to Nationalism*, edited by Anke K. Finger. Translated by Kenneth Kronenberg. Urbana: University of Illinois Press, 2003.

Fortune, Gabrielle. '"Mr Jones' Wives": War Brides, Marriage, Immigration and Identity Formation'. *Women's History Review* 15, no. 4 (2006): 587–99. doi.org/10.1080/09612020500530687.

Fox, James J. 'Emeritus Professor Derek Freeman'. Academy of the Social Sciences in Australia. www.assa.edu.au/fellowship/fellow/deceased/396 (site discontinued).

France, Christine, National Trust of Australia (New South Wales) and S. H. Ervin Museum and Art Gallery. *Merioola and After*. Sydney: The National Trust of Australia (NSW), 1986.

Francis, Niki. 'Churcher, 1931–2015'. The Australian Women's Register. www.womenaustralia.info/biogs/AWE4846b.htm.

Francis, Niki. 'Dobson, Rosemary De Brissac (1920–2012)'. The Australian Women's Register. www.womenaustralia.info/biogs/AWE4848b.htm.

Francis, Niki. 'Women Who Caucus: Feminist Political Scientists'. womenaustralia.info/exhib/caucus/essay.html.

Frost, Annabel. 'Rosalie Gascoigne: My Country Childhood'. *Country Style*, December 1997, 19–21.

Galbraith, John Kenneth. *The Affluent Society*. London: Hamish Hamilton, 1958.

Gascoigne, Martin. *New Zealand Lives: The New Zealand Families of Rosalie Gascoigne and of Ben Gascoigne*. Griffith: Martin Gascoigne, 2005.

Gascoigne, Martin. *Rosalie Gascoigne: A Catalogue Raisonné*. Canberra: ANU Press, 2019. doi.org/10.22459/RG.2019.

Gascoigne, Martin. *Rosalie Gascoigne: Her New Zealand Origins*. Martin Gascoigne, 2012.

Gascoigne, Martin. 'Rosalie's Artists'. In *Rosalie Gascoigne*, edited by Kelly Gellatly, 35–44. Melbourne: Council of Trustees of the National Gallery of Victoria, 2008.

Gascoigne, Rosalie. 'Colin McCahon: Victory over Death'. *Art and Australia* 21, no. 4 (1984): 490.

Gascoigne, S. C. B. 'Allen, Clabon Walter (Cla) (1904–1987)'. *Australian Dictionary of Biography*. National Centre of Biography, The Australian National University. Published first in hardcopy 2007. adb.anu.edu.au/biography/allen-clabon-walter-cla-12129/text21729.

Gascoigne, S. C. B. 'The Artist-in-Residence'. In *From the Studio of Rosalie Gascoigne*, edited by Mary Eagle, 9–15. Canberra: The Australian National University Drill Hall Gallery, 2000.

Gellatly, Kelly. 'Rosalie Gascoigne: Making Poetry of the Commonplace'. In *Rosalie Gascoigne*, edited by Kelly Gellatly, 9–27. Melbourne: Council of Trustees of the National Gallery of Victoria, 2008.

Gellatly, Kelly, Martin Gascoigne, Deborah Clark and National Gallery of Victoria. *Rosalie Gascoigne*. Melbourne: National Gallery of Victoria, 2008.

Gibbney, Jim. *Canberra 1913–1953*. Canberra: Australian Government Publishing Service, 1988.

Gill, Eleanor Francis. *Decorative Work for the Beginner*. Walcha: Walcha Horticultural Society, 1959.

Goodger, Kay. 'Maintaining Sole Parent Families in New Zealand: An Historical Review'. *Social Policy Journal of New Zealand* 10 (2008). www.msd.govt.nz/about-msd-and-our-work/publications-resources/journals-and-magazines/social-policy-journal/spj10/maintaining-sole-parent-families-in-new-zealand.html.

Green, Pauline, ed. *Building the Collection*. Canberra: National Gallery of Australia, 2003.

Greenaway, Paul. 'Rosalie Gascoigne AM'. *Artlink* 19, no. 4 (1999).

Greer, Germaine. *The Female Eunuch*. London: MacGibbon & Kee, 1970.

Greer, Germaine. *The Obstacle Race: The Fortunes of Women Painters and Their Work*. London: Book Club Associates, 1980.

Grimshaw, Patricia. *Colonialism, Gender and Representations of Race: Issues in Writing Women's History in Australia and the Pacific*. Melbourne: History Department, University of Melbourne, 1994.

Grimshaw, Patricia. 'Gendered Settlements'. In *Creating a Nation 1788–1990*, edited by Patricia Grimshaw, Marilyn Lake, Ann McGrath, Marian Quartly, 177–203. Ringwood: Penguin Books Australia, 1994.

Grishin, Sasha. *Australian Art: A History*. Carlton: The Miegunyah Press, 2013.

Gruenert, Stefan and Menka Tsantefski. 'Responding to the Needs of Children and Parents in Families Experiencing Alcohol and Other Drug Problems'. *Prevention Research Quarterly* 17 (May 2012). findanexpert.unimelb.edu.au/scholarly work/344474-responding-to-the-needs-of-children-and-parents-in-families-experiencing-alcohol-and-other-drug-problem.

Gustafson, Barry. *The First 50 Years: A History of the New Zealand National Party*. Auckland: Reed Methuen, 1986.

Haese, Richard. *Permanent Revolution: Mike Brown and the Australian Avant-Garde 1953–1997*. Melbourne: The Miegunyah Press, 2011.

Hamann, Conrad. 'Grounds, Sir Roy Burman (1905–1981)'. *Australian Dictionary of Biography*. National Centre of Biography, The Australian National University. Published first in hardcopy 2007. adb.anu.edu.au/biography/grounds-sir-roy-burman-12571/text22635.

Hamilton, Lolita. 'Physicality and Process: Representing an Evolving Practice through the Embodied Experience'. MA thesis, University of Wollongong, 2010.

Hancock, W. K. *The Battle of Black Mountain: An Episode of Canberra's Environmental History*. Canberra: Department of Economic History, Research School of Social Sciences, The Australian National University, 1974.

'Helen Bailey Bayly's Photo Album'. RSAA Picture Gallery. www.mso.anu.edu.au/gallery3/index.php/before2003/helen_bailey.

Hendrick, Harry. 'Children's Emotional Well-Being and Mental Health in Early Post-Second World War Britain: The Case of Unrestricted Hospital Visiting'. *Clio Medica* 71 (2003): 213–42. doi.org/10.1163/9789004333567_012.

Heritage New Zealand Pouhere Taonga. 'The National Art Gallery and Dominion Museum (Former), 7 Buckle Street, Mt Cook, Wellington'. www.heritage.org.nz/list-details/1409/National-Art-Gallery-and-Dominion-Museum-Former.

Hilary, Edmund. *Nothing Venture, Nothing Win*. London: Hodder & Stoughton, 1975.

Hinchco, Brian. 'A History of Middle Schooling in New Zealand'. EduSearch: New Zealand's Education Information Online. www.edusearch.co.nz/articles/3/article.htm?descriptions=&article=0000000157 (site discontinued).

Hogan, Janet and Queensland Art Gallery. *Diverse Visions: Twelve Australian Mid to Late Career Artists: Charles Blackman, Mike Brown, Ray Cooke, Rosalie Gascoigne, Inge King, Robert Klippel, Les Kossatz, Alun Leach-Jones, John Perceval, Gareth Sansom, Gordon Shepherdson, John Wolseley*. South Brisbane: Queensland Art Gallery, 1991.

Holland, Alison. 'Innovation, Art Practice and Japan–Australia Cultural Exchange during the 1970s and 1980s'. *Asia Pacific Journal of Arts and Cultural Management* 9, no. 1 (December 2012): 24–31.

Hoorn, Jeannette. 'Know My Name: Australian Women Artists 1900 to Now'. *Australian and New Zealand Journal of Art* 22, no. 1 (2022): 128–32. doi.org/10.1080/14434318.2022.2076035.

Horne, Donald. *The Lucky Country: Australia in the Sixties*. Ringwood: Penguin, 1964.

Ikäheimo, Heikki. 'A Vital Human Need: Recognition as Inclusion in Personhood'. *European Journal of Political Theory* 8, no. 31 (2009): 31–45. doi.org/10.1177/1474885108096958.

Jacobs, Genevieve. 'Rosalie Gascoigne'. *Art and Australia*, no. 44 (2006): 110–13.

John Curtin Prime Ministerial Library. 'Austerity, Liberty and Victory'. john.curtin.edu.au/legacyex/economy.html.

Jopling, Louise. *Twenty Years of My Life*. London: John Lane, 1925.

Karpel, Mark A. 'Family Secrets: I. Conceptual and Ethical Issues in the Relational Context. II. Ethical and Practical Considerations in Therapeutic Management'. *Family Process* 19, no. 3 (September 1980): 295–306. doi.org/10.1111/j.1545-5300.1980.00295.x.

Kent, Bruce. 'Packard, William Percival (Bill) (1925–2009)'. Obituaries Australia, National Centre of Biography, The Australian National University. oa.anu.edu.au/obituary/packard-willam-percival-bill-27128/text34674.

King, Nicola. *Memory, Narrative, Identity: Remembering the Self*. Edinburgh: Edinburgh University Press, 2000. doi.org/10.1515/9780748611164.

Kirker, Anne, Ian Wedde and Ewen McDonald. *Rosalie Gascoigne—Colin McCahon: Sense of Place*. Sydney: Ivan Dougherty Gallery and the University of New South Wales, 1990. Exhibition catalogue. On the occasion of the sesquicentenary of New Zealand.

'Know My Name Episode 6: Rosalie Gascoigne'. ABC Listen, 26 October 2021. Based on interview with Mary Lou Jelbart in 1994. www.abc.net.au/radionational/programs/the-art-show/know-my-name-ep-6:-rosalie-gascoigne/13607726.

Lawrence, D. H. *The Rainbow*. Harmondsworth, Middlesex: Penguin Books in association with William Heinemann Limited, 1950. First published in 1915.

Leese, P. J., B. Piatek and L. Curyllo-Klag, eds. *The British Migrant Experience, 1700–2000: An Anthology*. Basingstoke and New York: Palgrave Macmillan, 2002.

Levertov, Denise. 'Two Artists: I Rosalie Gascoigne II Memphis Wood'. *Meanjin* 41, no. 1 (1982): 20–2.

Lewin, Ben. *The Dunera Boys*. South Melbourne: Thomas Nelson, 1991.

MacDonald, Vici and Rosalie Gascoigne. *Rosalie Gascoigne*. Sydney: Regaro, 1997.

Malcolm, Janet. *The Silent Woman: Sylvia Plath & Ted Hughes*. Australia: Picador, 1994.

Marsh, Anne. 'Know My Name: Australian Women Artists 1900 to Now: An Historical Context'. *Artlink* 41, no.1 (April 2021). www.artlink.com.au/articles/4894/know-my-name-australian-women-artists-1900-to-now-/.

Maslow, A. H. 'A Theory of Human Motivation'. *Psychological Review* 50, no. 4 (1943): 370–96. doi.org/10.1037/h0054346.

McCallum, John. 'A Review of Field Club Research on the Northern Offshore Islands'. *Tane: The Journal of the Auckland University Field Club* 29 (1983): 223–46.

McCaughey, Patrick. *Strange Country: Why Australian Painting Matters*. Carlton: The Miegunyah Press, 2014.

McDonald, Ewen. 'There Are Only Lovers and Others: An Interview with Rosalie Gascoigne'. *Antic* 8 (December 1990): 10–13.

McQueen, Humphrey. *Suburbs of the Sacred*. Ringwood: Penguin, 1988.

Mendelssohn, Joanna. 'Beauty and Audacity: Know My Name Presents a New, Female Story of Australian Art, A Review: Know My Name: Australian Women Artists 1900 to Now, National Gallery of Australia'. *Conversation*, 17 November 2020. theconversation.com/beauty-and-audacity-know-my-name-presents-a-new-female-story-of-australian-art-150139.

Menzies, Robert. *The Measure of the Years*. London: Cassell, 1970.

Miller, Sarah, Cruthers Family and Perth Institute of Contemporary Arts. *In the Company of Women: 100 Years of Australian Women's Art from the Cruthers Collection*. Northbridge: Perth Institute for Contemporary Arts, 1995.

Mollison, James and Anne Gray. 'James Mollison in Conversation with Anne Gray, Head of Australian Art'. In *Building the Collection*, edited by Pauline Green, 23–31. Canberra: National Gallery of Australia, 2003.

Mollison, James and Steven Heath. 'Rosalie Gascoigne in Her Own Words'. In *Material as Landscape: Rosalie Gascoigne*, edited by Deborah Edwards, 7–8. Sydney: Trustees of the Art Gallery of New South Wales, 1997.

Moran, Louise. 'University House Ladies Drawing Room, Australian National University (1956–2002)'. The Australian Women's Register. www.womenaustralia.info/biogs/AWE4783b.htm.

Murray, Peta. 'Things That Fall Over: Women's Playwriting, Poetics and the (Anti-) Musical'. MA thesis, Queensland University of Technology, 2011.

Museum of Australian Democracy at Old Parliament House. 'National Capital Development Commission Act 1957'. www.foundingdocs.gov.au/item-sdid-114.html.

Museums Victoria. 'First Australian Exhibition of Women's Work, Exhibition Building, Melbourne, 23 Oct–30 Nov 1907'. Program. collections.museumsvictoria.com.au/items/2198527.

National Gallery of Australia. 'About Know My Name'. nga.gov.au/knowmyname/about/.

National Gallery of Victoria. *Found and Gathered: Rosalie Gascoigne | Lorraine Connelly-Northey*. Media release. www.ngv.vic.gov.au/wp-content/uploads/2021/08/NGV-MR_Rosalie-Gascoigne-Lorraine-Connelly-Northey-2.pdf.

National Gallery of Victoria. 'Rosalie Gascoigne: Landscape—Place, Memory, Experience'. www.ngv.vic.gov.au/wp-content/uploads/2014/10/ngv_edu_edres_gascoigne_landscape.pdf.

Neill, J. C. *The New Zealand Tunnelling Company, 1915–1919*. Auckland: Whitcombe & Tombs, 1922.

Nelson, Camilla. 'The Female Eunuch at 50, Germaine Greer's Fearless, Feminist Masterpiece'. *Conversation*, 9 October 2020. theconversation.com/friday-essay-the-female-eunuch-at-50-germaine-greers-fearless-feminist-masterpiece-147437.

Neuhouser, Frederick. *Rousseau's Theodicy of Self-Love: Evil, Rationality and the Drive for Recognition*. Oxford: Oxford University Press, 2008. doi.org/10.1093/acprof:oso/9780199542673.001.0001.

Neuman, Klaus and National Archives of Australia. *In the Interest of National Security: Civilian Internment in Australia During World War II*. Canberra: National Archives of Australia, 2006.

Nolan, Melanie. *Breadwinning: New Zealand Women and the State*. Christchurch: Canterbury University Press, 2000.

North, Ian. 'Rosalie Gascoigne: Signs of Light'. In *Australia: Venice Biennale 1982*, 47–68. Melbourne: Visual Arts Board of the Australia Council with the assistance of the Australian Department of Foreign Affairs, 1982.

North, Ian and Gary Catalano. *Australia, Venice Biennale 1982: Works by Peter Booth & Rosalie Gascoigne*. Melbourne: Visual Arts Board of the Australia Council with the assistance of the Australian Department of Foreign Affairs, 1982.

North, Ian, John Cattapan and University of South Australia Art Museum. *Expanse: Aboriginalities, Spatialities and the Politics of Ecstasy: An Exhibition: Jon Cattapan, Rosalie Gascoigne, Antony Hamilton, Kathleen Petyarre, Imants Tillers*. Adelaide: University of South Australia Art Museum, 1998.

Northey, Heather, J. A. Asher and M. Asher. *Auckland Girls' Grammar School: The First Hundred Years 1888–1988*. Auckland: Auckland Grammar School Old Girls' Association, 1988.

O'Brien, Gregory. 'Plain Air / Plain Song'. In *Rosalie Gascoigne: Plain Air*, edited by Gregory O'Brien, Paula Savage and City Gallery Wellington, 21–4. Wellington: City Gallery Wellington and Victoria University Press, 2004.

O'Brien, Gregory, Paula Savage and City Gallery Wellington. *Rosalie Gascoigne: Plain Air*. Wellington: City Gallery Wellington and Victoria University Press, 2004.

O'Brien, Margaret. *Designed Flower Arrangement*. Sydney: Angus & Robertson, 1958.

O'Neil, W. M. 'Waterhouse, Eben Gowrie (1881–1977)'. *Australian Dictionary of Biography*. National Centre of Biography, The Australian National University. Published first in hardcopy 1990. adb.anu.edu.au/biography/waterhouse-eben-gowrie-8991/text15827.

Olney, James. *Memory & Narrative: The Weave of Life-Writing*. Chicago: University of Chicago Press, 1998.

Ossman, Susan, ed. *The Places We Share: Migration, Subjectivity and Global Mobility*. Lanham: Lexington Books, 2007.

Page, Geoff. *Darker and Lighter*. Wollongong: Five Islands Press, 2001.

Passerini, Luisa. 'A Passion for Memory'. *History Workshop Journal* 72 (Autumn 2011): 241–50. doi.org/10.1093/hwj/dbr033.

Passerini, Luisa. 'Women's Personal Narratives: Myths, Experiences, and Emotions'. In *Interpreting Women's Lives: Feminist Theory and Personal Narratives*, edited by Personal Narratives Group, 189–97. Bloomington: Indiana University Press, 1989.

Patkin, Benzion. *The Dunera Internees*. Stanmore: Cassell Australia, 1979.

Pattison, Stephen. *Shame: Theory, Therapy, Theology*. Cambridge: Cambridge University Press, 2000. doi.org/10.1017/CBO9780511612411.

Pawson. Eric. 'Cars and the Motor Industry: A Motorised Society'. Te Ara—the Encyclopedia of New Zealand. www.teara.govt.nz/en/cars-and-the-motor-industry/page-1.

Pearl, Cyril. *The Dunera Scandal*. Port Melbourne: Mandarin Australia, 1990.

Phillips, J. 'War and National Identity'. In *Culture and Identity in New Zealand*, edited by David Novitz and Bill Willmott, 91–109. Wellington: GP Books, 1989.

Phillips, Jock. 'Arts and the Nation: Major Themes of Cultural Nationalism, 1930 to 1970'. Te Ara—the Encyclopedia of New Zealand. www.teara.govt.nz/en/zoomify/45016/colin-mccahons-northland-panels-1958.

Phillips, Jock. *A Man's Country? The Image of the Pakeha Male—A History*. Auckland: Penguin Books, 1987.

Piper, Alana and Ana Stevenson. 'The Long History of Gender Violence in Australia, and Why It Matters Today'. *Conversation*, 15 July 2019. theconversation.com/the-long-history-of-gender-violence-in-australia-and-why-it-matters-today-119927.

Poot, Jacques. 'Trans-Tasman Migration, Transnationalism and Economic Development in Australasia'. Motu Working Paper 09-05 (May 2009). motu-www.motu.org.nz/wpapers/09_05.pdf.

Portelli, Alessandro. *The Death of Luigi Trastulli and Other Stories: Form and Meaning in Oral History*. Edited by Michael Frisch. New York: State University of New York Press, 1991.

Preston, Edwina. *Bad Art Mother*. Mile End: Wakefield Press, 2022.

Rilke, Rainer Maria. *Letters to a Young Poet*. Translated by Stephen Mitchell. New York: Random House, 1984.

Roberts, Alan and Australian Academy of Science. *A Big, Bold, Simple Concept: A History of the Australian Academy of Science Dome.* Canberra: Australian Academy of Science, 2010.

Roberts, Pen. 'Discovering Tradition in Post-War Japan'. Australian War Memorial, 6 October 2010. www.awm.gov.au/blog/2010/10/06/discovering-tradition-in-post-war-japan/.

Rogers, Joyce and Lorraine Kloppman. *Australian Flower Arranging.* London: Paul Hamlyn, 1968.

Royal Buscombe. 'Royal Buscombe Collection'. The Field Museum. sites.google.com/a/fieldmuseum.org/pacific-web/Home/collections--collectors/recent-new-acquisitions-1/recent-new-acquisitions (site discontinued). See collections-anthropology.fieldmuseum.org/catalogue/1263188.

Ruvigny and Raineval, Melville Amadeus Henry Douglas Heddle de La Caillemotte de Massue de Ruvigny. *The Plantagenet Roll of the Blood Royal: The Mortimer-Percy Roll.* London: Melville & Company, 1911.

'S. C. B. Gascoigne, M.Sc'. *Craccum* 12, no. 9 (28 July 1938): 3.

Salmon, Catherine and Katrin Schumann. *The Secret Power of Middle Children: How Middleborns Can Harness Their Unexpected and Remarkable Abilities.* New York: Penguin, 2011.

Savage, Paula. 'Introduction'. In *Rosalie Gascoigne: Plain Air*, edited by Gregory O'Brien, 9–13. Wellington: City Gallery Wellington and Victoria University Press, 2004.

Sayers, Andrew. *Australian Art.* Oxford: Oxford University Press, 2001.

Scarlett, Ken. 'Robert Klippel: Australia's Greatest Sculptor'. *Sculpture* 23, no. 3 (April 2004). sculpturemagazine.art/robert-klippel-australias-greatest-sculptor/.

Schneider, Carl D. *Shame, Exposure and Privacy.* New York: W. W. Norton, 1977.

Schneider, Cynthia P. 'Culture Communicates: US Diplomacy That Works'. In *The New Public Diplomacy: Soft Power in International Relations*, edited by Jan Melissen, 147–68. Basingstoke: Palgrave MacMillan, 2005. doi.org/10.1057/9780230554931_8.

Seitz, William. *The Art of Assemblage.* New York: The Museum of Modern Art, 1961.

Seligman, Linda. *Theories of Counseling and Psychotherapy: Systems, Strategies, and Skills.* 2nd ed. New Jersey: Pearson Merrill Prentice Hall, 2006.

Shephard, Sue. *The Surprising Life of Constance Spry.* London: Macmillan, 2010.

Sherratt, Tim. 'A Wartime Observatory Observed'. Discontents, 3 January 1996. discontents.com.au/tag/ben-gascoigne.

Shimbo, Shoso. 'Ikebana to Contemporary Art: Rosalie Gascoigne'. Proceedings of the Asian Conference on Cultural Studies, Osaka, Japan, 2013. papers.iafor.org/wp-content/uploads/conference-proceedings/ACCS/ACCS2013_proceedings.pdf.

Simms, Marian. 'Writing the History of Australian Women'. Labour History 34 (May 1978): 93–101. doi.org/10.2307/27508313.

Sinclair, Keith and Trudie McNaughton. *A History of the University of Auckland, 1883–1983.* Auckland: Auckland University Press, 1983.

Smith, Bernard and Terry Smith. *Australian Painting 1788–1990.* 3rd ed. Melbourne: Oxford University Press, 1991.

Smith, Terry. 'Kngwarreye Woman Abstract Painter'. In *Emily Kngwarreye,* edited by Jennifer Isaacs, 25. Sydney: Craftsman House, 1998.

Smith, Terry. 'The Provincialism Problem'. *Artforum XIII* 1 (September 1974): 54–9.

Sparke, Eric. *Canberra 1954–1980.* Canberra: Australian Government Publishing Service, 1988.

Sparnon, Norman. *A Guide to Japanese Floral Arrangement.* Tokyo: Shufonotomo and Ure Smith, 1969.

Sparnon, Norman. *The Magic of Camellias: Creative Ideas for Japanese Flower Arrangement.* Sydney: Ure Smith, 1968.

Speck, Catherine. 'Nora Heysen'. In *Know My Name,* edited by N. Bullock, K. Cole, D. Hart and E. Pitt, 190–1. Canberra: National Gallery of Australia, 2020.

Statistics New Zealand. 'The New Zealand Official Year-Book, 1916'. www3.stats.govt.nz/New_Zealand_Official_Yearbooks/1916/NZOYB_1916.html.

Statistics New Zealand. 'The New Zealand Official Year-Book, 1928'. www3.stats.govt.nz/New_Zealand_Official_Yearbooks/1928/NZOYB_1928.html#idsect1_1_16796.

Statistics New Zealand. 'The New Zealand Official Year-Book, 1931'. www3.stats.govt.nz/New_Zealand_Official_Yearbooks/1931/NZOYB_1931.html.

Statistics New Zealand. 'The New Zealand Official Year-Book, 1936'. www3.stats.govt.nz/New_Zealand_Official_Yearbooks/1936/NZOYB_1936.html#idsect1_1_71879.

Statistics New Zealand. 'The New Zealand Official Year-Book, 1943'. www3.stats.govt.nz/New_Zealand_Official_Yearbooks/1943/NZOYB_1943.html#idchapter_1_4984.

Steedman, Carolyn. *Past Tenses: Essays on Writing, Autobiography and History*. London: Rivers Oran Press, 1992.

Stephen, Ann, Andrew McNamara and Philip Goad. *Modernism & Australia: Documents on Art, Design and Architecture 1917–1967*. Carlton: The Miegunyah Press, 2006.

Stephenson, Maxine. 'Thinking Historically: Maori and Settler Education'. In *Introduction to the History of New Zealand Education*, edited by Elizabeth Rata and Ros Sullivan. North Shore: Pearson, 2009.

'The Story of Studio Nundah: Oral History Interview with Michael Legrand'. thetocumwalarchive.photoaccess.org.au/html/006_nundah.htm (site discontinued).

Strickland, Katrina. *Affairs of the Heart: Love and Power in the Art World*. Carlton: Melbourne University Press, 2013.

Sugar, Vera. 'Manet Portraying Life'. *Fresh* (Roehampton University Students' Union magazine), no. 7 (February 2013): 16–17.

Summers, Anne. *Damned Whores and God's Police: The Colonization of Women in Australia*. Ringwood: Penguin Books, 1975.

Swarbrick, Nancy. 'Primary and Secondary Education—Teachers'. Te Ara—the Encyclopedia of New Zealand'. www.teara.govt.nz/en/primary-and-secondary-education/8.

Thapan, Meenakshi, ed. *Transnational Migration and the Politics of Identity. Vol. 1, Women and Migration in Asia*. New Delhi/Thousand Oaks/London: Sage Publications, 2005.

Thomas, Daniel. 'Art Museums in Australia: A Personal Account'. National Museum of Australia. nma.gov.au/research/understanding-museums/DThomas_2011.html.

Thomas, Daniel. 'Rhythm & Lift-Off'. In *Rosalie Gascoigne: Plain Air*, edited by Gregory O'Brien, 15–20. Wellington: City Gallery Wellington and Victoria University Press, 2004.

Thomas, Daniel. 'Smith, Grace Cossington (1892–1984)'. Australian Dictionary of Biography, National Centre of Biography, The Australian National University. Published first in hardcopy 1988. adb.anu.edu.au/biography/smith-grace-cossington-8469/text14893.

Trevelyan, Jill. *Peter McLeavey: The Life and Times of a New Zealand Art Dealer.* Wellington: Te Papa Press, 2013.

Tyler, Linda. 'Mcdonald, Mullions and Smith Architects: An Open Architecture for Auckland in the 1920s'. Proceedings of the 30th annual conference of the Society of Architectural Historians, Australia and New Zealand, Gold Coast, Queensland, 2013. www.sahanz.net/wp-content/uploads/S15_02_Tyler_McDonald-Mullions-and-Smith-Architects.pdf.

United States Census Bureau. '1910 Census: Volume 1. Population, General Report and Analysis'. 1913. www.census.gov/library/publications/1913/dec/vol-1-population.html.

Ward, Lucina. 'Art Current (1972–1984)'. In *Building the Collection*, edited by Pauline Green, 148–63. Canberra: National Gallery of Australia, 2003.

Waterhouse, Jill. *University House: As They Experienced It.* Canberra: University House, The Australian National University, 2004.

Wedde, Ian. 'Where Was the Best Art This Summer?'. *New Zealand Art News* 1, no. 1 (1984).

White, Georgina. *Light Fantastic: Dance Floor Courtship in New Zealand.* Auckland: Harper Collins Publishers, 2007.

Wildlife Preservation Society of Queensland. 'Monograph 1—Catalyst for Action: Formation of a Conservation Society'. Historical Papers. wildlife.org.au/wp-content/uploads/2022/06/Monograph-1.pdf.

Wilford, Thomas M. 'Elsie Walker Case'. Statement by the minister of justice, Wellington, New Zealand, 1929. paperspast.natlib.govt.nz/parliamentary/AJHR1929-I.2.3.2.33.

Williams, Christine. *Green Power: Environmentalists Who Have Changed the Face of Australia.* South Melbourne: Thomas C. Lothian, 2006.

Williams, Raymond. 'The Bloomsbury Fraction'. In *Problems in Material and Culture: Selected Essays*, 148–69. London: Verso Editions and NLB, 1980.

Woititz, Janet Geringer. *Adult Children of Alcoholics.* Expanded ed. Deerfield Beach: Health Communications, 1990.

Woolf, Virginia. *A Room of One's Own.* Camberwell: Penguin Books, 2009. First published 1928.

Yska, Redmer. *Truth: The Rise and Fall of the People's Paper.* Nelson: Craig Potton, 2010.

Index

Note: Page numbers in *italics* indicate illustrations. Page numbers with 'n' indicate footnotes.

www.ingramcontent.com/pod-product-compliance
Lightning Source LLC
LaVergne TN
LVHW020503100826
845148LV00003B/688

* 9 7 8 1 7 6 0 4 6 6 5 5 8 *